2

Hina matsuri

Masao Ohtake

HINA MATSURI Vol.2

CONTENTS

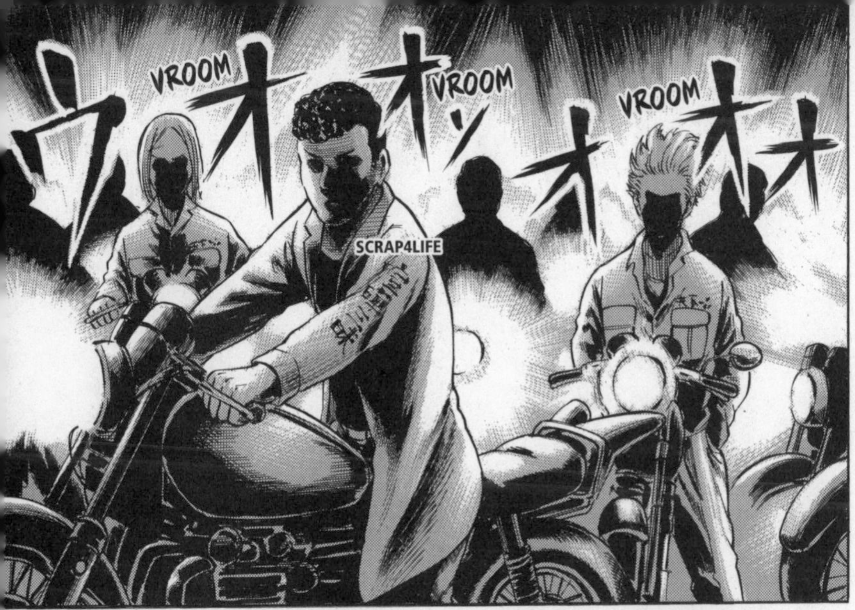
VROOM
VROOM
VROOM
ウオオッオオオオ
SCRAP4LIFE

CHAPTER 6

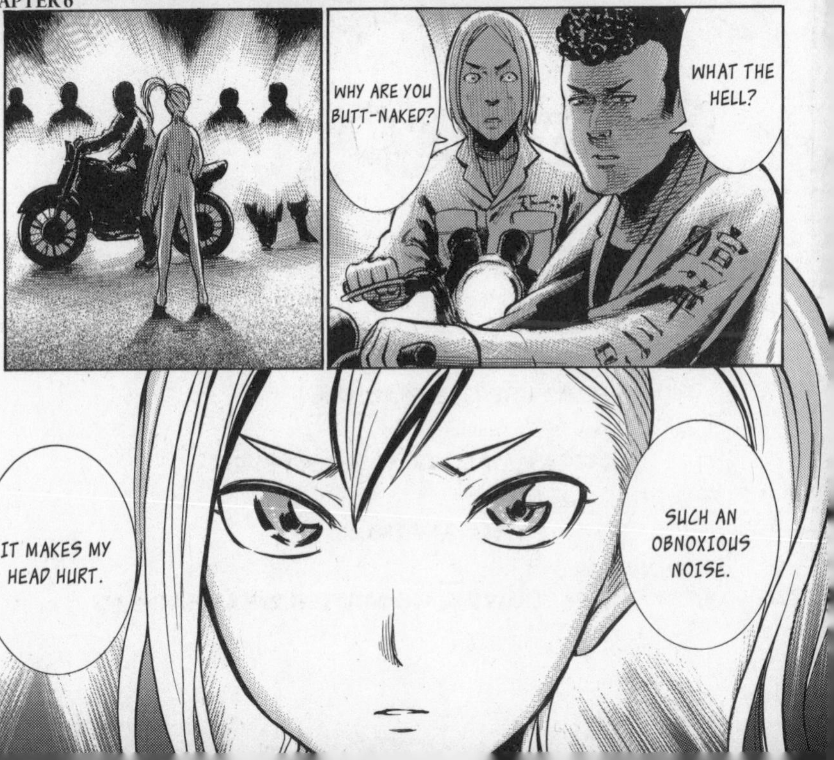
WHAT THE HELL?
WHY ARE YOU BUTT-NAKED?
SUCH AN OBNOXIOUS NOISE.
IT MAKES MY HEAD HURT.

CHAPTER 6
HOW TO HAVE A PSYCHOKINETIC SHOWDOWN

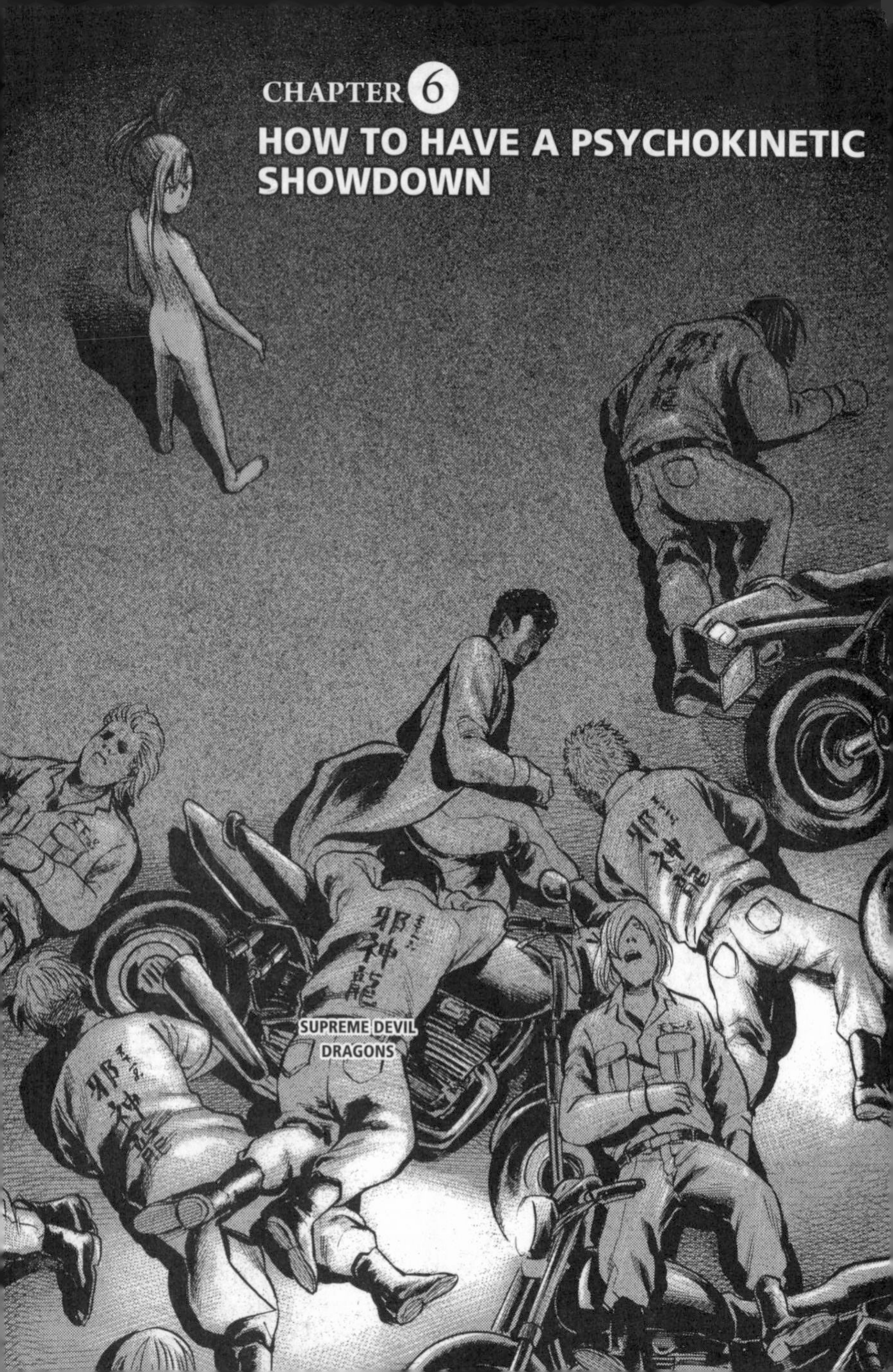
SUPREME DEVIL DRAGONS

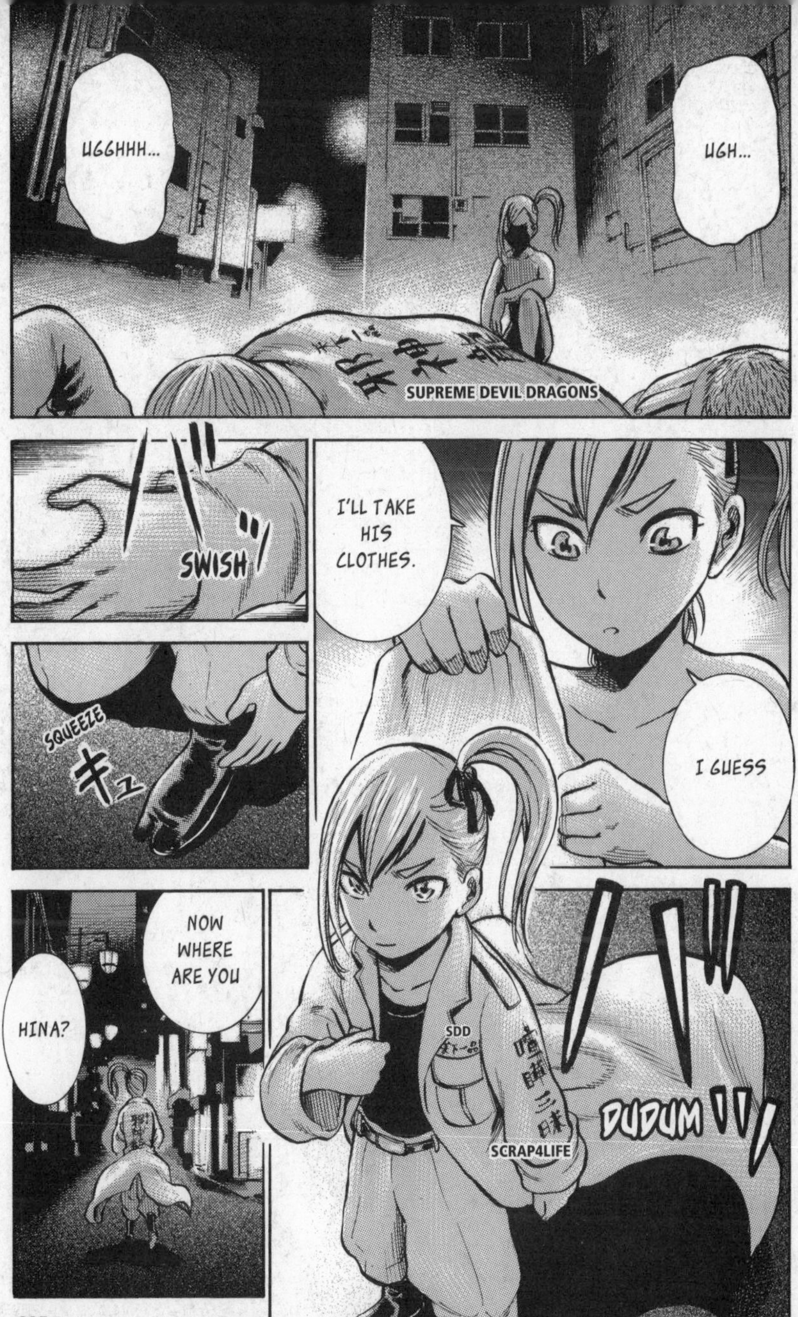
UGH...
UGGHHH...
SUPREME DEVIL DRAGONS
I'LL TAKE HIS CLOTHES.
I GUESS
SWISH
SQUEEZE
キュ
DUDUM
SDD
SCRAP4LIFE
NOW WHERE ARE YOU
HINA?

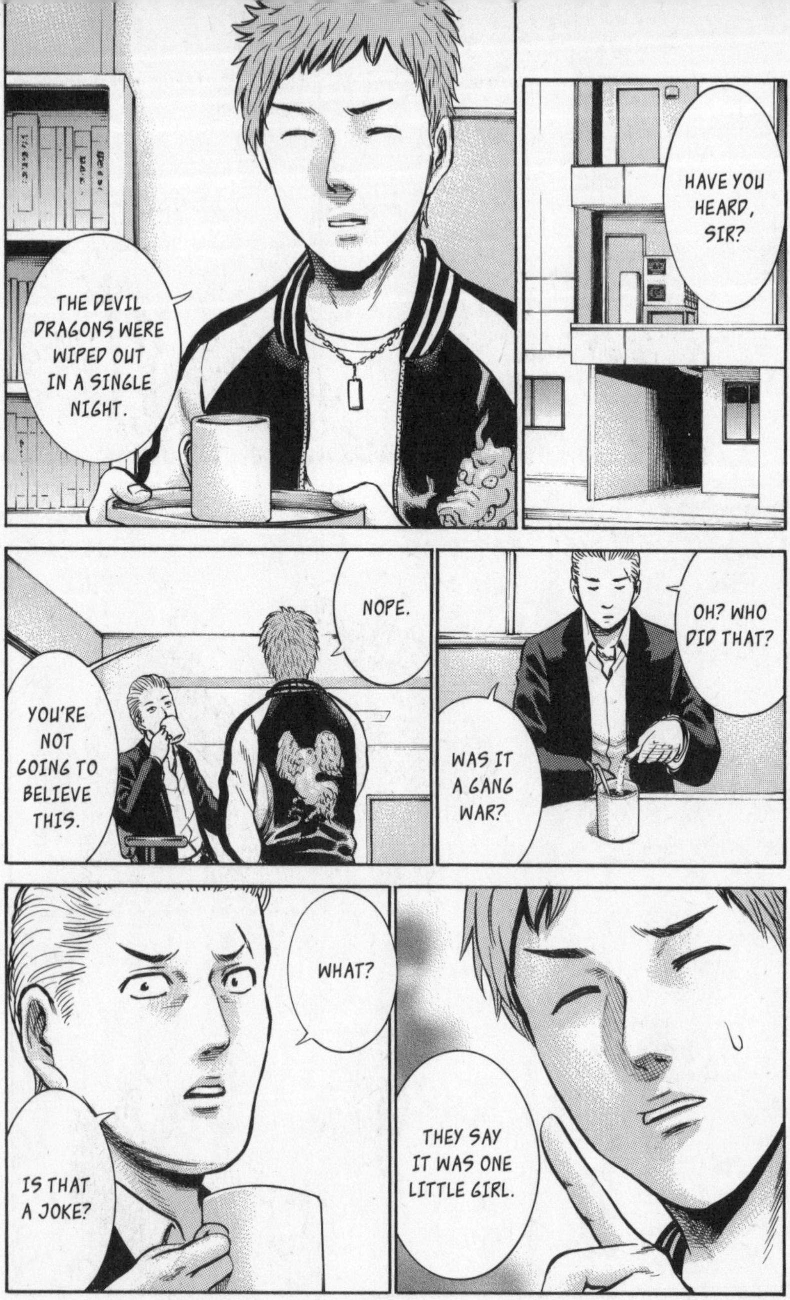
HAVE YOU HEARD, SIR?
THE DEVIL DRAGONS WERE WIPED OUT IN A SINGLE NIGHT.
OH? WHO DID THAT?
WAS IT A GANG WAR?
NOPE.
YOU'RE NOT GOING TO BELIEVE THIS.
THEY SAY IT WAS ONE LITTLE GIRL.
WHAT?
IS THAT A JOKE?

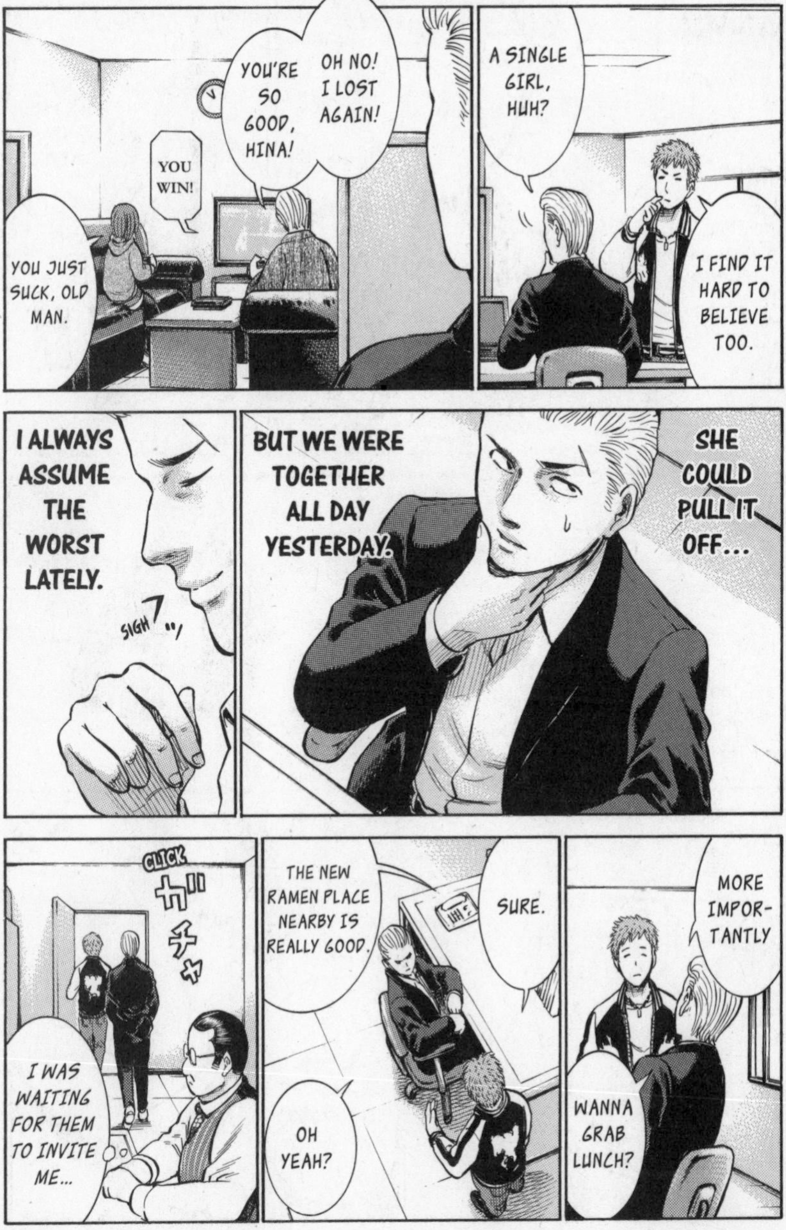
A SINGLE GIRL, HUH?
I FIND IT HARD TO BELIEVE TOO.
OH NO! I LOST AGAIN!
YOU'RE SO GOOD, HINA!
YOU WIN!
YOU JUST SUCK, OLD MAN.
SHE COULD PULL IT OFF...
BUT WE WERE TOGETHER ALL DAY YESTERDAY.
I ALWAYS ASSUME THE WORST LATELY.
SIGH
MORE IMPORTANTLY
WANNA GRAB LUNCH?
SURE.
THE NEW RAMEN PLACE NEARBY IS REALLY GOOD.
OH YEAH?
CLICK
I WAS WAITING FOR THEM TO INVITE ME...

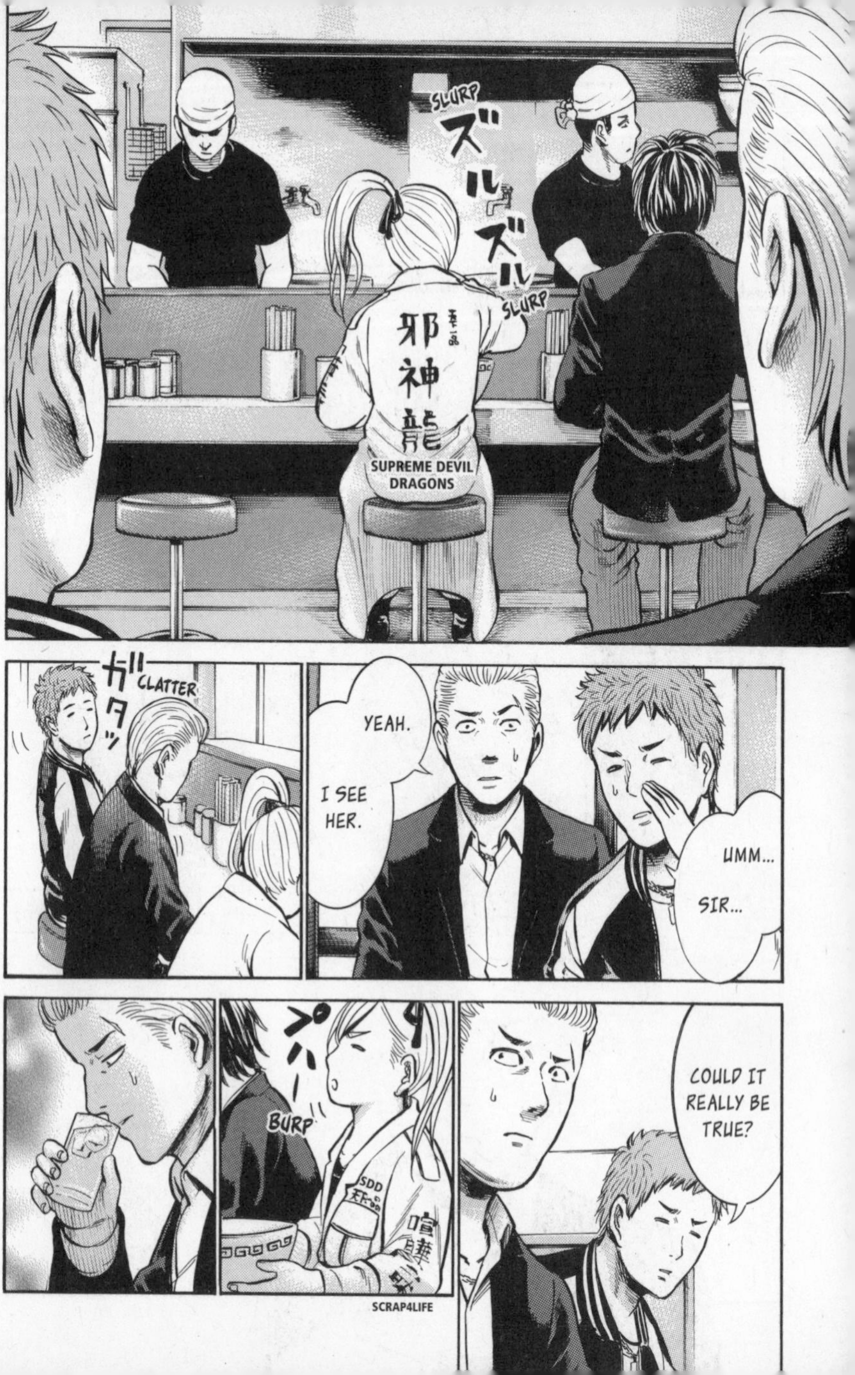
SLURP
ズル
ズル
SLURP
邪神龍
SUPREME DEVIL DRAGONS
UMM...
SIR...
YEAH.
I SEE HER.
ガタッ
CLATTER
COULD IT REALLY BE TRUE?
プハー
BURP
SDD

SCRAP4LIFE

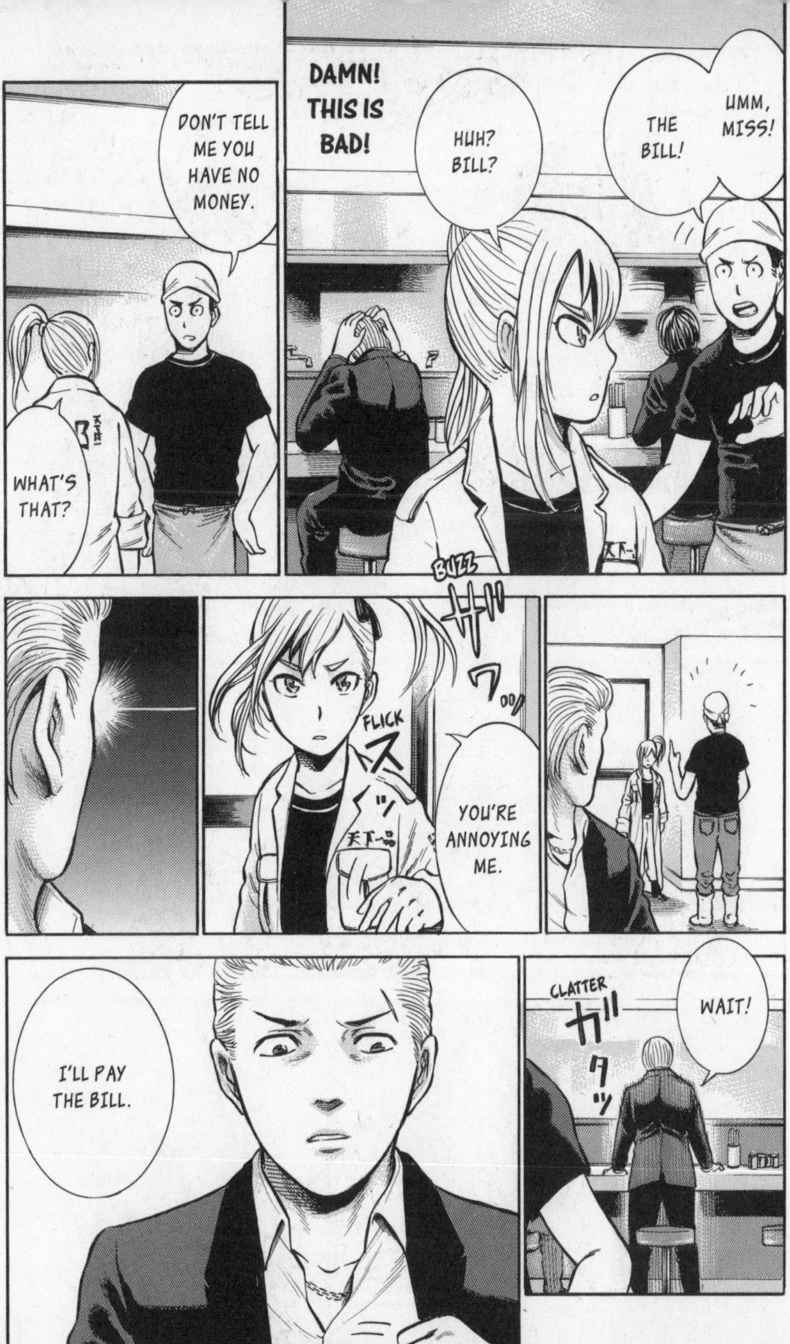
UMM, MISS!
THE BILL!
HUH? BILL?
DAMN! THIS IS BAD!
DON'T TELL ME YOU HAVE NO MONEY.
WHAT'S THAT?
BUZZ
YOU'RE ANNOYING ME.
FLICK
WAIT!
CLATTER
I'LL PAY THE BILL.

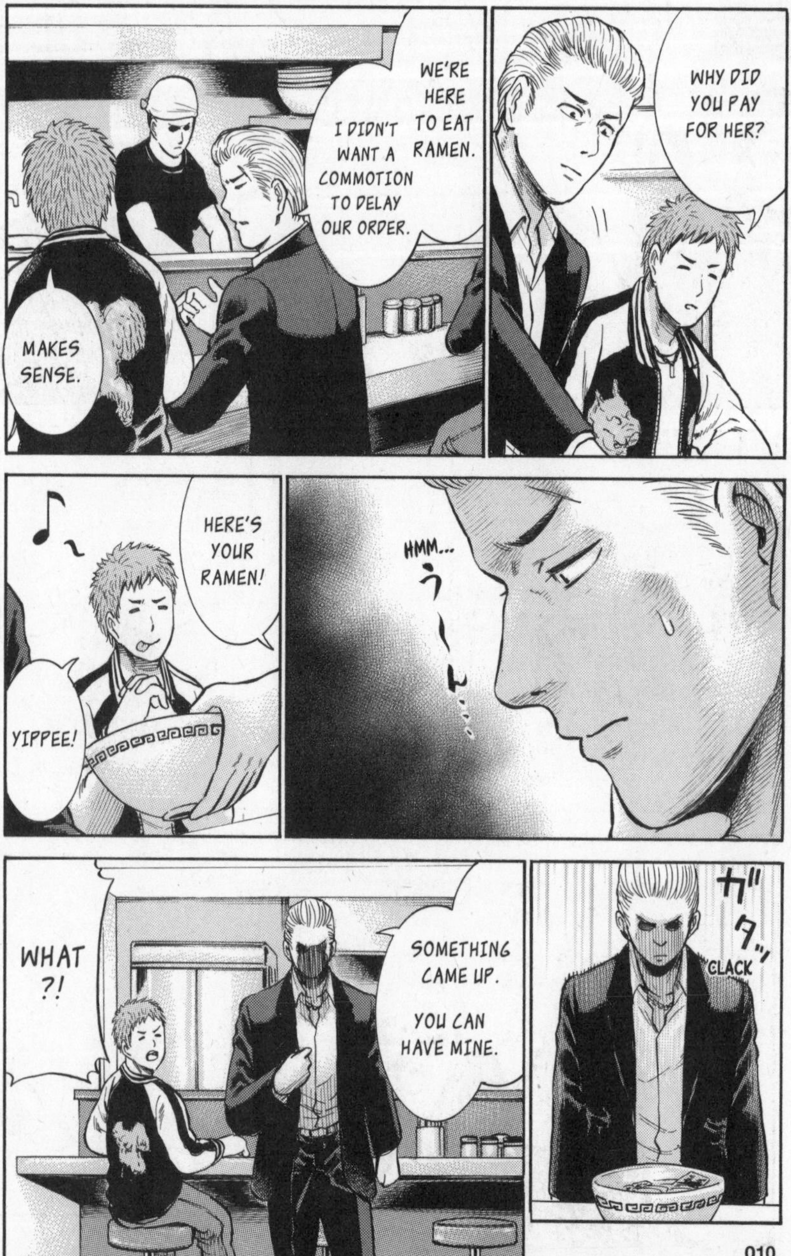
WHY DID YOU PAY FOR HER?
WE'RE HERE TO EAT RAMEN.
I DIDN'T WANT A COMMOTION TO DELAY OUR ORDER.
MAKES SENSE.
HMM...
うーん...
HERE'S YOUR RAMEN!
YIPPEE!
ガタッ
CLACK
SOMETHING CAME UP.
YOU CAN HAVE MINE.
WHAT?!

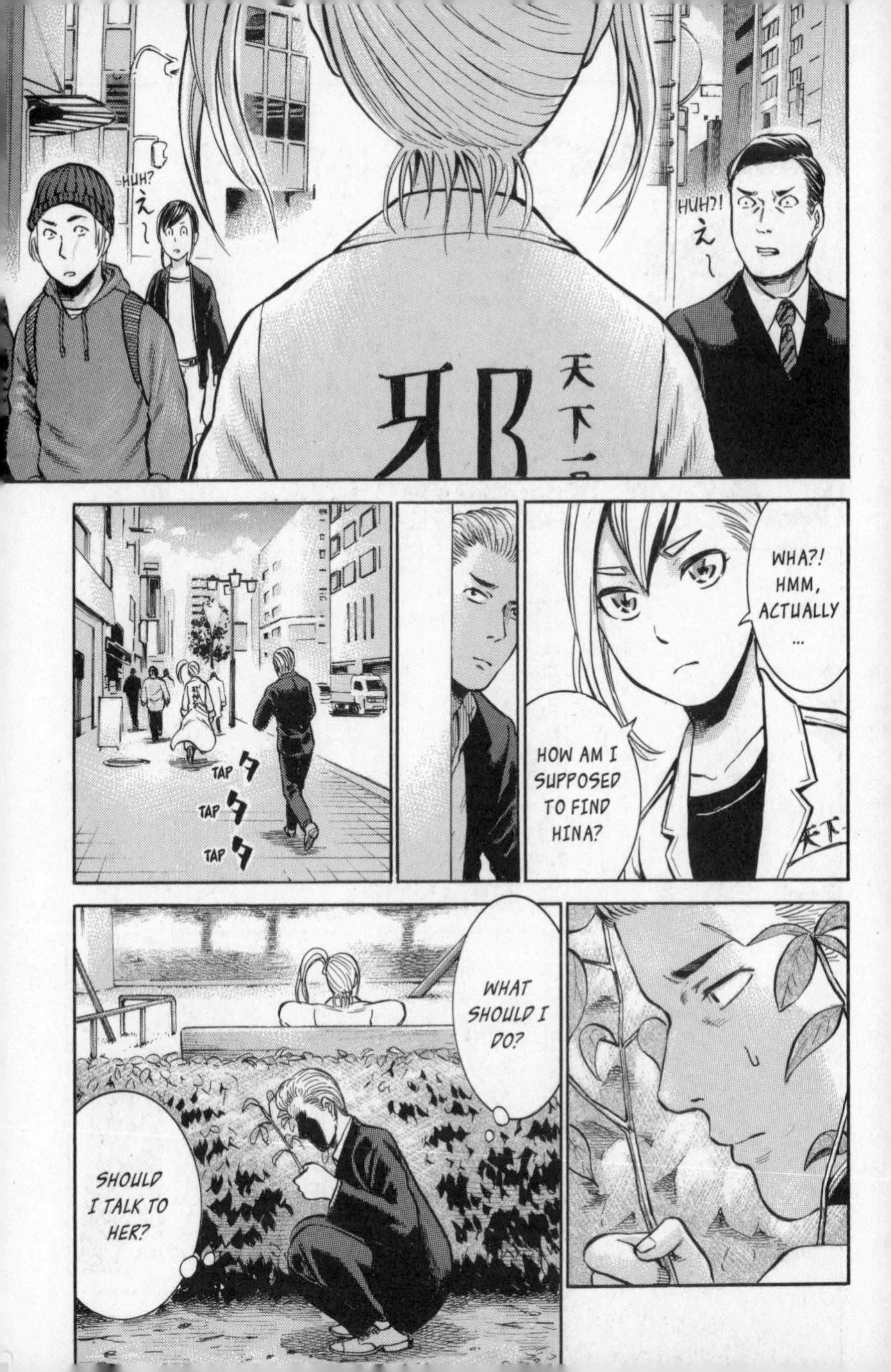
HUH?!
え～
HUH?
え～
WHA?! HMM, ACTUALLY ...
HOW AM I SUPPOSED TO FIND HINA?
TAP タ
TAP タ
TAP タ
WHAT SHOULD I DO?
SHOULD I TALK TO HER?

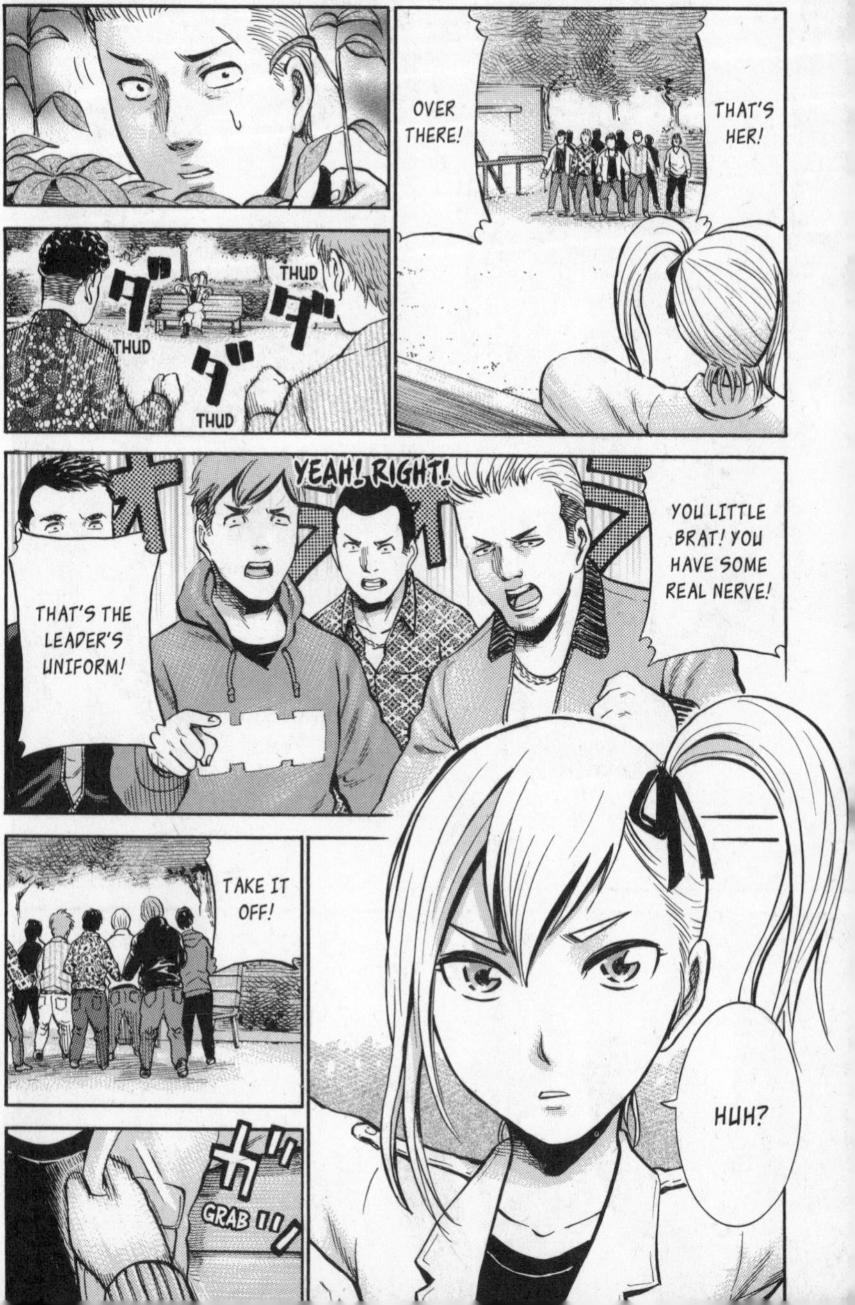
THAT'S HER!
OVER THERE!
THUD
THUD
THUD
YOU LITTLE BRAT! YOU HAVE SOME REAL NERVE!
YEAH! RIGHT!
THAT'S THE LEADER'S UNIFORM!
HUH?
TAKE IT OFF!
GRAB!!

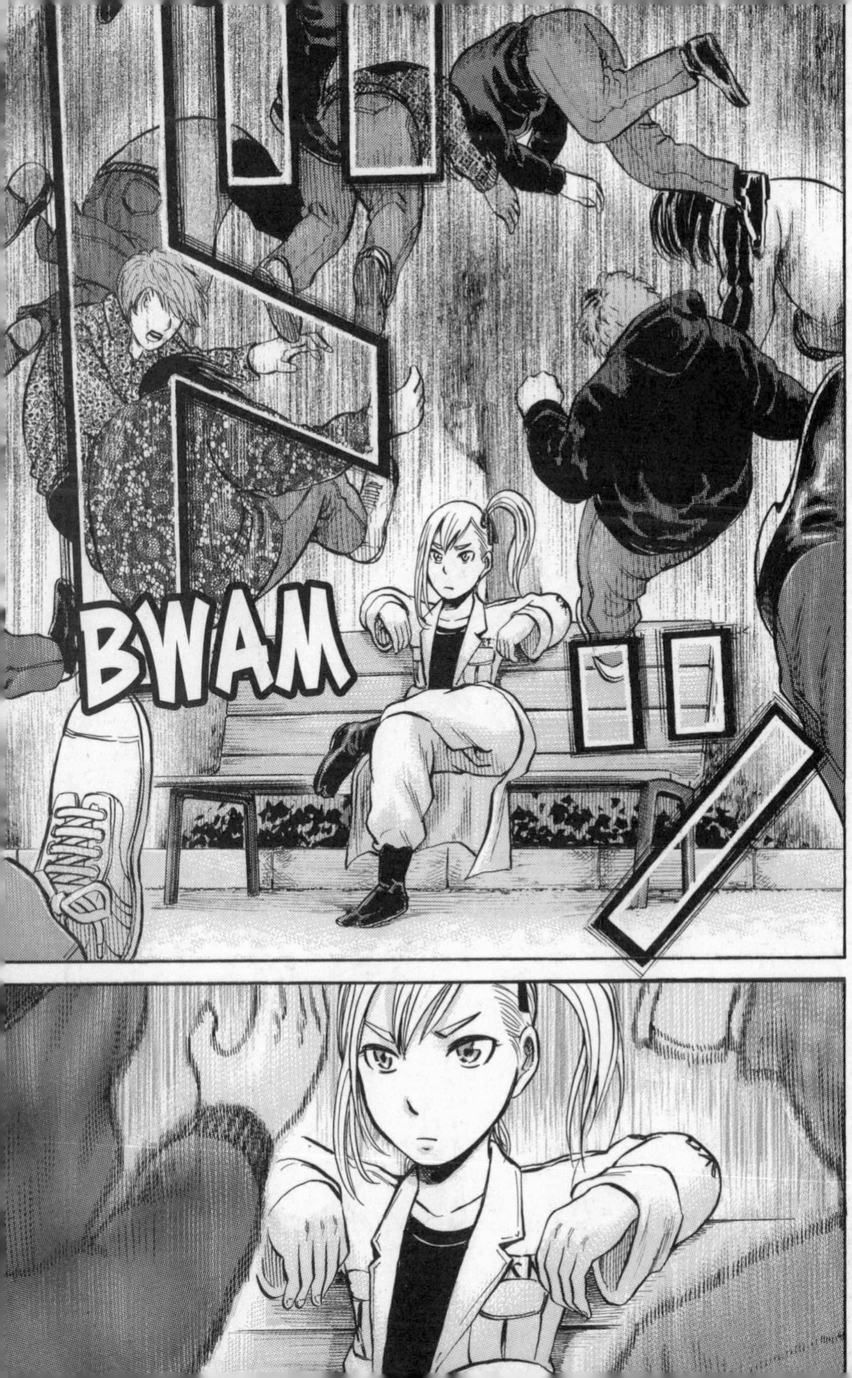
BWAM

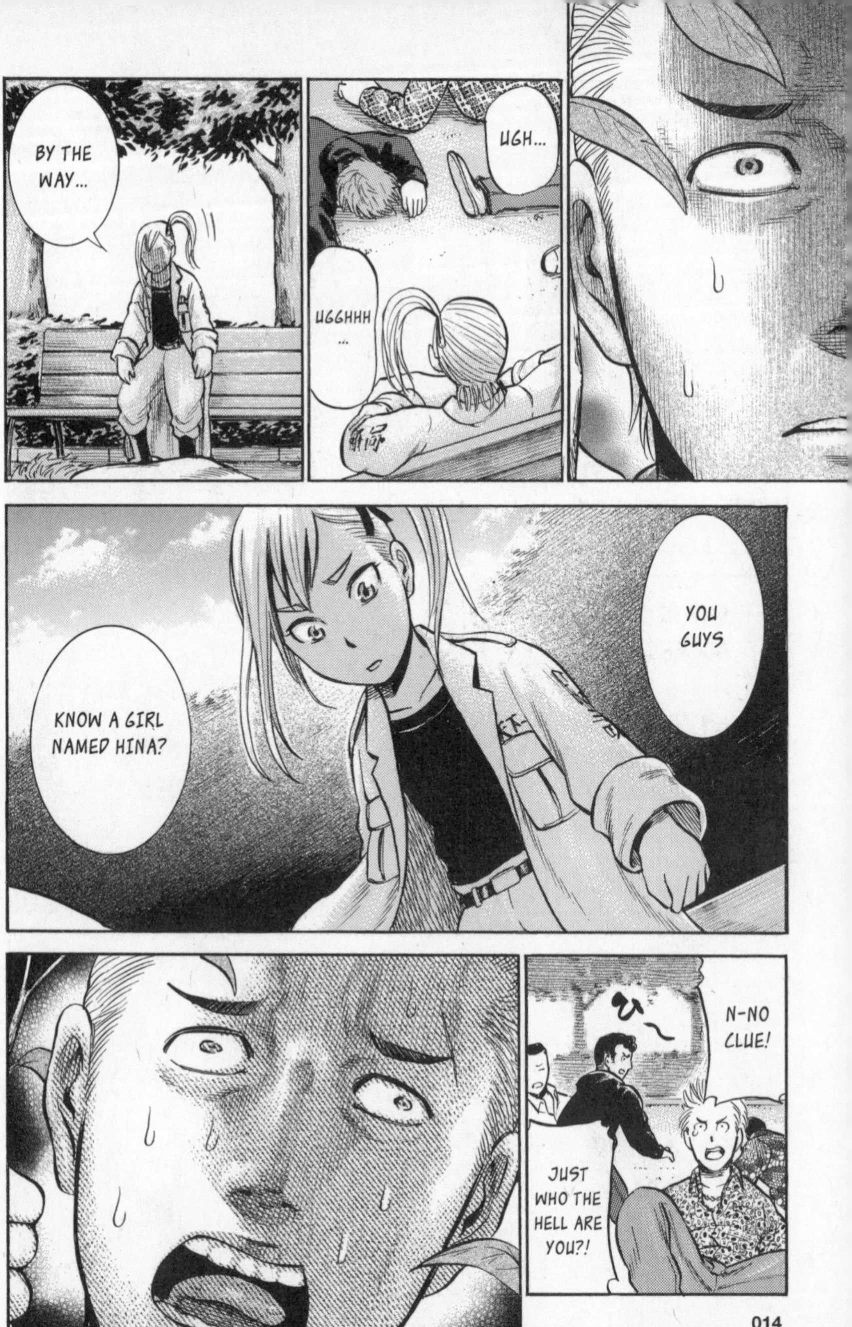
UGH...
UGGHHH ...
BY THE WAY...
YOU GUYS
KNOW A GIRL NAMED HINA?
N-NO CLUE!
ひ~
JUST WHO THE HELL ARE YOU?!

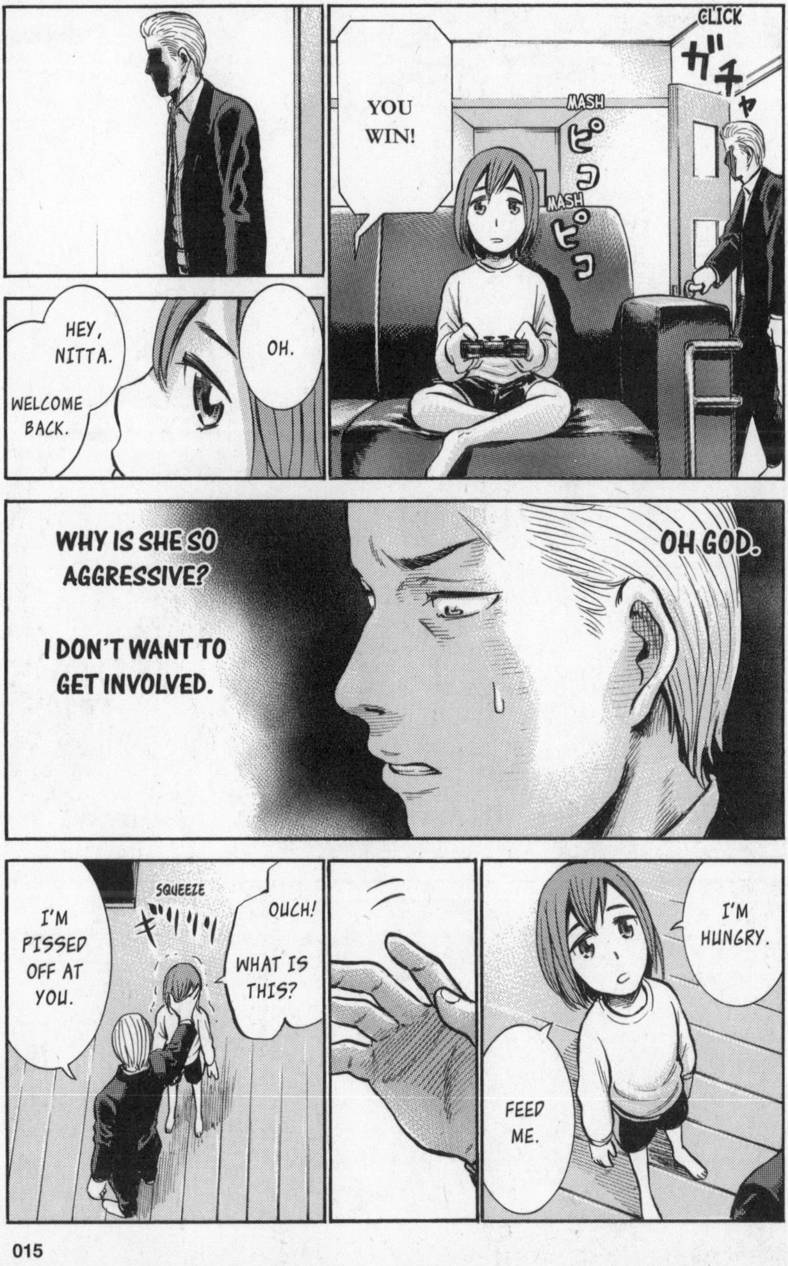
CLICK
ガチャ
MASH
ピコ
MASH
ピコ
YOU WIN!
OH.
HEY, NITTA.
WELCOME BACK.
OH GOD.
WHY IS SHE SO AGGRESSIVE?
I DON'T WANT TO GET INVOLVED.
I'M HUNGRY.
FEED ME.
OUCH!
WHAT IS THIS?
SQUEEZE
ギリリリ
I'M PISSED OFF AT YOU.

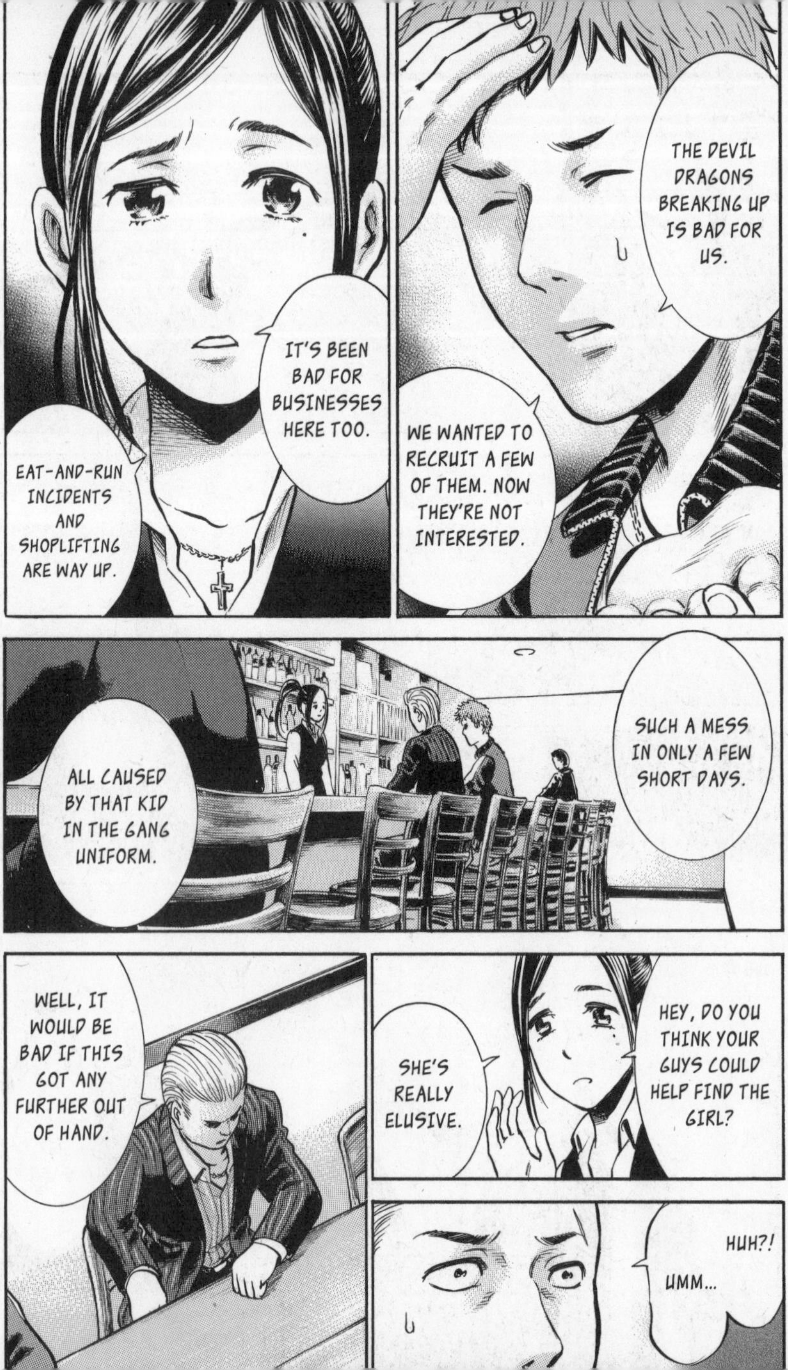
THE DEVIL DRAGONS BREAKING UP IS BAD FOR US.
WE WANTED TO RECRUIT A FEW OF THEM. NOW THEY'RE NOT INTERESTED.
IT'S BEEN BAD FOR BUSINESSES HERE TOO.
EAT-AND-RUN INCIDENTS AND SHOPLIFTING ARE WAY UP.
SUCH A MESS IN ONLY A FEW SHORT DAYS.
ALL CAUSED BY THAT KID IN THE GANG UNIFORM.
HEY, DO YOU THINK YOUR GUYS COULD HELP FIND THE GIRL?
SHE'S REALLY ELUSIVE.
HUH?!
UMM...
WELL, IT WOULD BE BAD IF THIS GOT ANY FURTHER OUT OF HAND.

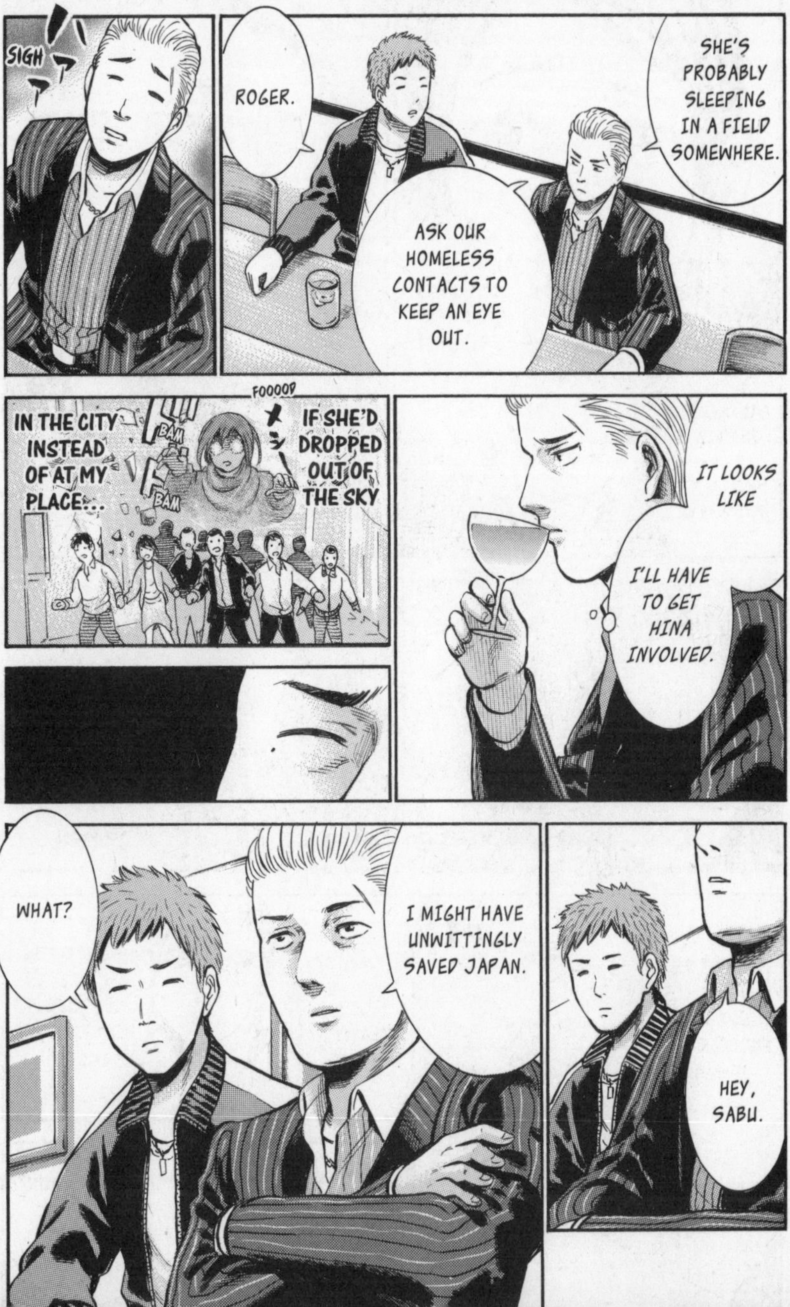
SHE'S PROBABLY SLEEPING IN A FIELD SOMEWHERE.
ROGER.
ASK OUR HOMELESS CONTACTS TO KEEP AN EYE OUT.
SIGH
IT LOOKS LIKE
I'LL HAVE TO GET HINA INVOLVED.
IF SHE'D DROPPED OUT OF THE SKY
FOOOOD
BAM
BAM
IN THE CITY INSTEAD OF AT MY PLACE...
HEY, SABU.
I MIGHT HAVE UNWITTINGLY SAVED JAPAN.
WHAT?

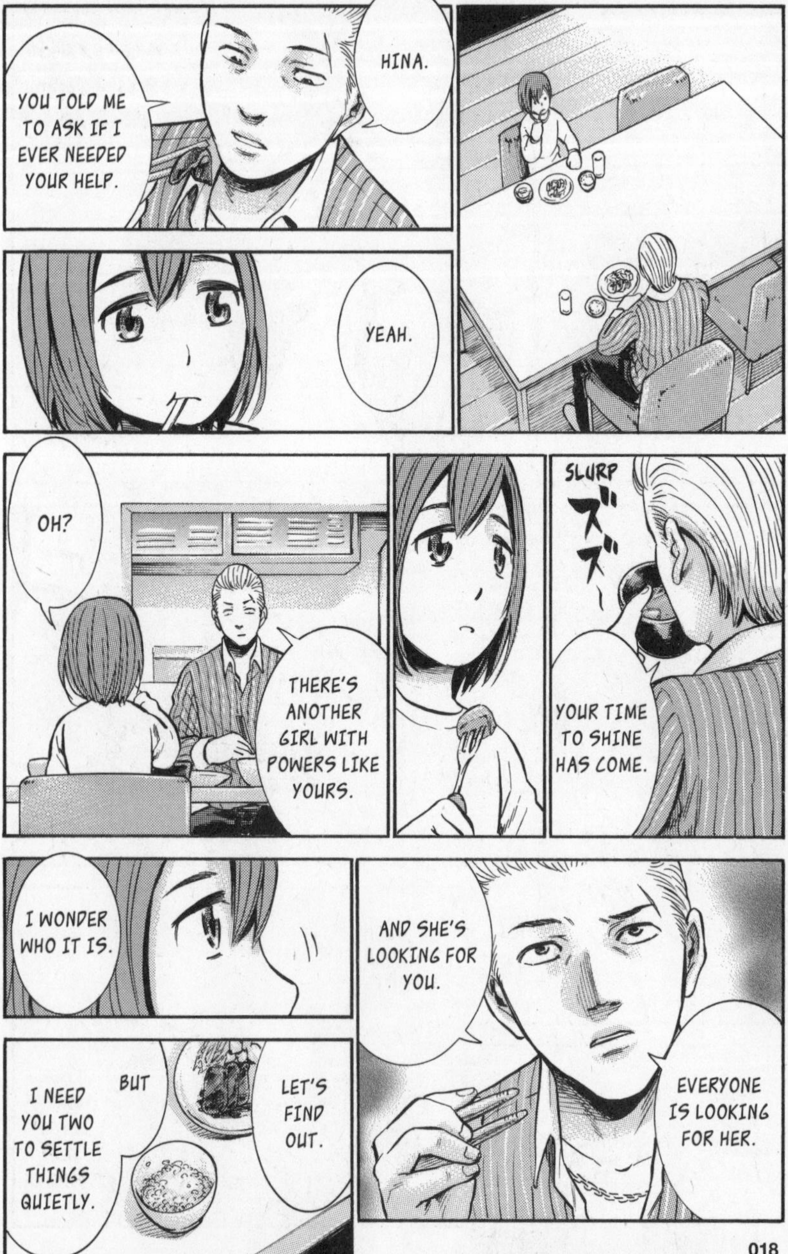

HINA.
YOU TOLD ME TO ASK IF I EVER NEEDED YOUR HELP.
YEAH.
SLURP
ズズ~
YOUR TIME TO SHINE HAS COME.
THERE'S ANOTHER GIRL WITH POWERS LIKE YOURS.
OH?
AND SHE'S LOOKING FOR YOU.
EVERYONE IS LOOKING FOR HER.
I WONDER WHO IT IS.
LET'S FIND OUT.
BUT
I NEED YOU TWO TO SETTLE THINGS QUIETLY.

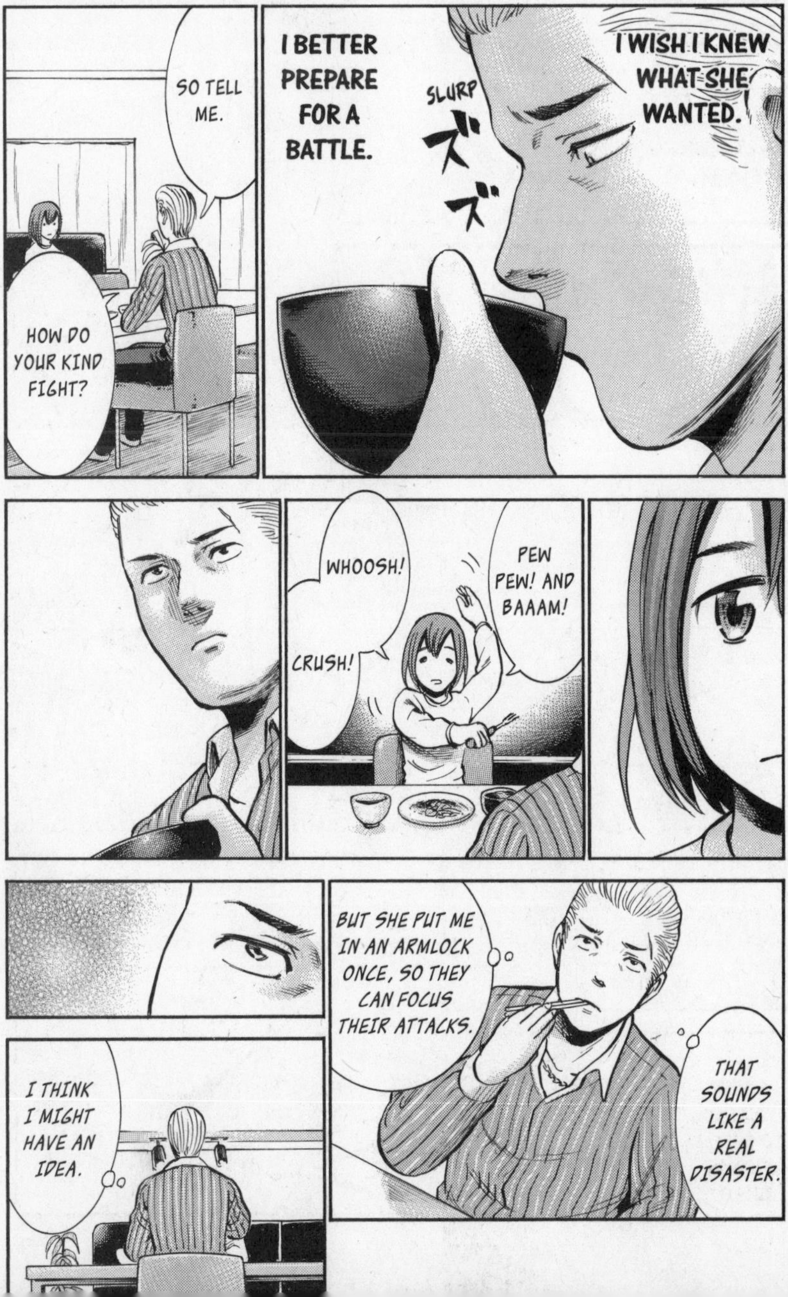
I WISH I KNEW WHAT SHE WANTED.
SLURP
ズズ
I BETTER PREPARE FOR A BATTLE.
SO TELL ME.
HOW DO YOUR KIND FIGHT?
PEW PEW! AND BAAAM!
WHOOSH!
CRUSH!
THAT SOUNDS LIKE A REAL DISASTER.
BUT SHE PUT ME IN AN ARMLOCK ONCE, SO THEY CAN FOCUS THEIR ATTACKS.
I THINK I MIGHT HAVE AN IDEA.

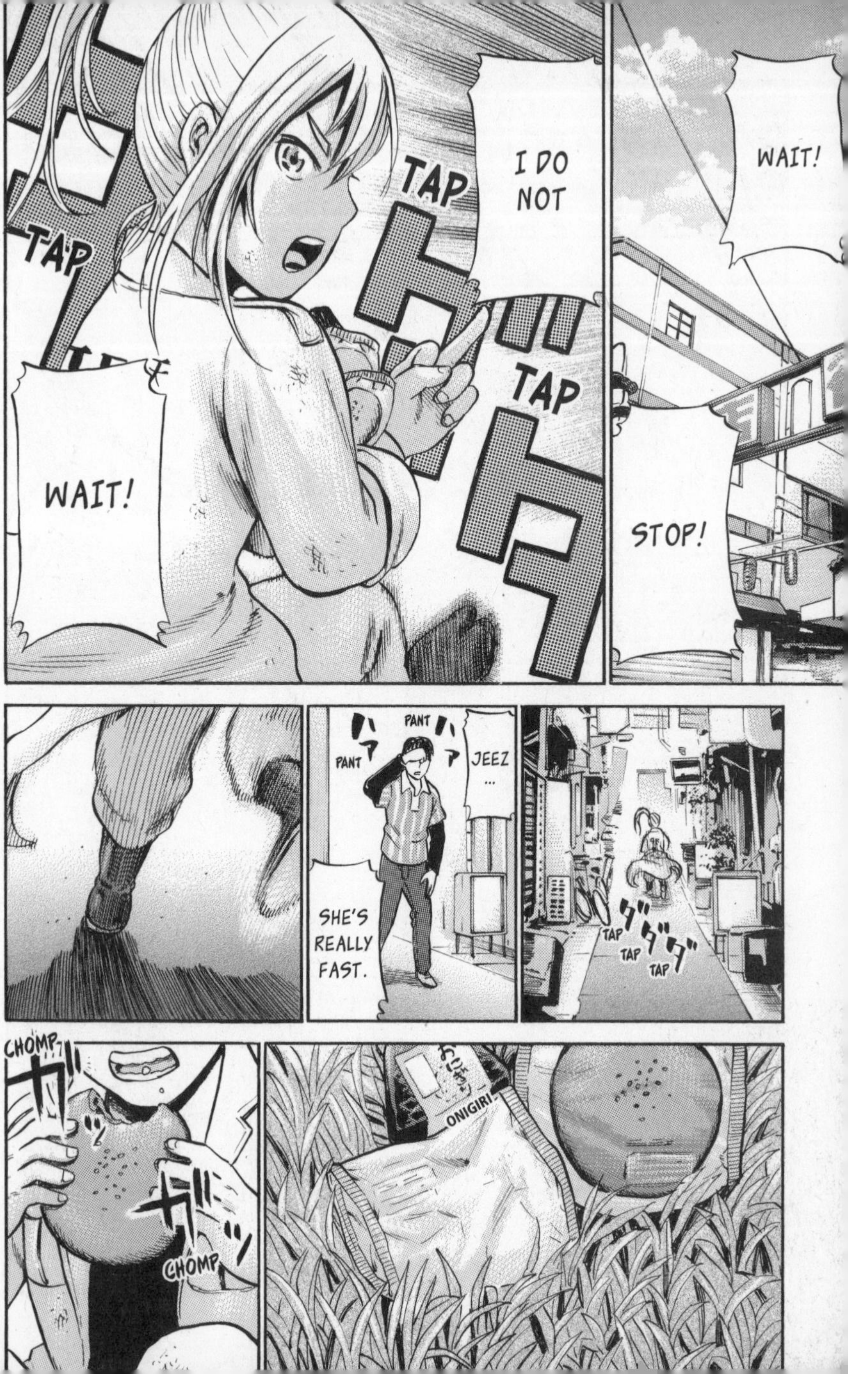

WAIT!
STOP!
I DO NOT
TAP
TAP
TAP
WAIT!
TAP
TAP
TAP
PANT
JEEZ ...
PANT
SHE'S REALLY FAST.
ONIGIRI
CHOMP
CHOMP

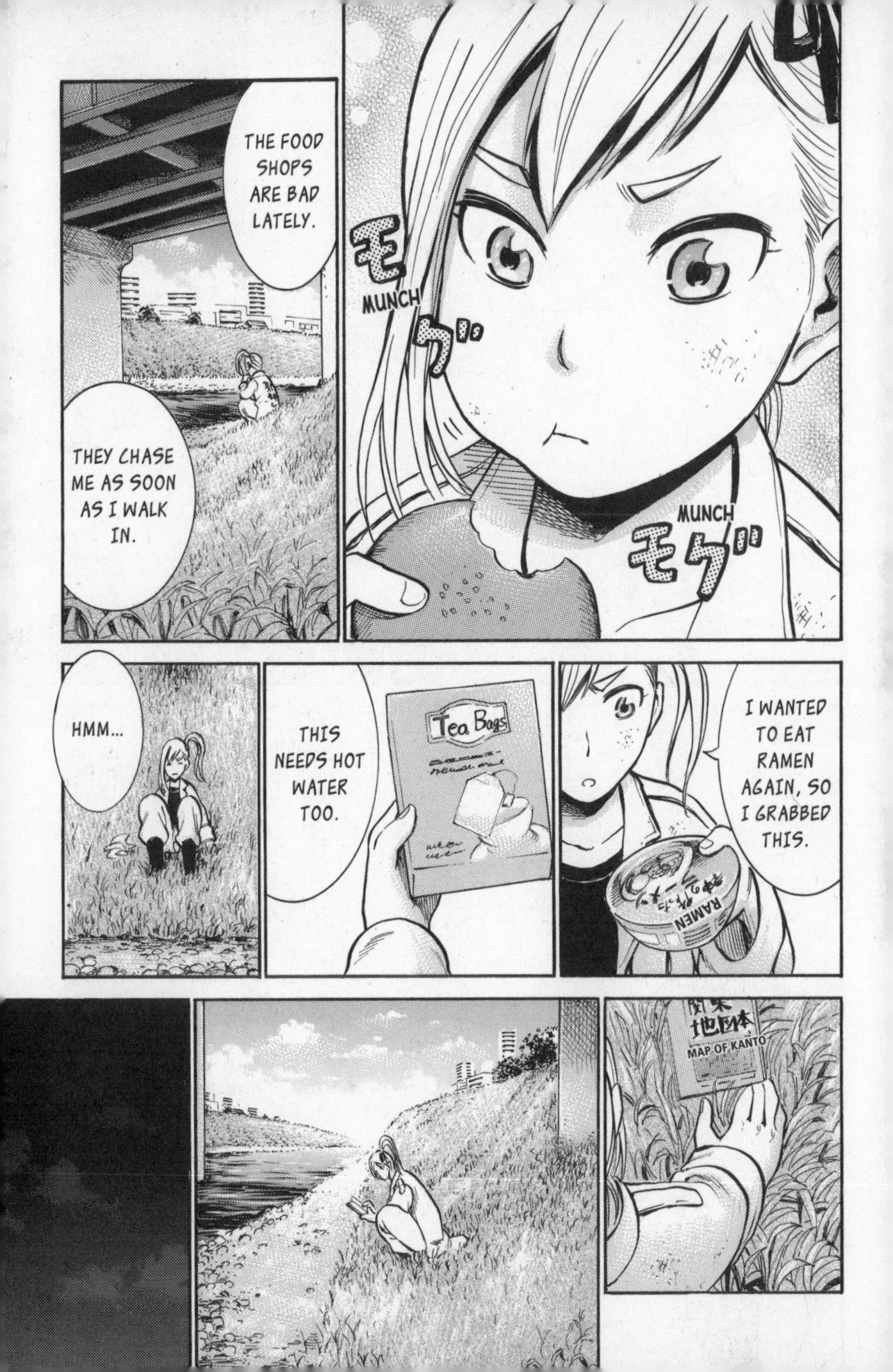
モグ
MUNCH
モグ
MUNCH
THE FOOD SHOPS ARE BAD LATELY.
THEY CHASE ME AS SOON AS I WALK IN.
I WANTED TO EAT RAMEN AGAIN, SO I GRABBED THIS.
RAMEN
Tea Bags
THIS NEEDS HOT WATER TOO.
HMM...
関東地図本
MAP OF KANTO

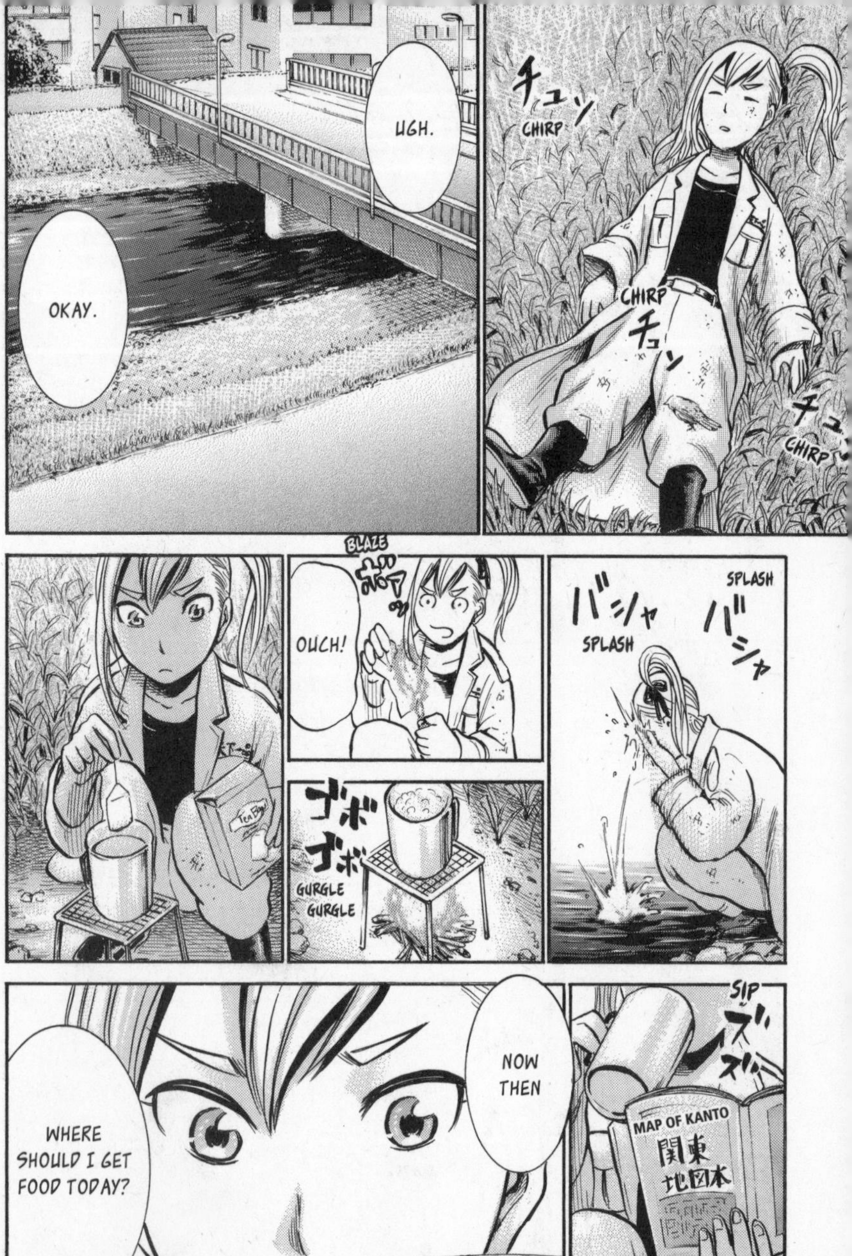
チュン
CHIRP
CHIRP
チュン
チュ
CHIRP
UGH.
OKAY.
バシャ
SPLASH
SPLASH
バシャ
BLAZE
OUCH!
GURGLE
GURGLE
SIP
MAP OF KANTO
関東
地図本
NOW THEN
WHERE SHOULD I GET FOOD TODAY?

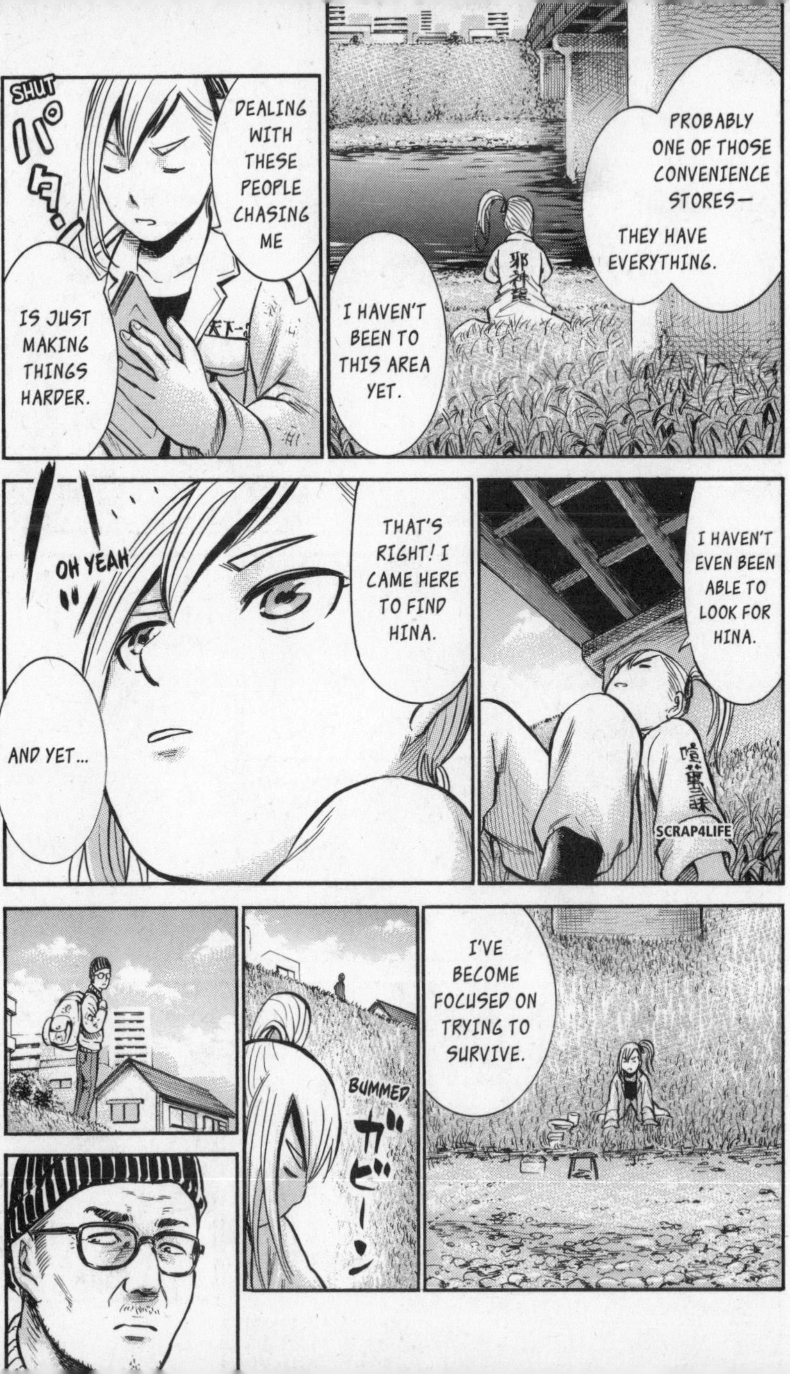
PROBABLY ONE OF THOSE CONVENIENCE STORES—
THEY HAVE EVERYTHING.
I HAVEN'T BEEN TO THIS AREA YET.
SHUT
DEALING WITH THESE PEOPLE CHASING ME
IS JUST MAKING THINGS HARDER.
I HAVEN'T EVEN BEEN ABLE TO LOOK FOR HINA.
SCRAP4LIFE
OH YEAH
THAT'S RIGHT! I CAME HERE TO FIND HINA.
AND YET...
I'VE BECOME FOCUSED ON TRYING TO SURVIVE.
BUMMED

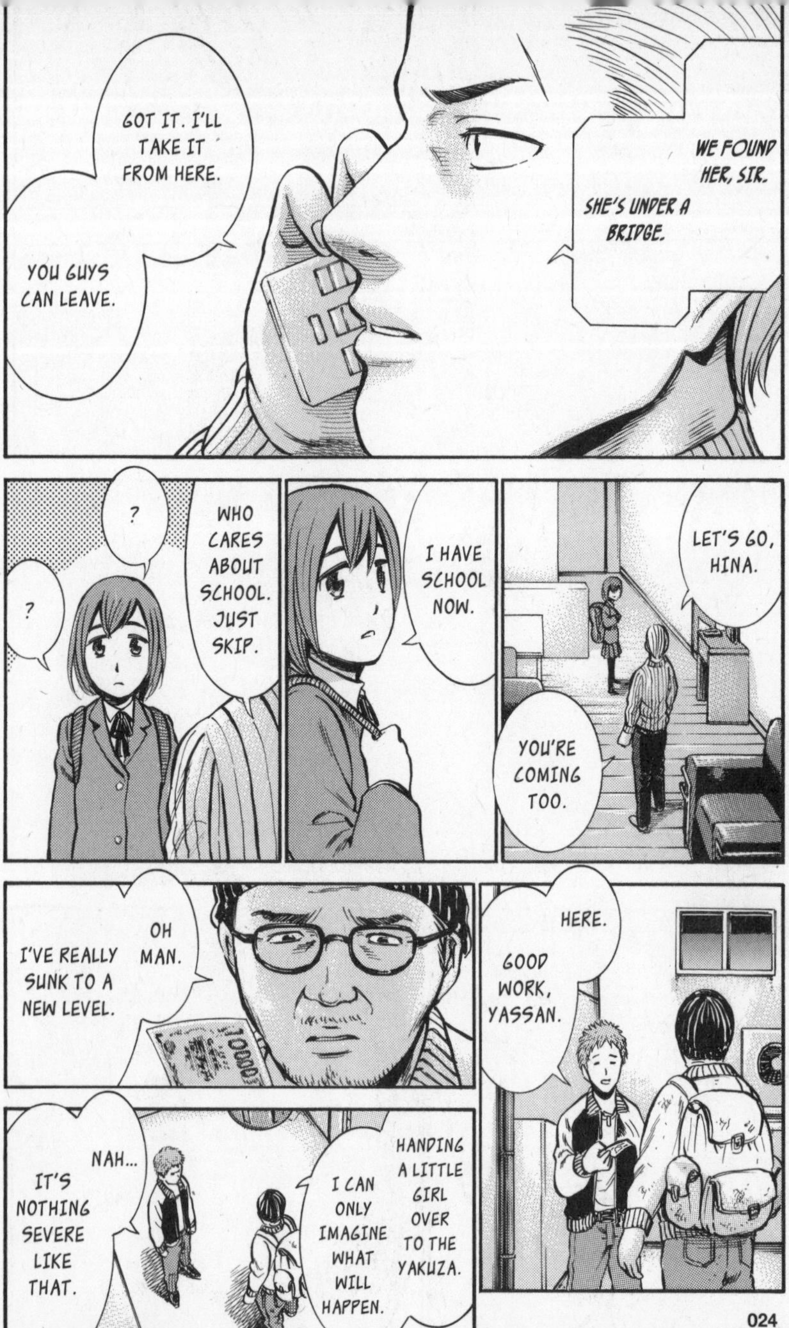
WE FOUND HER, SIR.
SHE'S UNDER A BRIDGE.
GOT IT. I'LL TAKE IT FROM HERE.
YOU GUYS CAN LEAVE.
LET'S GO, HINA.
YOU'RE COMING TOO.
I HAVE SCHOOL NOW.
WHO CARES ABOUT SCHOOL. JUST SKIP.
?
?
HERE.
GOOD WORK, YASSAN.
OH MAN.
I'VE REALLY SUNK TO A NEW LEVEL.
HANDING A LITTLE GIRL OVER TO THE YAKUZA.
I CAN ONLY IMAGINE WHAT WILL HAPPEN.
NAH...
IT'S NOTHING SEVERE LIKE THAT.

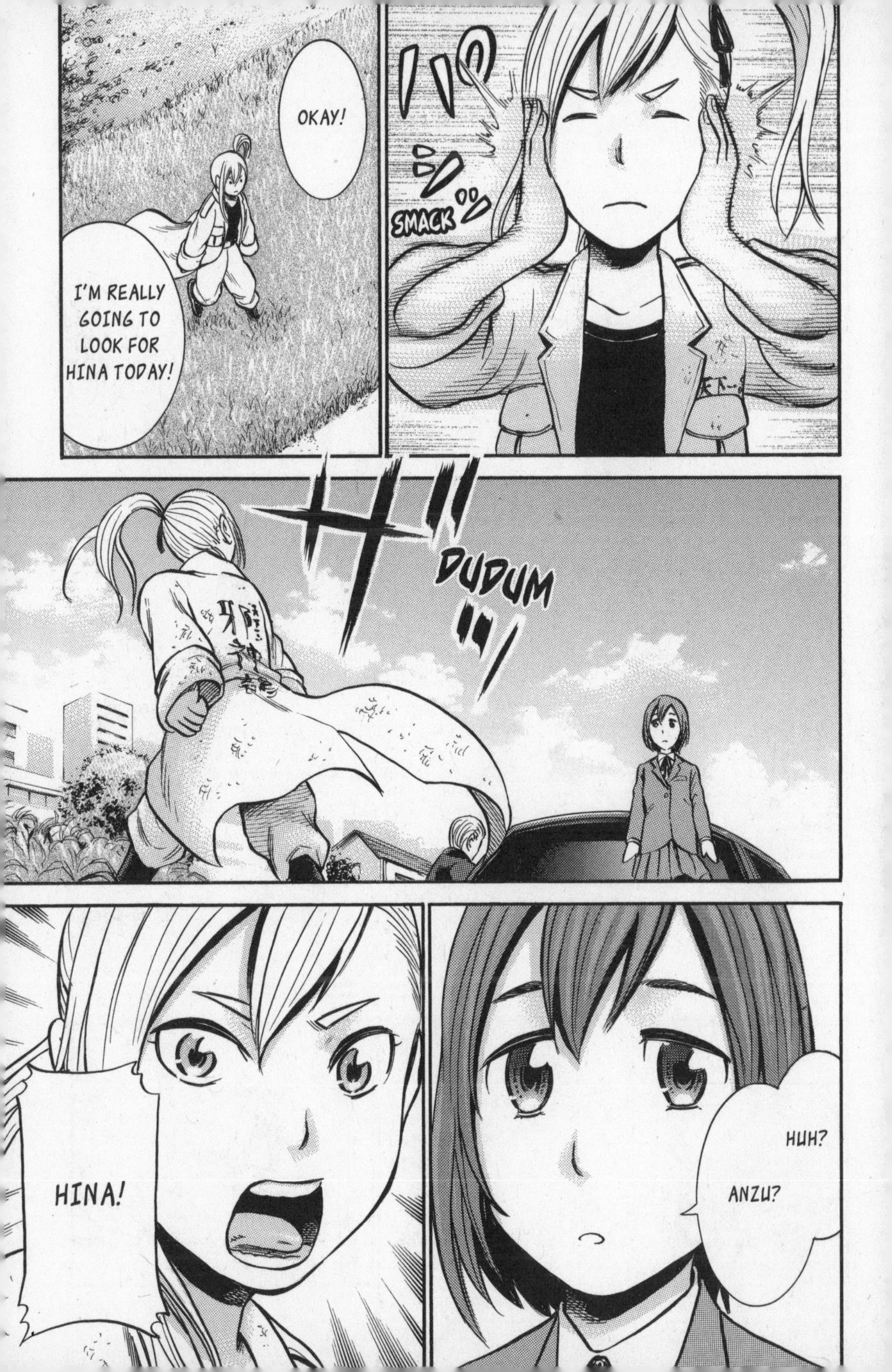
SMACK
OKAY!
I'M REALLY GOING TO LOOK FOR HINA TODAY!
DUDUM
HUH?
ANZU?
HINA!

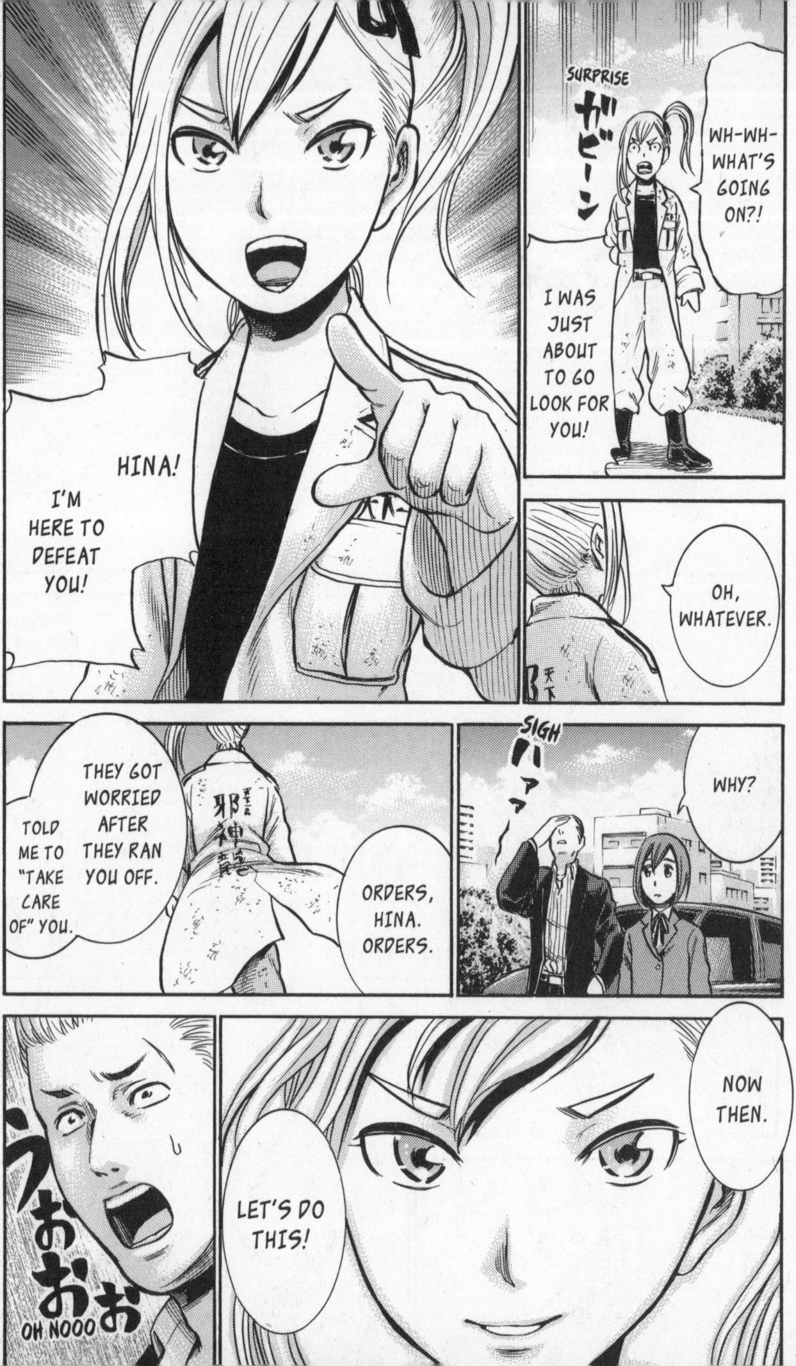
SURPRISE
ガビーン
WH-WH-WHAT'S GOING ON?!
I WAS JUST ABOUT TO GO LOOK FOR YOU!
OH, WHATEVER.
HINA!
I'M HERE TO DEFEAT YOU!
SIGH
ハァー
WHY?
ORDERS, HINA. ORDERS.
THEY GOT WORRIED AFTER THEY RAN YOU OFF.
TOLD ME TO "TAKE CARE OF" YOU.
NOW THEN.
LET'S DO THIS!
うおおお
OH NOOO

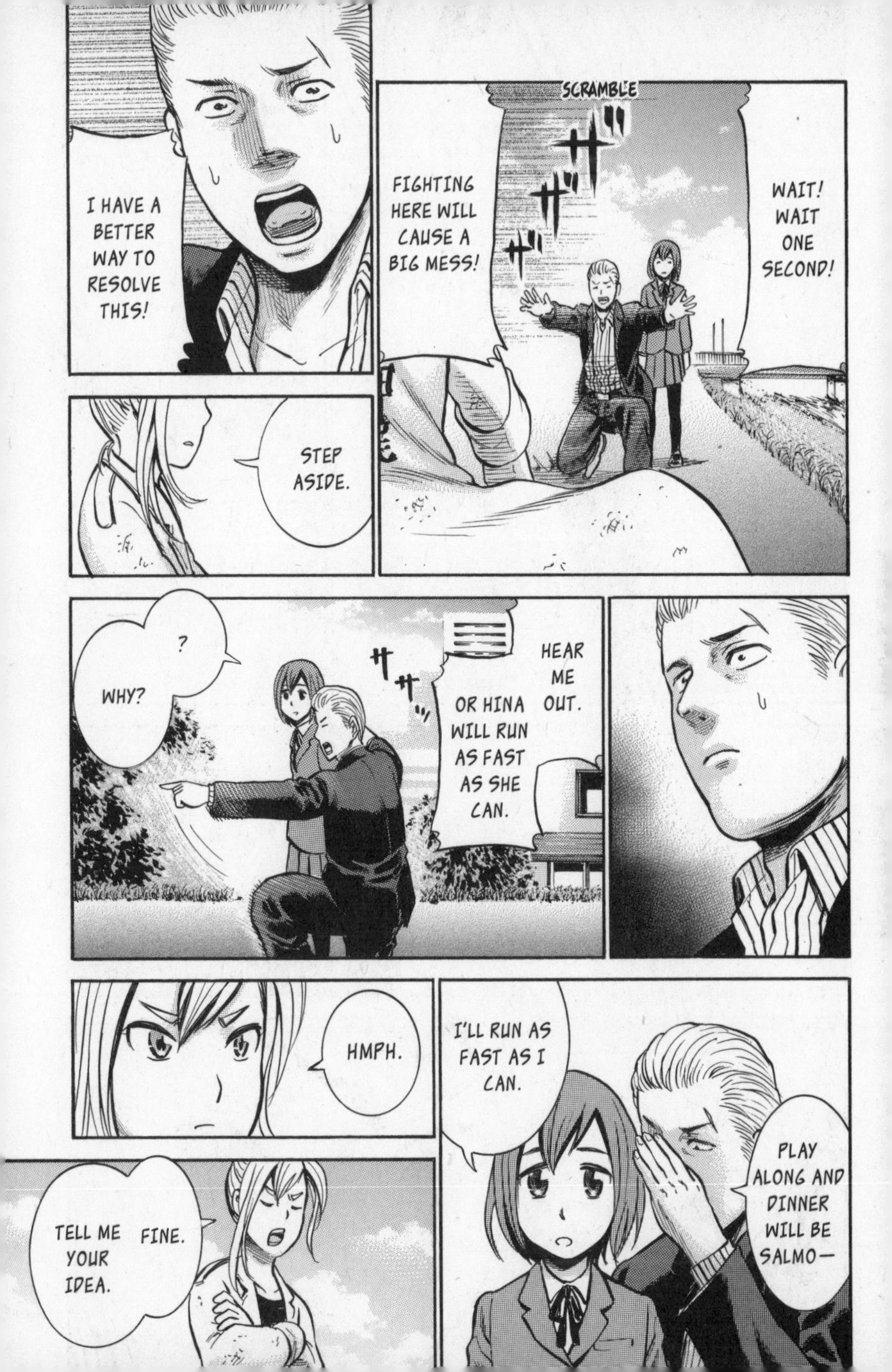
SCRAMBLE
WAIT! WAIT ONE SECOND!
FIGHTING HERE WILL CAUSE A BIG MESS!
I HAVE A BETTER WAY TO RESOLVE THIS!
STEP ASIDE.
HEAR ME OUT.
OR HINA WILL RUN AS FAST AS SHE CAN.
?
WHY?
PLAY ALONG AND DINNER WILL BE SALMO—
I'LL RUN AS FAST AS I CAN.
HMPH.
FINE.
TELL ME YOUR IDEA.

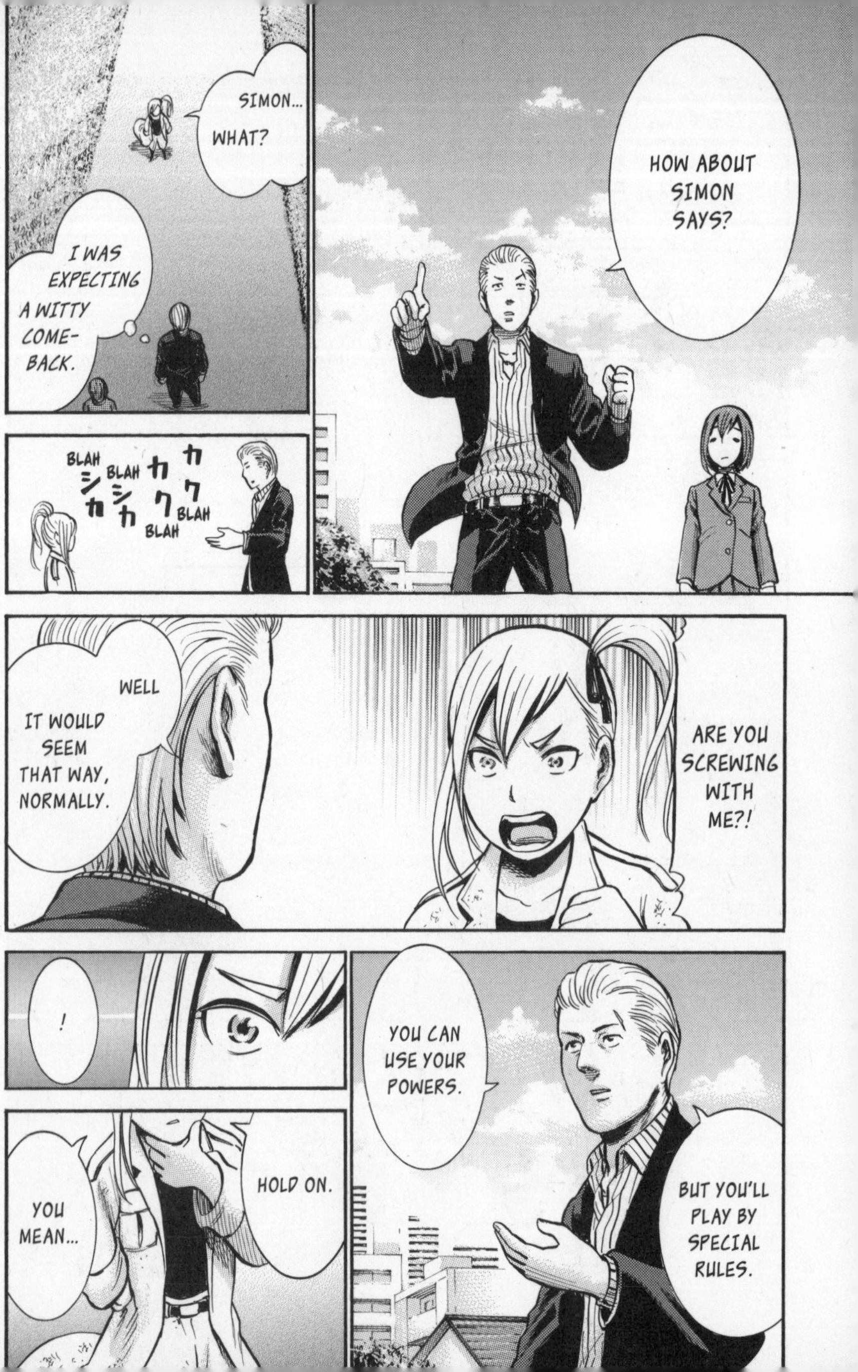
HOW ABOUT SIMON SAYS?
SIMON... WHAT?
I WAS EXPECTING A WITTY COME-BACK.
カク カク
BLAH BLAH BLAH BLAH
シカ シカ
ARE YOU SCREWING WITH ME?!
WELL
IT WOULD SEEM THAT WAY, NORMALLY.
YOU CAN USE YOUR POWERS.
BUT YOU'LL PLAY BY SPECIAL RULES.
!
HOLD ON.
YOU MEAN...

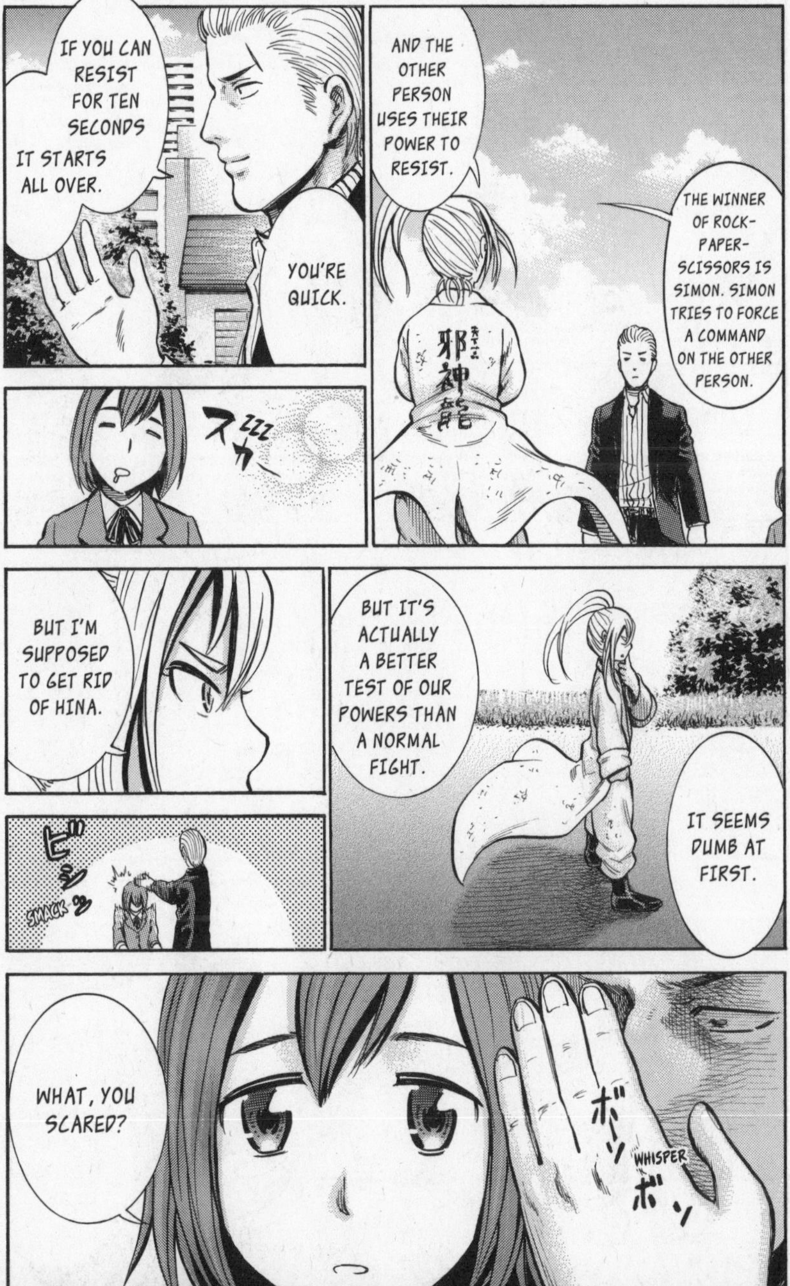
THE WINNER OF ROCK-PAPER-SCISSORS IS SIMON. SIMON TRIES TO FORCE A COMMAND ON THE OTHER PERSON.
AND THE OTHER PERSON USES THEIR POWER TO RESIST.
IF YOU CAN RESIST FOR TEN SECONDS IT STARTS ALL OVER.
YOU'RE QUICK.
スカー
ZZZ
IT SEEMS DUMB AT FIRST.
BUT IT'S ACTUALLY A BETTER TEST OF OUR POWERS THAN A NORMAL FIGHT.
BUT I'M SUPPOSED TO GET RID OF HINA.
ビシッ
SMACK
WHAT, YOU SCARED?
ボソッ
WHISPER
ボソッ

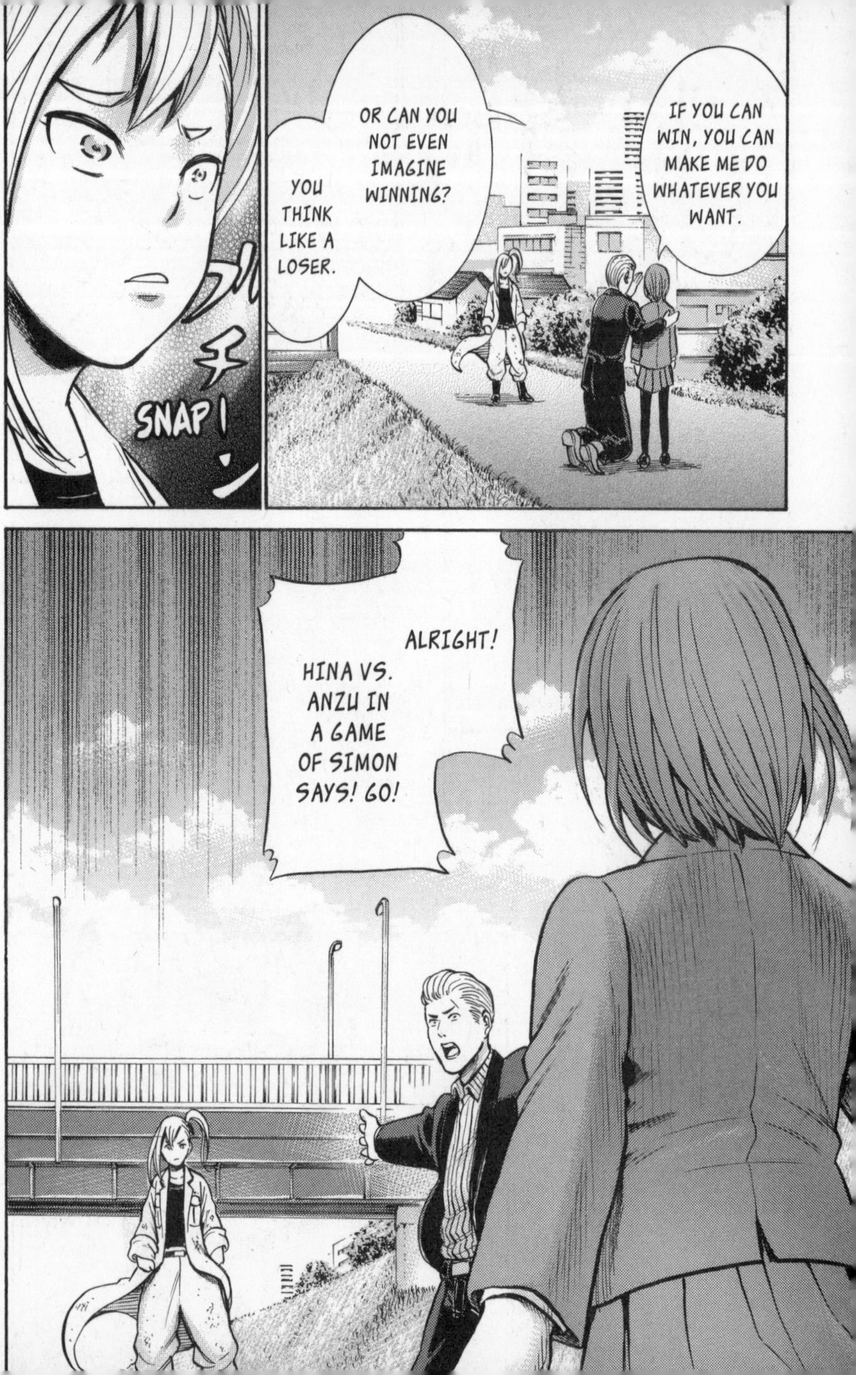
IF YOU CAN WIN, YOU CAN MAKE ME DO WHATEVER YOU WANT.
OR CAN YOU NOT EVEN IMAGINE WINNING?
YOU THINK LIKE A LOSER.
チ
SNAP!
ALRIGHT!
HINA VS. ANZU IN A GAME OF SIMON SAYS! GO!

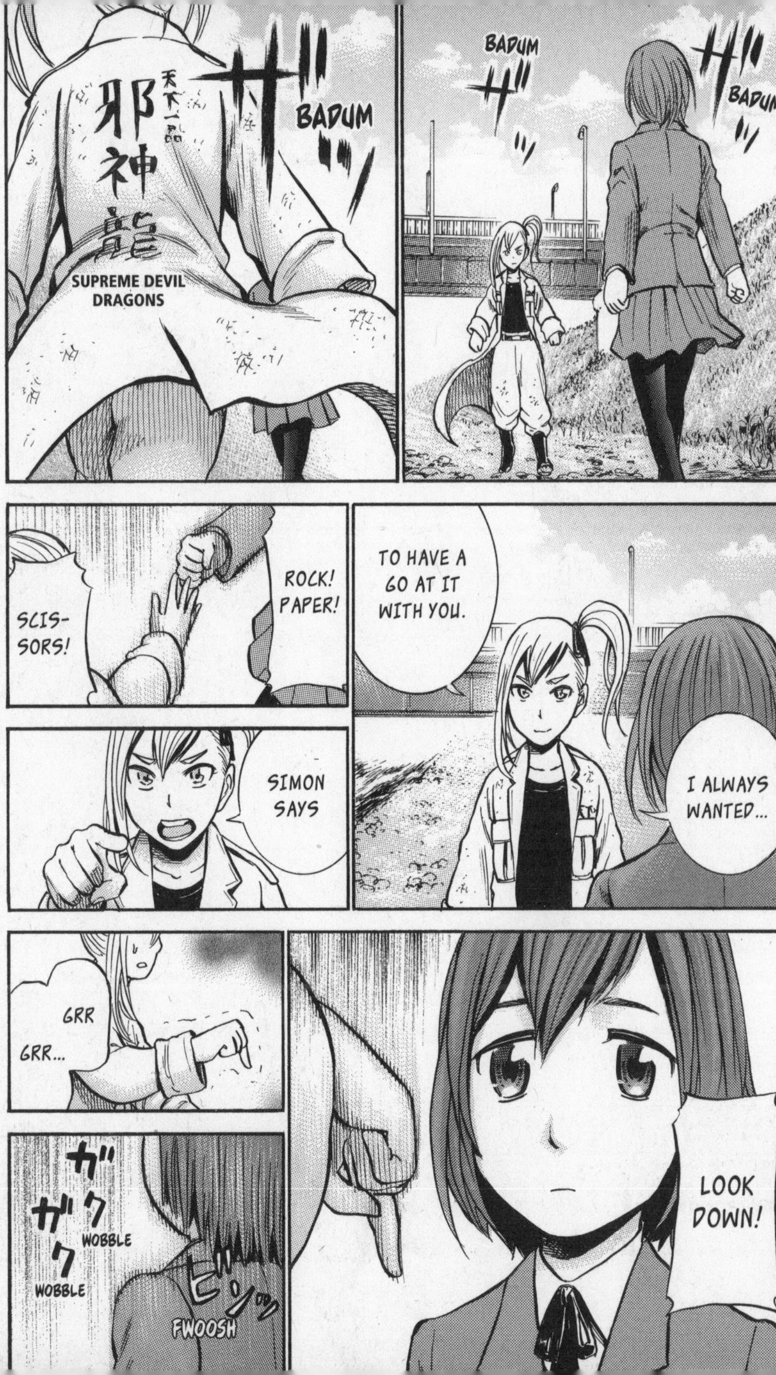

BADUM
BADUM
邪神龍
SUPREME DEVIL DRAGONS
BADUM
I ALWAYS WANTED...
TO HAVE A GO AT IT WITH YOU.
ROCK! PAPER!
SCIS-SORS!
SIMON SAYS
LOOK DOWN!
GRR GRR...
WOBBLE
WOBBLE
FWOOSH

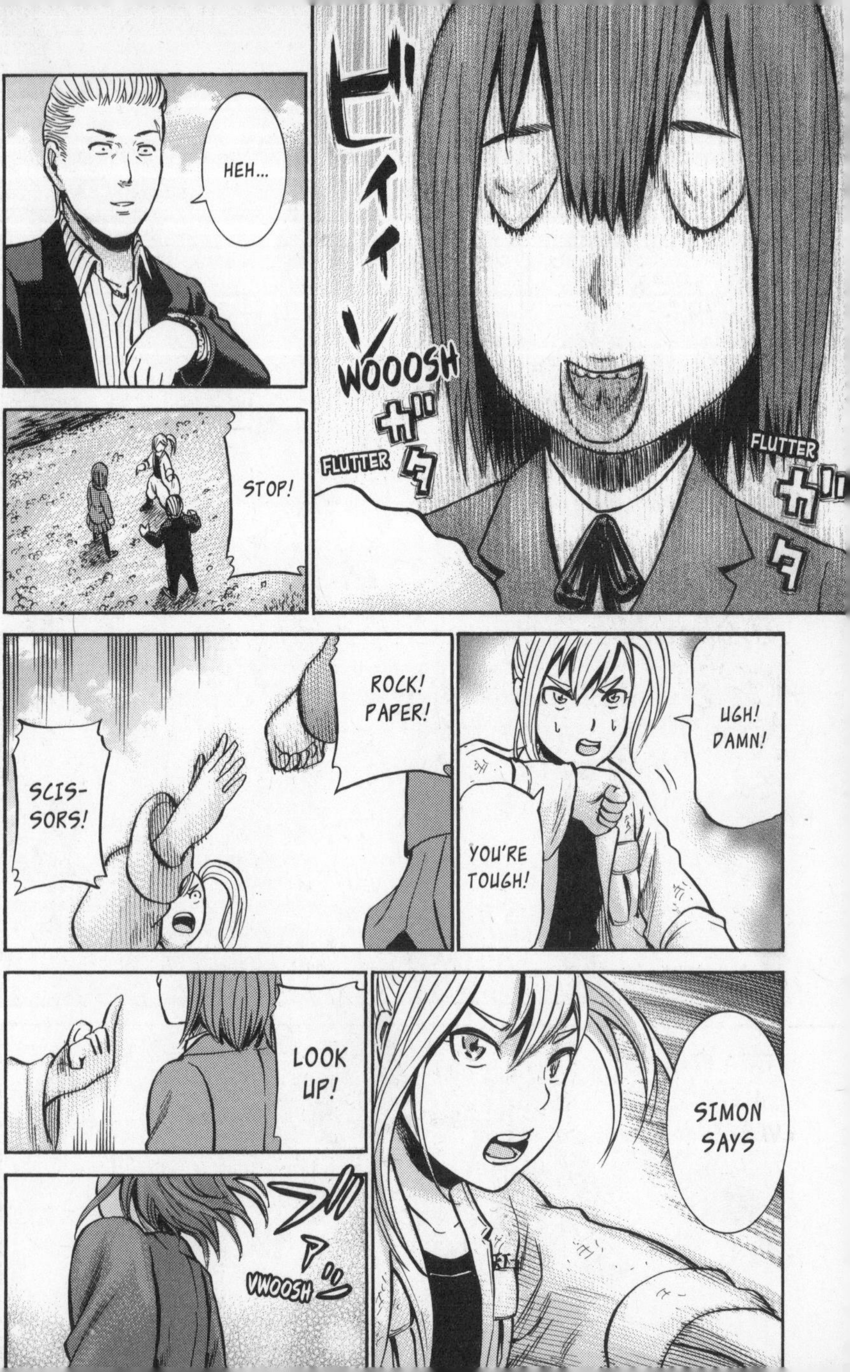
WOOOSH
FLUTTER
FLUTTER
HEH...
STOP!
UGH! DAMN!
YOU'RE TOUGH!
ROCK! PAPER!
SCIS-SORS!
SIMON SAYS
LOOK UP!
VWOOSH

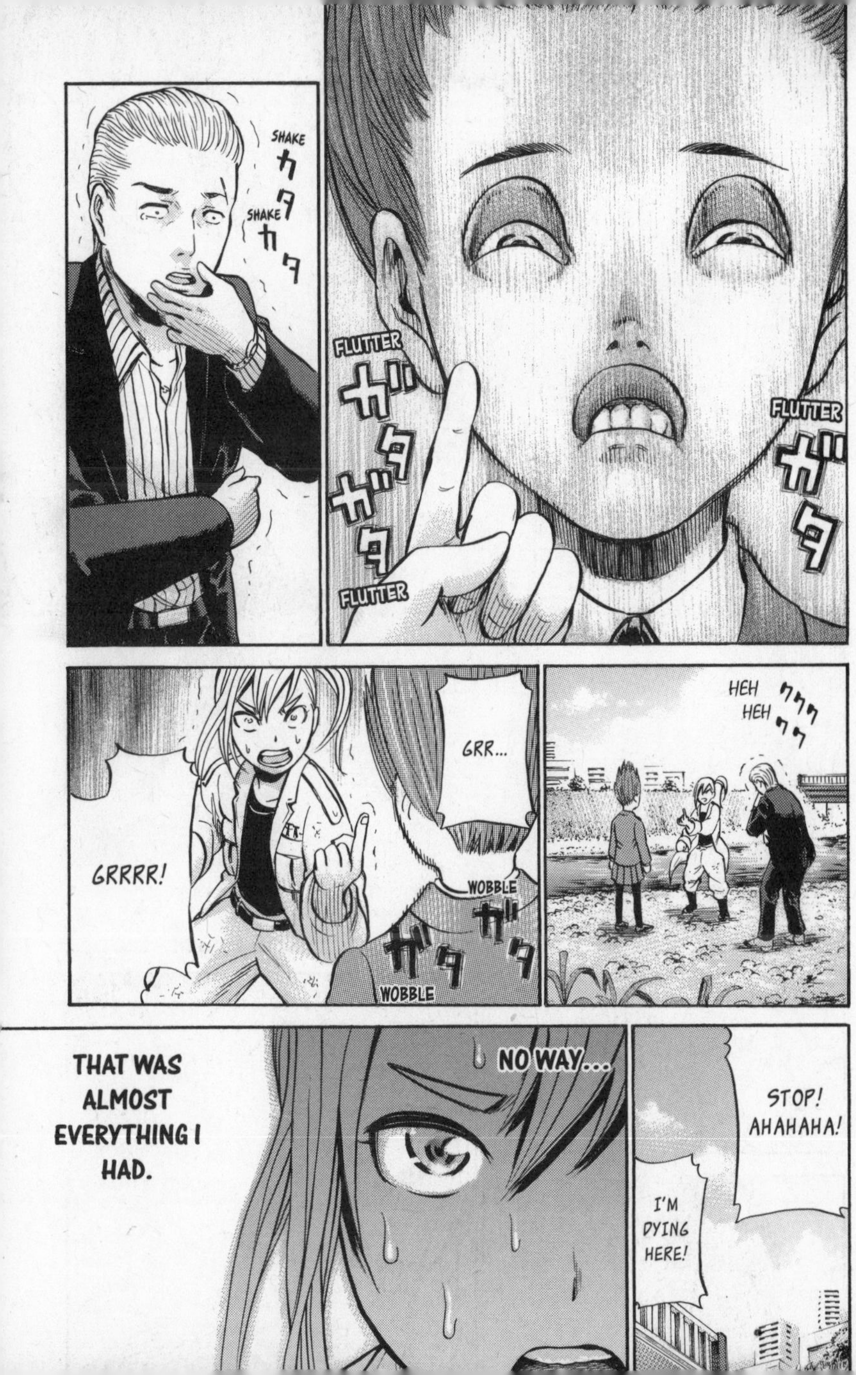
FLUTTER
ガタ
FLUTTER
ガタ
ガタ
FLUTTER
SHAKE
カタ
SHAKE
カタ
HEH HEH
ククク
クク
GRR...
WOBBLE
ガタ
ガタ
WOBBLE
GRRRR!
STOP! AHAHAHA!
I'M DYING HERE!
NO WAY...
THAT WAS ALMOST EVERYTHING I HAD.

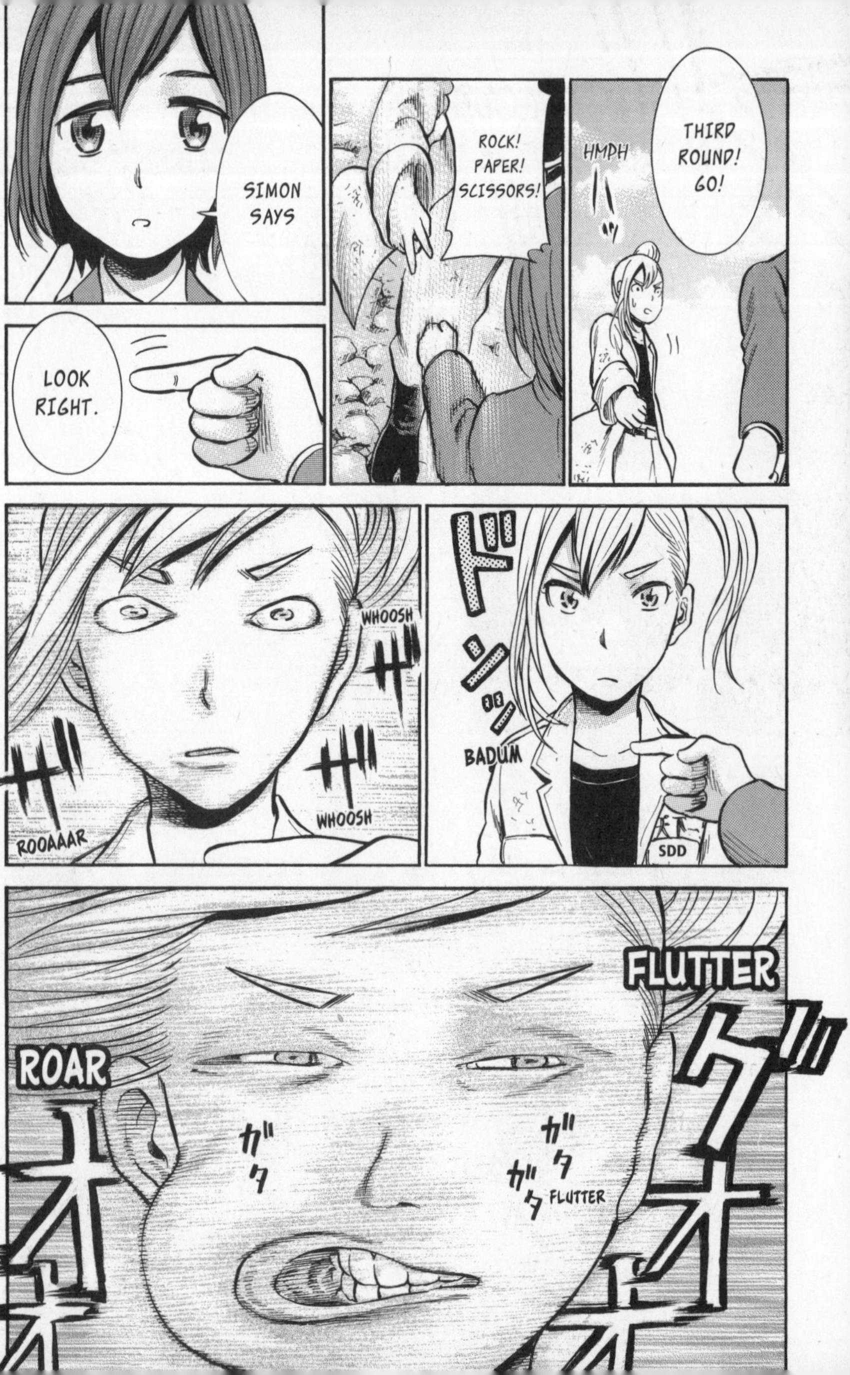
THIRD ROUND! GO!
HMPH
ROCK! PAPER! SCISSORS!
SIMON SAYS
LOOK RIGHT.
BADUM
SDD
WHOOSH
WHOOSH
ROOAAAR
FLUTTER
FLUTTER
ROAR

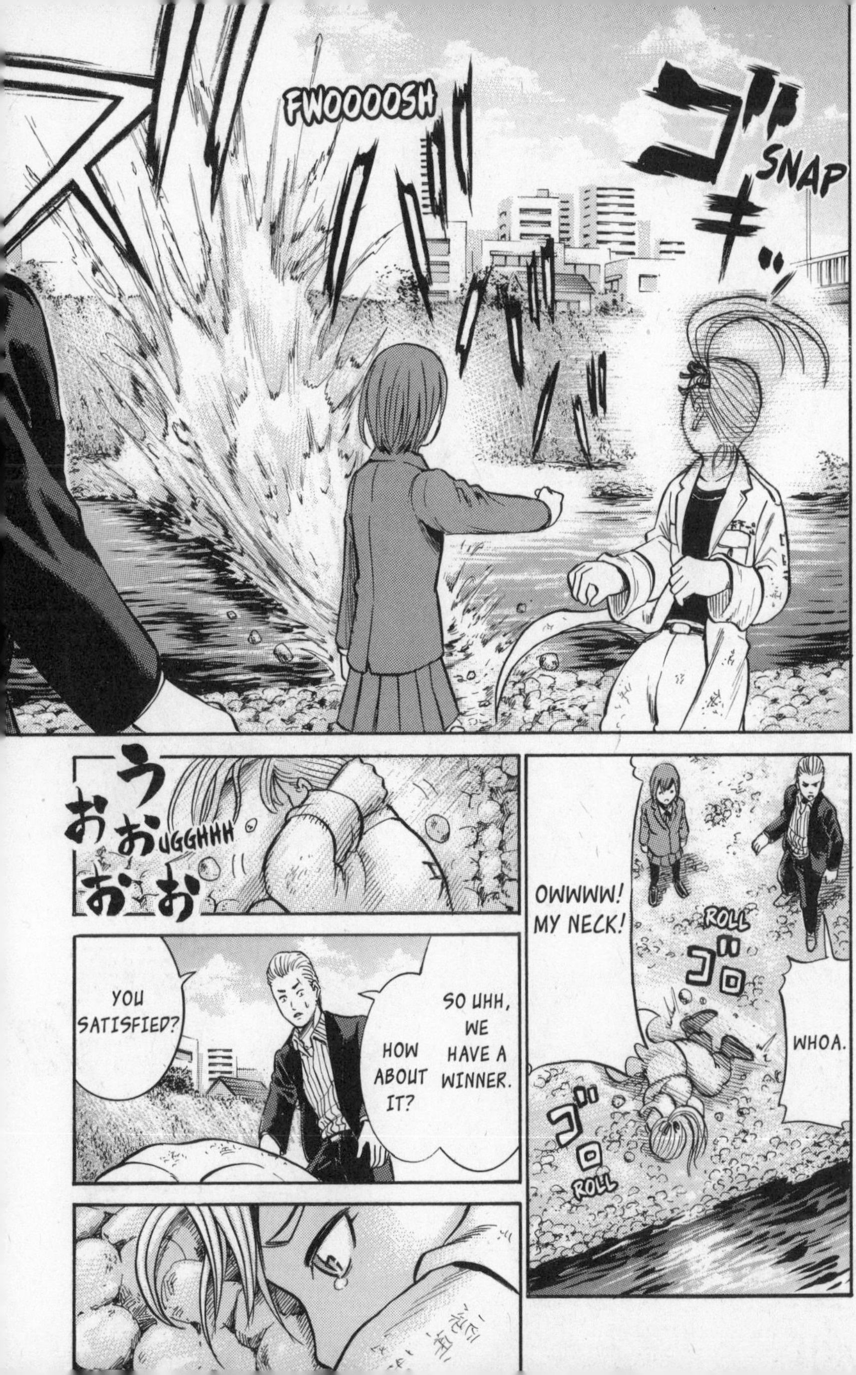

ゴキッ
SNAP
FWOOOOSH
OWWWW! MY NECK!
ROLL
ゴロ
WHOA.
ゴロ
ROLL
うおおおお
UGGHHH
SO UHH, WE HAVE A WINNER.
HOW ABOUT IT?
YOU SATISFIED?

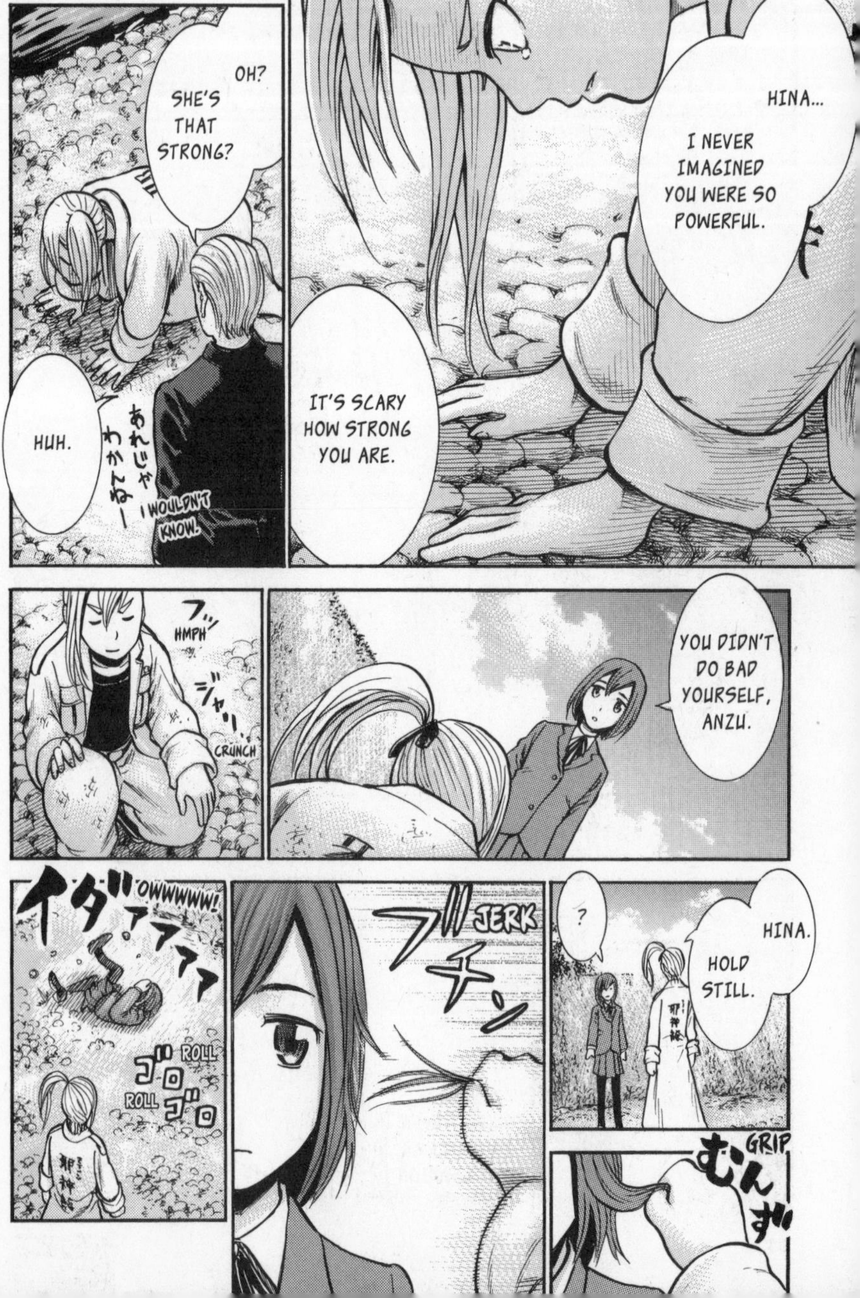
HINA...
I NEVER IMAGINED YOU WERE SO POWERFUL.
IT'S SCARY HOW STRONG YOU ARE.
OH?
SHE'S THAT STRONG?
HUH.
あれじゃわかんねー
I WOULDN'T KNOW.
YOU DIDN'T DO BAD YOURSELF, ANZU.
フッ
HMPH
ジャリ…
CRUNCH
HINA.
HOLD STILL.
?
むんず
GRIP
ブチン
JERK
イダァァァァ
OWWWWW!
ゴロゴロ
ROLL ROLL

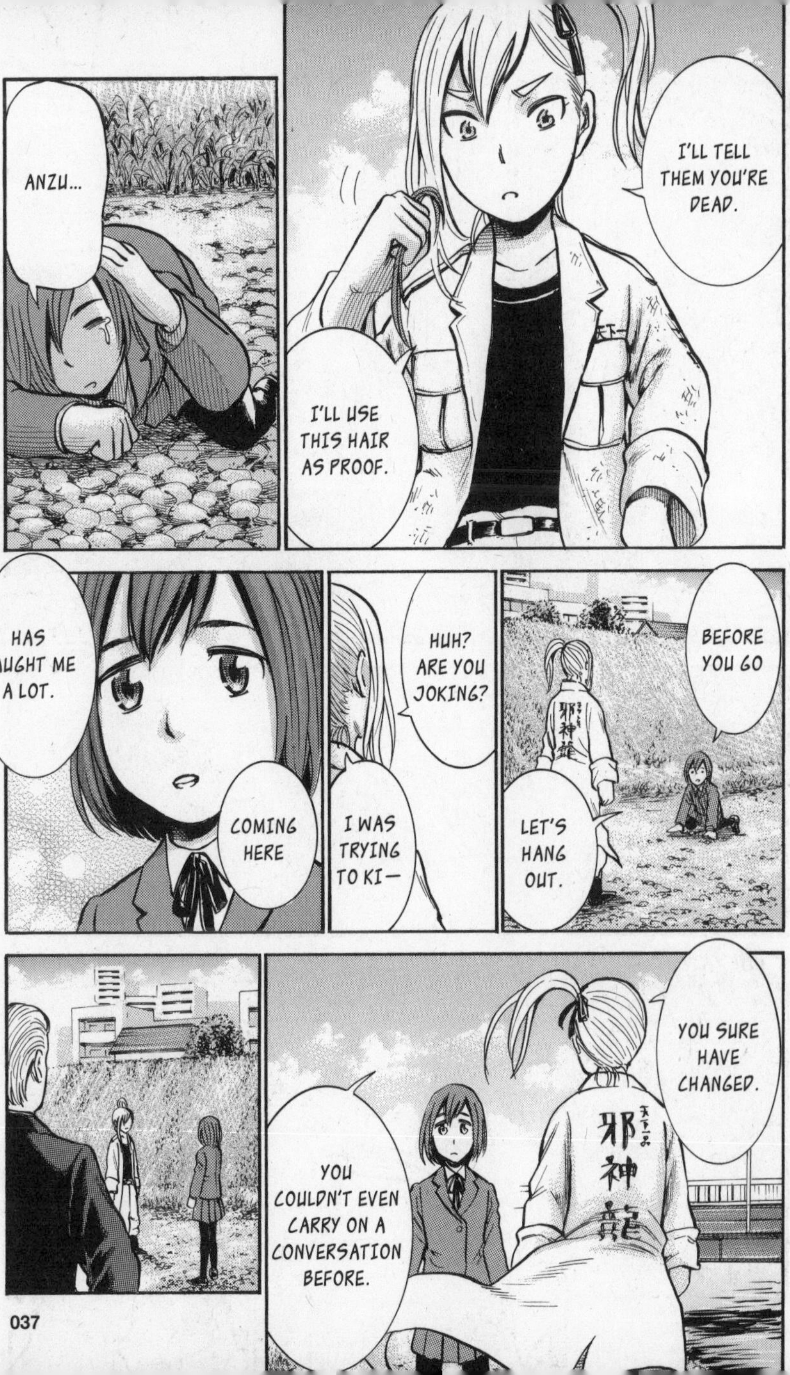
I'LL TELL THEM YOU'RE DEAD.
I'LL USE THIS HAIR AS PROOF.
ANZU...
BEFORE YOU GO
LET'S HANG OUT.
邪神龍
HUH? ARE YOU JOKING?
I WAS TRYING TO KI—
COMING HERE
HAS TAUGHT ME A LOT.
YOU SURE HAVE CHANGED.
YOU COULDN'T EVEN CARRY ON A CONVERSATION BEFORE.

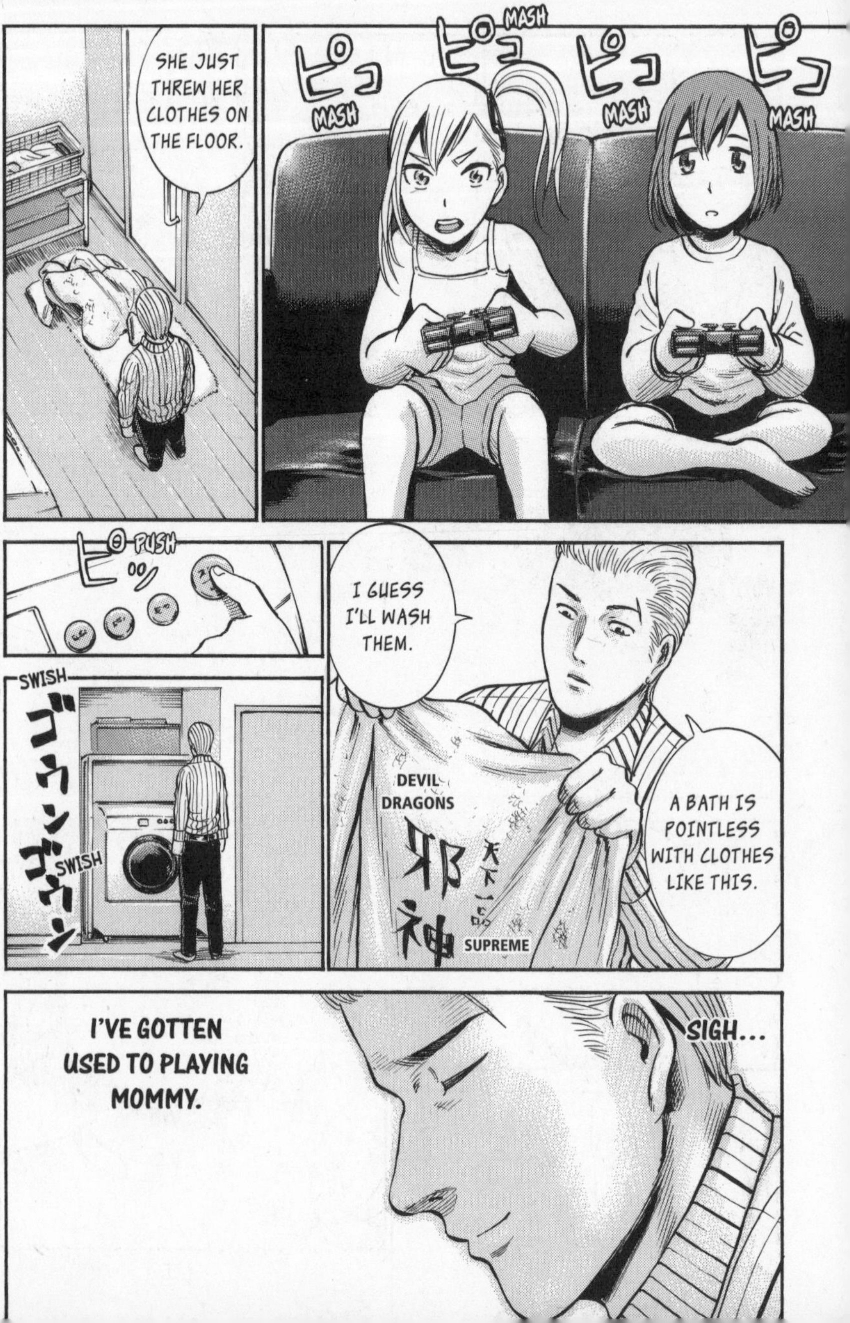

ピコ
MASH
ピコ
MASH
ピコ
MASH
ピコ
MASH
SHE JUST THREW HER CLOTHES ON THE FLOOR.
I GUESS I'LL WASH THEM.
DEVIL DRAGONS
邪神
SUPREME
A BATH IS POINTLESS WITH CLOTHES LIKE THIS.
PUSH
SWISH
ゴウンゴウン
SWISH
SIGH...
I'VE GOTTEN USED TO PLAYING MOMMY.

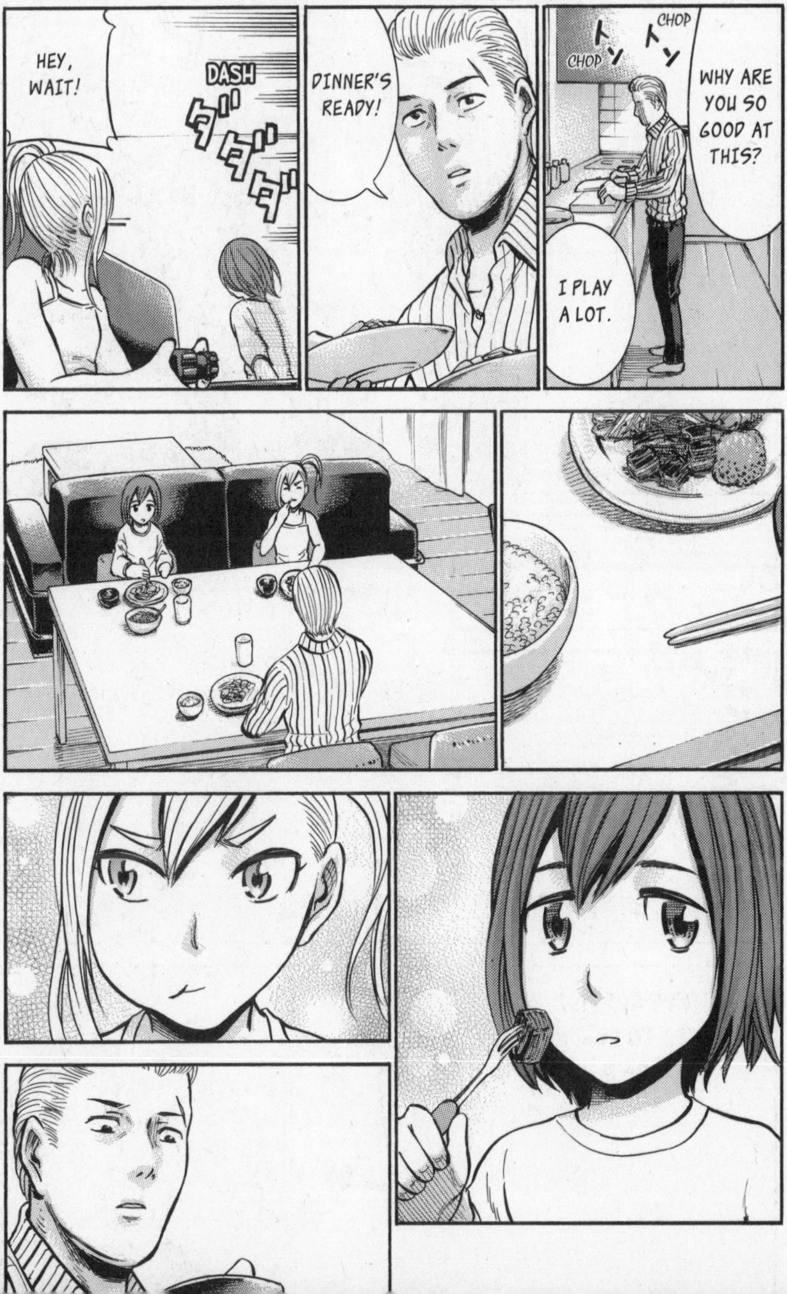
WHY ARE YOU SO GOOD AT THIS?
CHOP
トン
CHOP
トン
I PLAY A LOT.
DINNER'S READY!
DASH
ダダダ
HEY, WAIT!

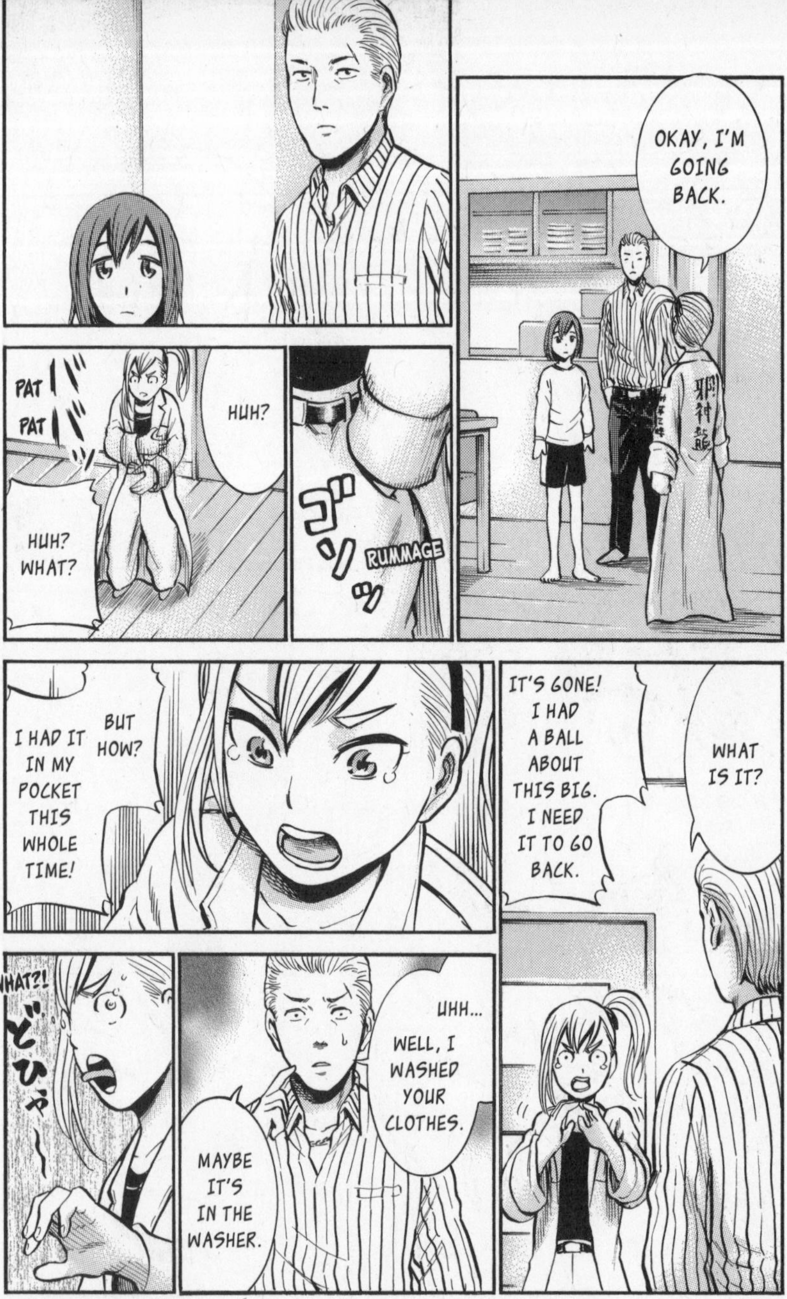
OKAY, I'M GOING BACK.
ゴソッ
RUMMAGE
HUH?
PAT PAT
HUH? WHAT?
WHAT IS IT?
IT'S GONE! I HAD A BALL ABOUT THIS BIG. I NEED IT TO GO BACK.
BUT HOW?
I HAD IT IN MY POCKET THIS WHOLE TIME!
UHH...
WELL, I WASHED YOUR CLOTHES.
MAYBE IT'S IN THE WASHER.
WHAT?!
どひゃ～

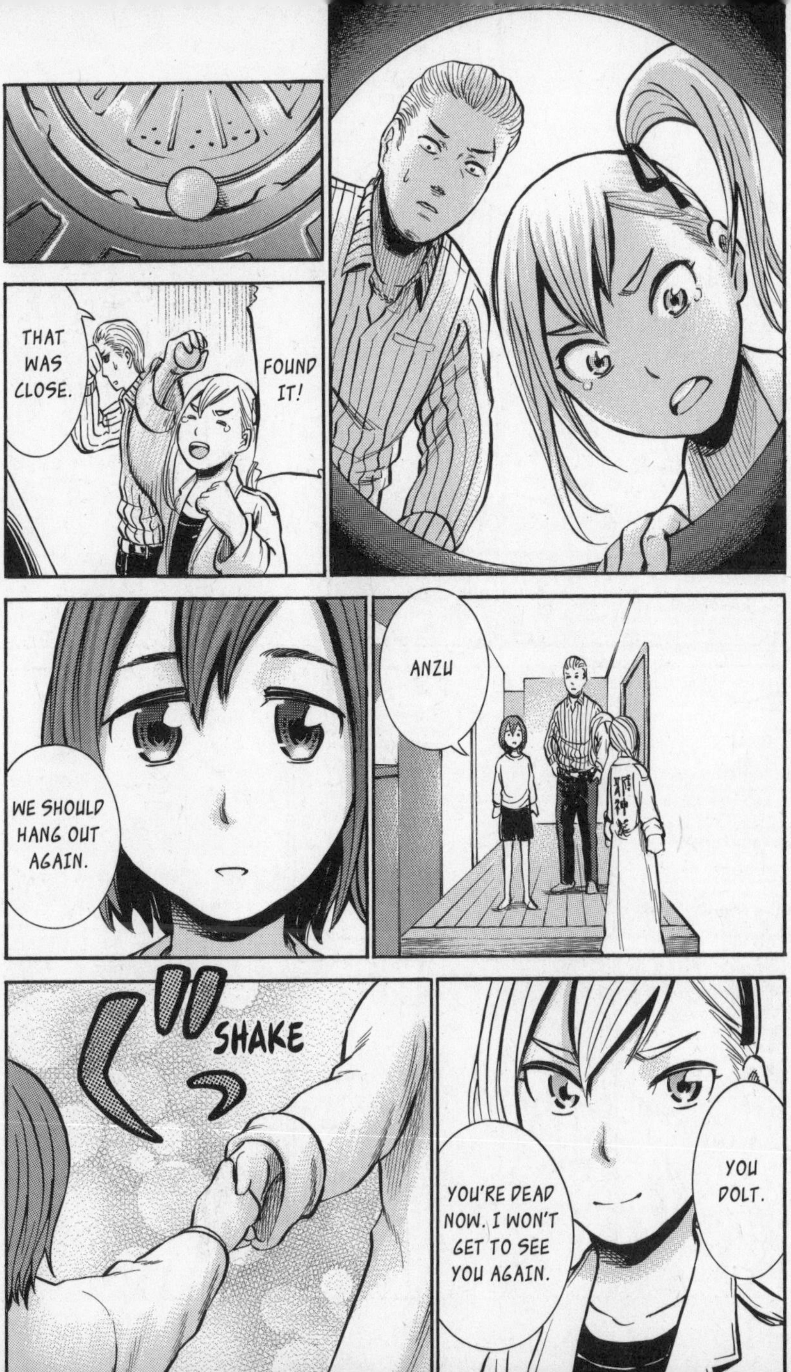
FOUND IT!
THAT WAS CLOSE.
ANZU
WE SHOULD HANG OUT AGAIN.
YOU DOLT.
YOU'RE DEAD NOW. I WON'T GET TO SEE YOU AGAIN.
SHAKE

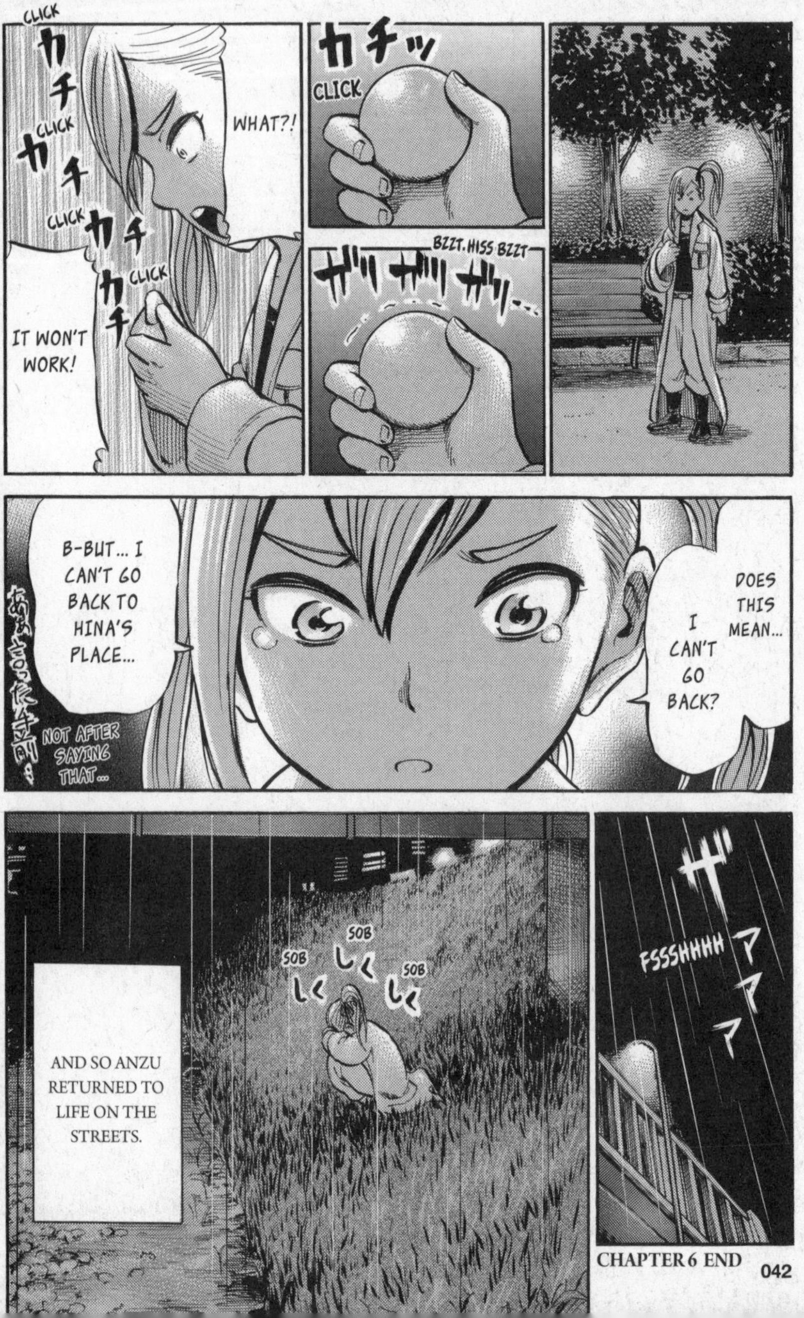

カチッ
CLICK
BZZT.HISS BZZT
ザリ ザリ ザリ...
CLICK
カチ
CLICK
カチ
CLICK
カチ
CLICK
カチ
WHAT?!
IT WON'T WORK!
DOES THIS MEAN... I CAN'T GO BACK?
B-BUT... I CAN'T GO BACK TO HINA'S PLACE...
NOT AFTER SAYING THAT...
ザアアア
FSSSHHHH
SOB
しく
SOB
しく
SOB
しく
AND SO ANZU RETURNED TO LIFE ON THE STREETS.

CHAPTER 6 END

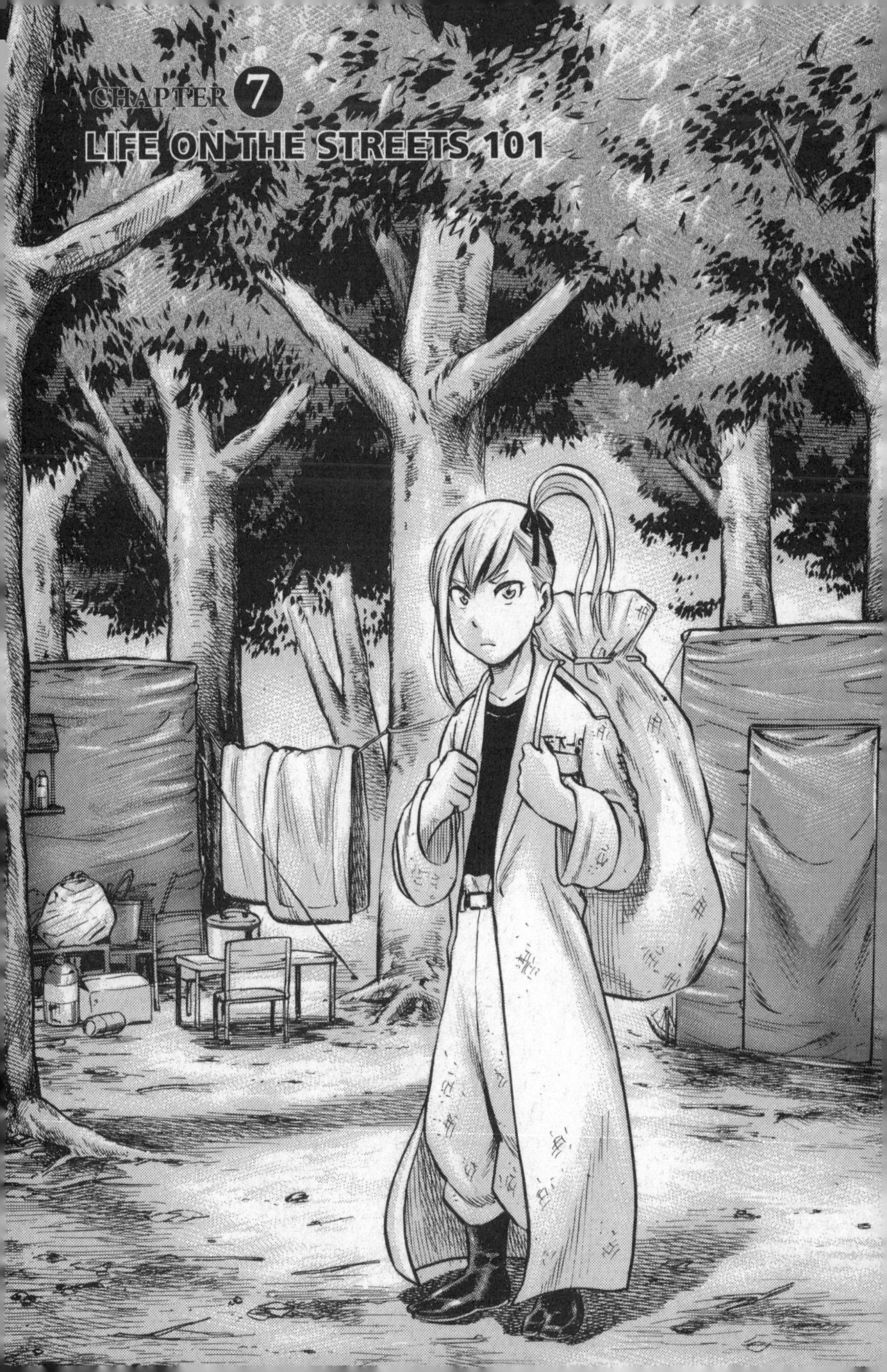
CHAPTER 7
LIFE ON THE STREETS 101

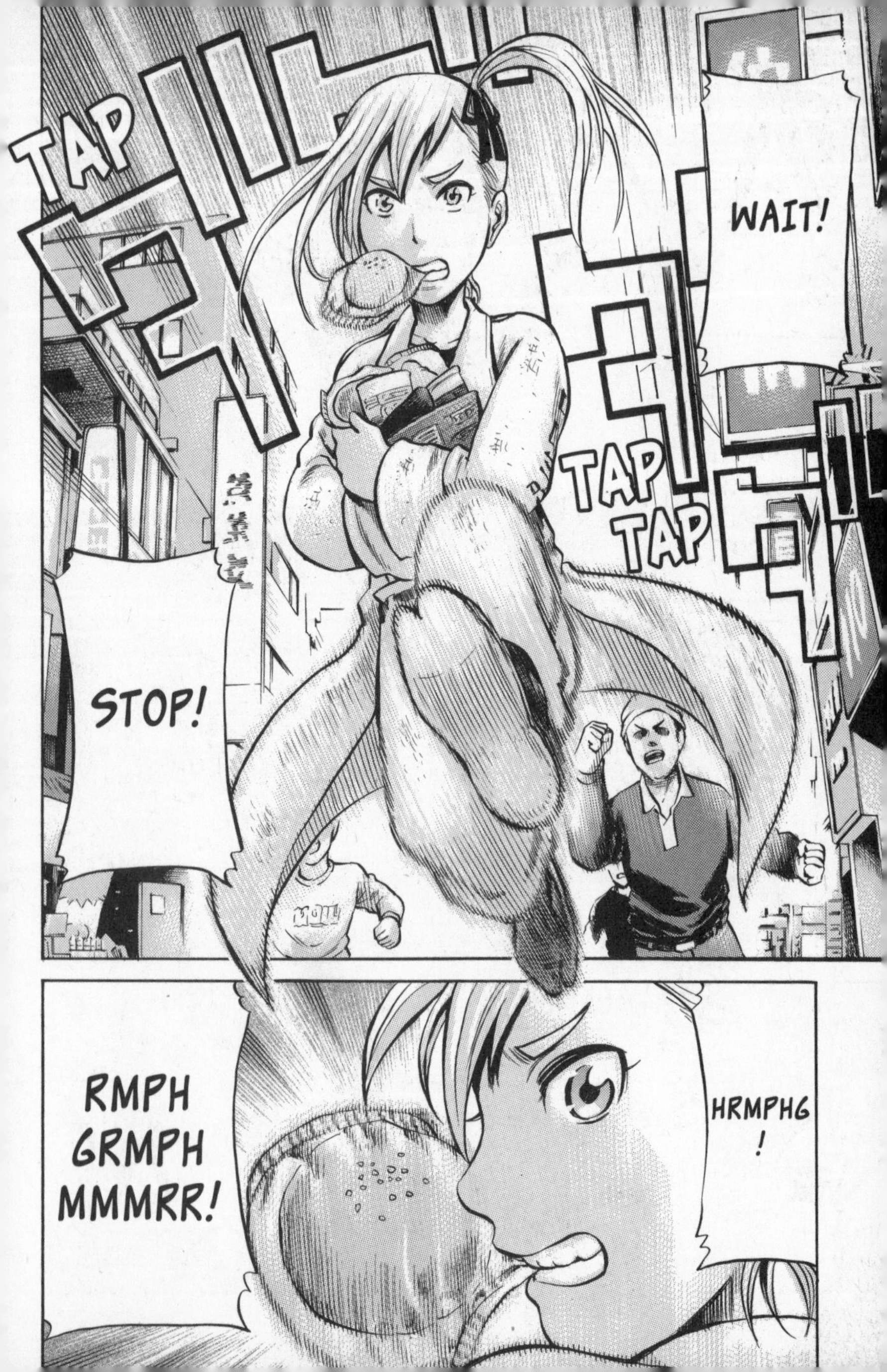
WAIT!
TAP
TAP
TAP
STOP!
HRMPHG
!
RMPH
GRMPH
MMMRR!

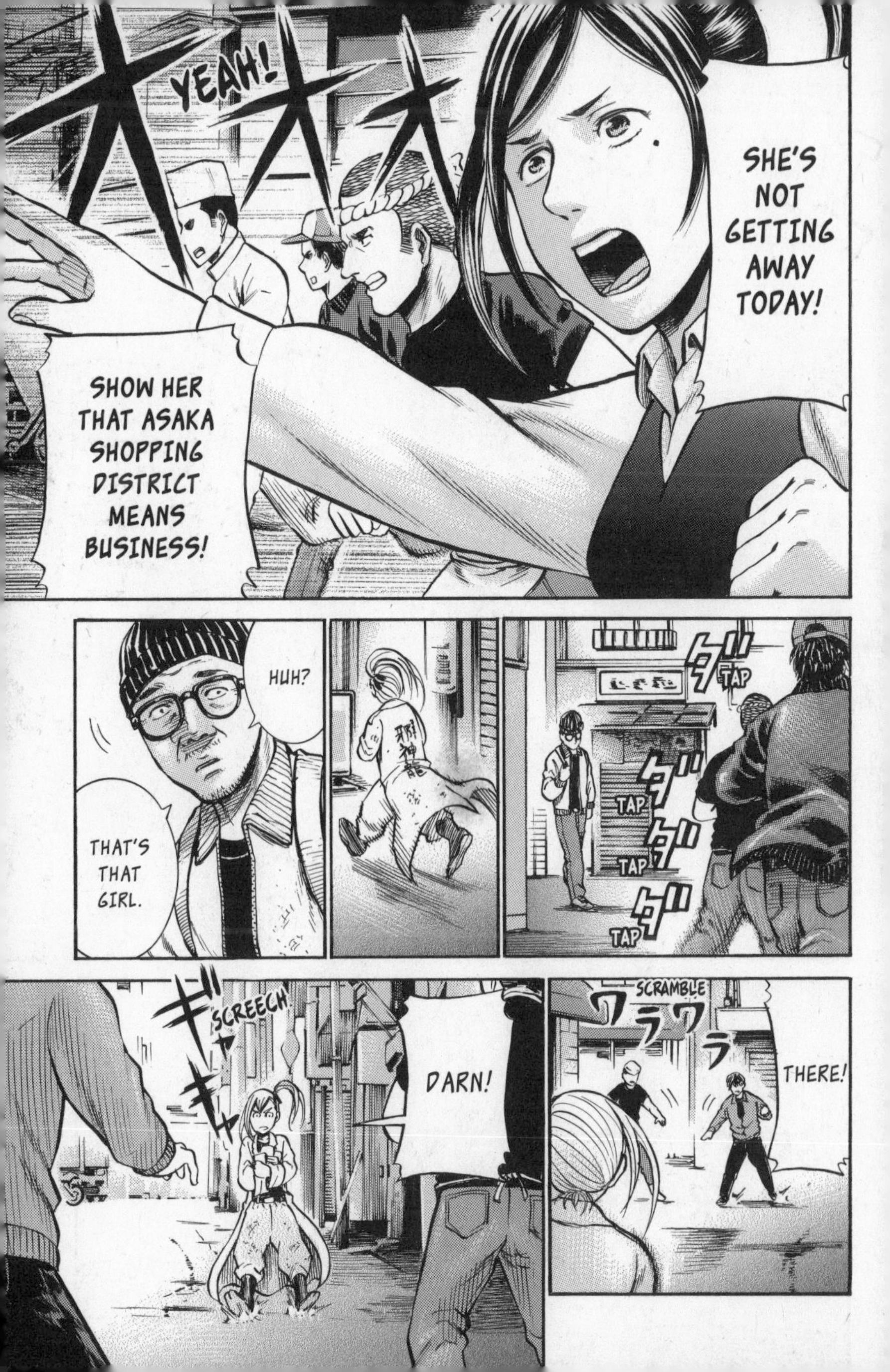
SHE'S NOT GETTING AWAY TODAY!
SHOW HER THAT ASAKA SHOPPING DISTRICT MEANS BUSINESS!
YEAH!
TAP
TAP
TAP
TAP
HUH?
THAT'S THAT GIRL.
SCRAMBLE
THERE!
DARN!
SCREECH

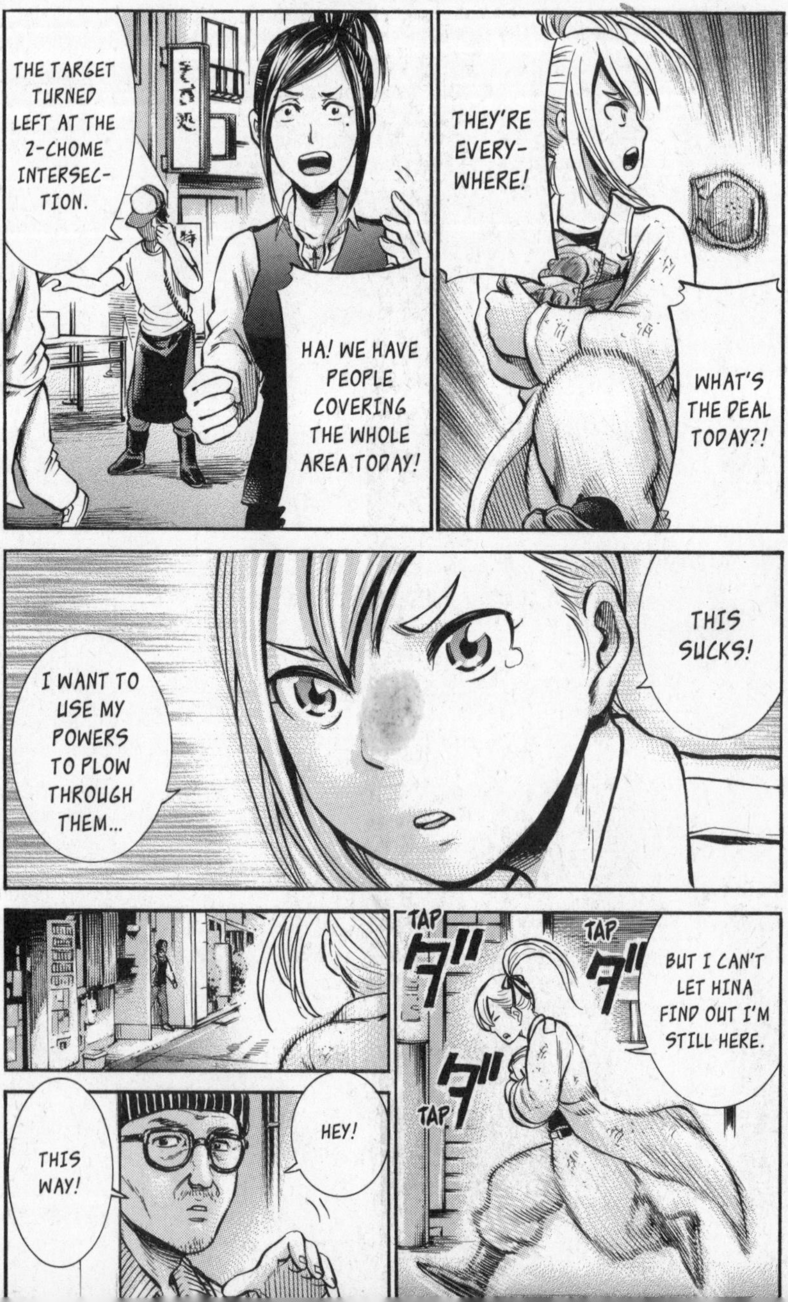
THEY'RE EVERY-WHERE!
WHAT'S THE DEAL TODAY?!
THE TARGET TURNED LEFT AT THE 2-CHOME INTERSEC-TION.
HA! WE HAVE PEOPLE COVERING THE WHOLE AREA TODAY!
THIS SUCKS!
I WANT TO USE MY POWERS TO PLOW THROUGH THEM...
TAP
TAP
BUT I CAN'T LET HINA FIND OUT I'M STILL HERE.
TAP
HEY!
THIS WAY!

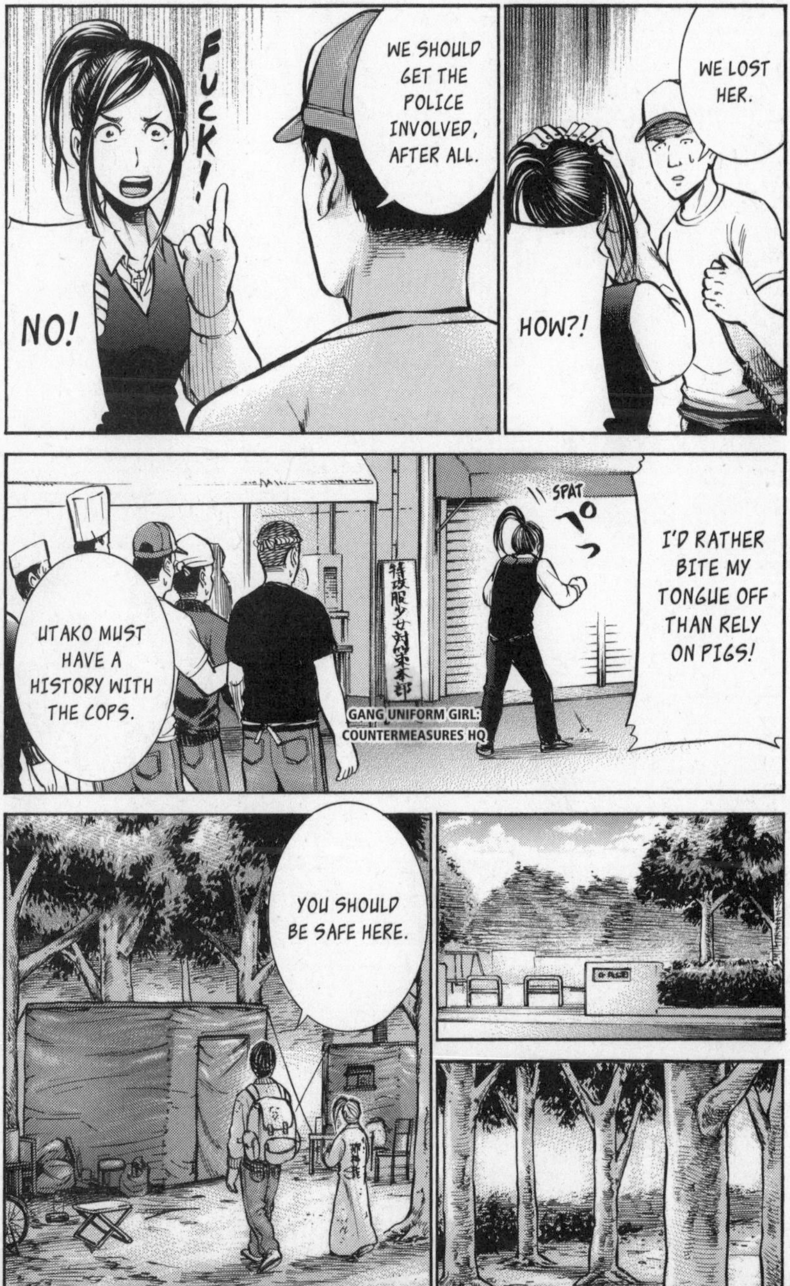
WE LOST HER.
HOW?!
WE SHOULD GET THE POLICE INVOLVED, AFTER ALL.
FUCK!!
NO!
I'D RATHER BITE MY TONGUE OFF THAN RELY ON PIGS!
SPAT
GANG UNIFORM GIRL: COUNTERMEASURES HQ
UTAKO MUST HAVE A HISTORY WITH THE COPS.
YOU SHOULD BE SAFE HERE.

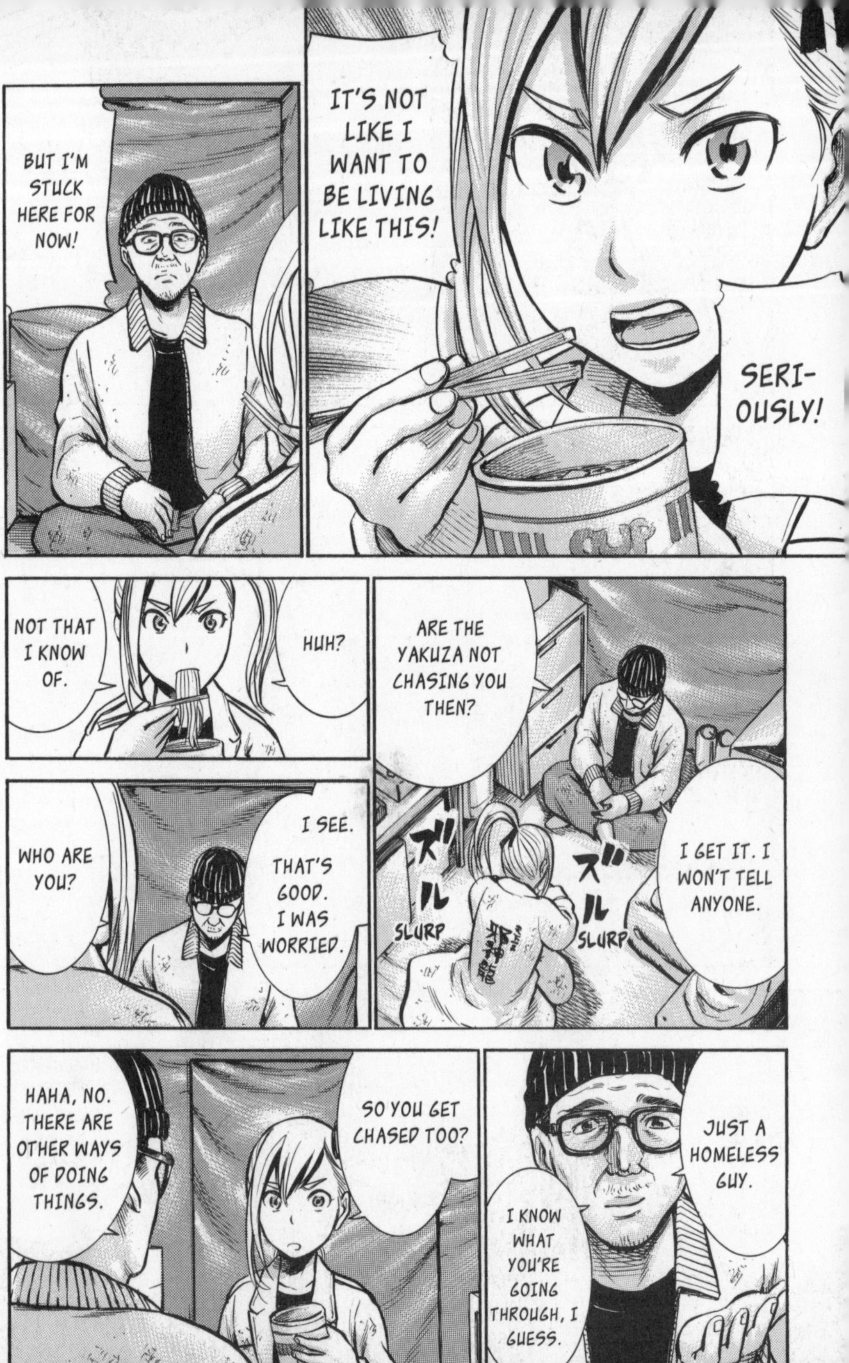
IT'S NOT LIKE I WANT TO BE LIVING LIKE THIS!
SERI-OUSLY!
BUT I'M STUCK HERE FOR NOW!
ARE THE YAKUZA NOT CHASING YOU THEN?
I GET IT. I WON'T TELL ANYONE.
ズル
SLURP
ズル
SLURP
HUH?
NOT THAT I KNOW OF.
I SEE.
THAT'S GOOD. I WAS WORRIED.
WHO ARE YOU?
JUST A HOMELESS GUY.
I KNOW WHAT YOU'RE GOING THROUGH, I GUESS.
SO YOU GET CHASED TOO?
HAHA, NO. THERE ARE OTHER WAYS OF DOING THINGS.

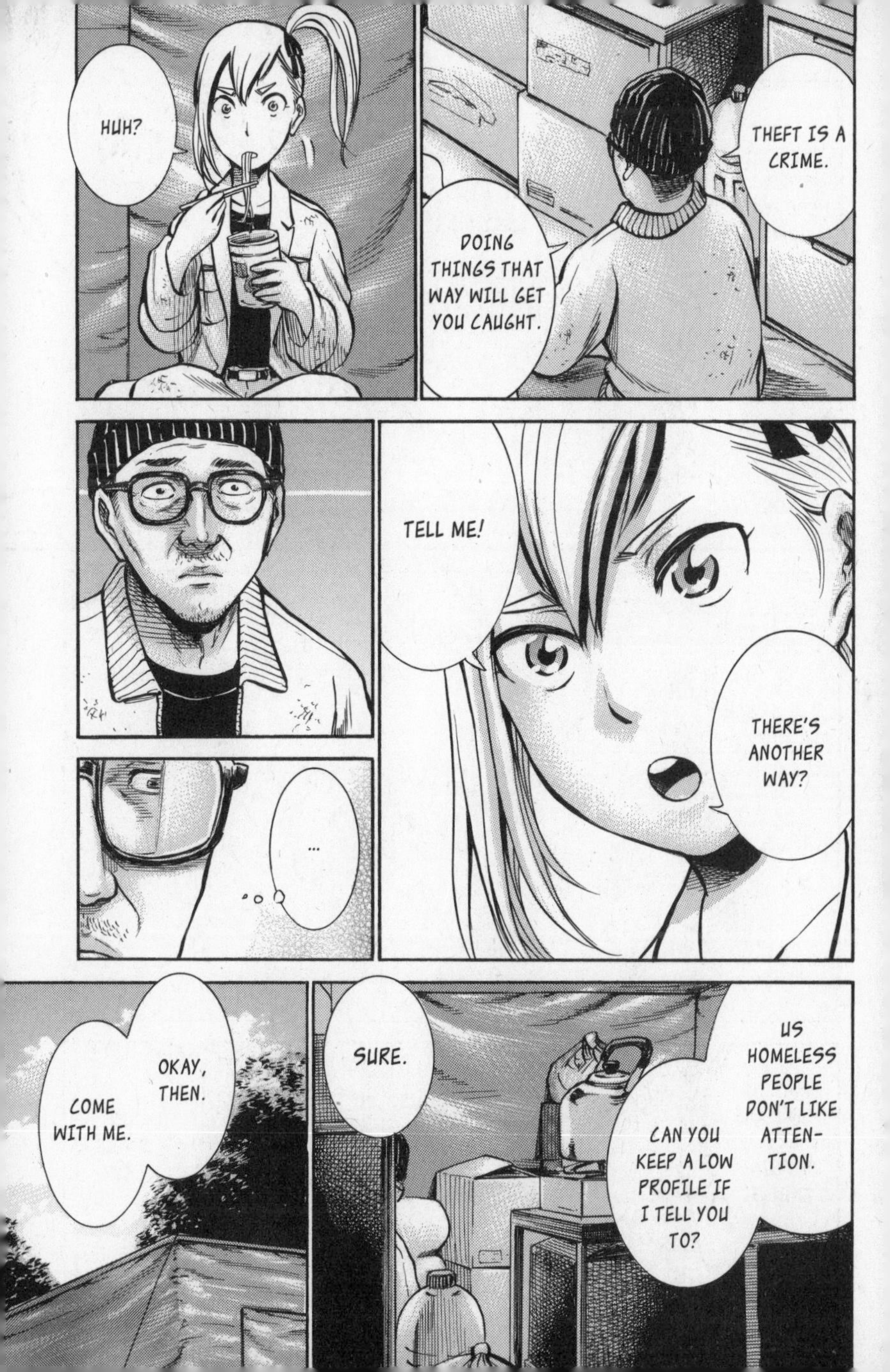
THEFT IS A CRIME.
DOING THINGS THAT WAY WILL GET YOU CAUGHT.
HUH?
THERE'S ANOTHER WAY?
TELL ME!
...
US HOMELESS PEOPLE DON'T LIKE ATTEN-TION.
CAN YOU KEEP A LOW PROFILE IF I TELL YOU TO?
SURE.
OKAY, THEN.
COME WITH ME.

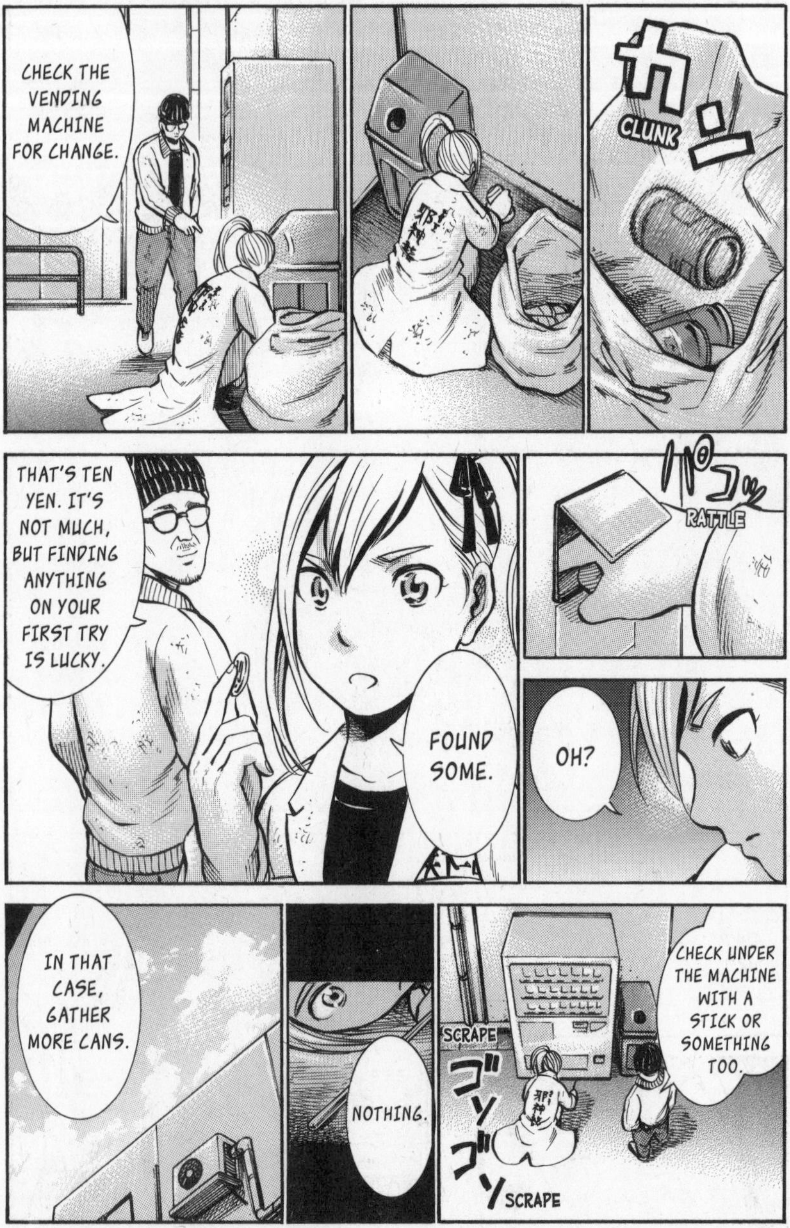
カン
CLUNK
CHECK THE VENDING MACHINE FOR CHANGE.
パコッ
RATTLE
OH?
FOUND SOME.
THAT'S TEN YEN. IT'S NOT MUCH, BUT FINDING ANYTHING ON YOUR FIRST TRY IS LUCKY.
CHECK UNDER THE MACHINE WITH A STICK OR SOMETHING TOO.
SCRAPE
ゴソゴソ
SCRAPE
NOTHING.
IN THAT CASE, GATHER MORE CANS.

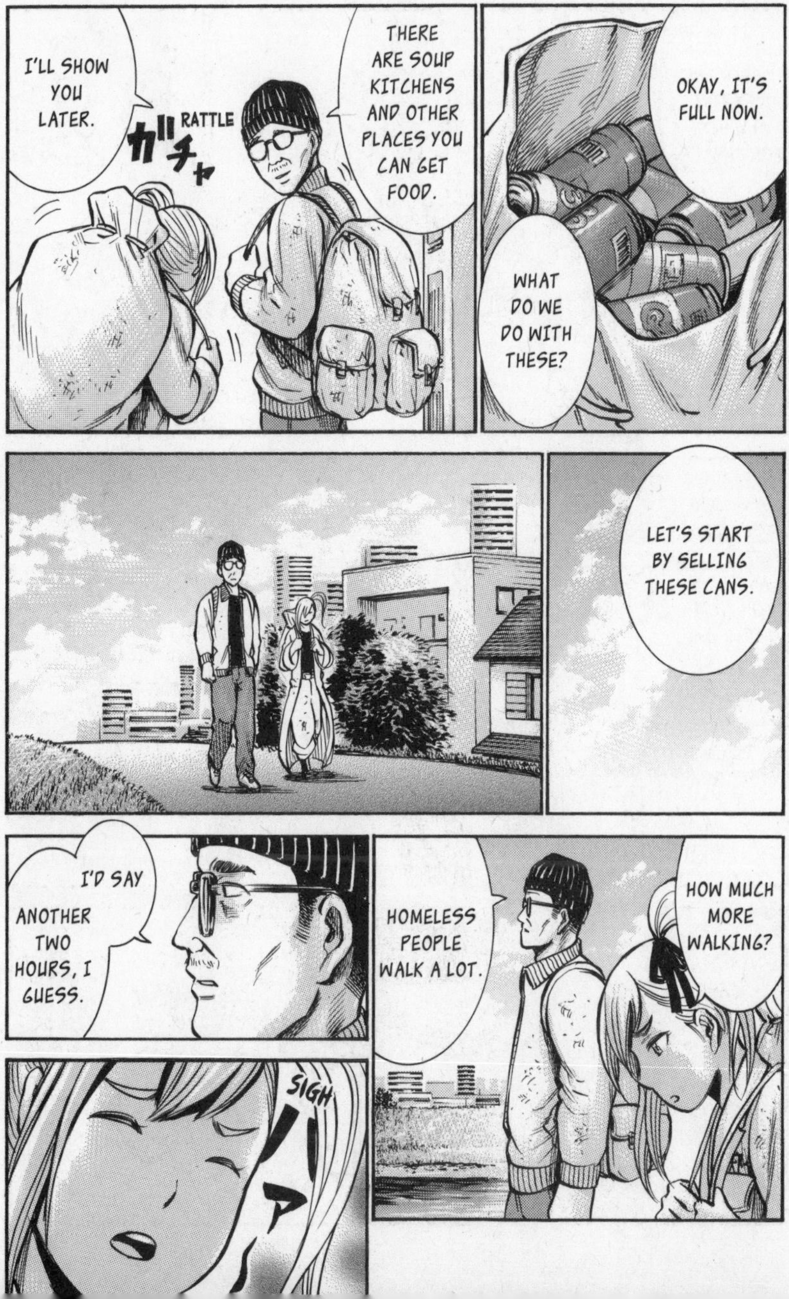
OKAY, IT'S FULL NOW.
WHAT DO WE DO WITH THESE?
THERE ARE SOUP KITCHENS AND OTHER PLACES YOU CAN GET FOOD.
ガチャ
RATTLE
I'LL SHOW YOU LATER.
LET'S START BY SELLING THESE CANS.
HOW MUCH MORE WALKING?
HOMELESS PEOPLE WALK A LOT.
I'D SAY
ANOTHER TWO HOURS, I GUESS.
SIGH

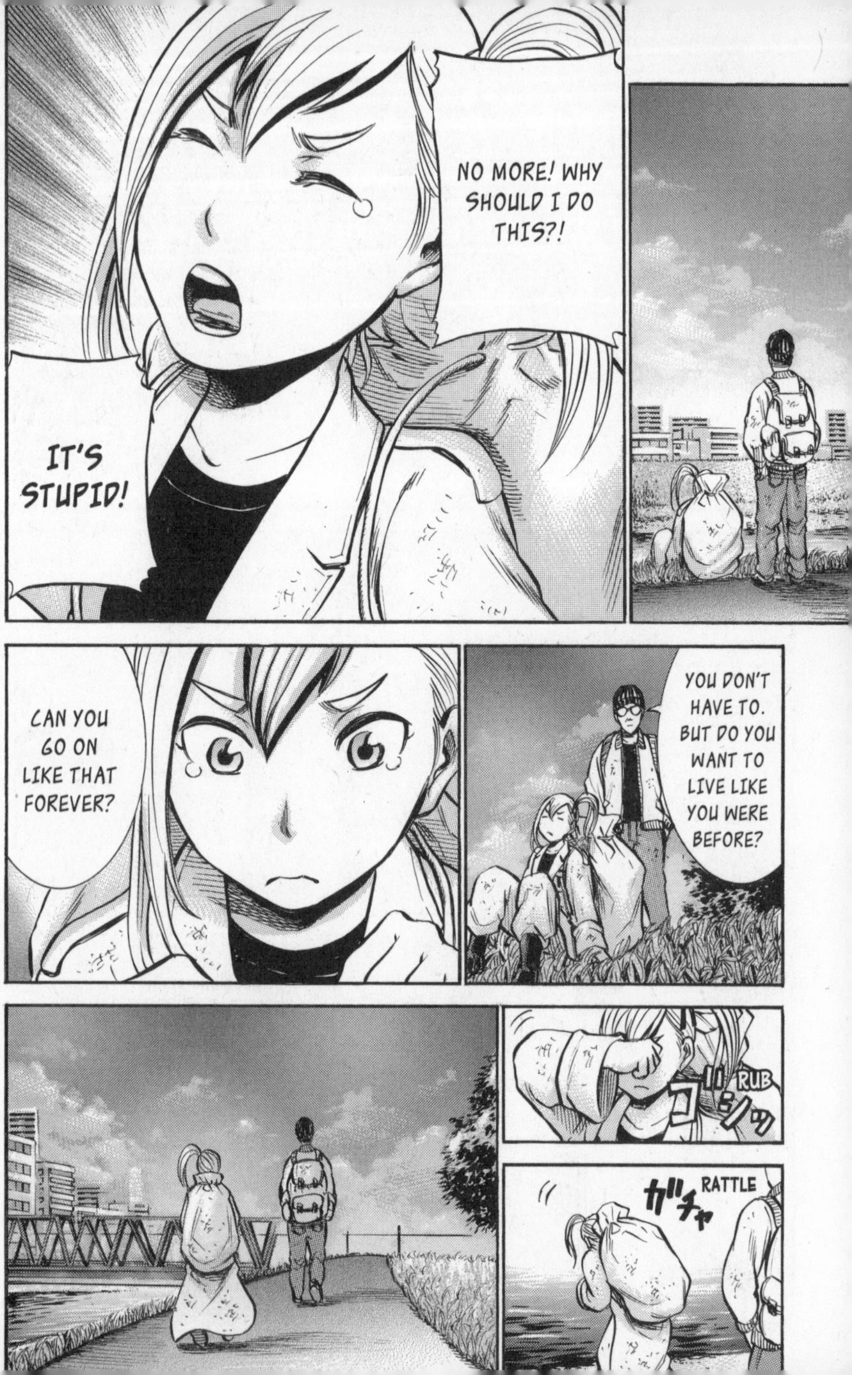
NO MORE! WHY SHOULD I DO THIS?!
IT'S STUPID!
YOU DON'T HAVE TO. BUT DO YOU WANT TO LIVE LIKE YOU WERE BEFORE?
CAN YOU GO ON LIKE THAT FOREVER?
ゴシッ
RUB
ガチャ
RATTLE

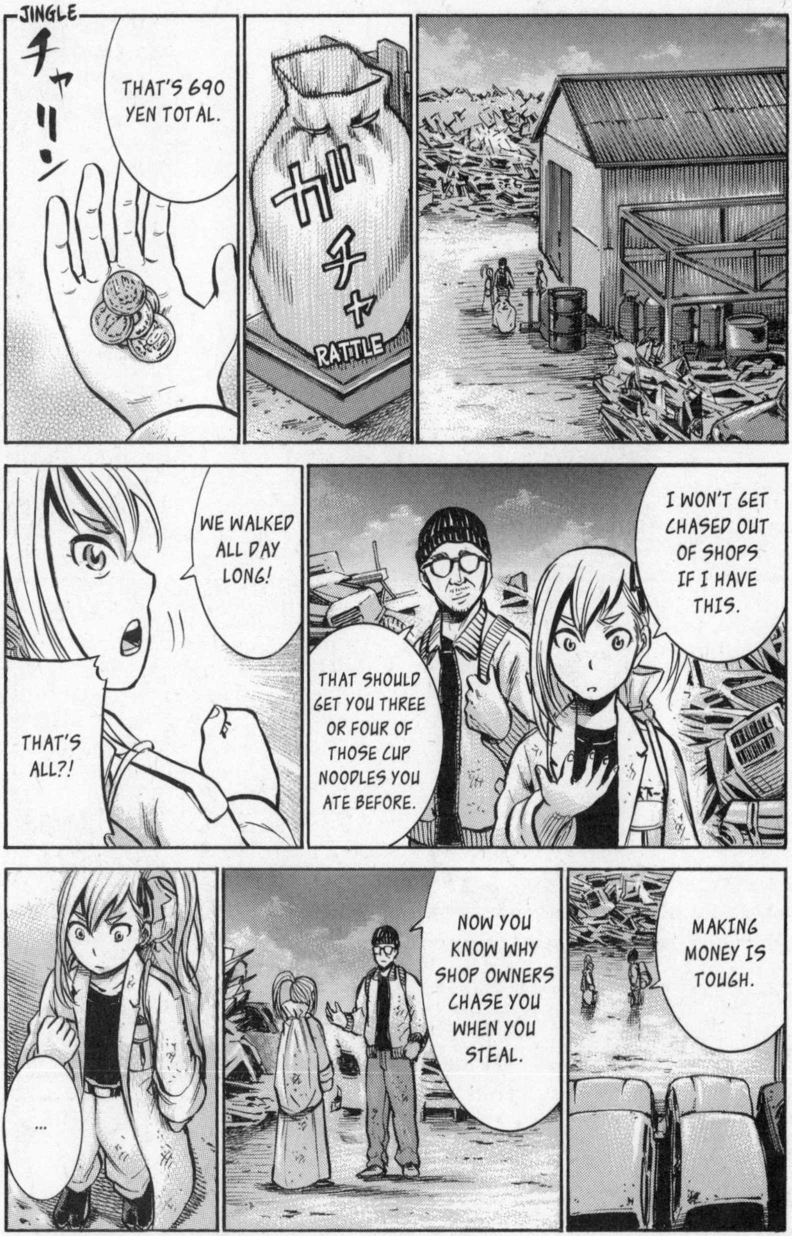
ガチャ
RATTLE
JINGLE
チャリン
THAT'S 690 YEN TOTAL.
I WON'T GET CHASED OUT OF SHOPS IF I HAVE THIS.
THAT SHOULD GET YOU THREE OR FOUR OF THOSE CUP NOODLES YOU ATE BEFORE.
WE WALKED ALL DAY LONG!
THAT'S ALL?!
MAKING MONEY IS TOUGH.
NOW YOU KNOW WHY SHOP OWNERS CHASE YOU WHEN YOU STEAL.
...

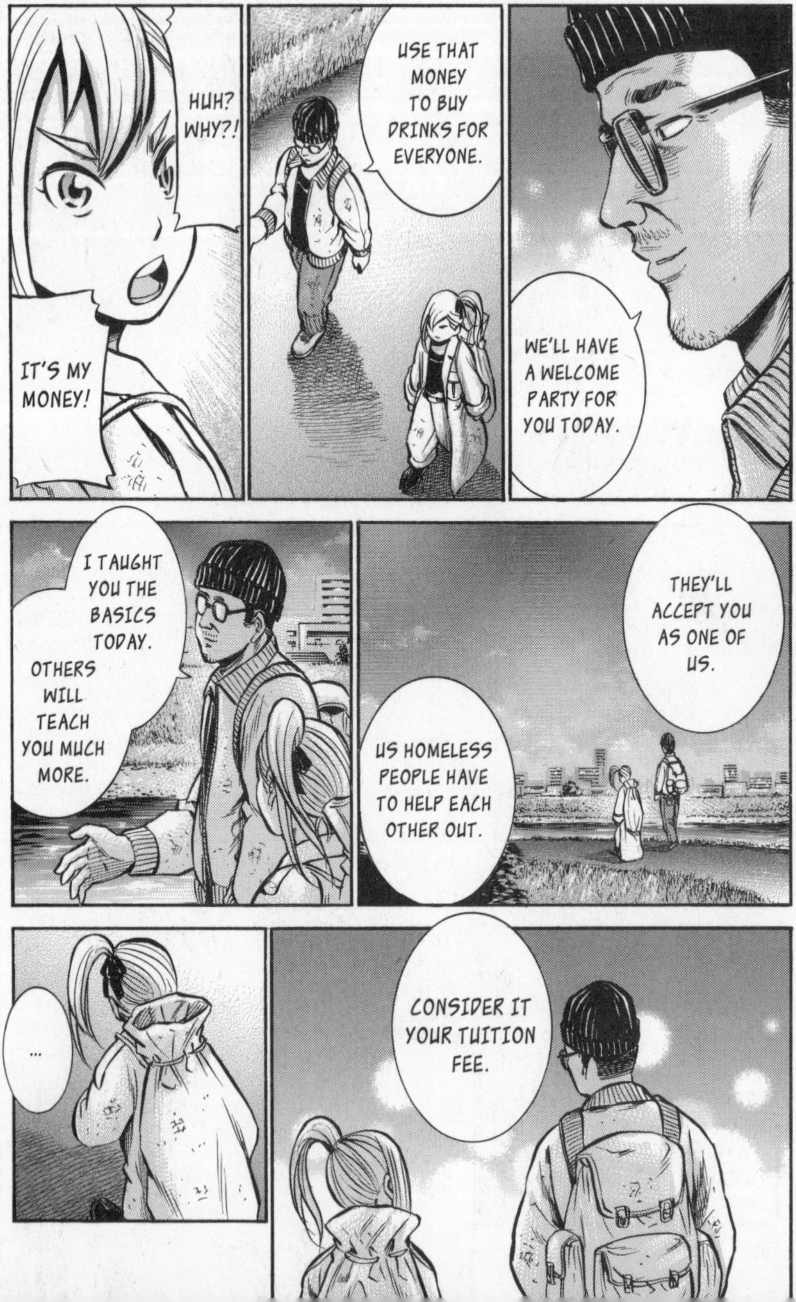
WE'LL HAVE A WELCOME PARTY FOR YOU TODAY.
USE THAT MONEY TO BUY DRINKS FOR EVERYONE.
HUH? WHY?!
IT'S MY MONEY!
THEY'LL ACCEPT YOU AS ONE OF US.
US HOMELESS PEOPLE HAVE TO HELP EACH OTHER OUT.
I TAUGHT YOU THE BASICS TODAY.
OTHERS WILL TEACH YOU MUCH MORE.
CONSIDER IT YOUR TUITION FEE.
...

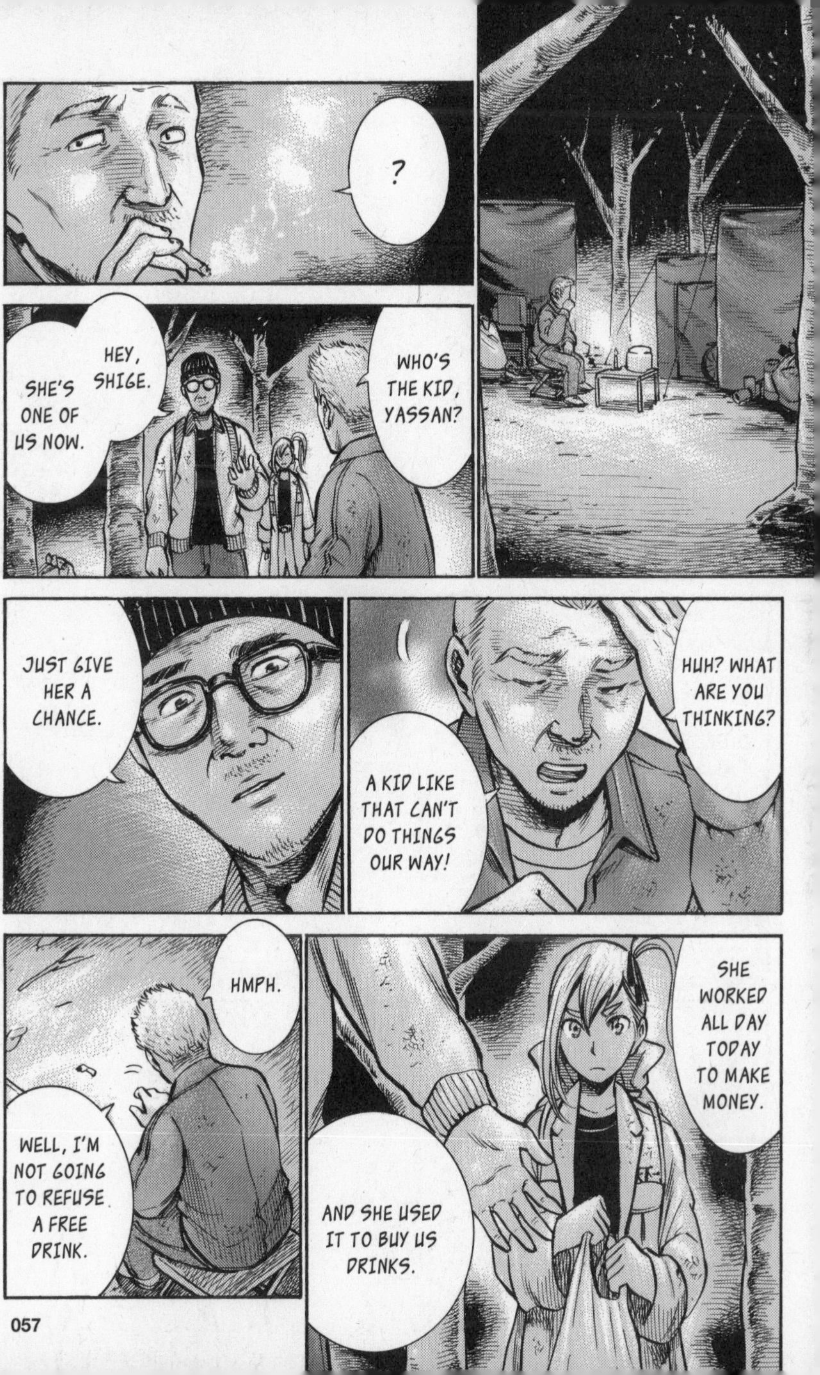
?
WHO'S THE KID, YASSAN?
HEY, SHIGE.
SHE'S ONE OF US NOW.
HUH? WHAT ARE YOU THINKING?
A KID LIKE THAT CAN'T DO THINGS OUR WAY!
JUST GIVE HER A CHANCE.
SHE WORKED ALL DAY TODAY TO MAKE MONEY.
AND SHE USED IT TO BUY US DRINKS.
HMPH.
WELL, I'M NOT GOING TO REFUSE A FREE DRINK.

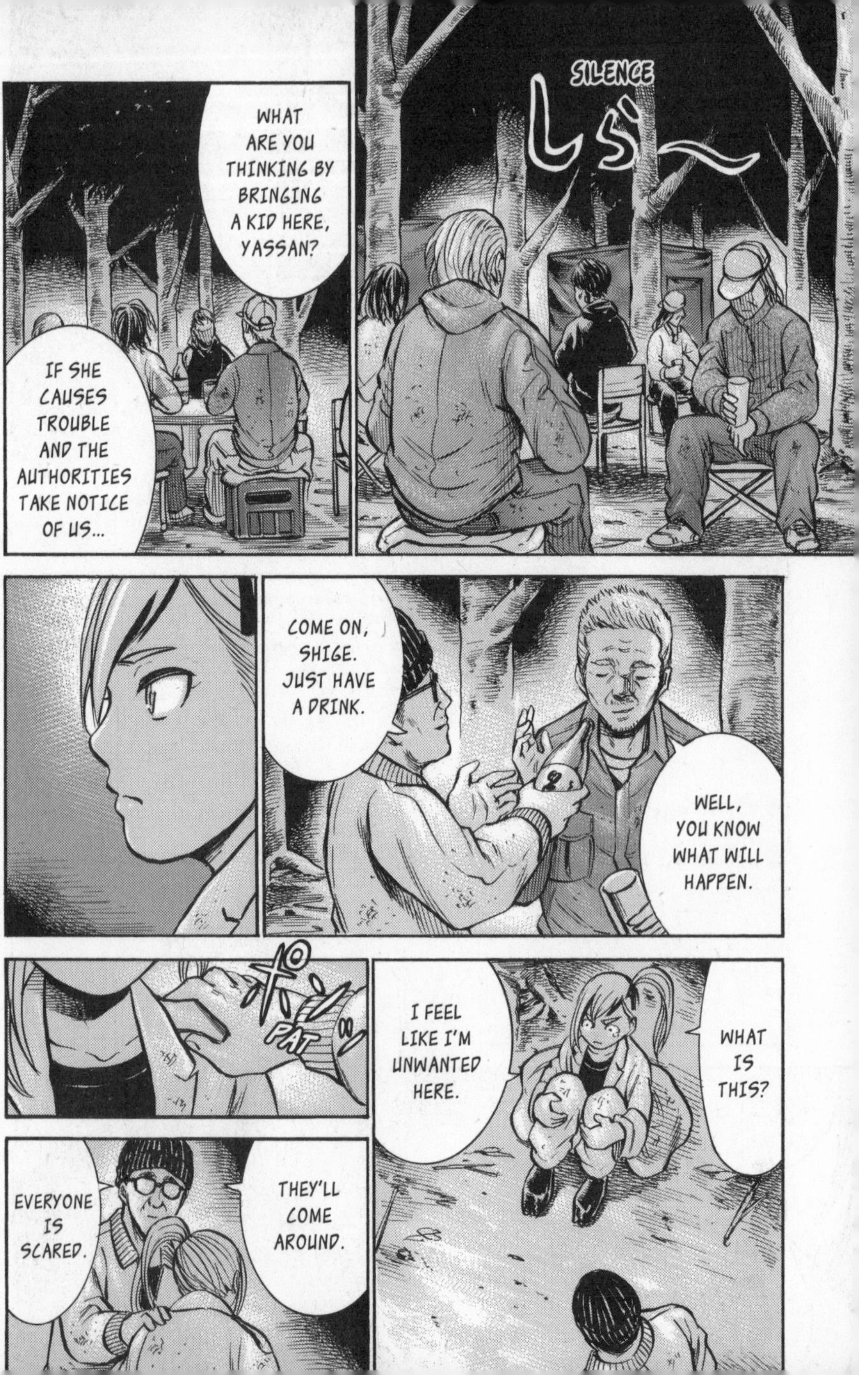
SILENCE
しら～
WHAT ARE YOU THINKING BY BRINGING A KID HERE, YASSAN?
IF SHE CAUSES TROUBLE AND THE AUTHORITIES TAKE NOTICE OF US...
COME ON, SHIGE. JUST HAVE A DRINK.
WELL, YOU KNOW WHAT WILL HAPPEN.
WHAT IS THIS?
I FEEL LIKE I'M UNWANTED HERE.
PAT
THEY'LL COME AROUND.
EVERYONE IS SCARED.

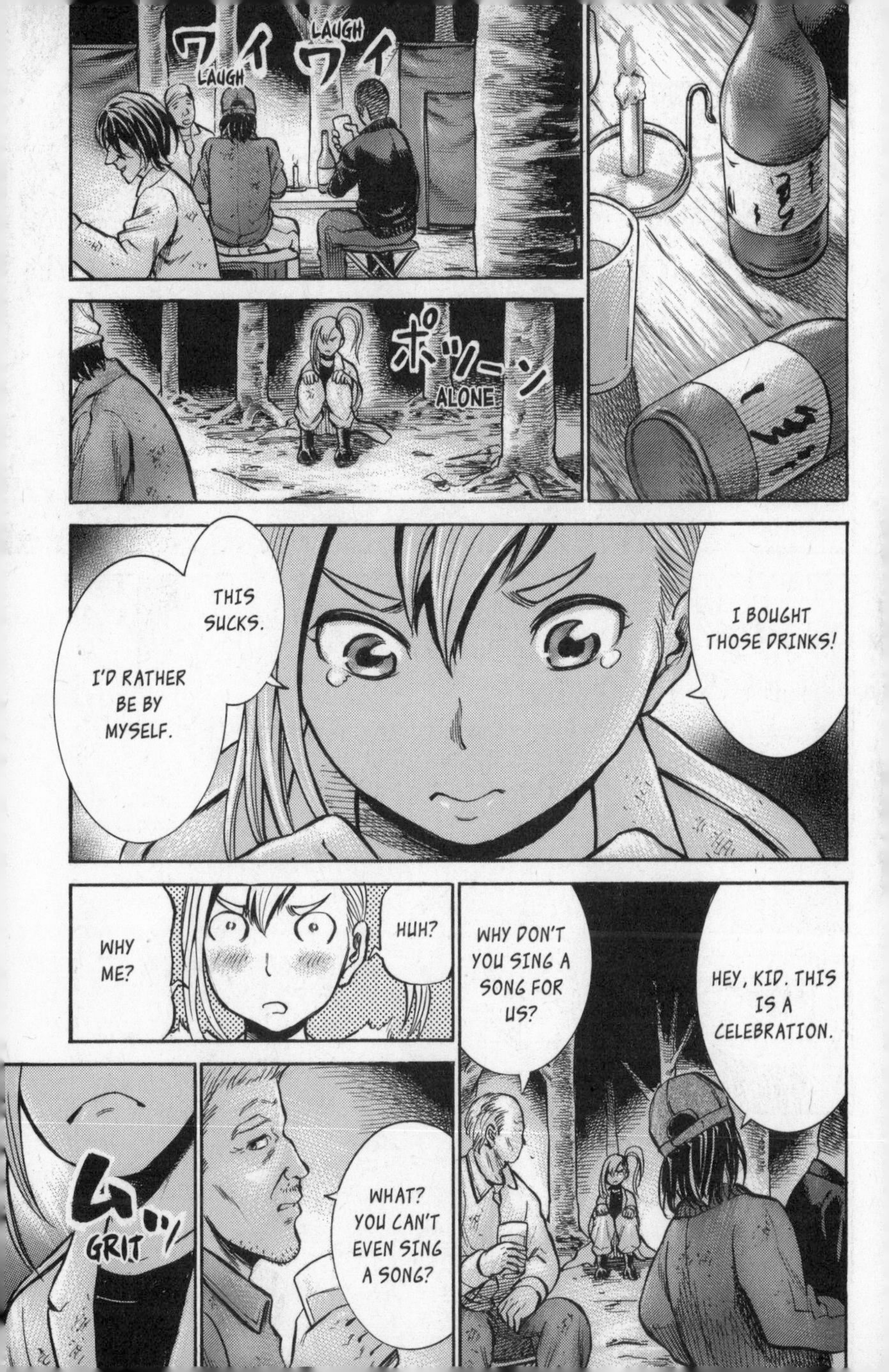
ワイワイ
LAUGH
LAUGH
ポツーン
ALONE
I BOUGHT THOSE DRINKS!
THIS SUCKS.
I'D RATHER BE BY MYSELF.
HEY, KID. THIS IS A CELEBRATION.
WHY DON'T YOU SING A SONG FOR US?
HUH?
WHY ME?
WHAT? YOU CAN'T EVEN SING A SONG?
ム…ッ
GRIT

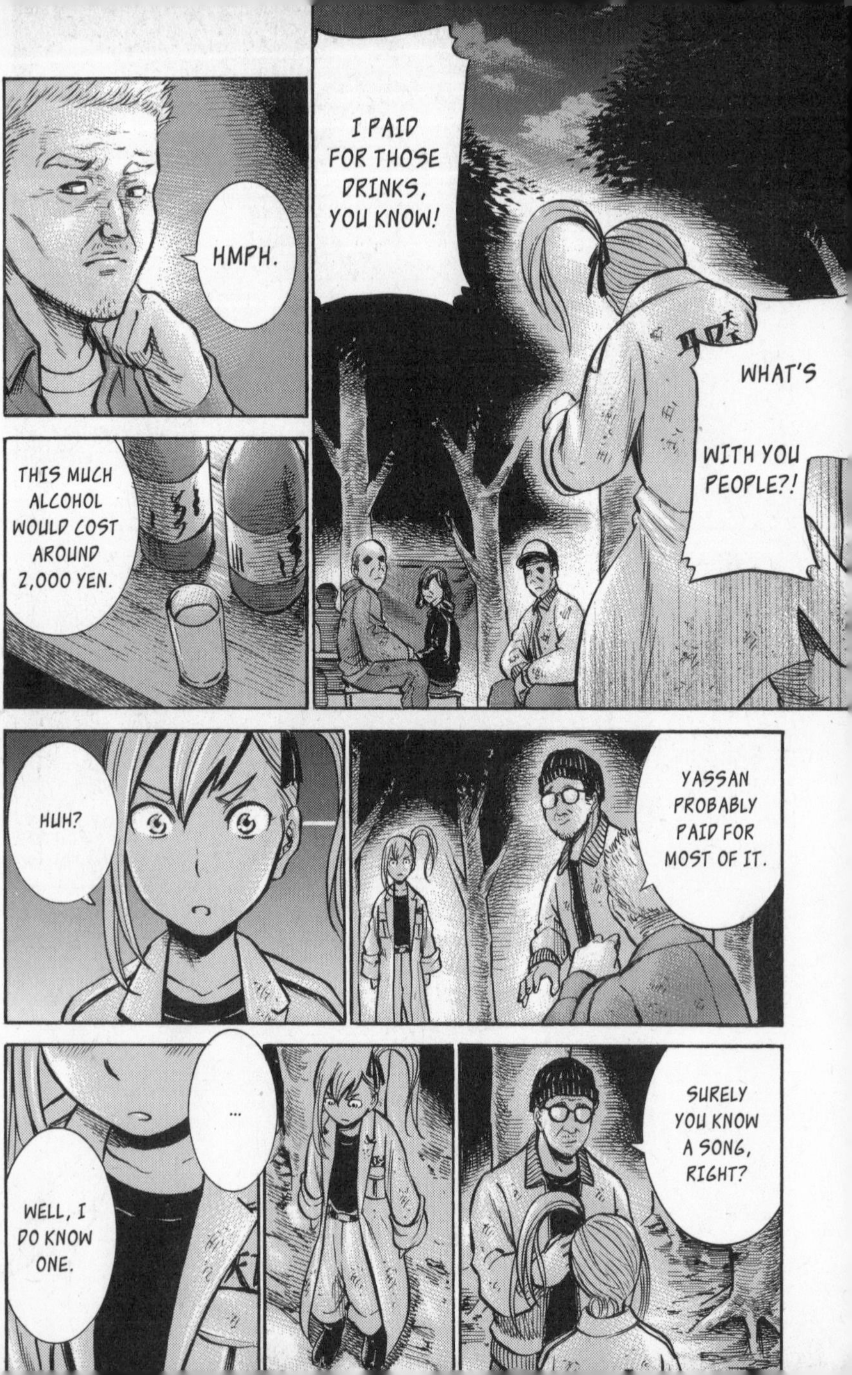
WHAT'S
WITH YOU PEOPLE?!
I PAID FOR THOSE DRINKS, YOU KNOW!
HMPH.
THIS MUCH ALCOHOL WOULD COST AROUND 2,000 YEN.
YASSAN PROBABLY PAID FOR MOST OF IT.
HUH?
SURELY YOU KNOW A SONG, RIGHT?
...
WELL, I DO KNOW ONE.

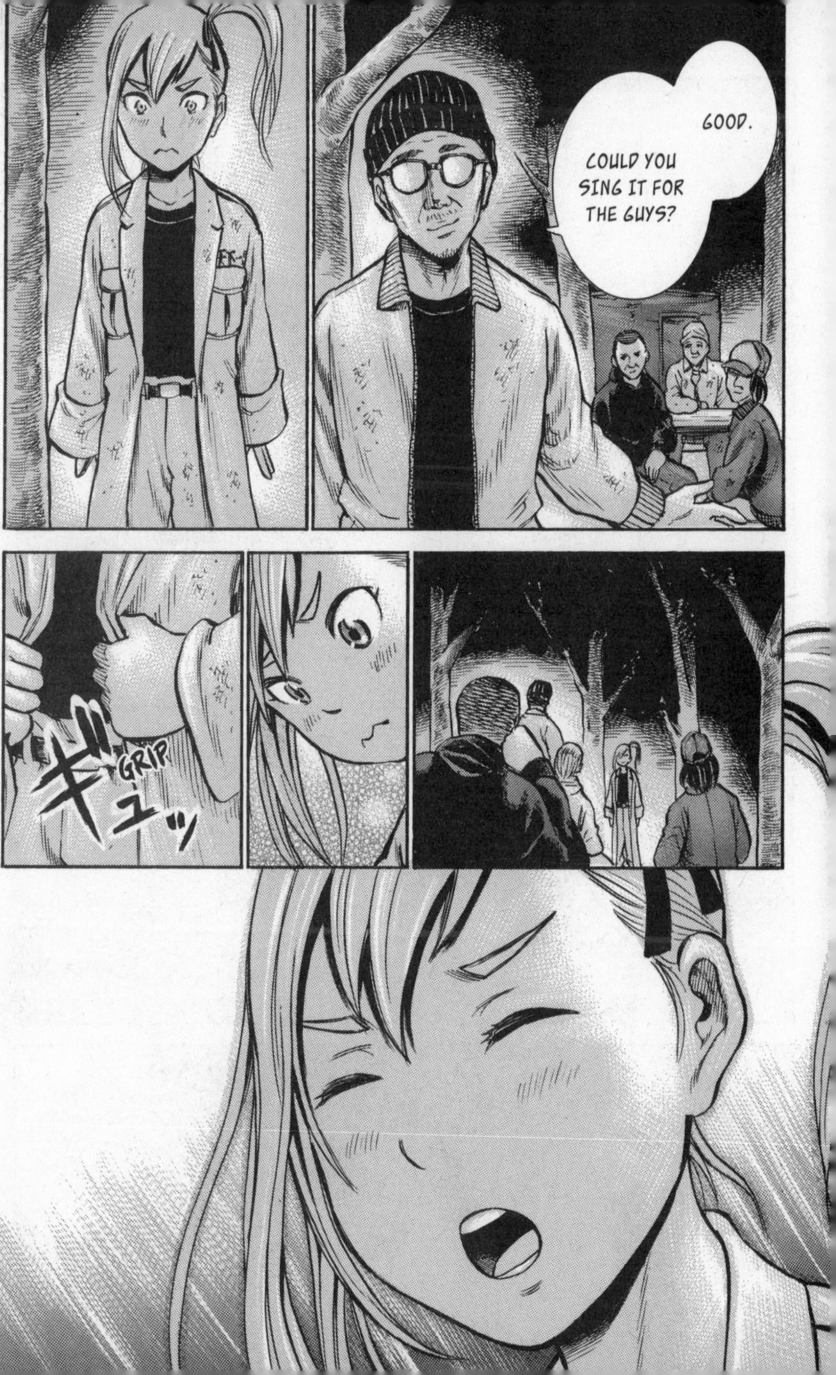
GOOD.
COULD YOU SING IT FOR THE GUYS?
GRIP
ギュッ

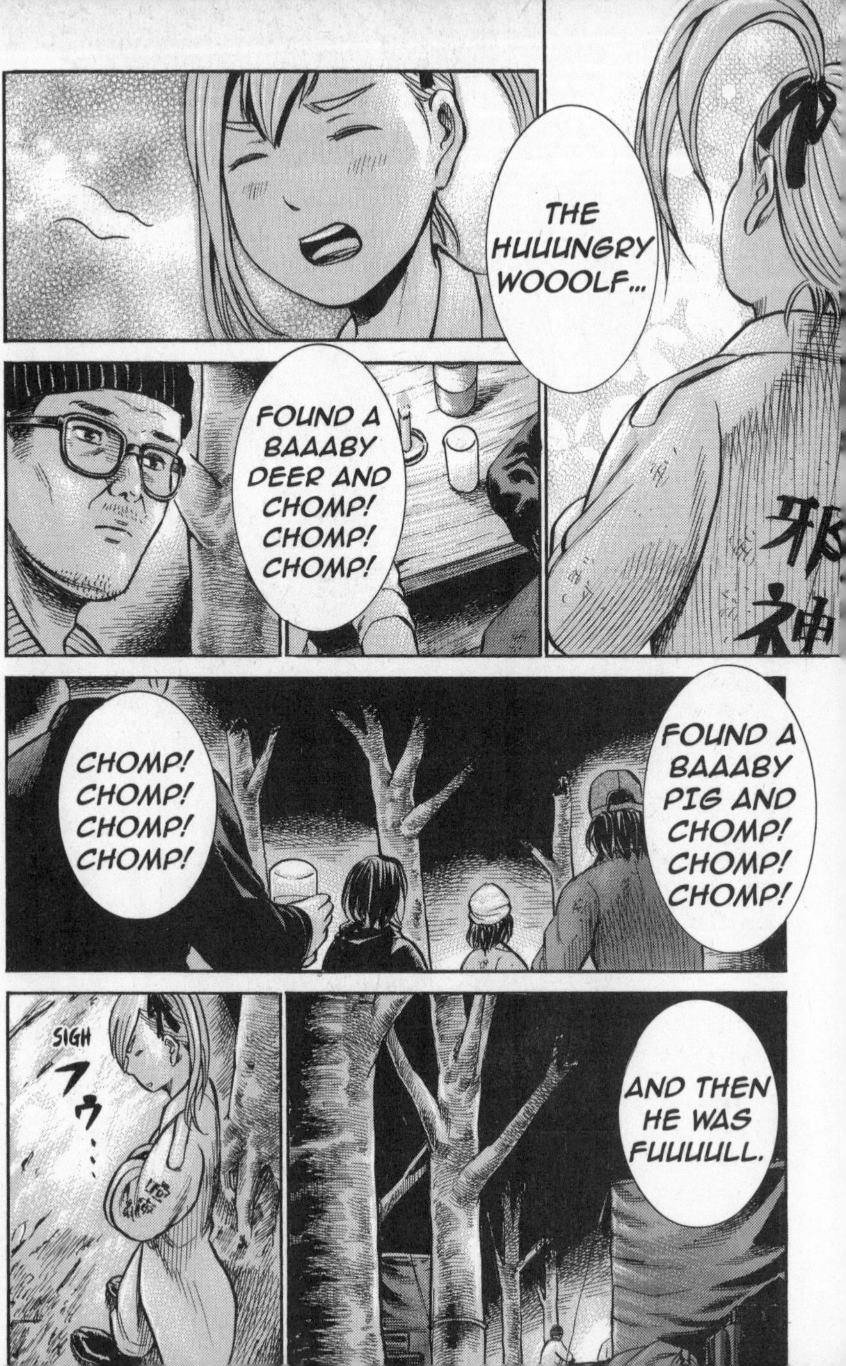
THE HUUUNGRY WOOOLF...
邪神
FOUND A BAAABY DEER AND CHOMP! CHOMP! CHOMP!
FOUND A BAAABY PIG AND CHOMP! CHOMP! CHOMP!
CHOMP! CHOMP! CHOMP! CHOMP!
AND THEN HE WAS FUUUULL.
SIGH
フゥ…

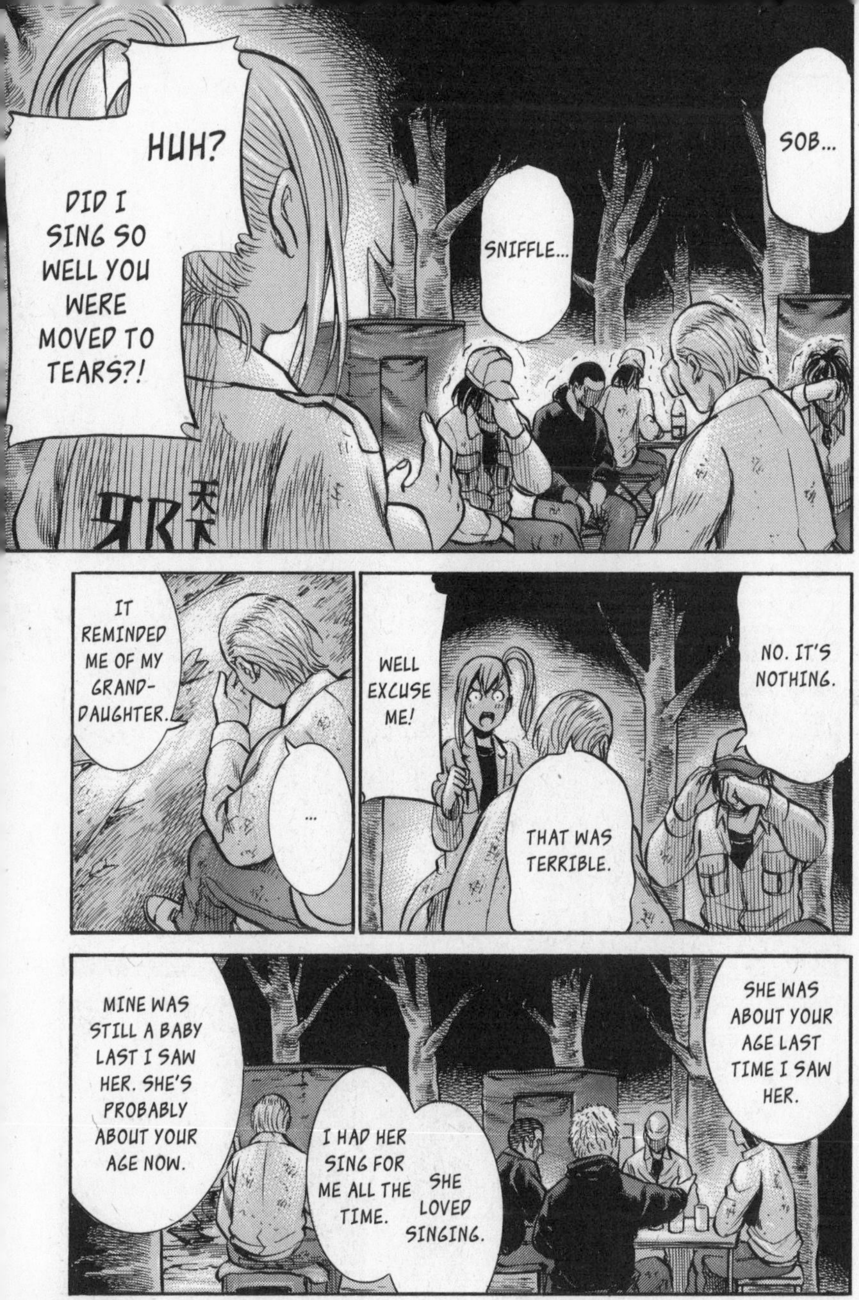
SOB...
SNIFFLE...
HUH?
DID I SING SO WELL YOU WERE MOVED TO TEARS?!
NO. IT'S NOTHING.
THAT WAS TERRIBLE.
WELL EXCUSE ME!
IT REMINDED ME OF MY GRAND-DAUGHTER.
...
SHE WAS ABOUT YOUR AGE LAST TIME I SAW HER.
SHE LOVED SINGING.
I HAD HER SING FOR ME ALL THE TIME.
MINE WAS STILL A BABY LAST I SAW HER. SHE'S PROBABLY ABOUT YOUR AGE NOW.

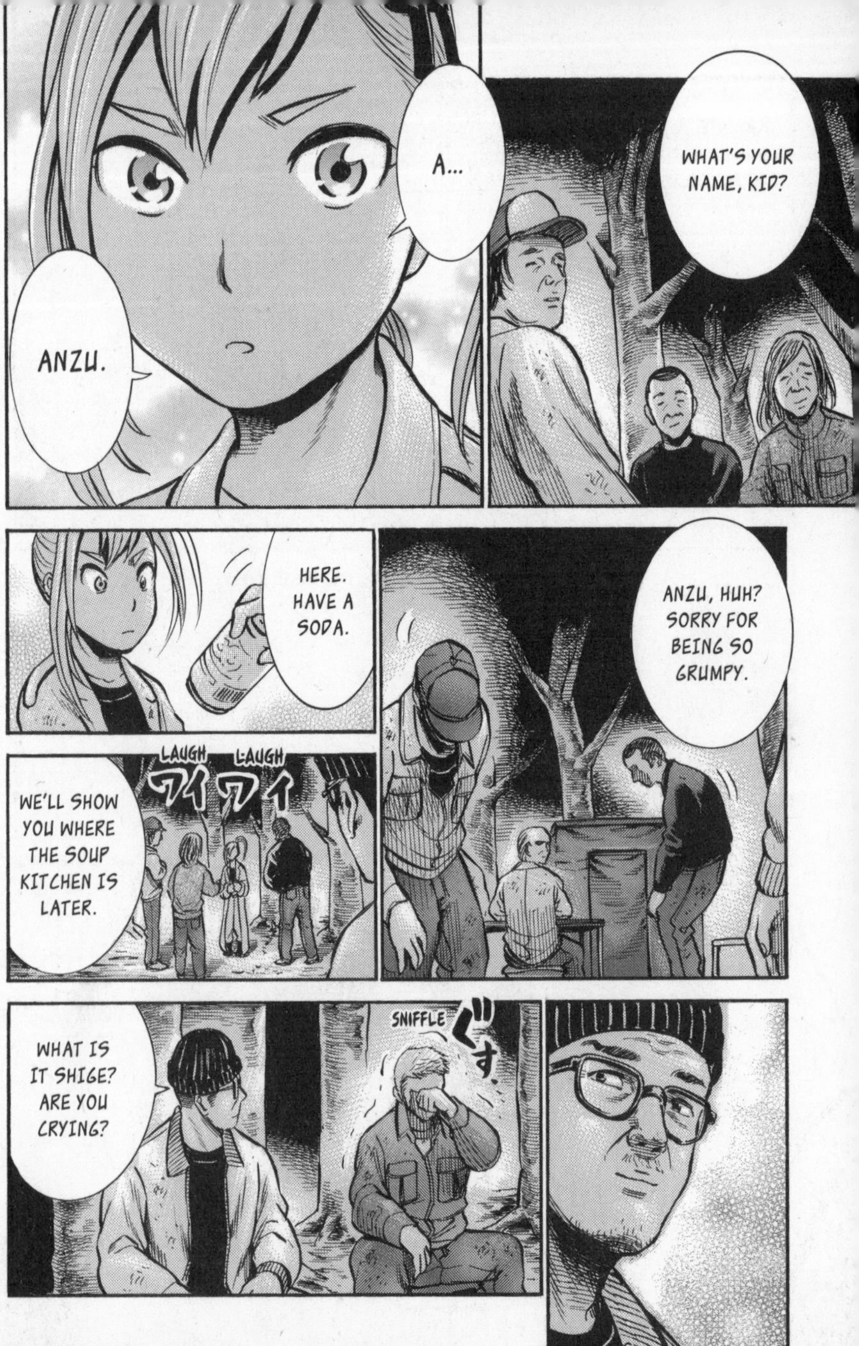
WHAT'S YOUR NAME, KID?
A...
ANZU.
ANZU, HUH? SORRY FOR BEING SO GRUMPY.
HERE. HAVE A SODA.
LAUGH LAUGH
ワイワイ
WE'LL SHOW YOU WHERE THE SOUP KITCHEN IS LATER.
SNIFFLE
ぐす
WHAT IS IT SHIGE? ARE YOU CRYING?

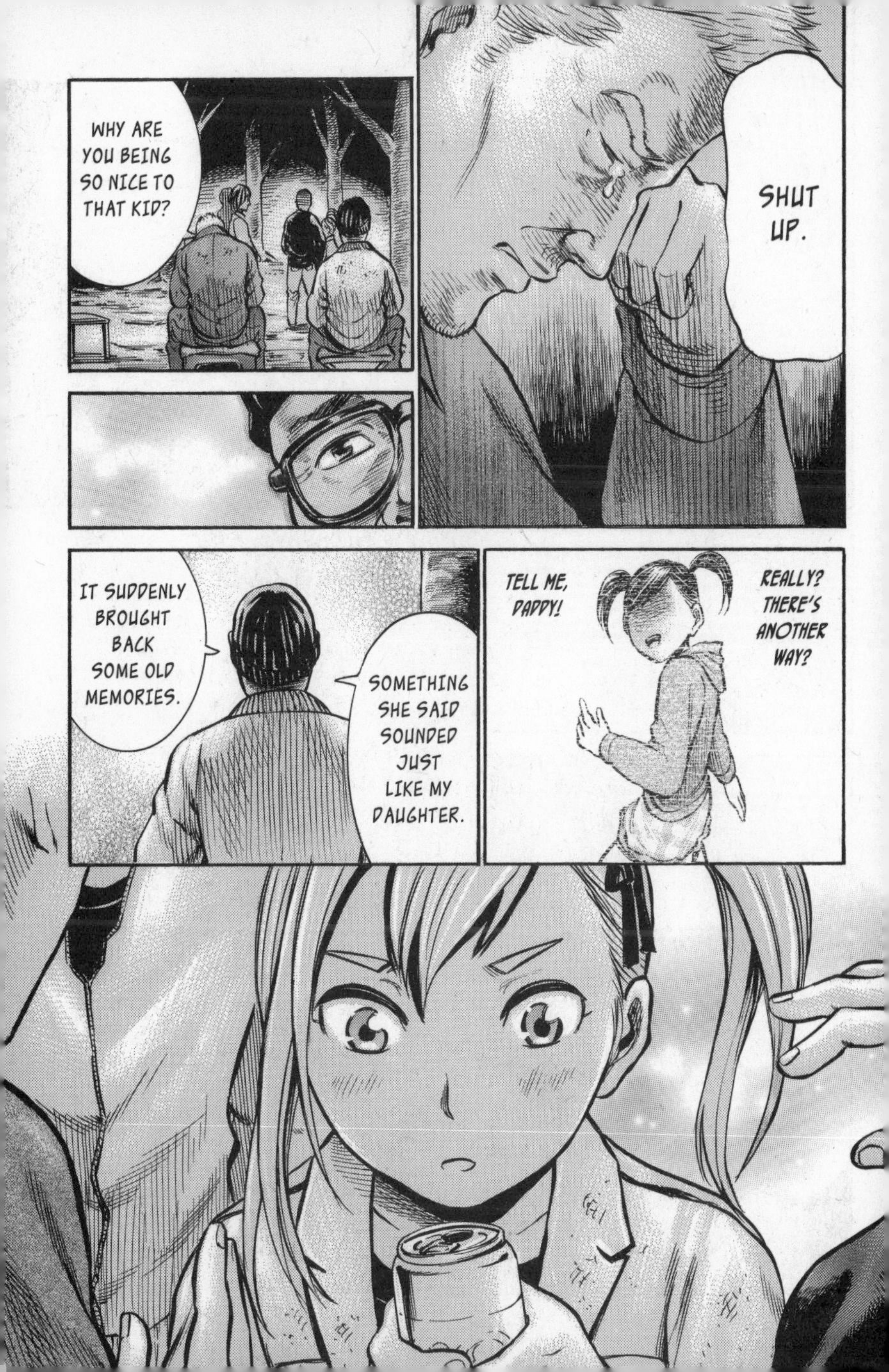
WHY ARE YOU BEING SO NICE TO THAT KID?
SHUT UP.
SOMETHING SHE SAID SOUNDED JUST LIKE MY DAUGHTER.
IT SUDDENLY BROUGHT BACK SOME OLD MEMORIES.
REALLY? THERE'S ANOTHER WAY?
TELL ME, DADDY!

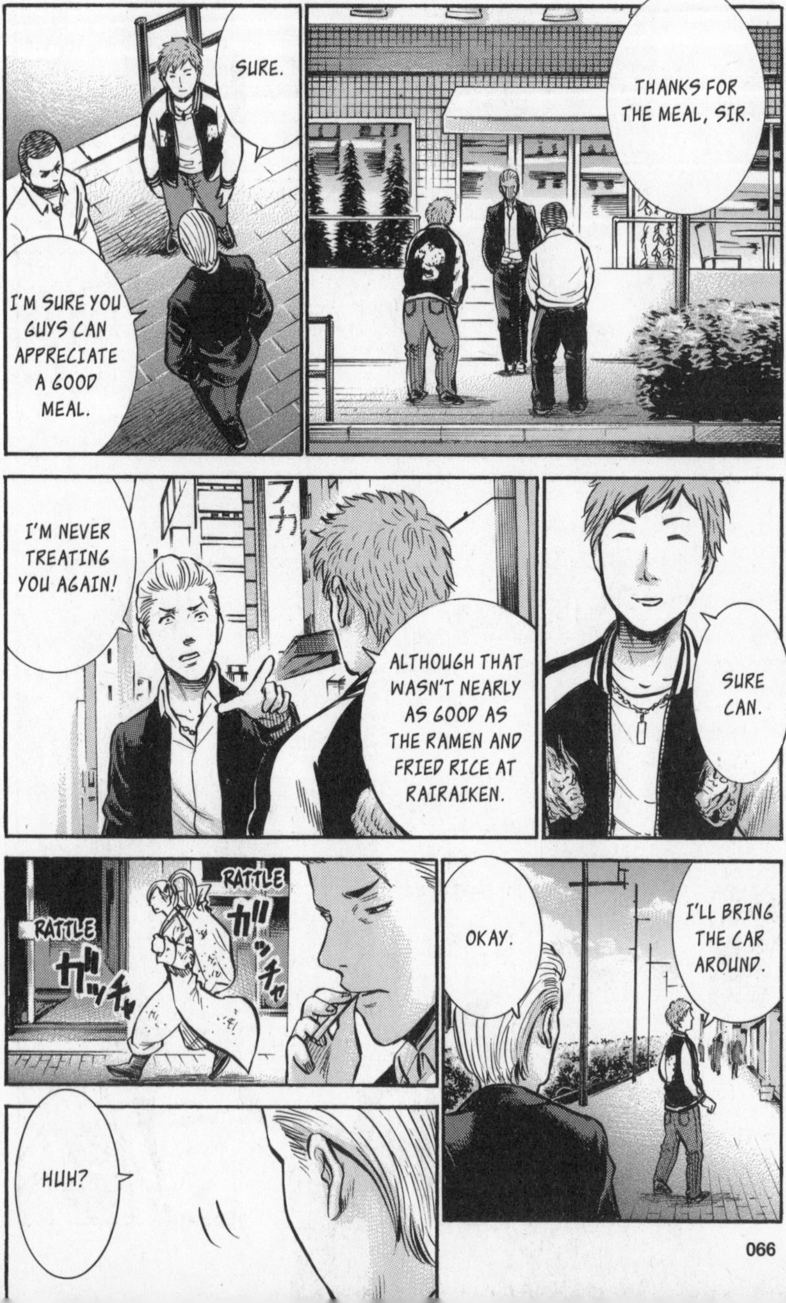
THANKS FOR THE MEAL, SIR.
SURE.
I'M SURE YOU GUYS CAN APPRECIATE A GOOD MEAL.
SURE CAN.
ALTHOUGH THAT WASN'T NEARLY AS GOOD AS THE RAMEN AND FRIED RICE AT RAIRAIKEN.
I'M NEVER TREATING YOU AGAIN!
I'LL BRING THE CAR AROUND.
OKAY.
RATTLE
ガッチャ
RATTLE
ガッチャ
HUH?

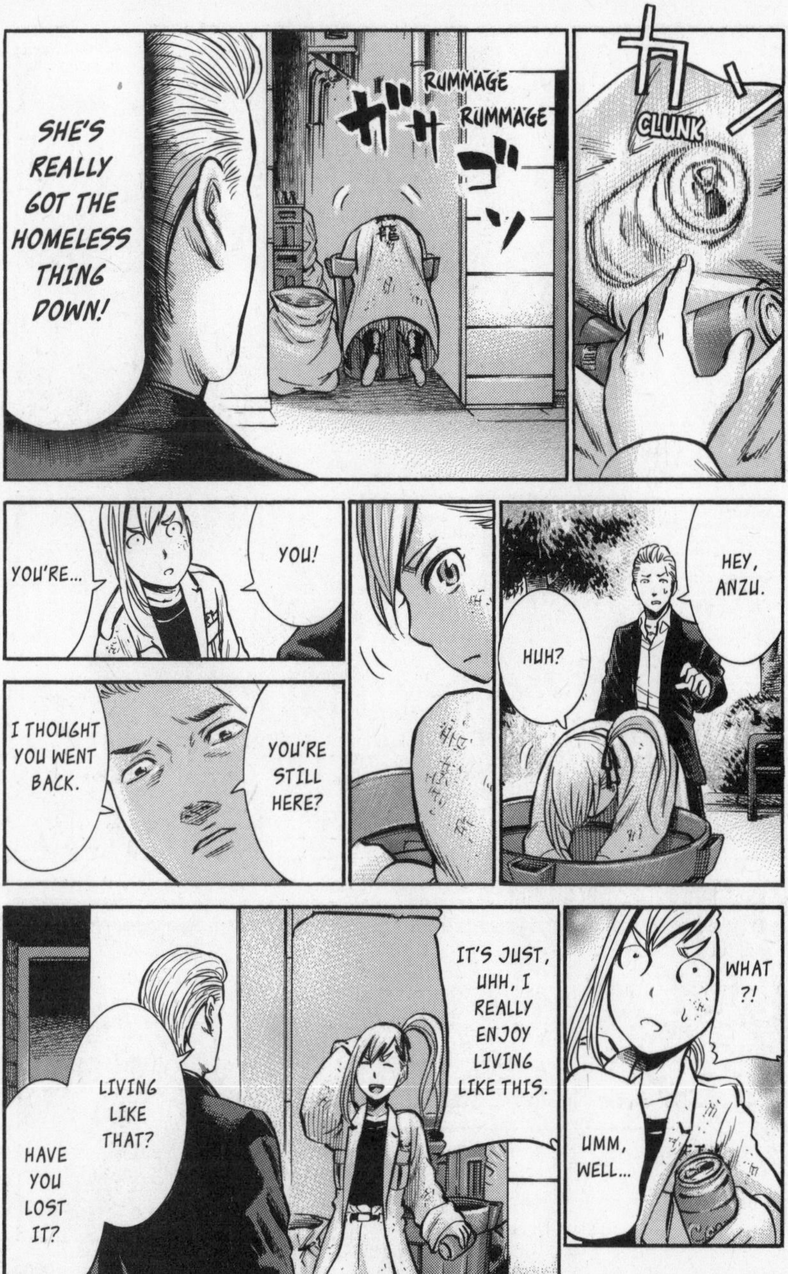

CLUNK
RUMMAGE RUMMAGE
ガサ
ゴッ
SHE'S REALLY GOT THE HOMELESS THING DOWN!
HEY, ANZU.
HUH?
YOU!
YOU'RE...
YOU'RE STILL HERE?
I THOUGHT YOU WENT BACK.
WHAT?!
UMM, WELL...
IT'S JUST, UHH, I REALLY ENJOY LIVING LIKE THIS.
LIVING LIKE THAT?
HAVE YOU LOST IT?

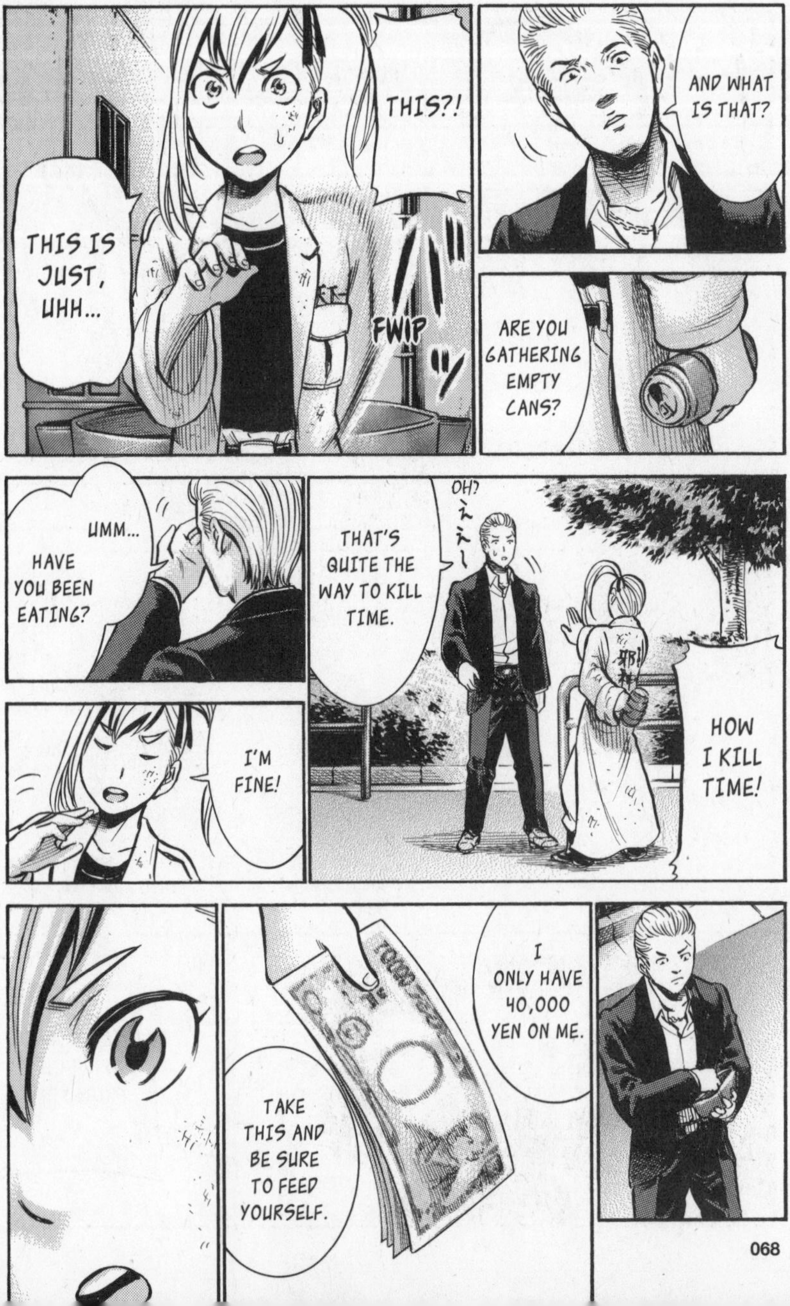
AND WHAT IS THAT?
ARE YOU GATHERING EMPTY CANS?
THIS?!
THIS IS JUST, UHH...
FWIP
HOW I KILL TIME!
OH?
ええ
THAT'S QUITE THE WAY TO KILL TIME.
UMM... HAVE YOU BEEN EATING?
I'M FINE!
I ONLY HAVE 40,000 YEN ON ME.
TAKE THIS AND BE SURE TO FEED YOURSELF.

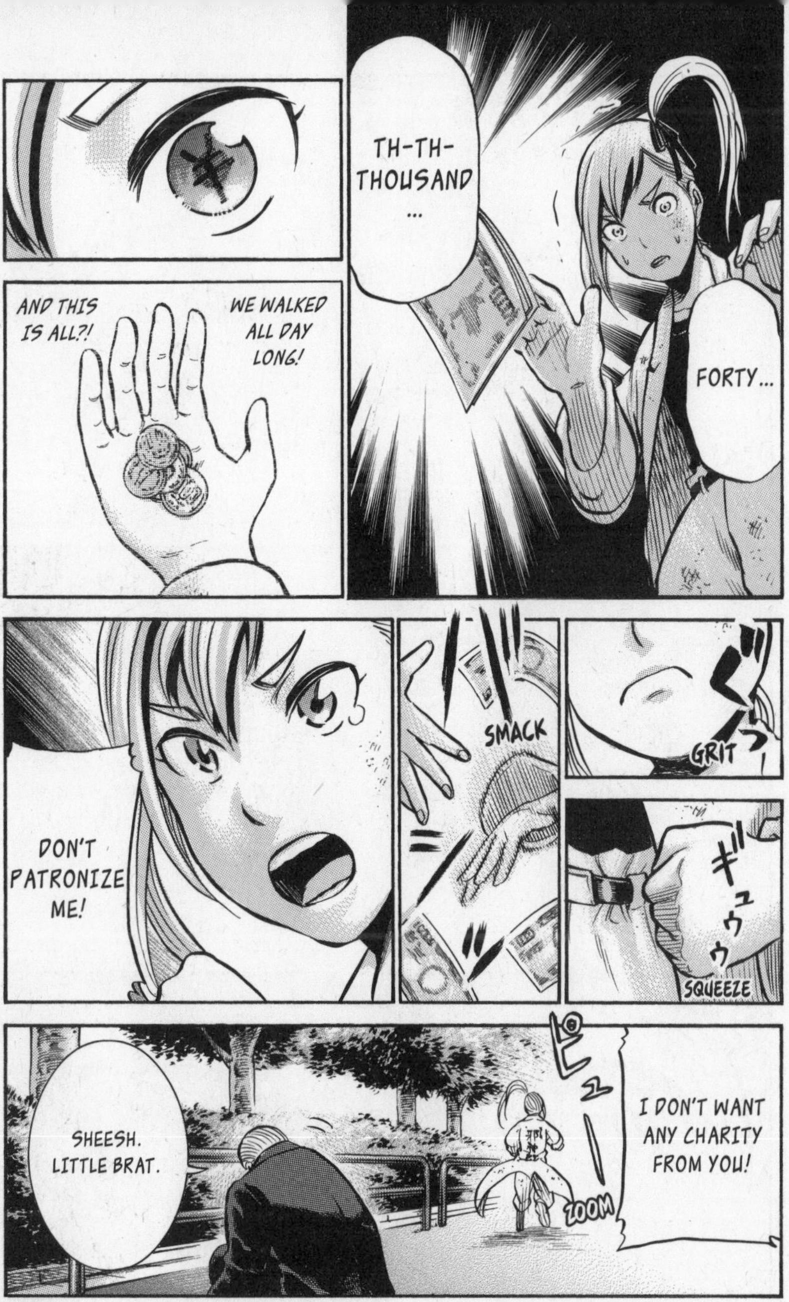
FORTY...
TH-TH-THOUSAND ...
WE WALKED ALL DAY LONG!
AND THIS IS ALL?!
GRIT
SQUEEZE
SMACK
DON'T PATRONIZE ME!
I DON'T WANT ANY CHARITY FROM YOU!
ZOOM
SHEESH. LITTLE BRAT.

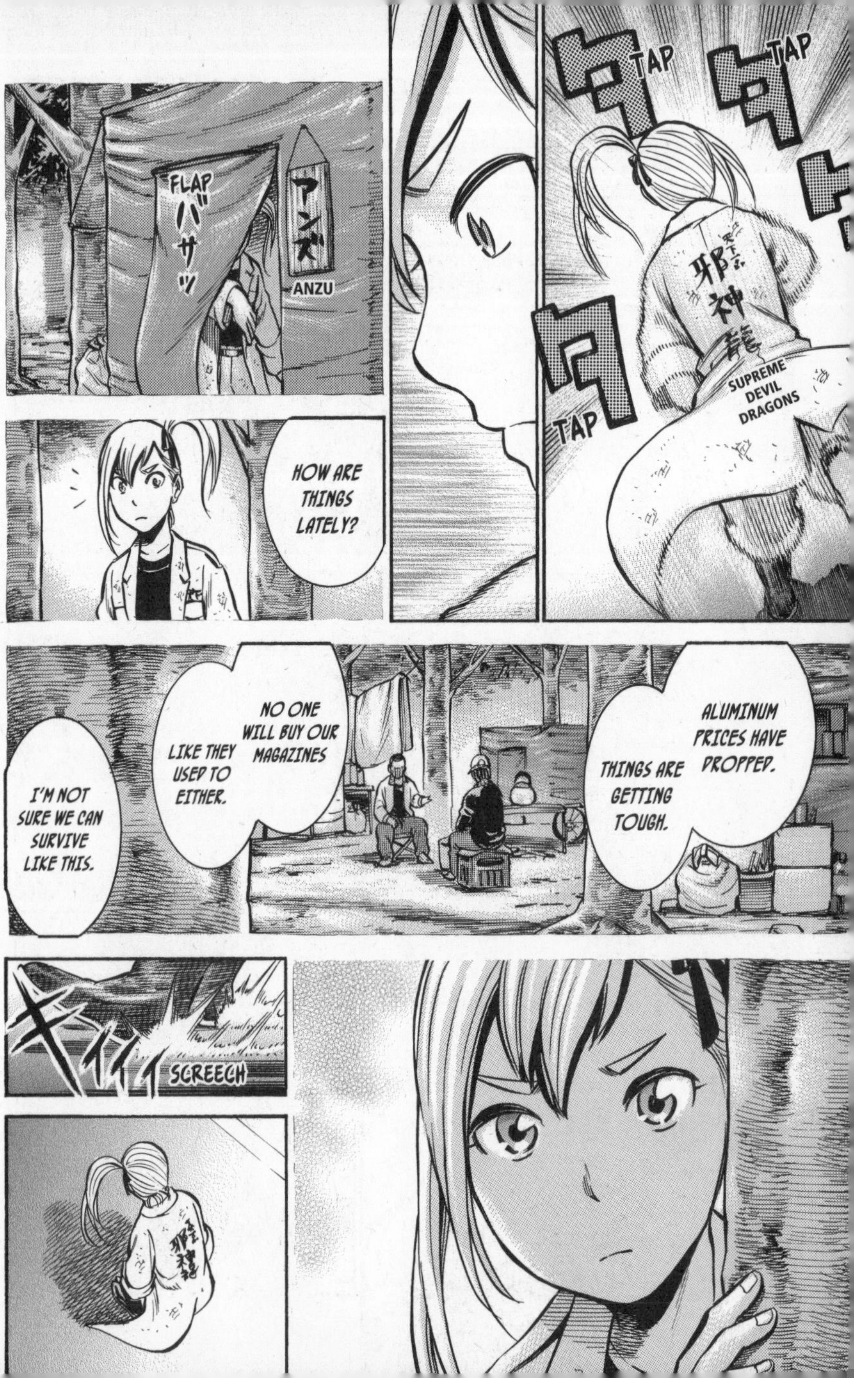
TAP
TAP
TAP
SUPREME DEVIL DRAGONS
FLAP
バサッ
アンズ
ANZU
HOW ARE THINGS LATELY?
ALUMINUM PRICES HAVE DROPPED.
THINGS ARE GETTING TOUGH.
NO ONE WILL BUY OUR MAGAZINES
LIKE THEY USED TO EITHER.
I'M NOT SURE WE CAN SURVIVE LIKE THIS.
SCREECH

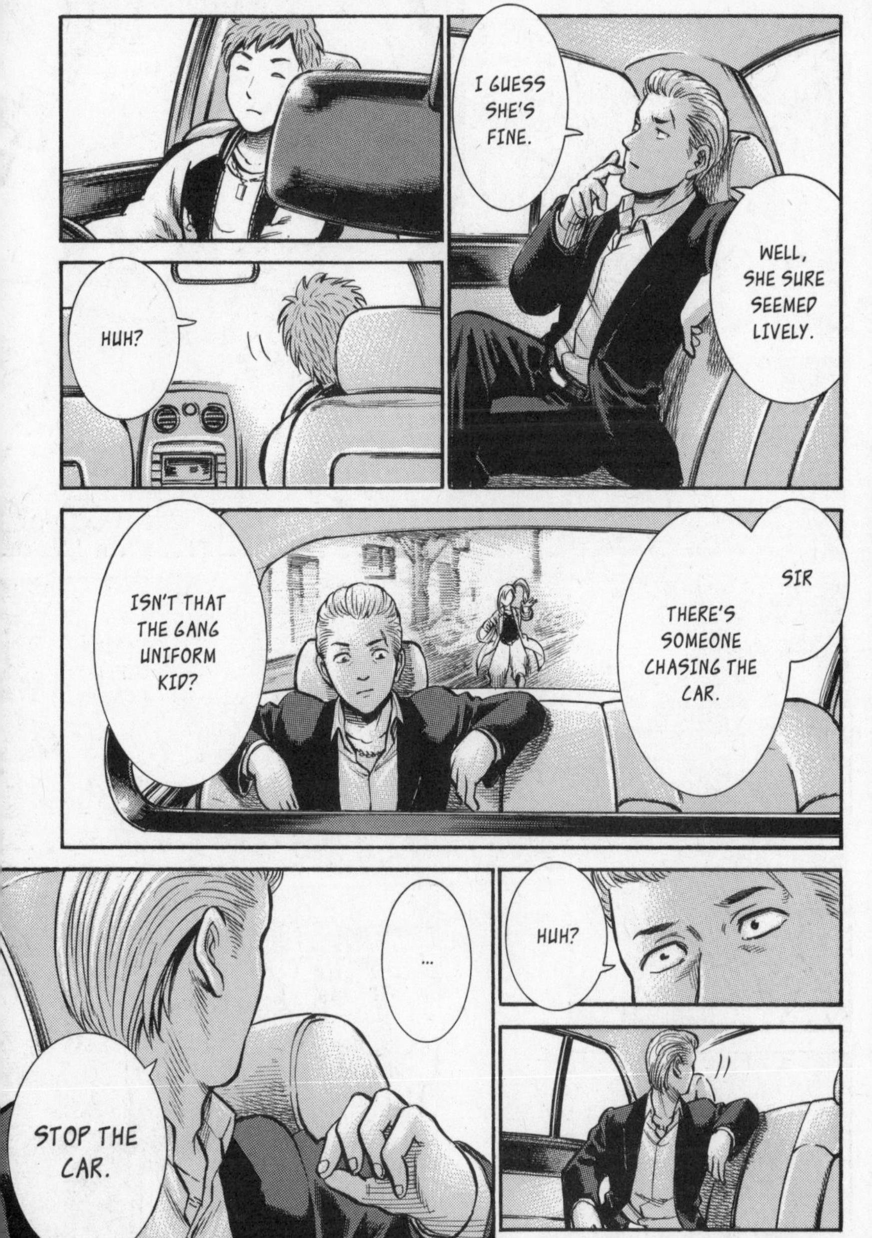
I GUESS SHE'S FINE.
WELL, SHE SURE SEEMED LIVELY.
HUH?
SIR
THERE'S SOMEONE CHASING THE CAR.
ISN'T THAT THE GANG UNIFORM KID?
HUH?
...
STOP THE CAR.

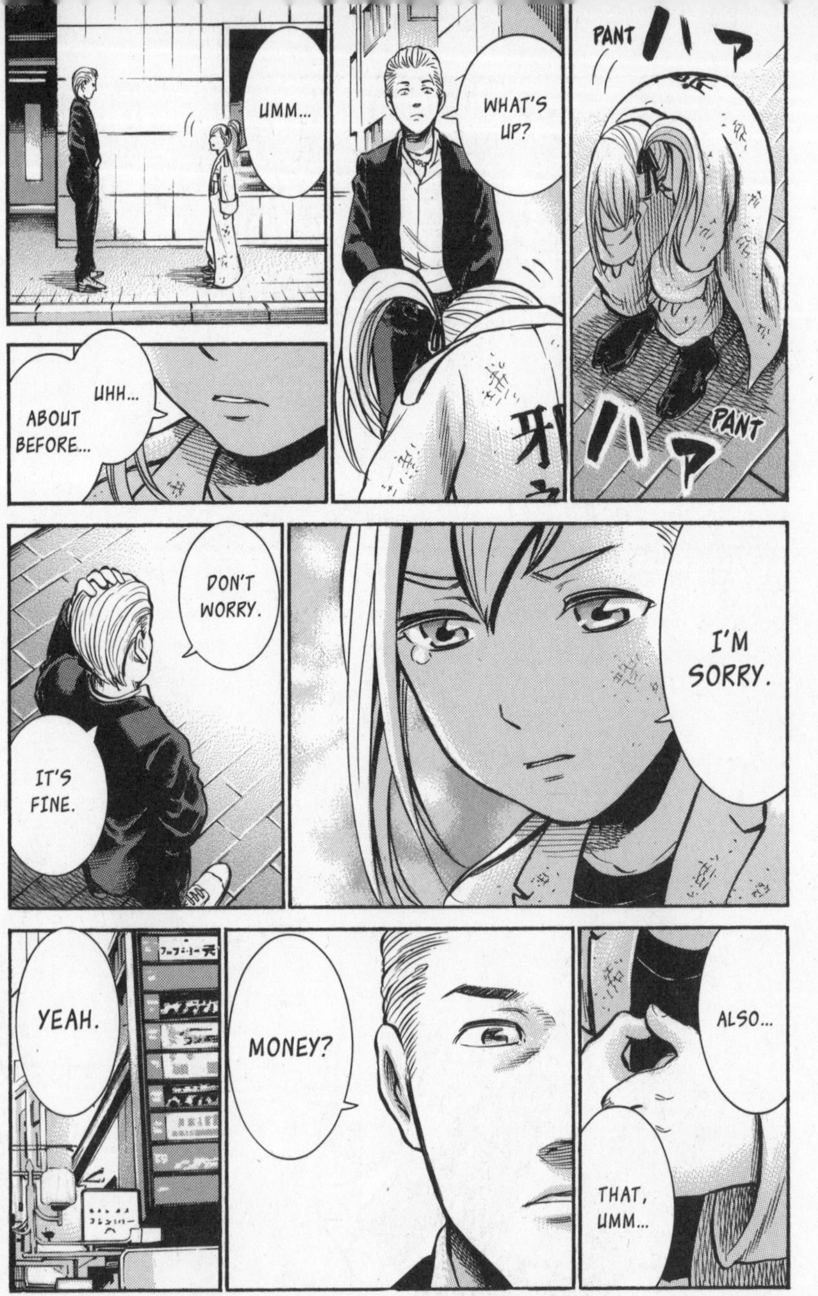
PANT
ハア
PANT
ハア
WHAT'S UP?
UMM...
UHH... ABOUT BEFORE...
I'M SORRY.
DON'T WORRY.
IT'S FINE.
ALSO...
THAT, UMM...
MONEY?
YEAH.

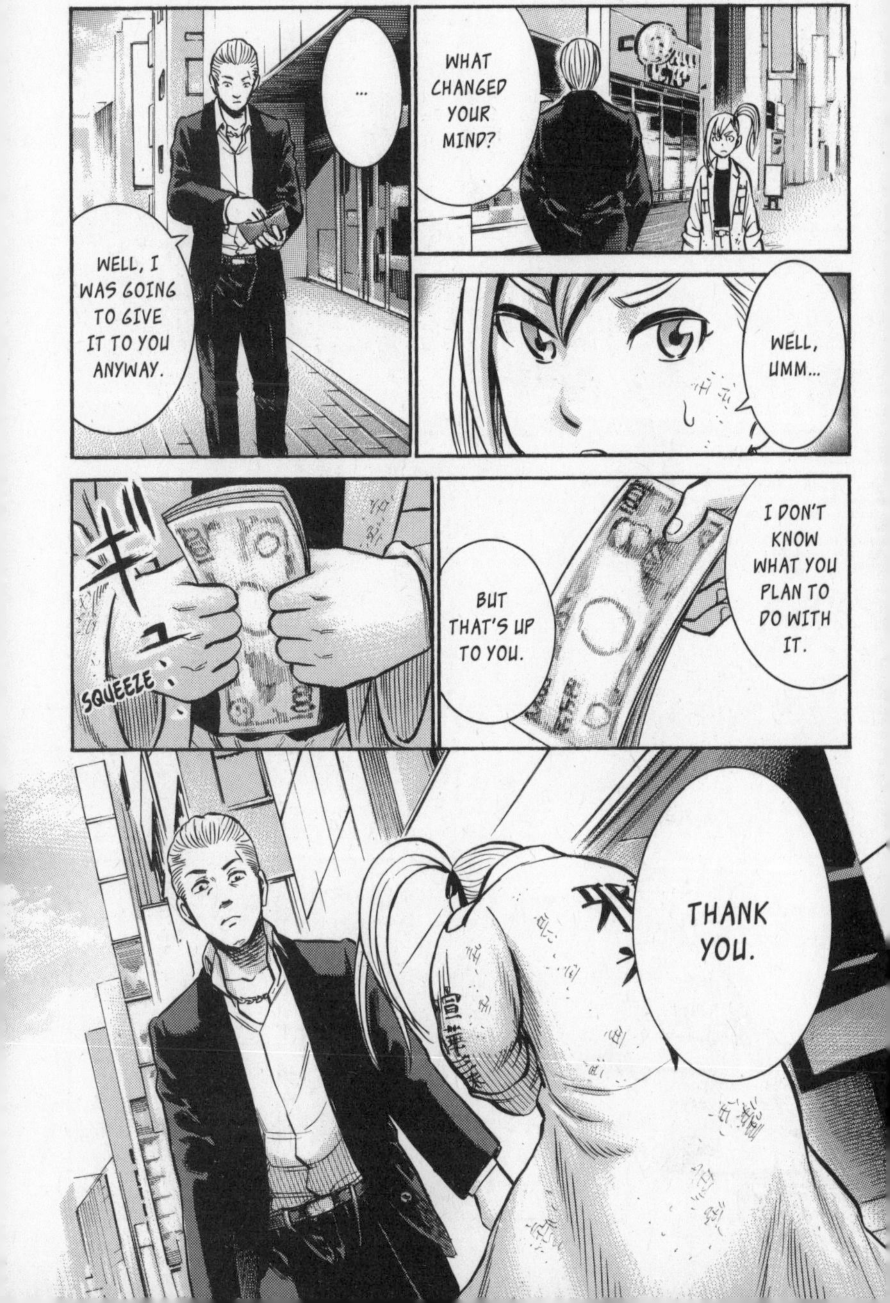
WHAT CHANGED YOUR MIND?
WELL, UMM...
...
WELL, I WAS GOING TO GIVE IT TO YOU ANYWAY.
I DON'T KNOW WHAT YOU PLAN TO DO WITH IT.
BUT THAT'S UP TO YOU.
SQUEEZE
THANK YOU.

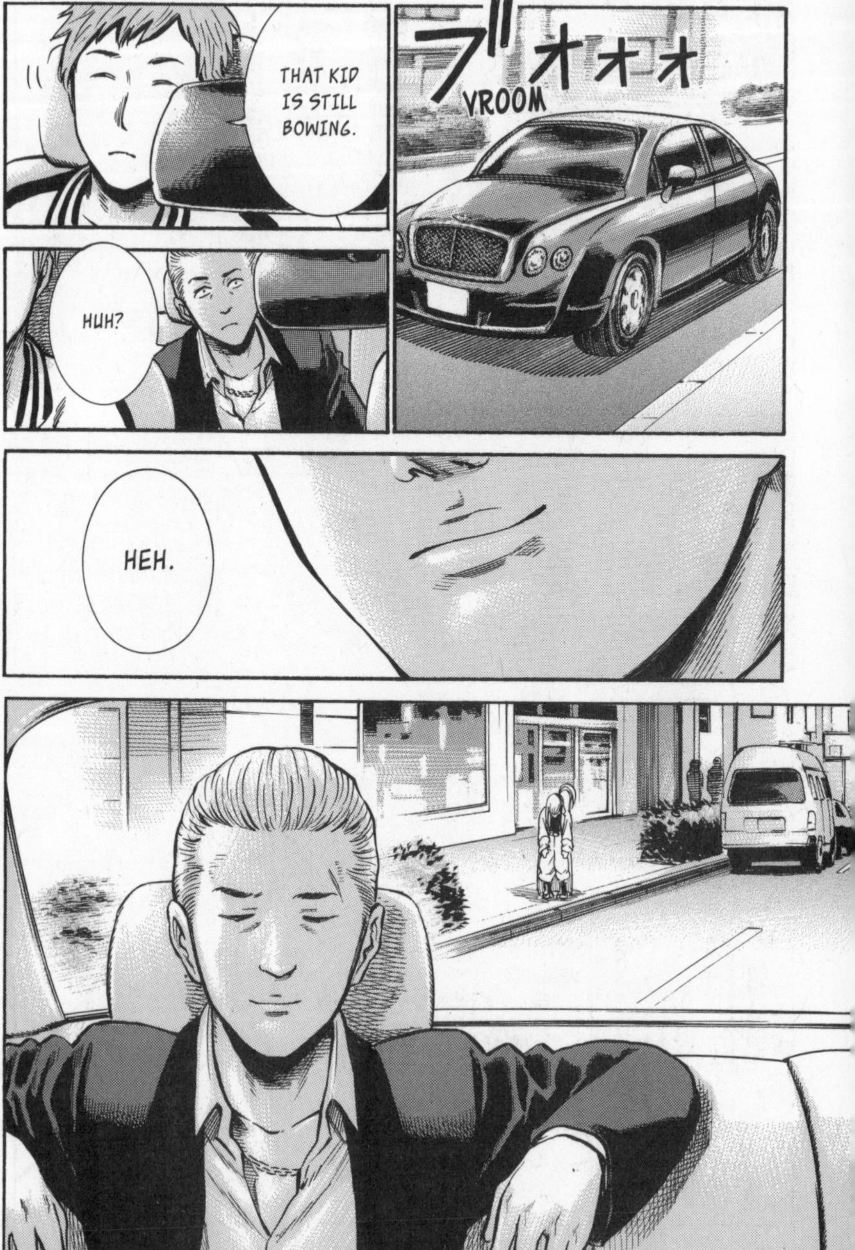
VROOM
THAT KID IS STILL BOWING.
HUH?
HEH.

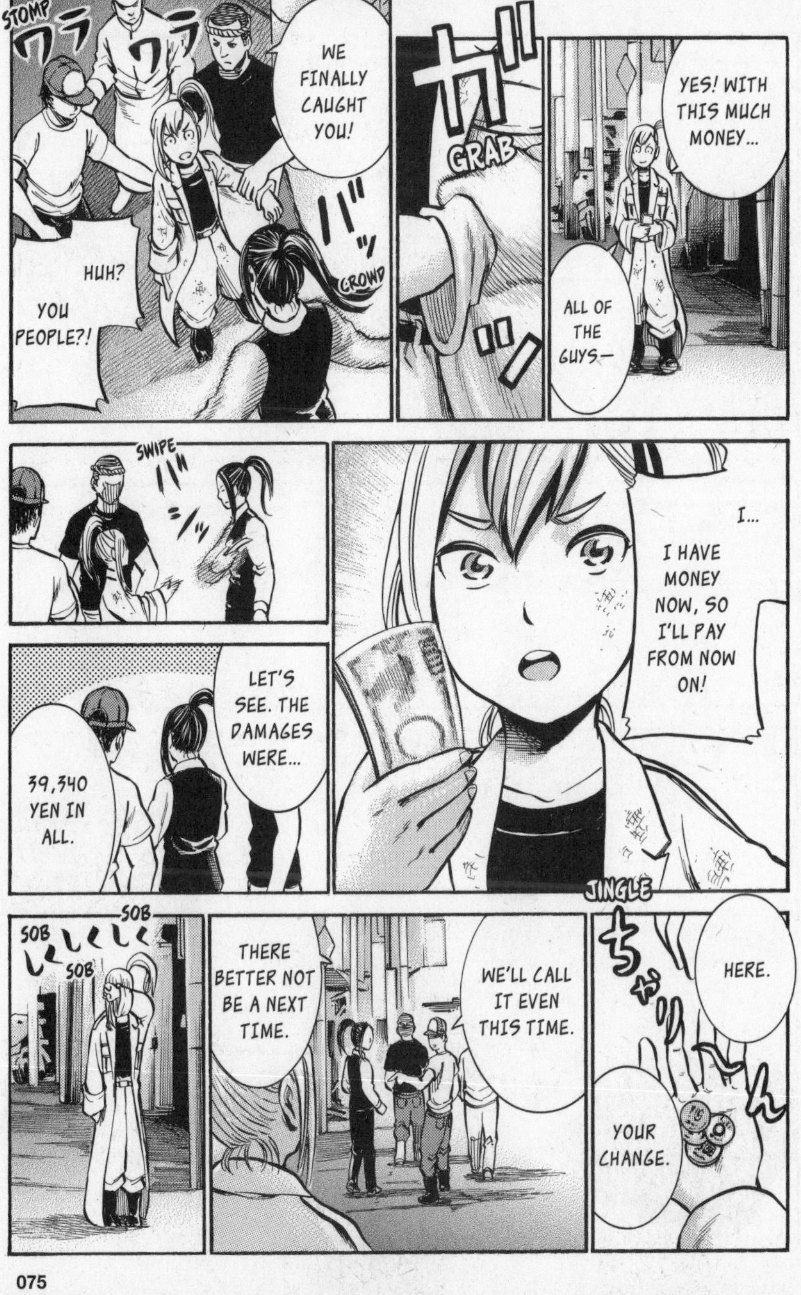
YES! WITH THIS MUCH MONEY...
ALL OF THE GUYS—
GRAB
WE FINALLY CAUGHT YOU!
STOMP
CROWD
HUH?
YOU PEOPLE?!
I...
I HAVE MONEY NOW, SO I'LL PAY FROM NOW ON!
SWIPE
LET'S SEE. THE DAMAGES WERE...
39,340 YEN IN ALL.
JINGLE
HERE.
YOUR CHANGE.
WE'LL CALL IT EVEN THIS TIME.
THERE BETTER NOT BE A NEXT TIME.
SOB
SOB
SOB

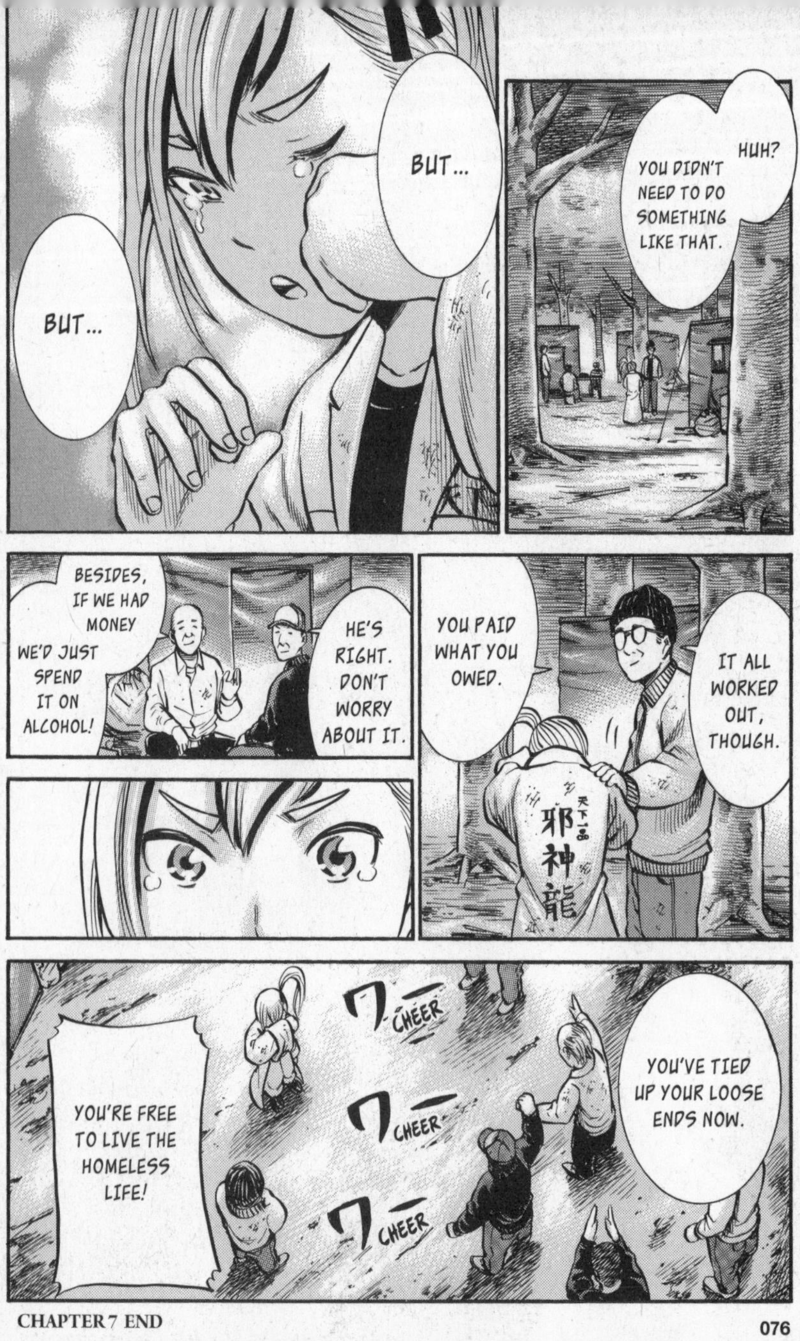
HUH?
YOU DIDN'T NEED TO DO SOMETHING LIKE THAT.
BUT...
BUT...
IT ALL WORKED OUT, THOUGH.
YOU PAID WHAT YOU OWED.
HE'S RIGHT. DON'T WORRY ABOUT IT.
BESIDES, IF WE HAD MONEY
WE'D JUST SPEND IT ON ALCOHOL!
天下一品
邪神龍
YOU'VE TIED UP YOUR LOOSE ENDS NOW.
ワー CHEER
ワー CHEER
ワー CHEER
YOU'RE FREE TO LIVE THE HOMELESS LIFE!

CHAPTER 7 END

CHAPTER 8

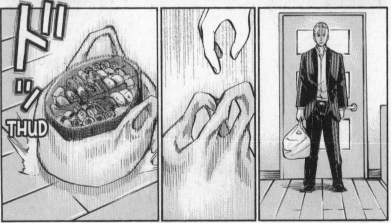

ドッ

THUD

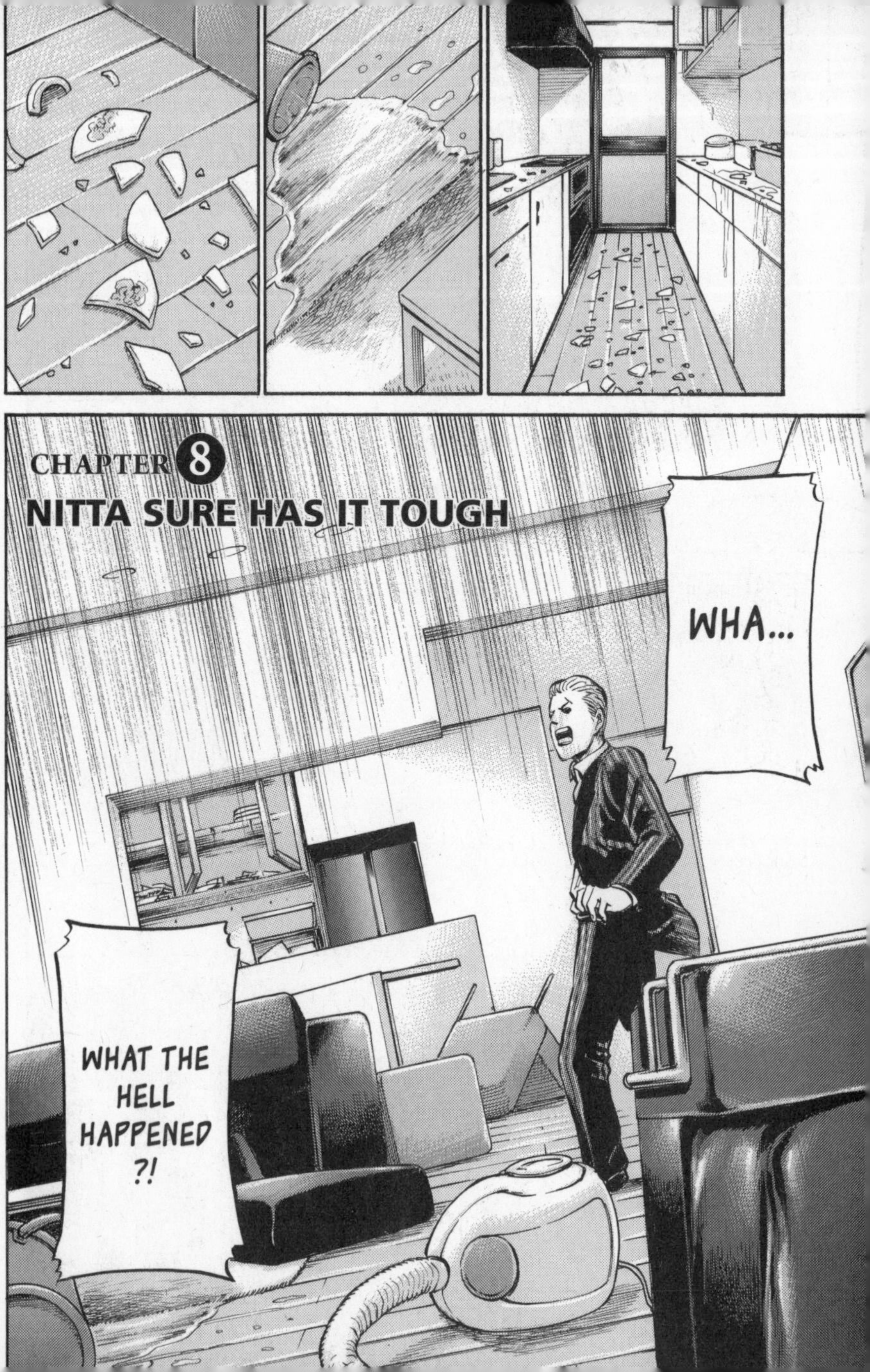
CHAPTER 8
NITTA SURE HAS IT TOUGH
WHA...
WHAT THE HELL HAPPENED ?!

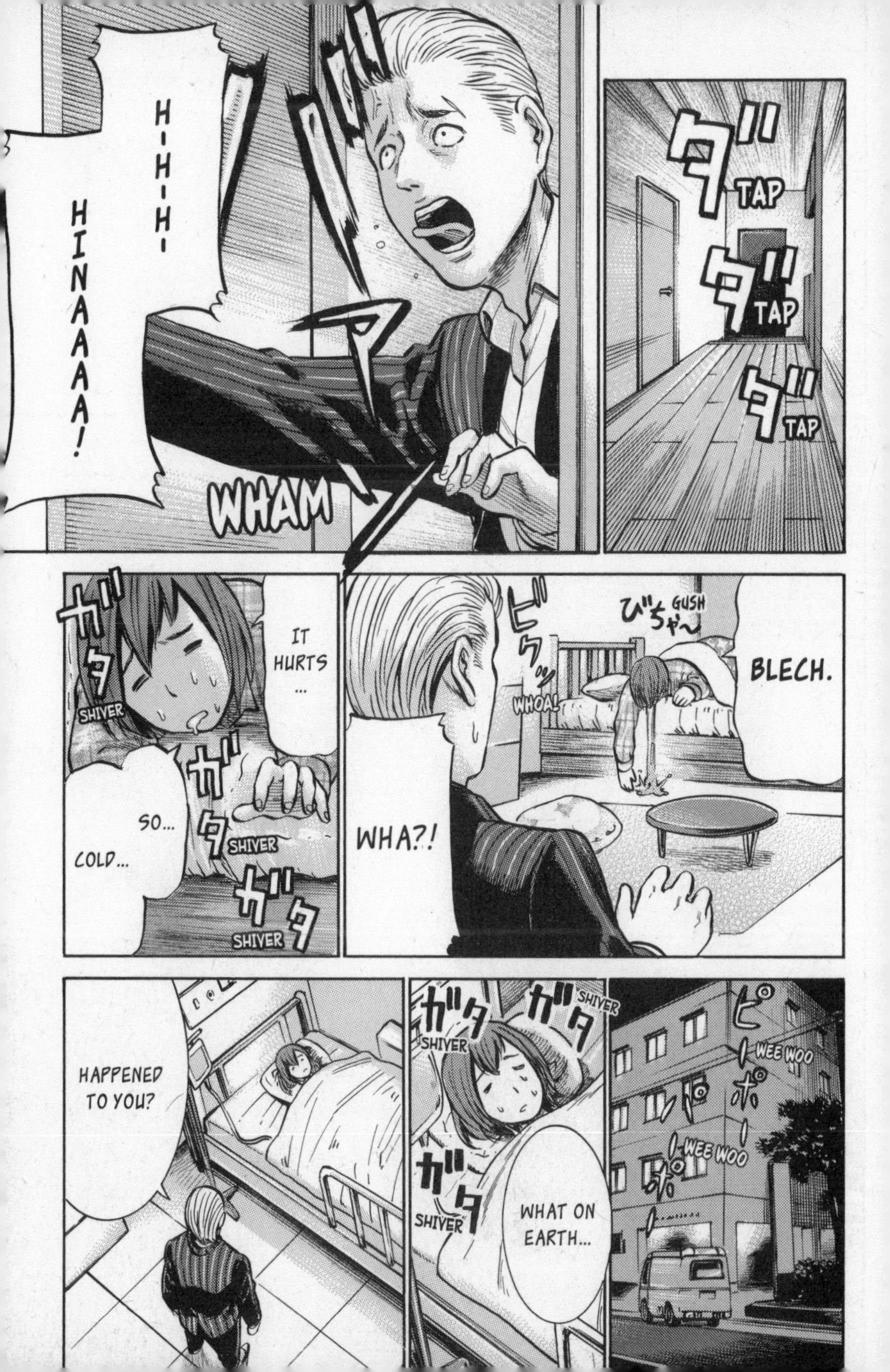

タ TAP
タ TAP
タ TAP
ダッ
WHAM
H-I-H-I-H-I- HINAAAAA!
BLECH.
びちゃ~ GUSH
ビクッ WHOA!
WHA?!
IT HURTS...
ガタ SHIVER
SO... COLD...
ガタ SHIVER
ガタ SHIVER
ピーポー WEE WOO
ピーポー WEE WOO
ガタ SHIVER
ガタ SHIVER
ガタ SHIVER
WHAT ON EARTH...
HAPPENED TO YOU?

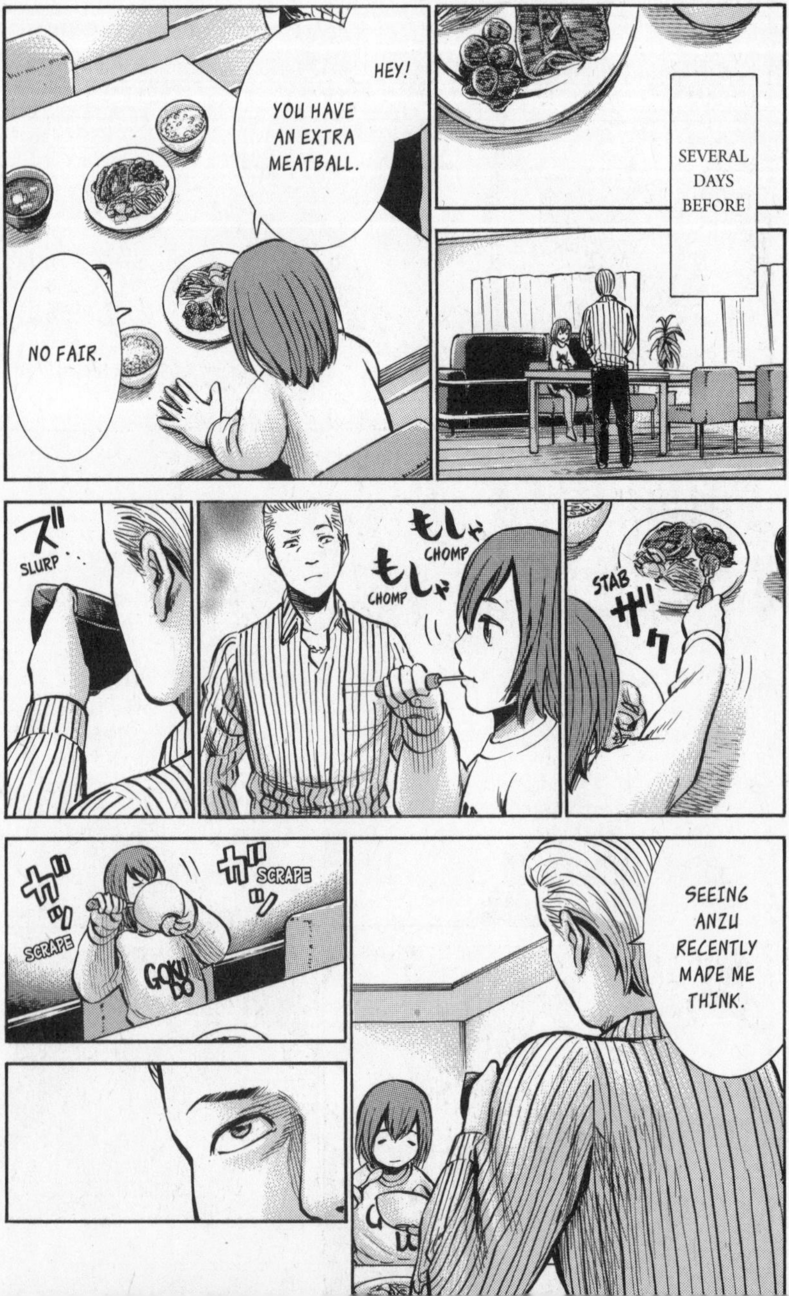
SEVERAL DAYS BEFORE
HEY!
YOU HAVE AN EXTRA MEATBALL.
NO FAIR.
ザク
STAB
もしゃ
CHOMP
もしゃ
CHOMP
ズ
SLURP
SEEING ANZU RECENTLY MADE ME THINK.
ガッ
SCRAPE
ガッ
SCRAPE
GOKUDO

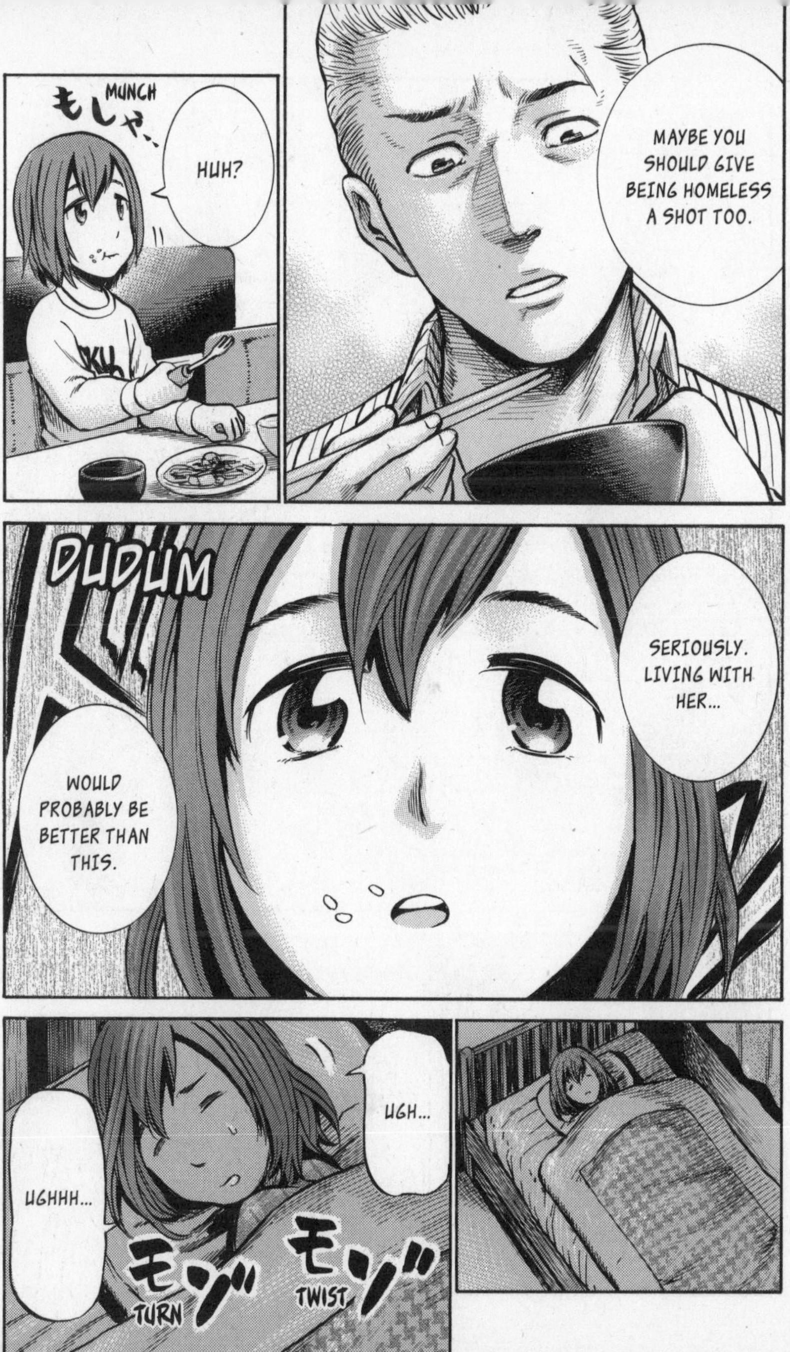
MAYBE YOU SHOULD GIVE BEING HOMELESS A SHOT TOO.
もしゃ...
MUNCH
HUH?
DUDUM
SERIOUSLY. LIVING WITH HER...
WOULD PROBABLY BE BETTER THAN THIS.
UGH...
UGHHH...
モゾ
TWIST
モゾ
TURN

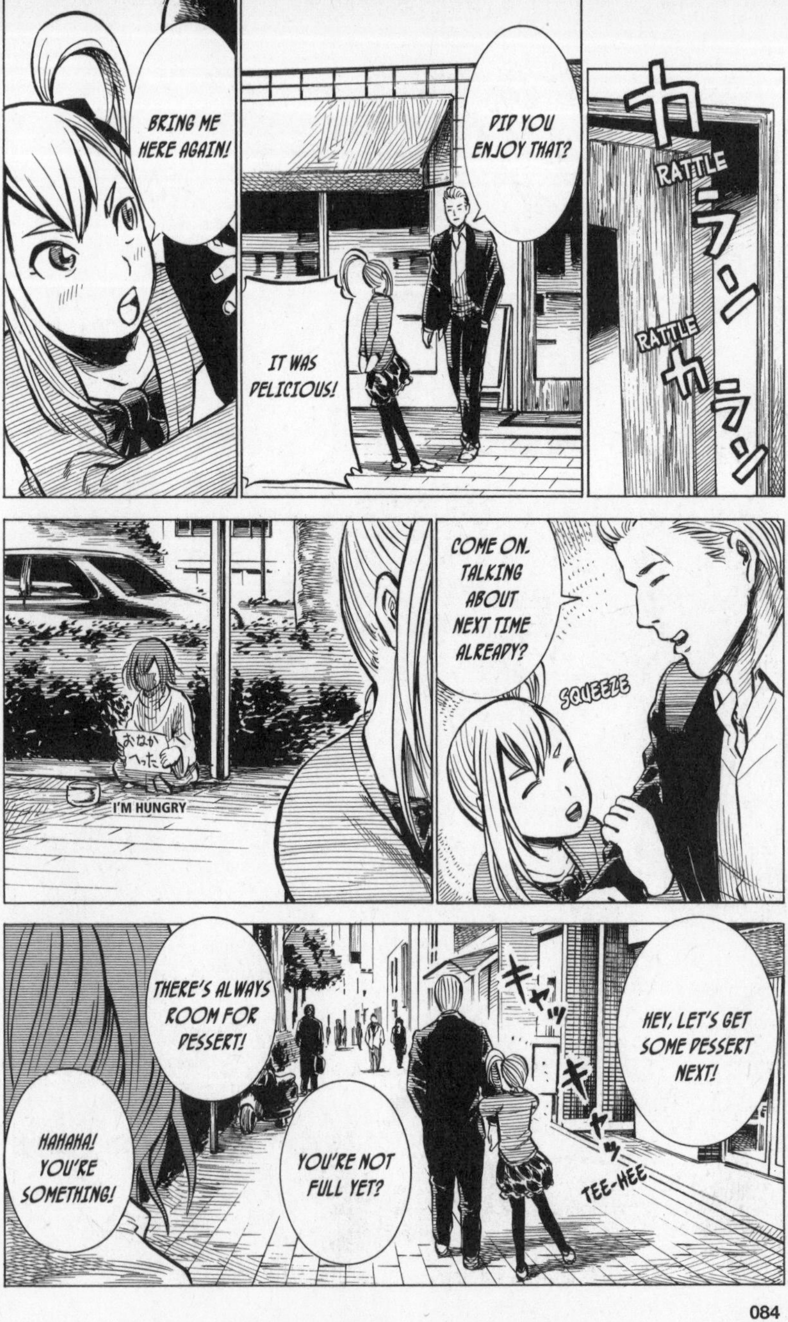
カラン
RATTLE
カラン
RATTLE
DID YOU ENJOY THAT?
IT WAS DELICIOUS!
BRING ME HERE AGAIN!
COME ON. TALKING ABOUT NEXT TIME ALREADY?
SQUEEZE
おなか へった
I'M HUNGRY
HEY, LET'S GET SOME DESSERT NEXT!
キャッ キャッ
TEE-HEE
YOU'RE NOT FULL YET?
THERE'S ALWAYS ROOM FOR DESSERT!
HAHAHA! YOU'RE SOMETHING!

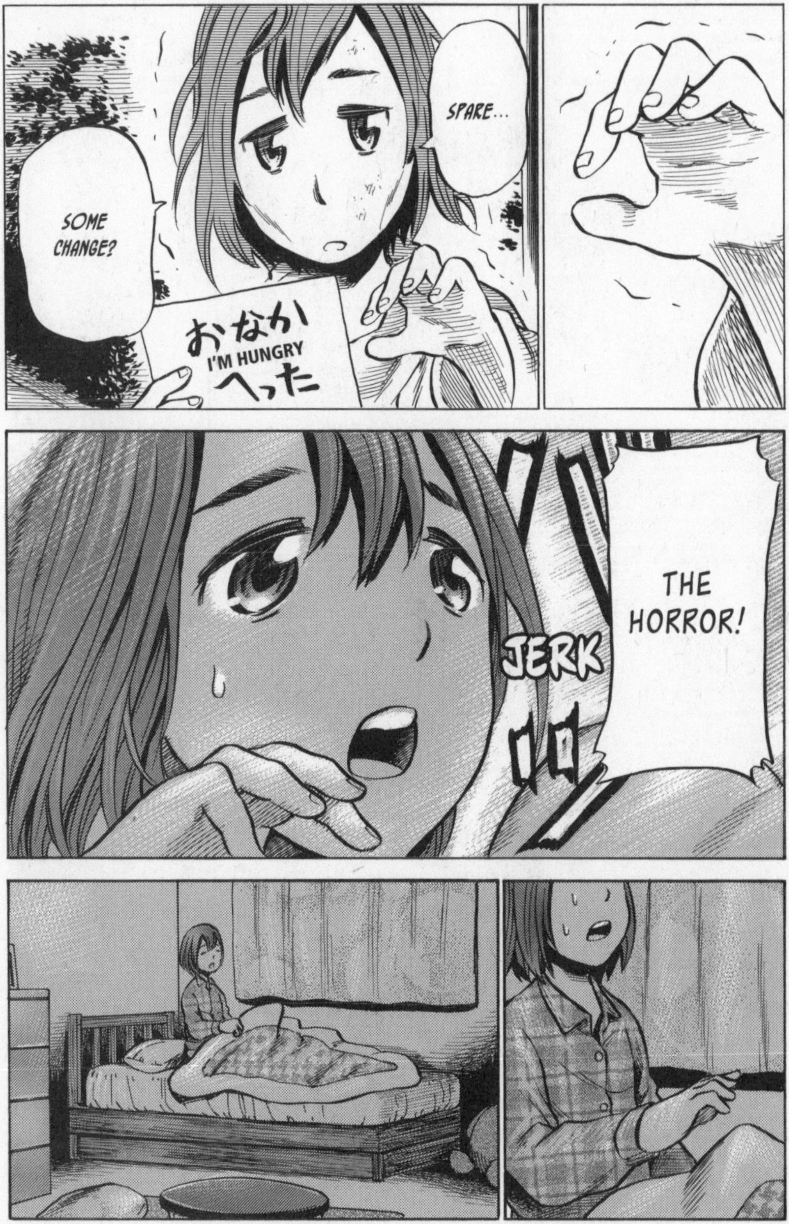
SPARE...
SOME CHANGE?
おなか
I'M HUNGRY
へった
THE HORROR!
JERK

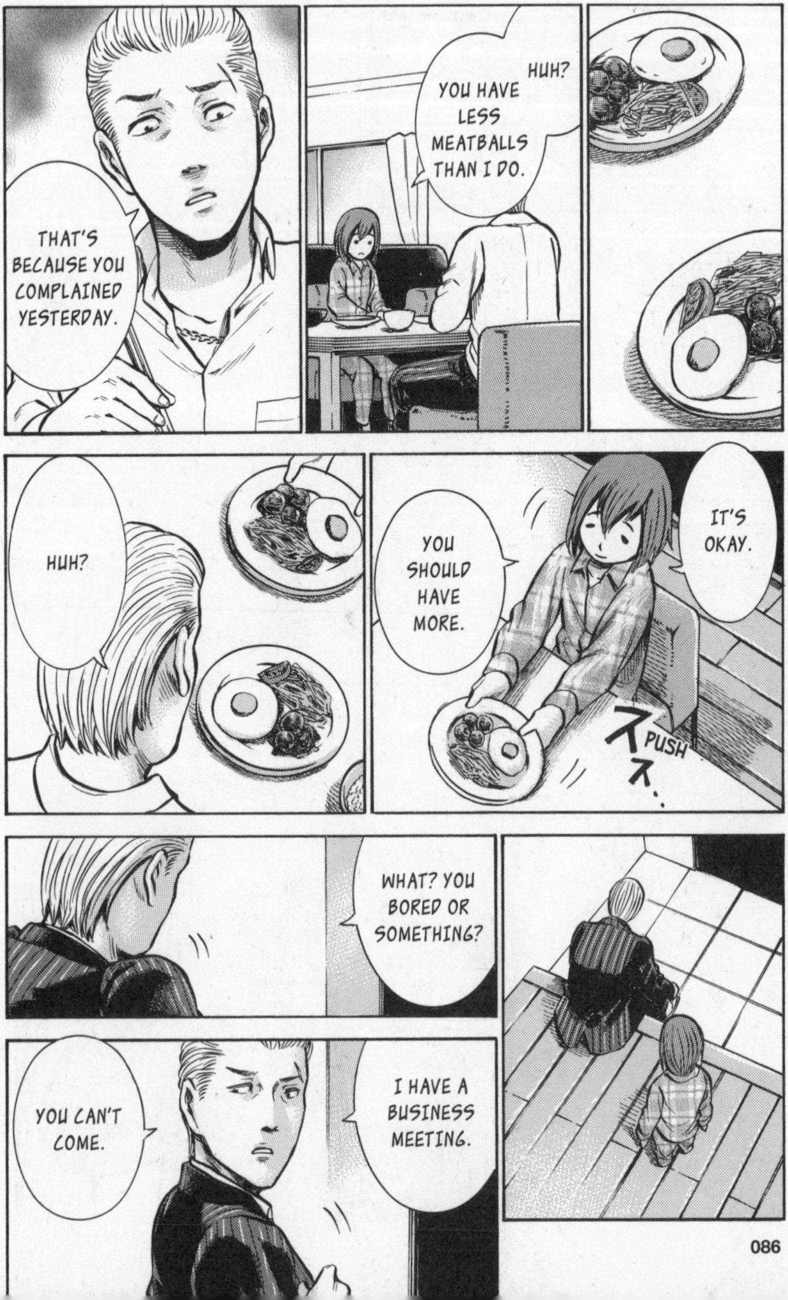
HUH? YOU HAVE LESS MEATBALLS THAN I DO.
THAT'S BECAUSE YOU COMPLAINED YESTERDAY.
IT'S OKAY.
YOU SHOULD HAVE MORE.
PUSH
HUH?
WHAT? YOU BORED OR SOMETHING?
I HAVE A BUSINESS MEETING.
YOU CAN'T COME.

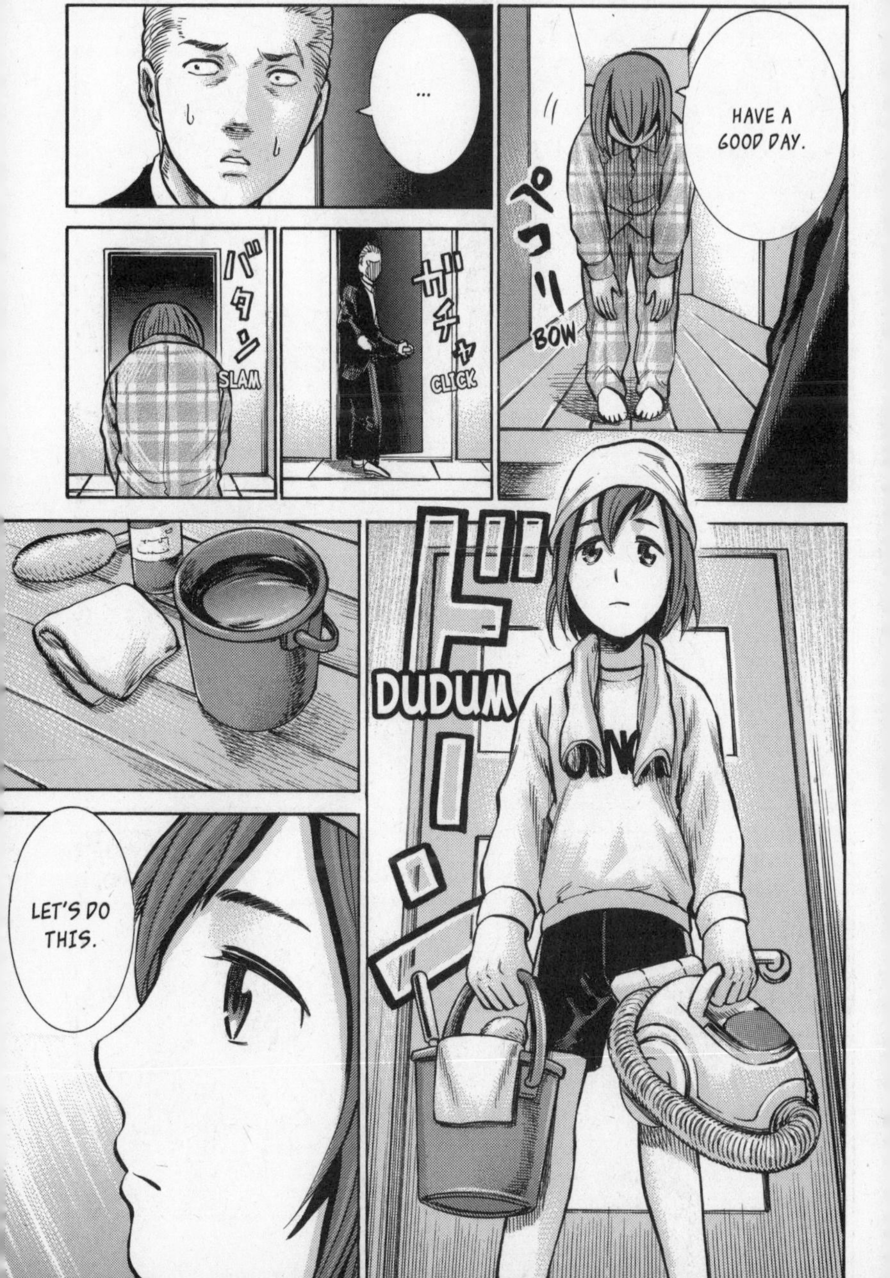
HAVE A GOOD DAY.
ペコリ
BOW
...
ガチャ
CLICK
バタン
SLAM
ドーン
DUDUM
LET'S DO THIS.

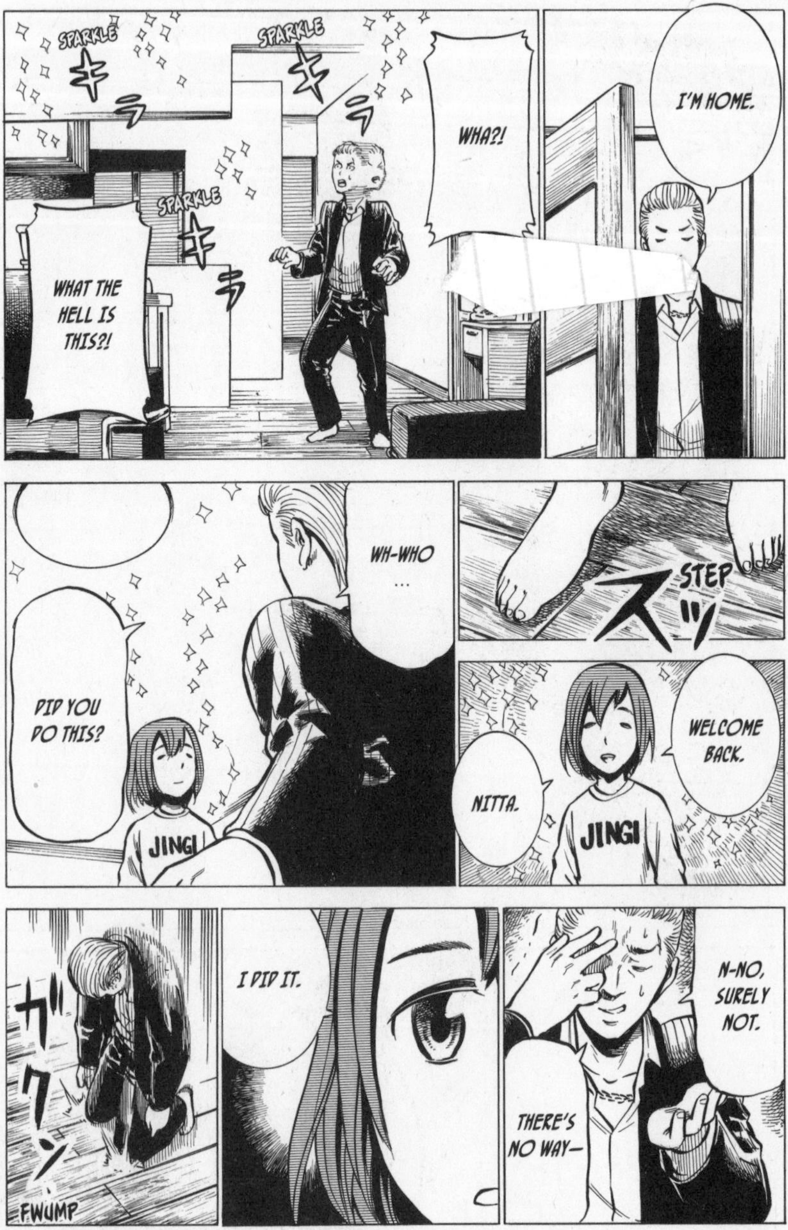
I'M HOME.
WHA?!
SPARKLE
SPARKLE
SPARKLE
WHAT THE HELL IS THIS?!
STEP
WELCOME BACK.
NITTA.
WH-WHO ...
DID YOU DO THIS?
N-NO, SURELY NOT.
THERE'S NO WAY—
I DID IT.
FWUMP

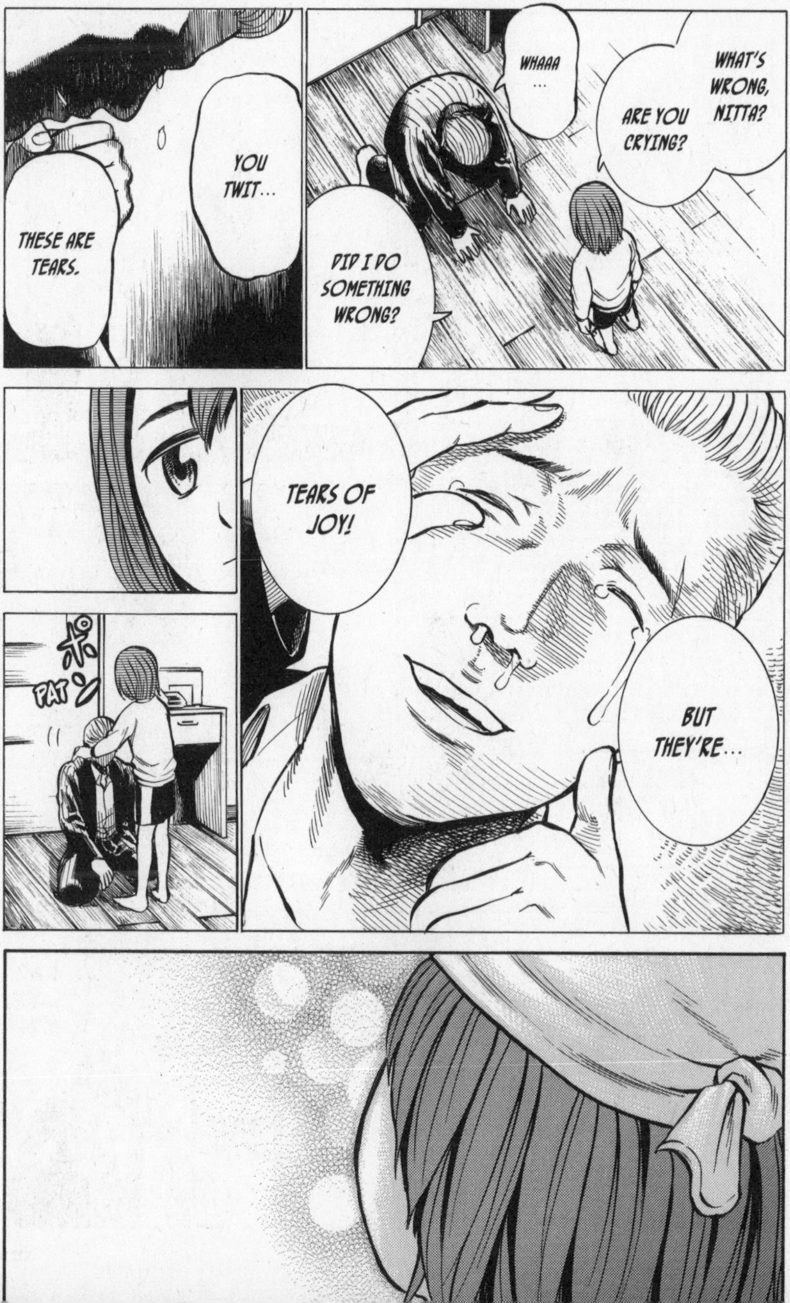
WHAT'S WRONG, NITTA?
ARE YOU CRYING?
WHAAA...
DID I DO SOMETHING WRONG?
YOU TWIT...
THESE ARE TEARS.
BUT THEY'RE...
TEARS OF JOY!
PAT

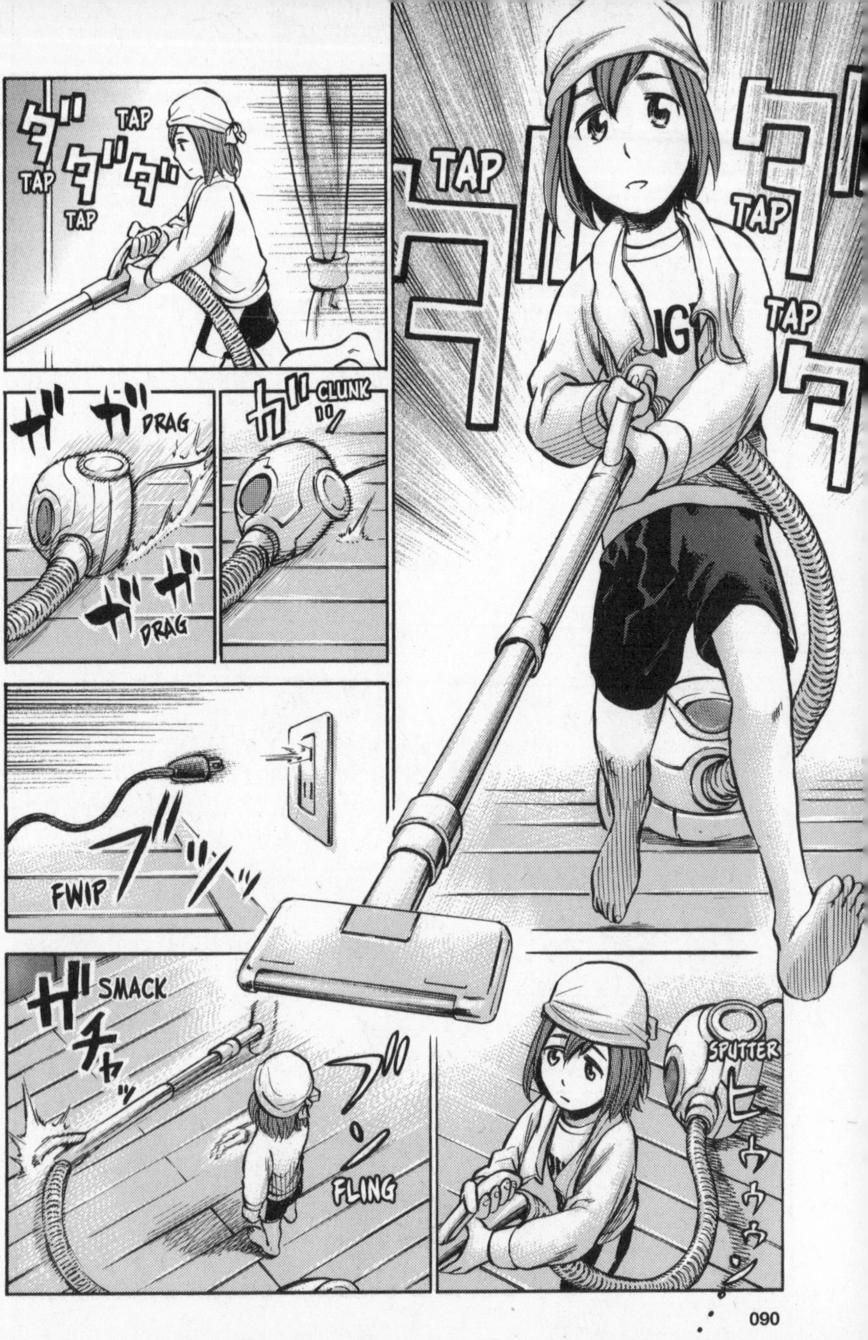

TAP
TAP
TAP
TAP
TAP
TAP
CLUNK
DRAG
DRAG
FWIP
SPUTTER
SMACK
FLING

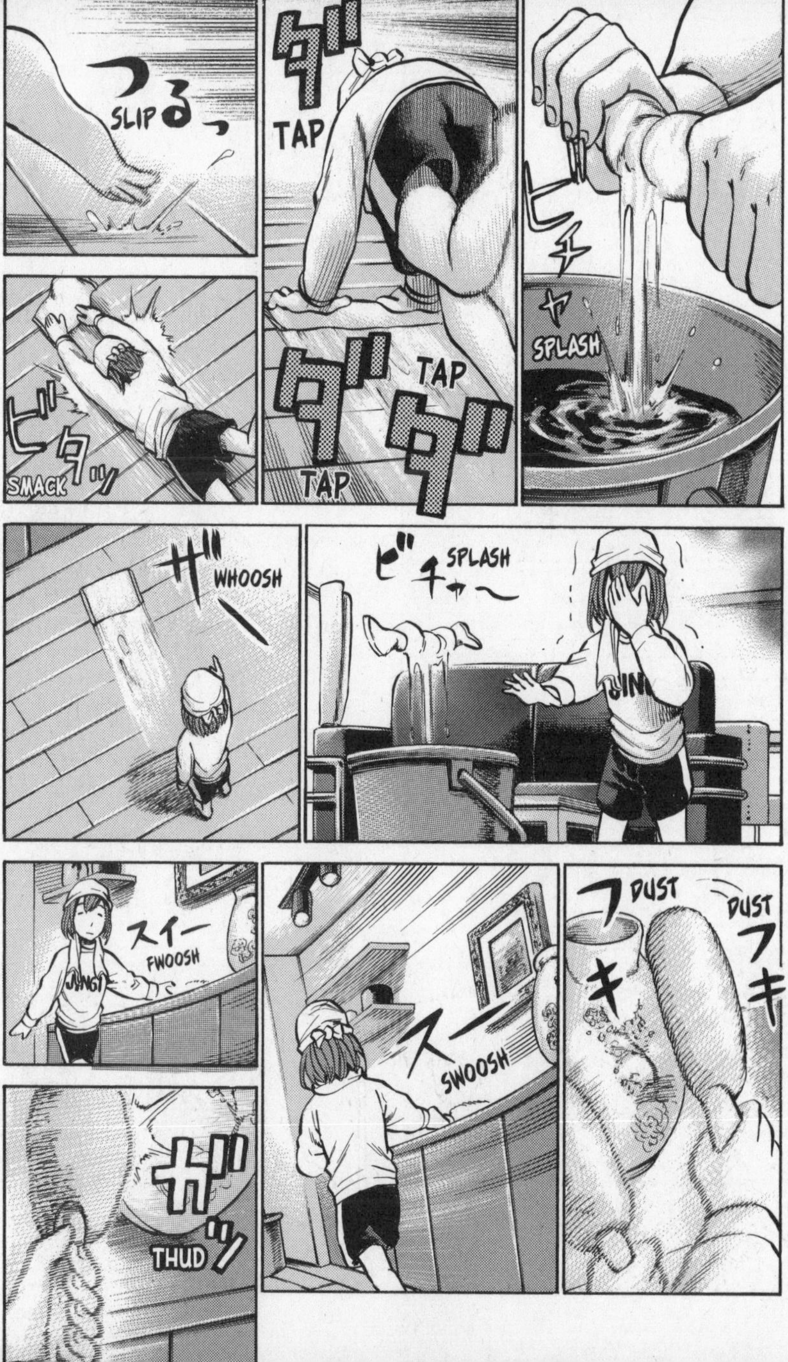
ピチャ
SPLASH
ダ
TAP
ダダ
TAP
TAP
つるっ
SLIP
ビタッ
SMACK
ビチャ〜
SPLASH
ザー
WHOOSH
フキ
DUST
フキ
DUST
スー
SWOOSH
スイー
FWOOSH
ガッ
THUD

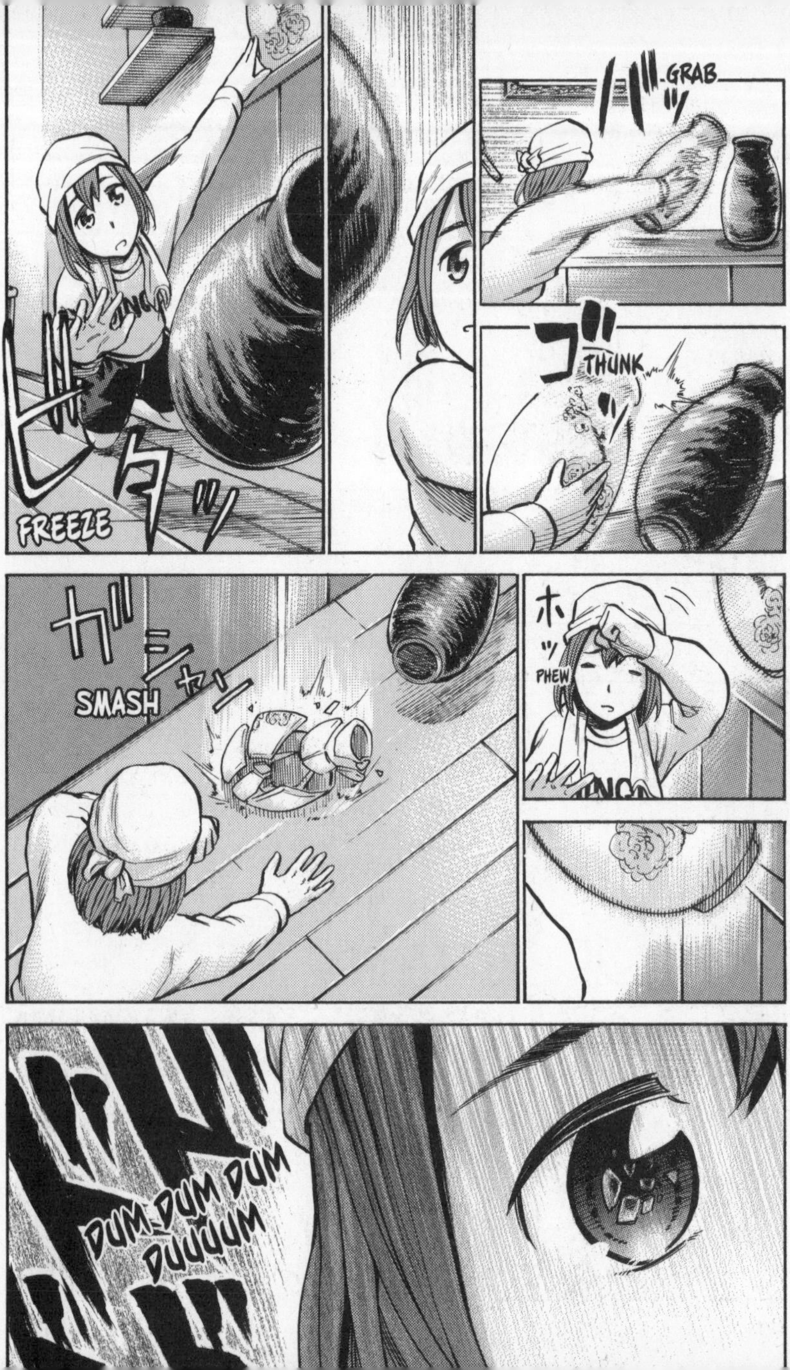

GRAB
ゴッ
THUNK
ピタッ
FREEZE
ホッ
PHEW
ガシャーン
SMASH
DUM DUM DUM DUUUUM

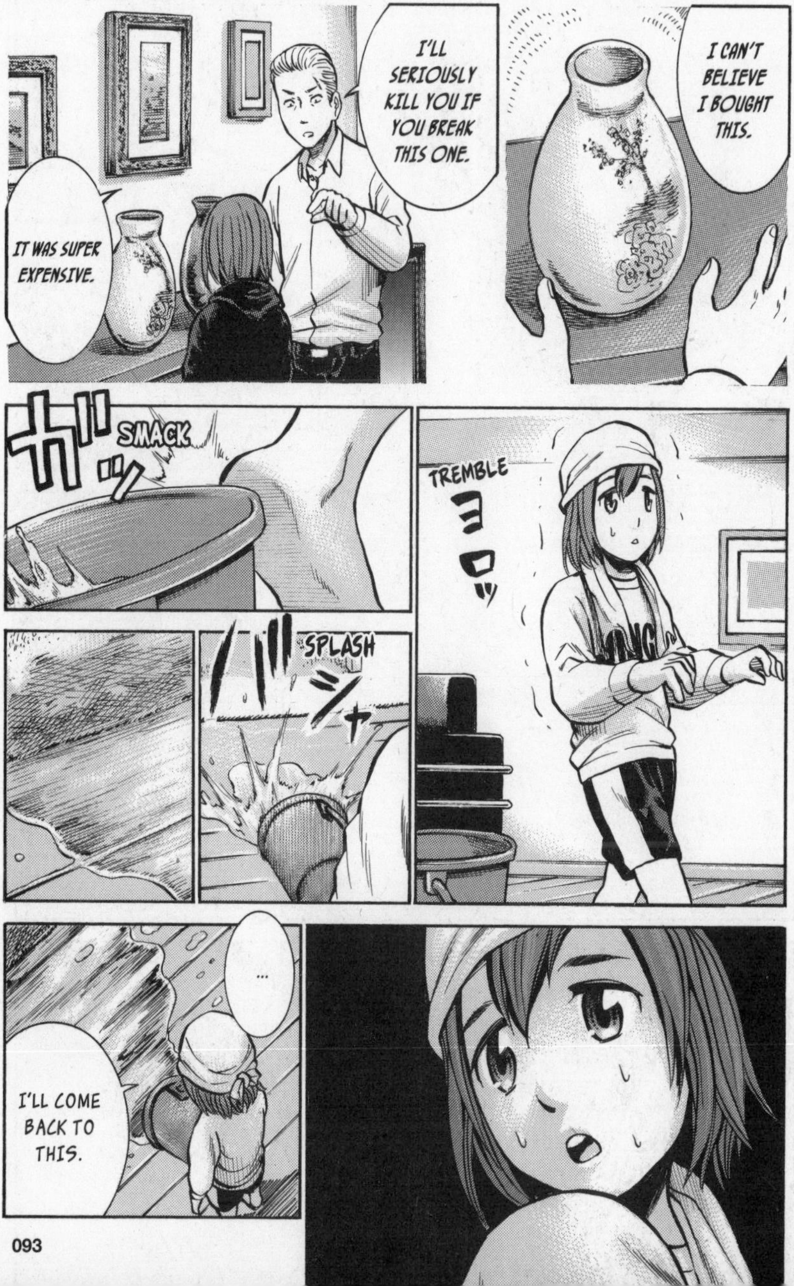
I CAN'T BELIEVE I BOUGHT THIS.
I'LL SERIOUSLY KILL YOU IF YOU BREAK THIS ONE.
IT WAS SUPER EXPENSIVE.
TREMBLE
ヨロッ
ガッ
SMACK
バシャ
SPLASH
...
I'LL COME BACK TO THIS.

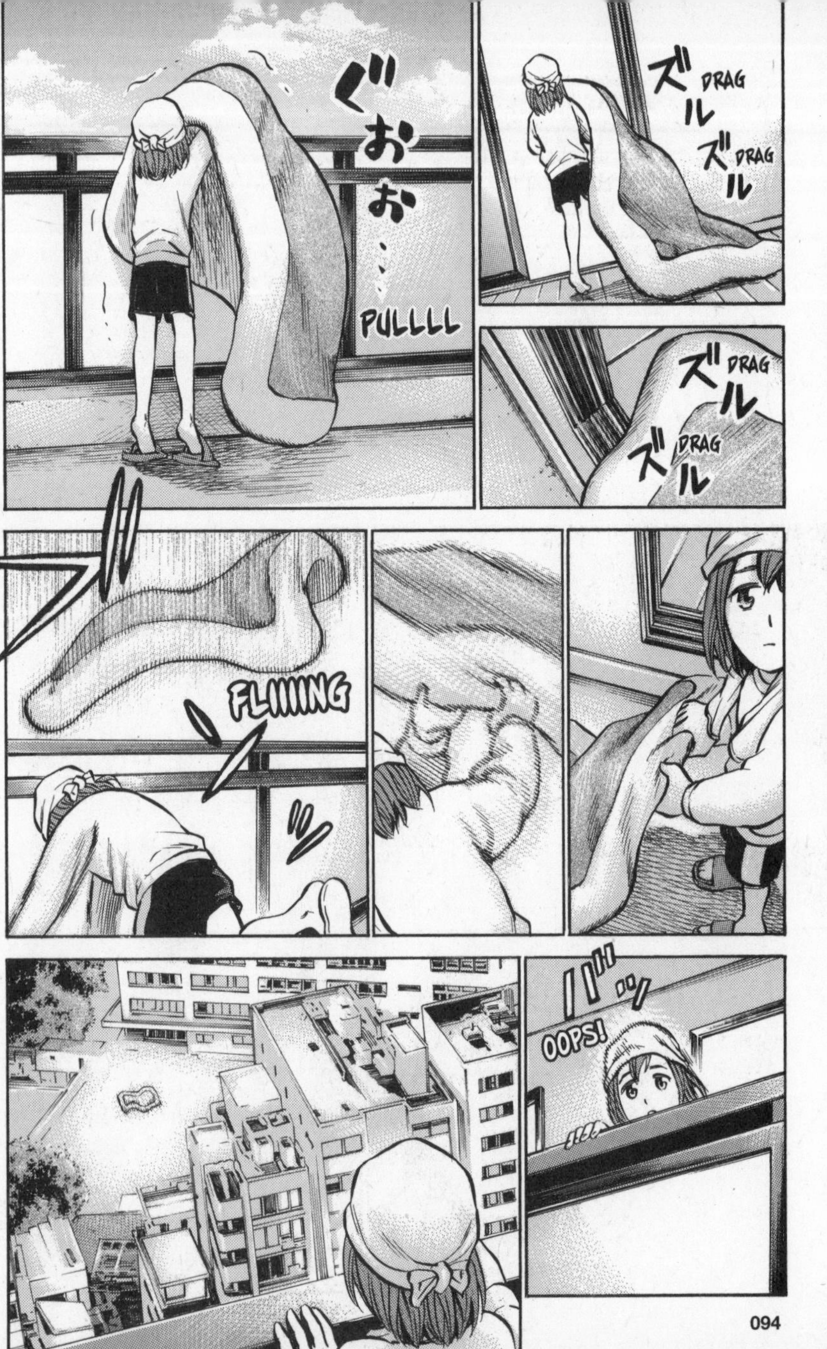
ズル DRAG
ズル DRAG
ズル DRAG
ズル DRAG
ぐおお…
PULLLLL
FLIIIING
バッ
OOPS!

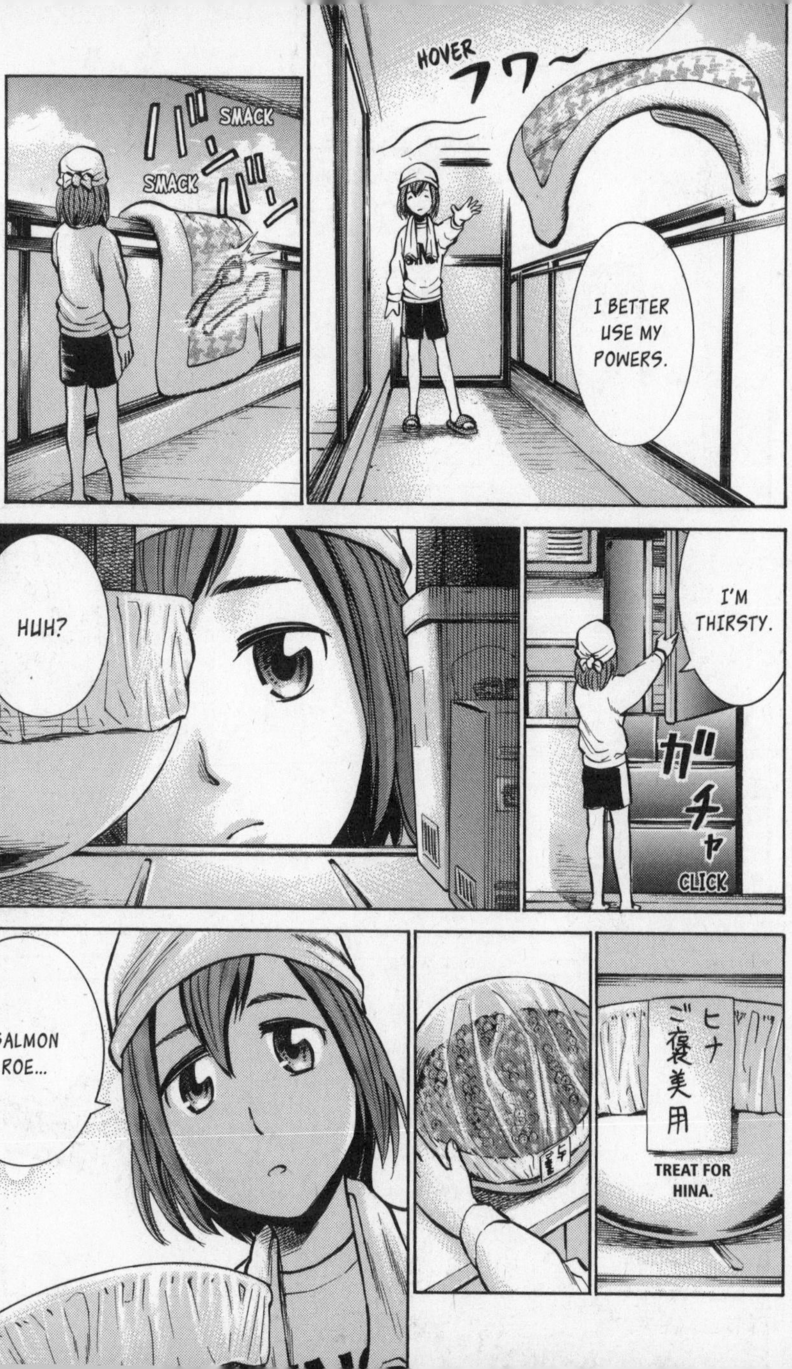
HOVER
フワ~
I BETTER USE MY POWERS.
SMACK
SMACK
I'M THIRSTY.
ガチャ
CLICK
HUH?
ヒナ
ご褒美用
TREAT FOR HINA.
SALMON ROE...

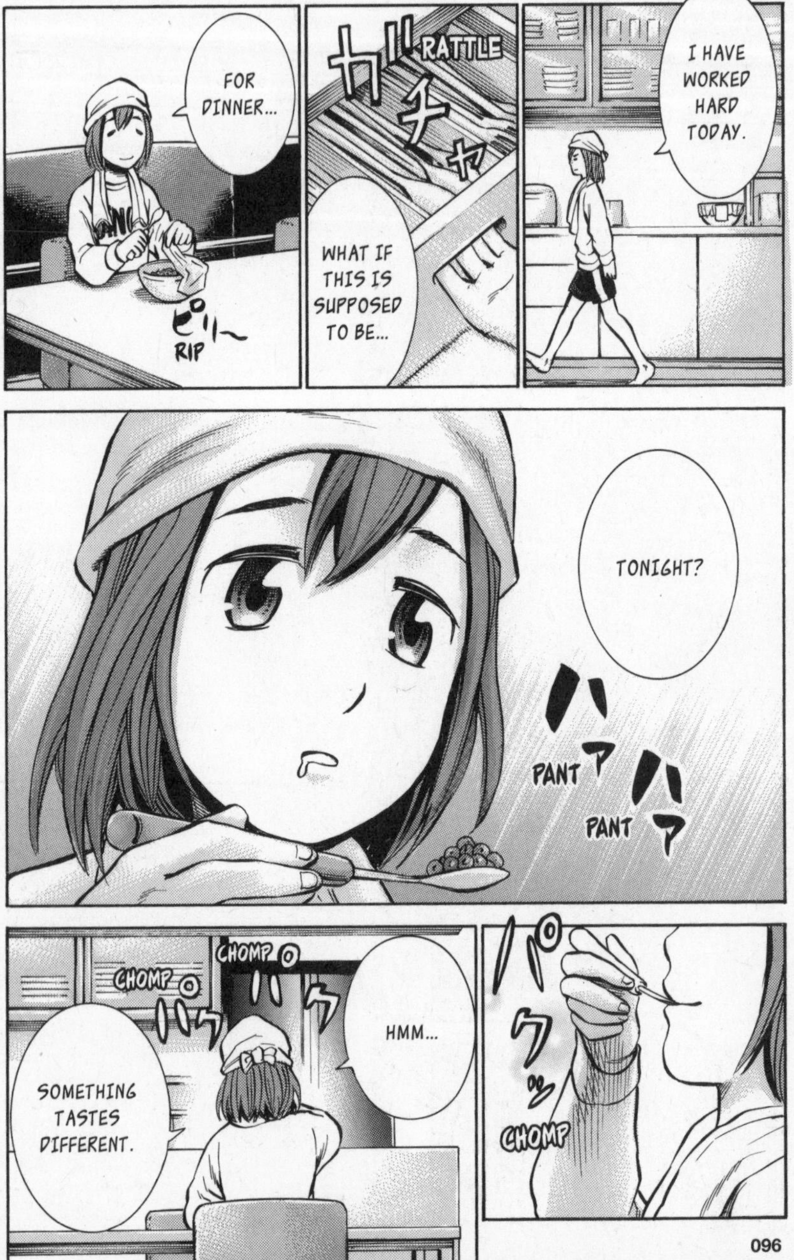
I HAVE WORKED HARD TODAY.
カチャ
RATTLE
WHAT IF THIS IS SUPPOSED TO BE...
FOR DINNER...
ピリー
RIP
TONIGHT?
ハァ
PANT
ハァ
PANT
パクッ
CHOMP
HMM...
パク
CHOMP
パク
CHOMP
SOMETHING TASTES DIFFERENT.

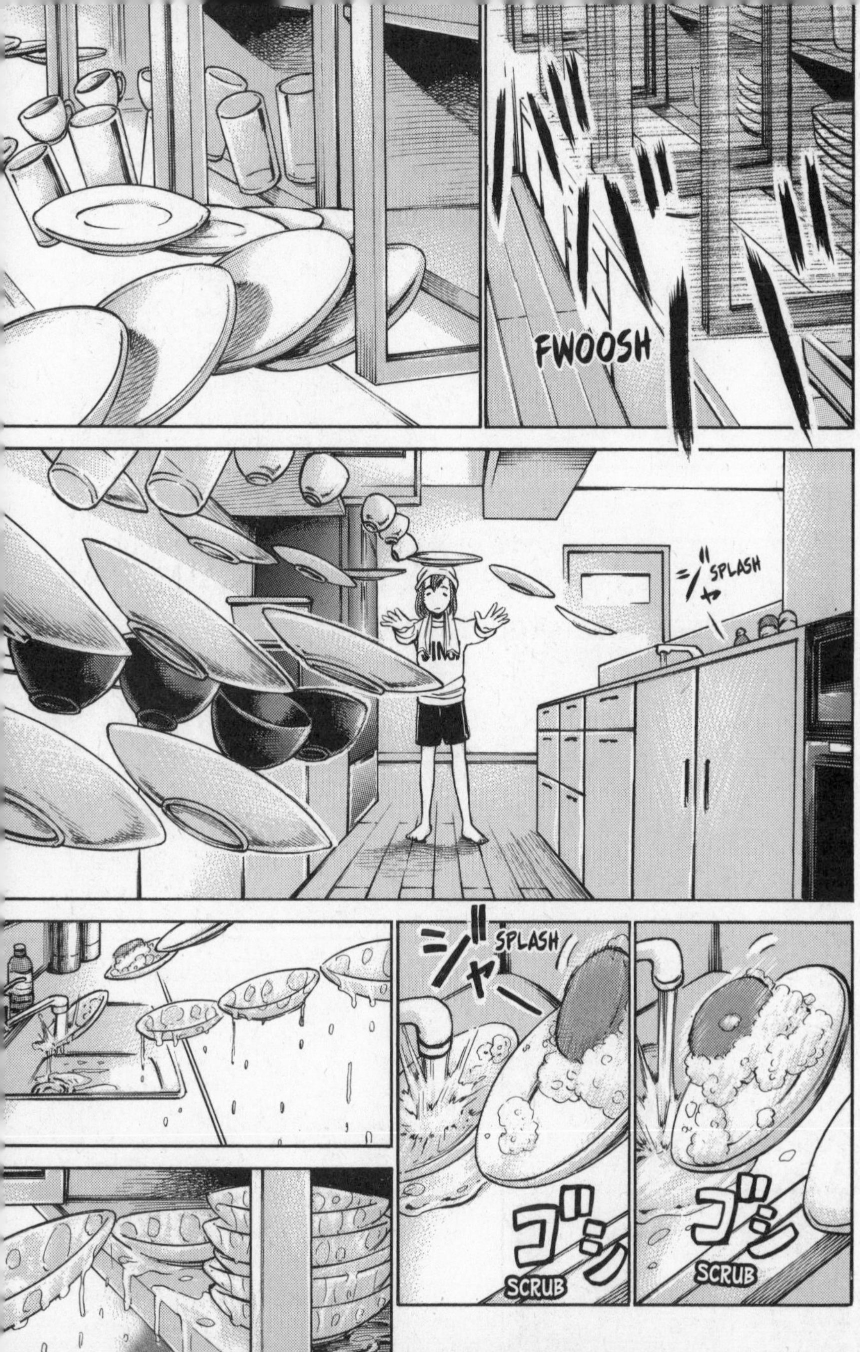
FWOOSH
ジャ
SPLASH
ゴシ
SCRUB
ジャー
SPLASH
ゴシ
SCRUB

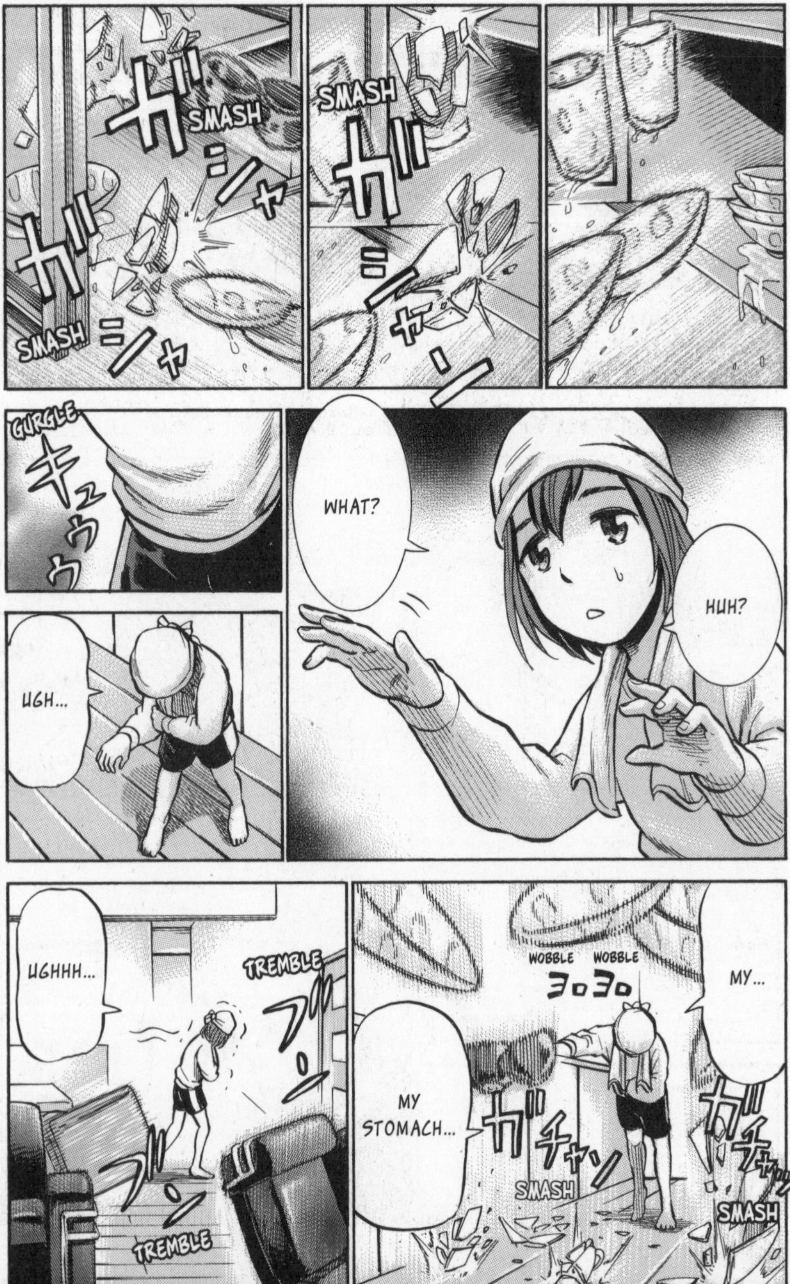
SMASH
ガシャーン
SMASH
ガシャ
SMASH
ガシャ
HUH?
WHAT?
GURGLE
キュウウ
UGH...
MY...
WOBBLE WOBBLE
ヨロヨロ
MY STOMACH...
ガチャン
SMASH
ガチャン
SMASH
UGHHH...
TREMBLE
TREMBLE

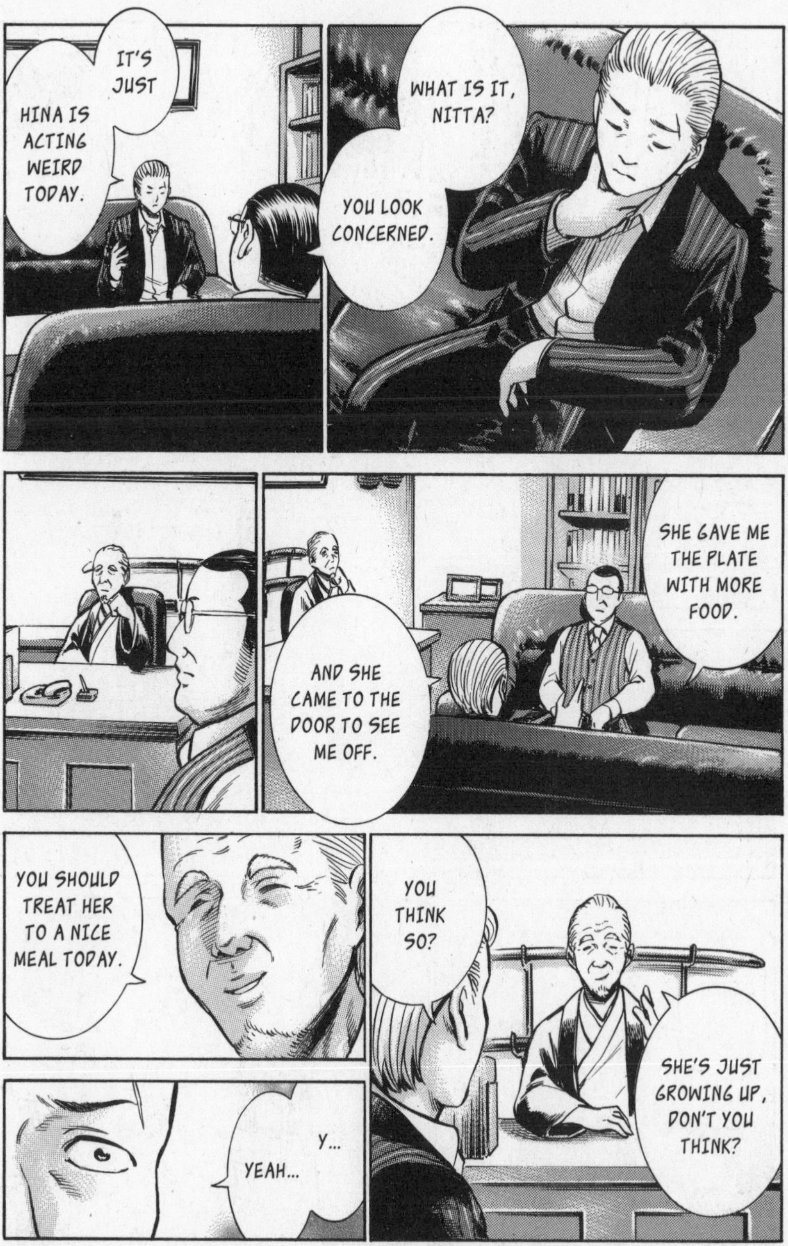
WHAT IS IT, NITTA?
YOU LOOK CONCERNED.
IT'S JUST
HINA IS ACTING WEIRD TODAY.
SHE GAVE ME THE PLATE WITH MORE FOOD.
AND SHE CAME TO THE DOOR TO SEE ME OFF.
YOU THINK SO?
SHE'S JUST GROWING UP, DON'T YOU THINK?
YOU SHOULD TREAT HER TO A NICE MEAL TODAY.
Y...
YEAH...

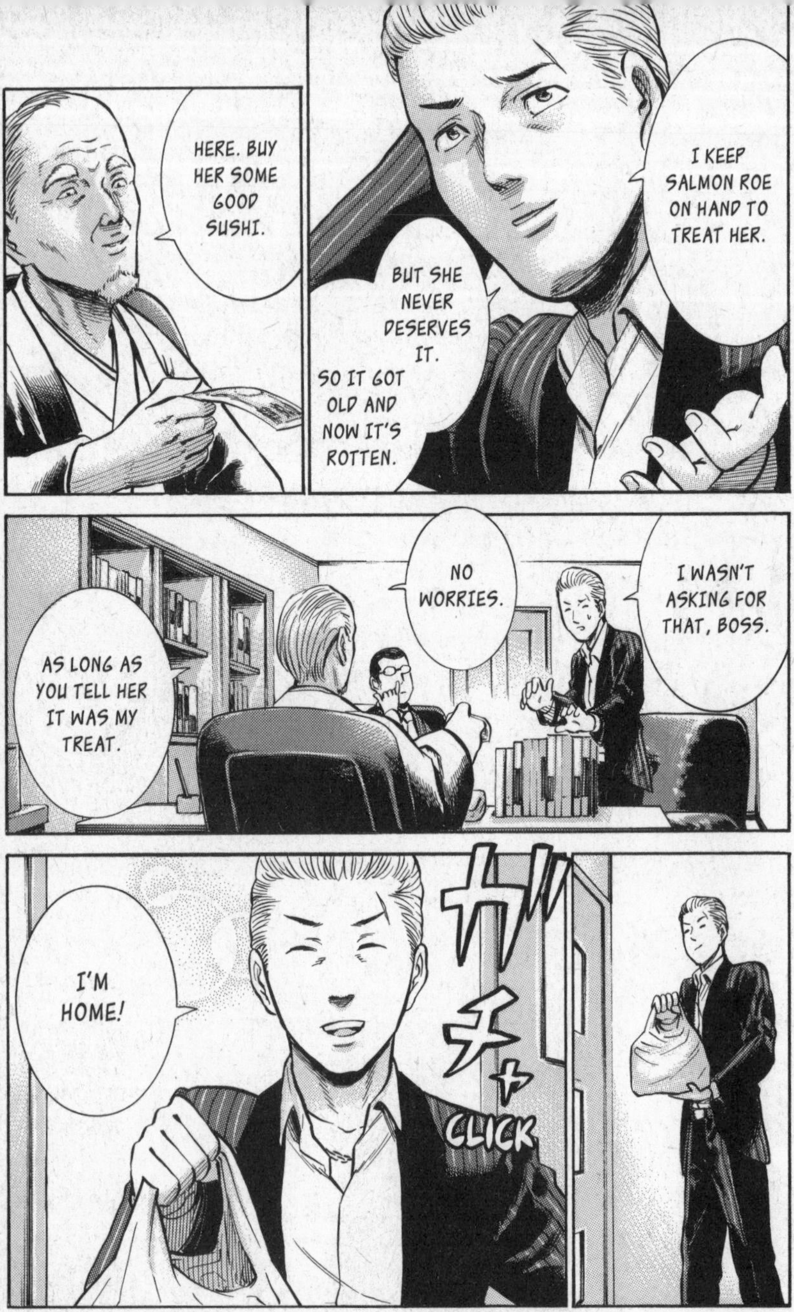
I KEEP SALMON ROE ON HAND TO TREAT HER.
BUT SHE NEVER DESERVES IT.
SO IT GOT OLD AND NOW IT'S ROTTEN.
HERE. BUY HER SOME GOOD SUSHI.
I WASN'T ASKING FOR THAT, BOSS.
NO WORRIES.
AS LONG AS YOU TELL HER IT WAS MY TREAT.
ガチャ
CLICK
I'M HOME!

CHAPTER 8 END

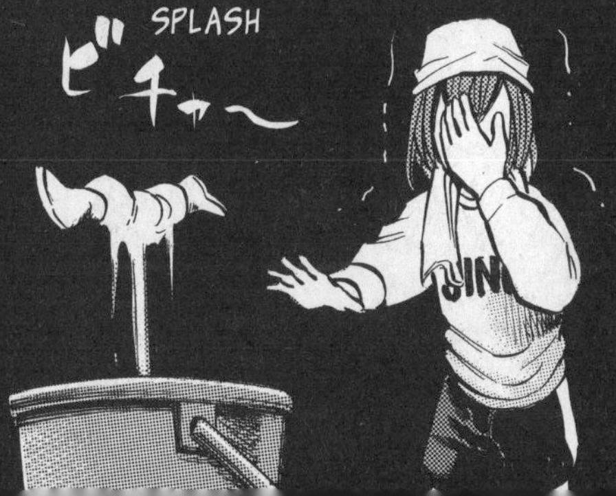
SPLASH
ビチャ～

CHAPTER 9
DISOWNED! ROCK 'N' ROLL FEVER

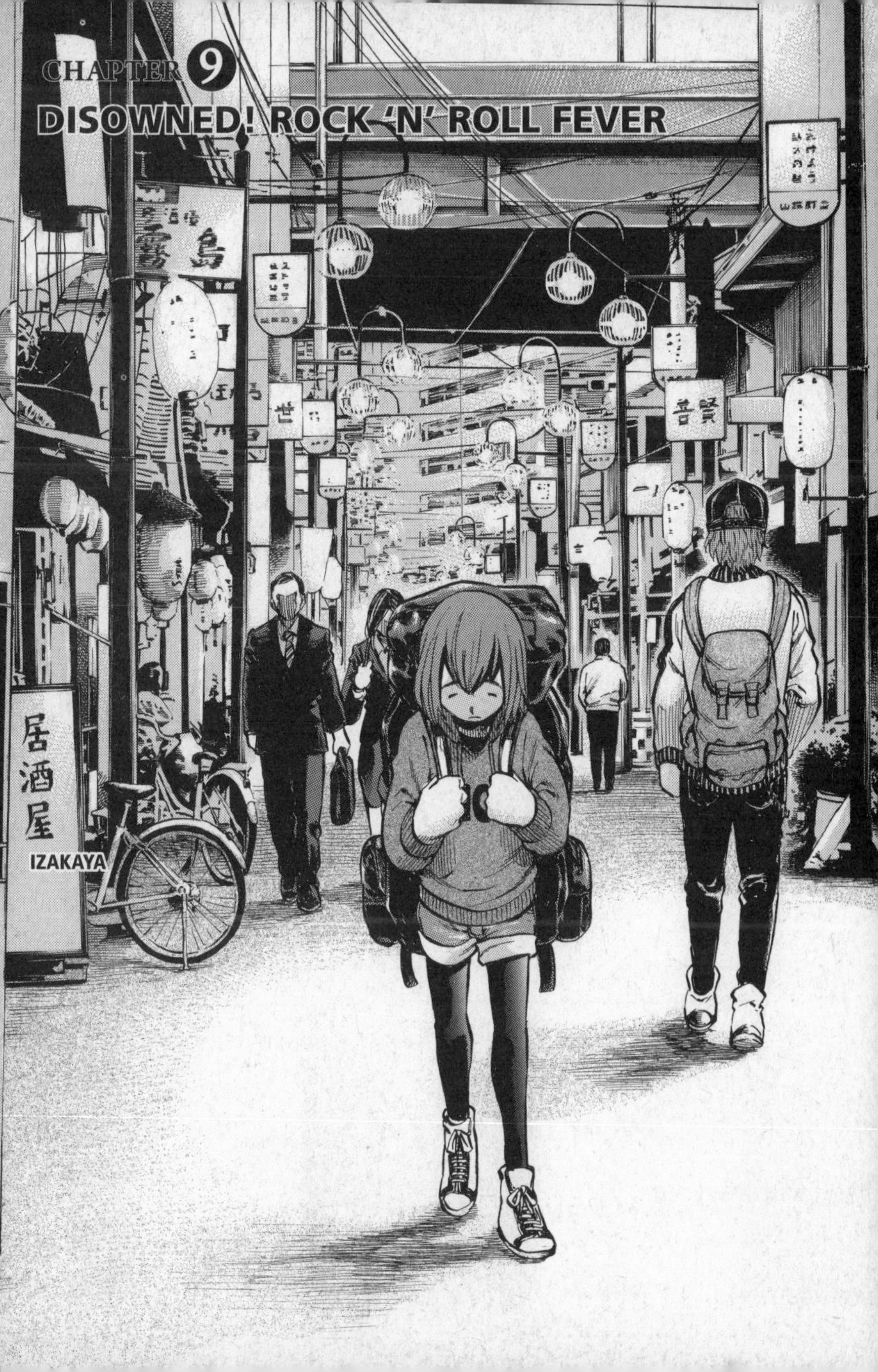

居酒屋
IZAKAYA

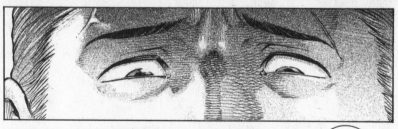

DO YOU SEE THIS? LOOK AT THIS MESS.

I LEFT IT UNTOUCHED WHILE YOU WERE IN THE HOSPITAL.

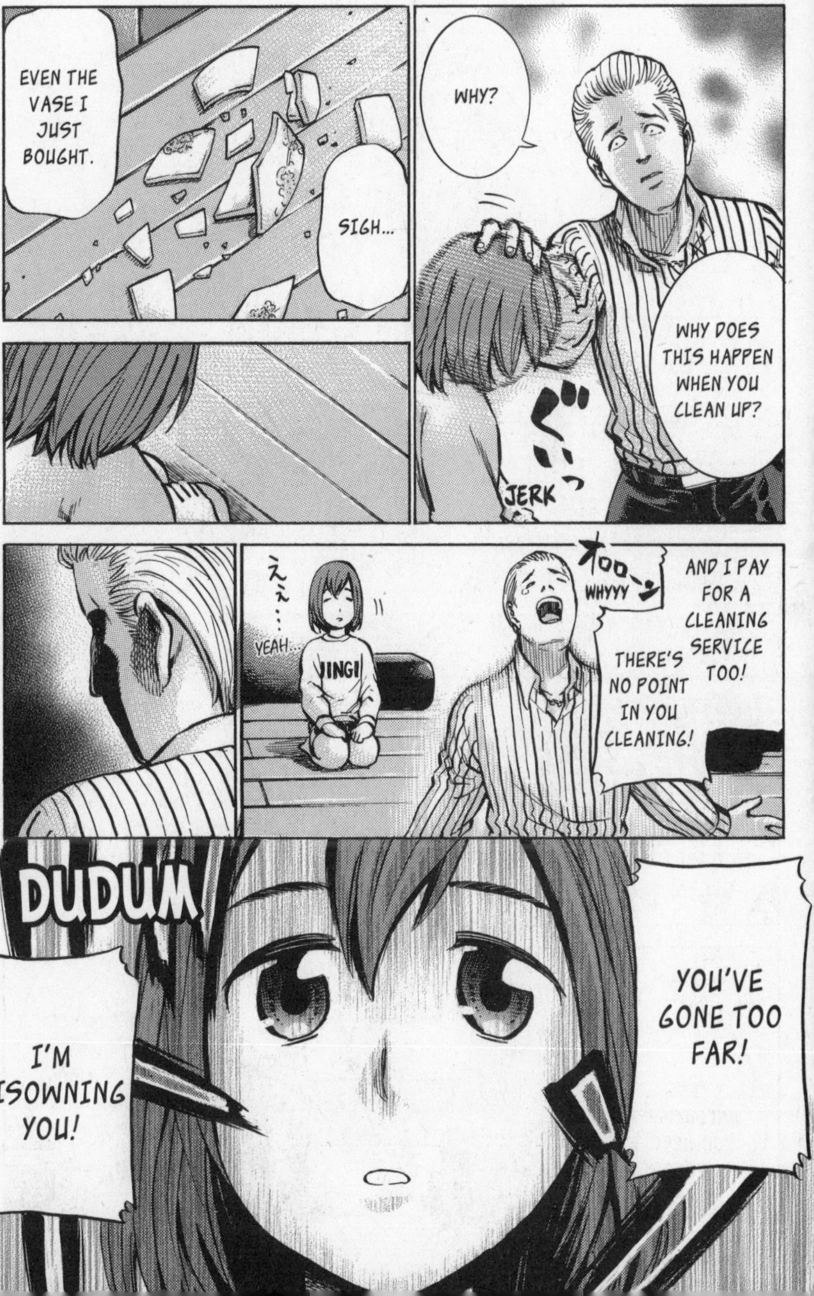
WHY?
WHY DOES THIS HAPPEN WHEN YOU CLEAN UP?
ぐいっ
JERK
EVEN THE VASE I JUST BOUGHT.
SIGH...
オロ〜ン
WHYYY
AND I PAY FOR A CLEANING SERVICE TOO!
THERE'S NO POINT IN YOU CLEANING!
ええ…
YEAH
JINGI
YOU'VE GONE TOO FAR!
DUDUM
I'M DISOWNING YOU!

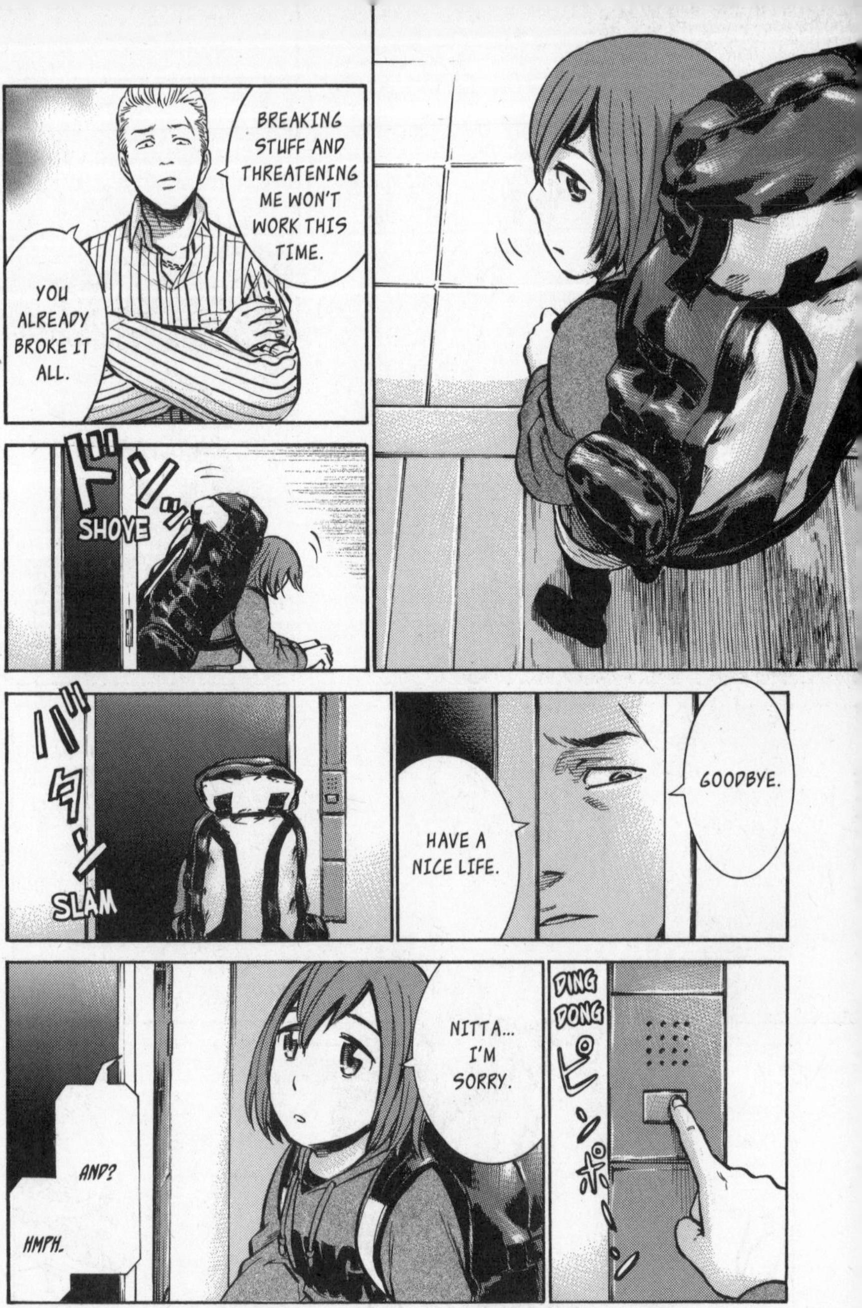
BREAKING STUFF AND THREATENING ME WON'T WORK THIS TIME.
YOU ALREADY BROKE IT ALL.
SHOVE
GOODBYE.
HAVE A NICE LIFE.
SLAM
DING DONG
NITTA... I'M SORRY.
AND?
HMPH.

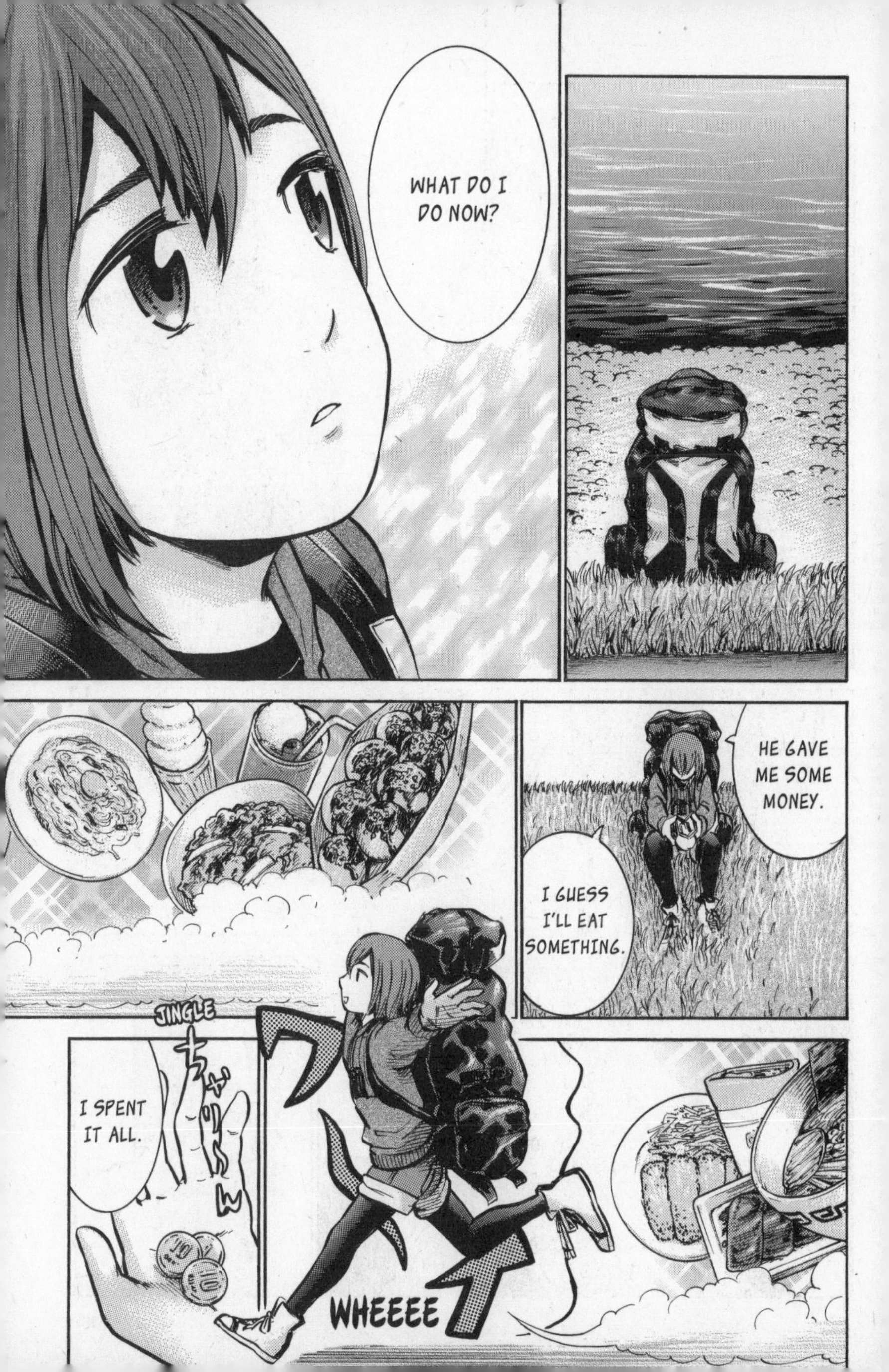
WHAT DO I DO NOW?
HE GAVE ME SOME MONEY.
I GUESS I'LL EAT SOMETHING.
WHEEEE
JINGLE
I SPENT IT ALL.

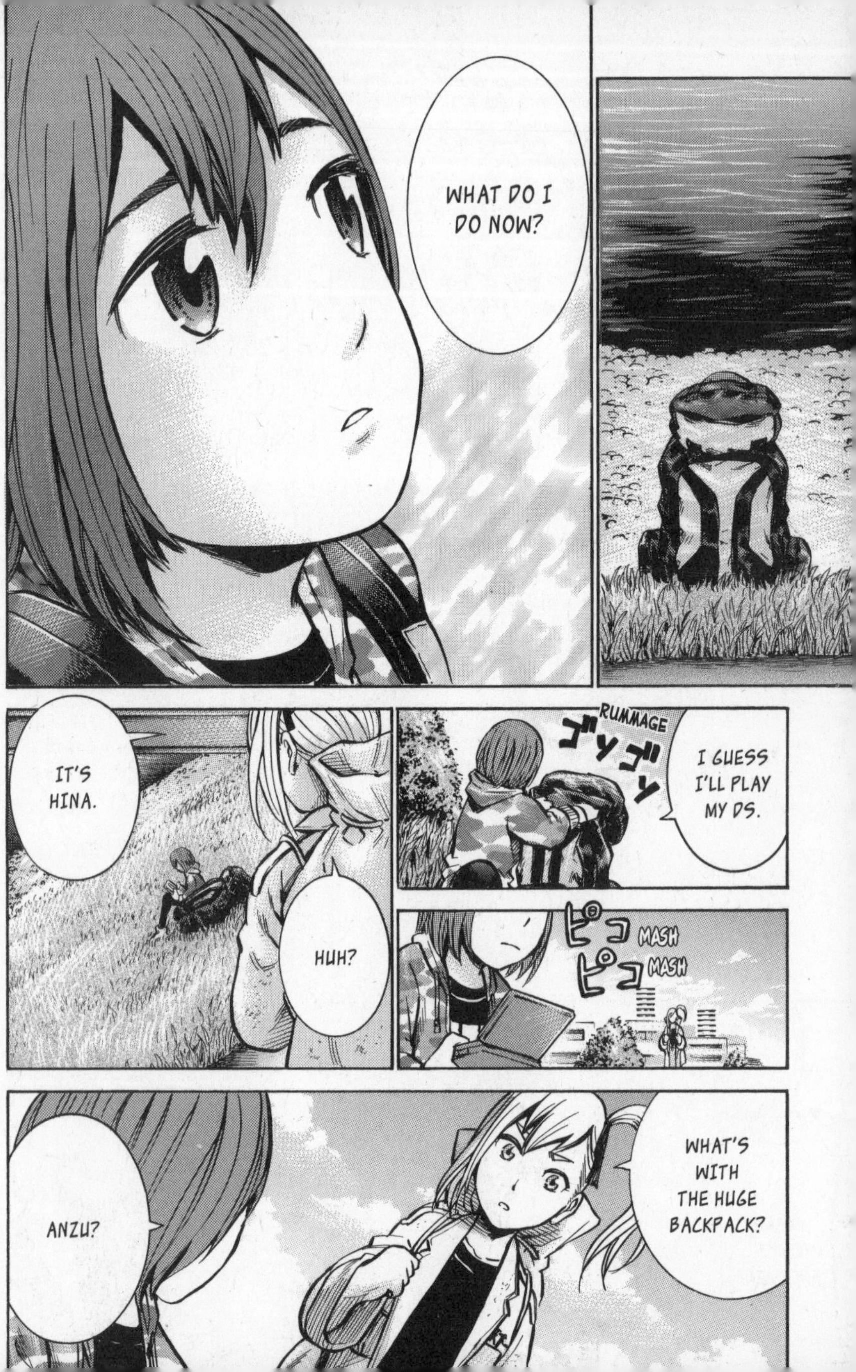
WHAT DO I DO NOW?
RUMMAGE
ゴソゴソ
I GUESS I'LL PLAY MY DS.
ピコ MASH
ピコ MASH
HUH?
IT'S HINA.
WHAT'S WITH THE HUGE BACKPACK?
ANZU?

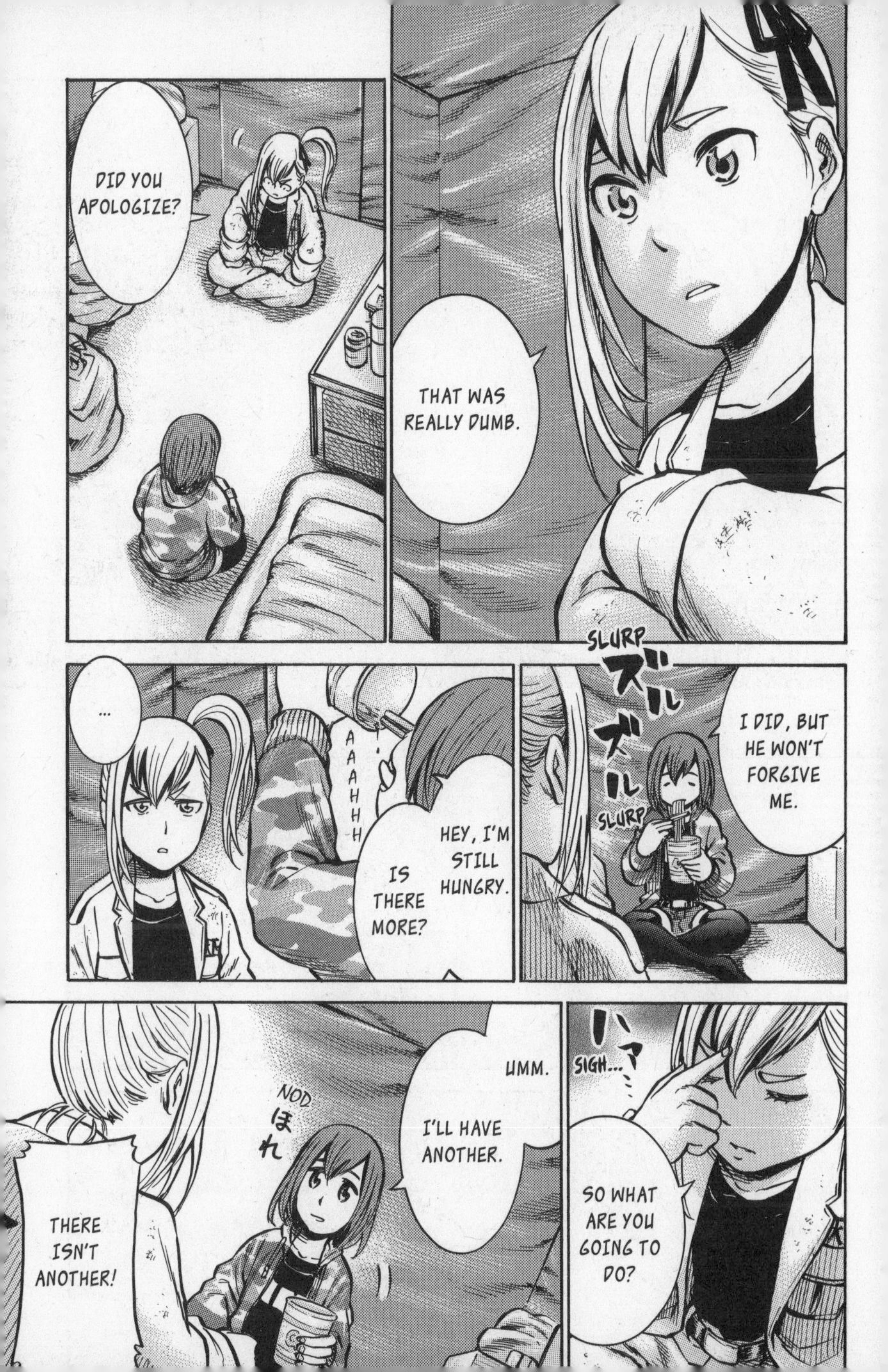
THAT WAS REALLY DUMB.
DID YOU APOLOGIZE?
SLURP
I DID, BUT HE WON'T FORGIVE ME.
SLURP
HEY, I'M STILL HUNGRY.
IS THERE MORE?
AAAHHH
...
SIGH...
SO WHAT ARE YOU GOING TO DO?
UMM.
I'LL HAVE ANOTHER.
NOD
THERE ISN'T ANOTHER!

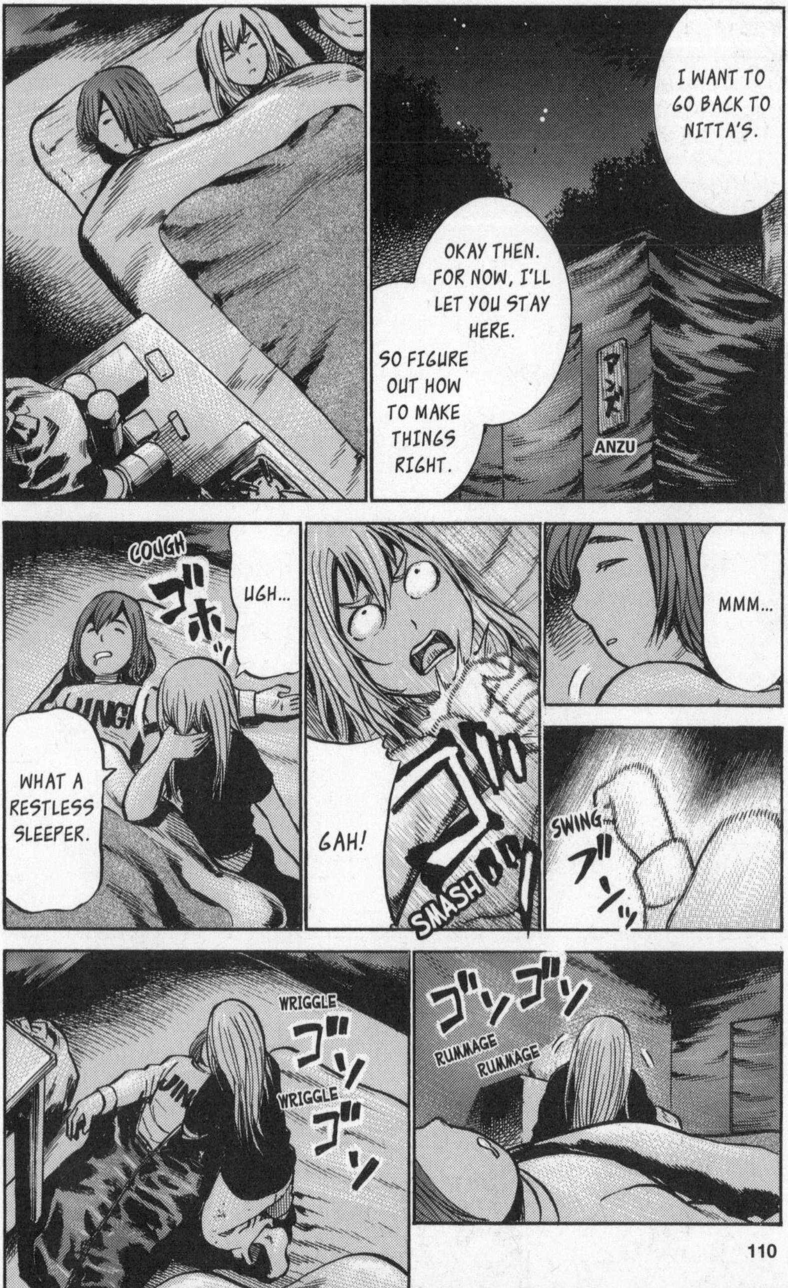
I WANT TO GO BACK TO NITTA'S.
OKAY THEN. FOR NOW, I'LL LET YOU STAY HERE.
SO FIGURE OUT HOW TO MAKE THINGS RIGHT.
ANZU
MMM...
SWING
GAH!
SMASH
UGH...
COUGH
WHAT A RESTLESS SLEEPER.
RUMMAGE
RUMMAGE
WRIGGLE
WRIGGLE

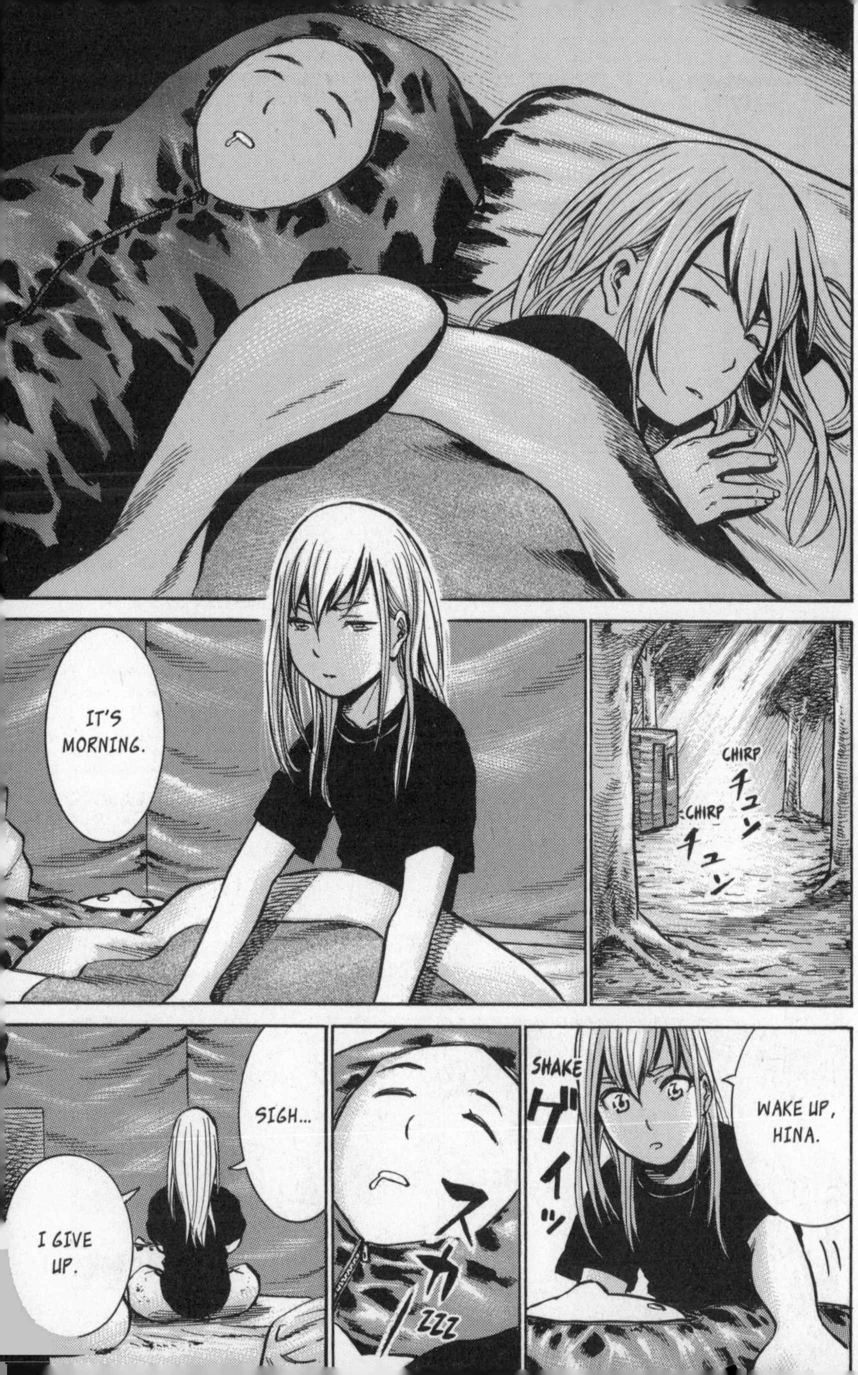
CHIRP
チュン
CHIRP
チュン
IT'S MORNING.
SHAKE
グイッ
WAKE UP, HINA.
スカー
ZZZ
SIGH...
I GIVE UP.

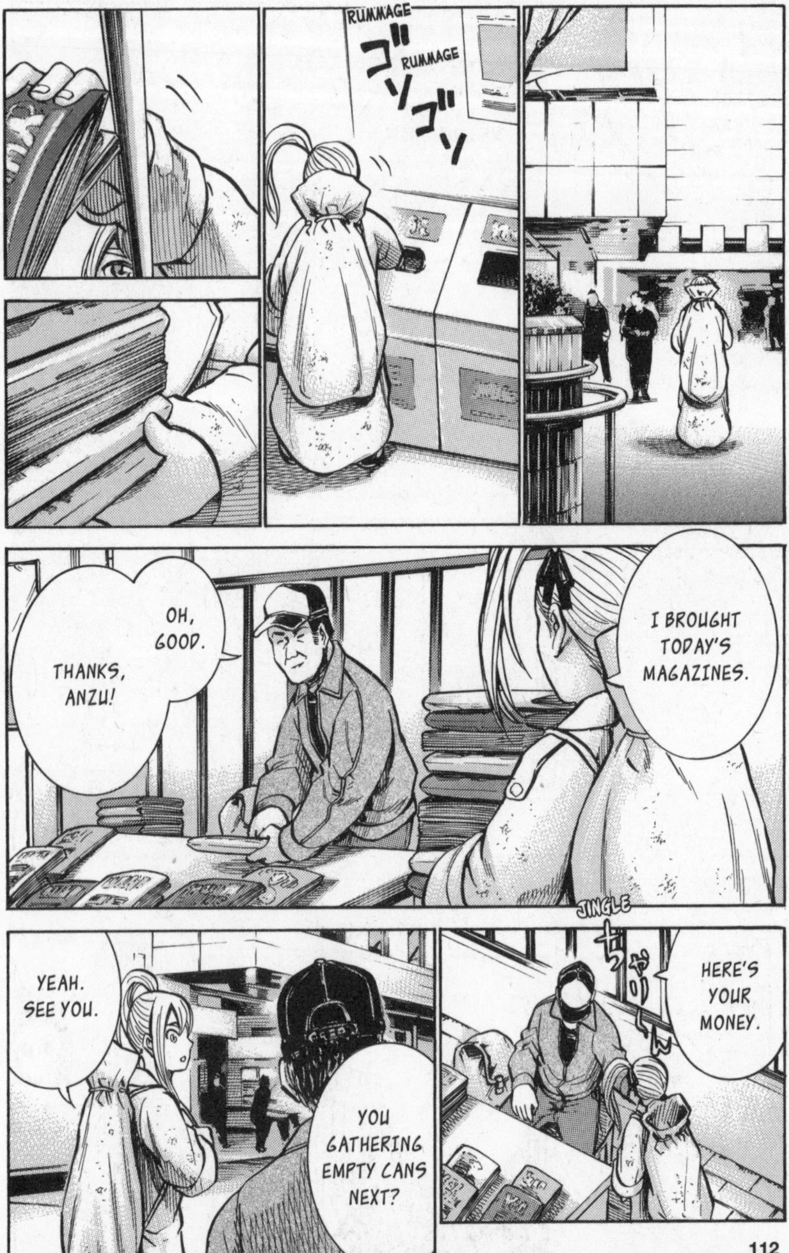
RUMMAGE
ゴソゴソ
RUMMAGE
I BROUGHT TODAY'S MAGAZINES.
OH, GOOD.
THANKS, ANZU!
JINGLE
ちゃりん
HERE'S YOUR MONEY.
YOU GATHERING EMPTY CANS NEXT?
YEAH. SEE YOU.

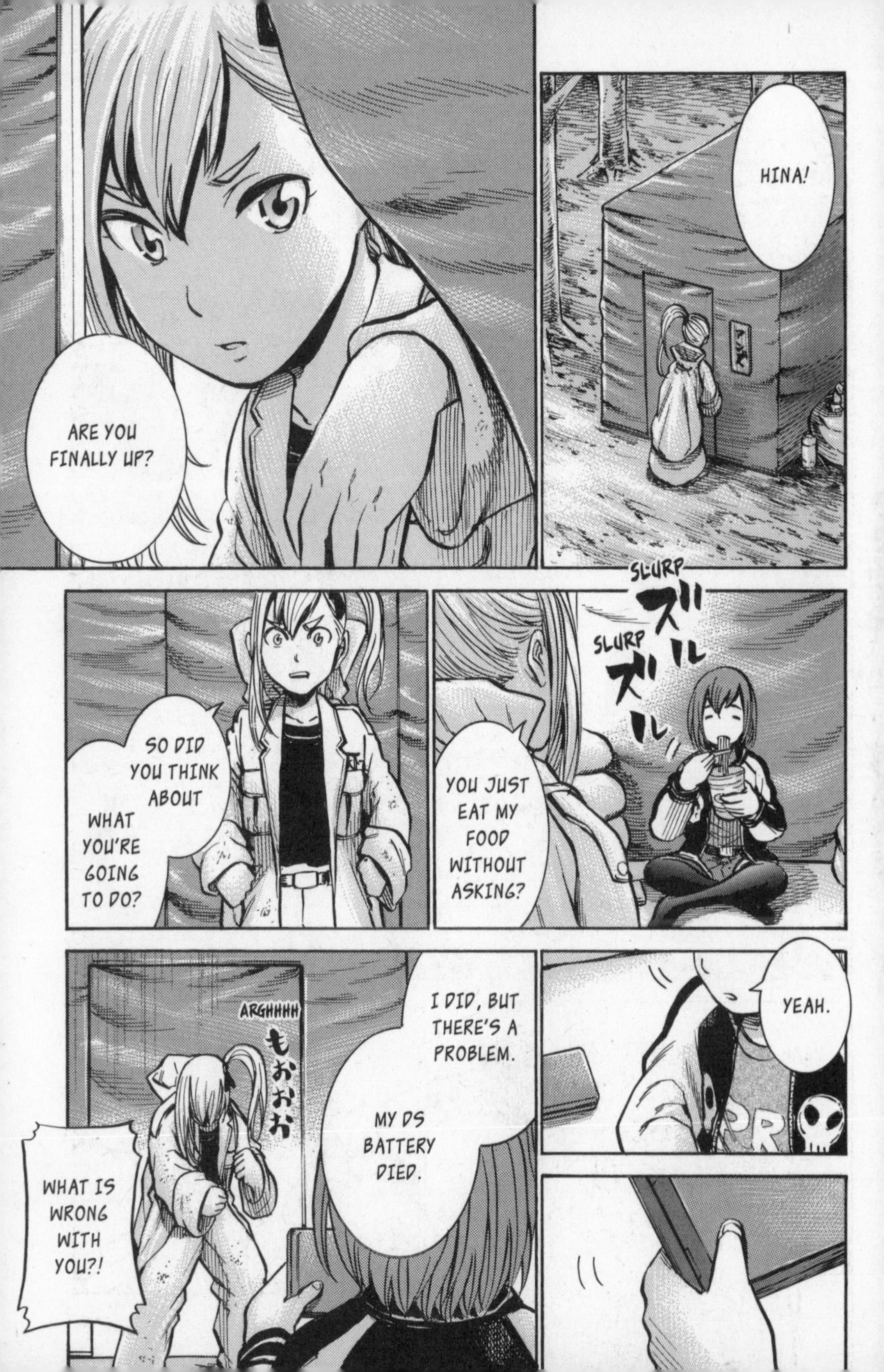
HINA!
ARE YOU FINALLY UP?
SLURP
ズル
SLURP
ズル
YOU JUST EAT MY FOOD WITHOUT ASKING?
SO DID YOU THINK ABOUT
WHAT YOU'RE GOING TO DO?
YEAH.
I DID, BUT THERE'S A PROBLEM.
MY DS BATTERY DIED.
ARGHHHH
もおおお
WHAT IS WRONG WITH YOU?!

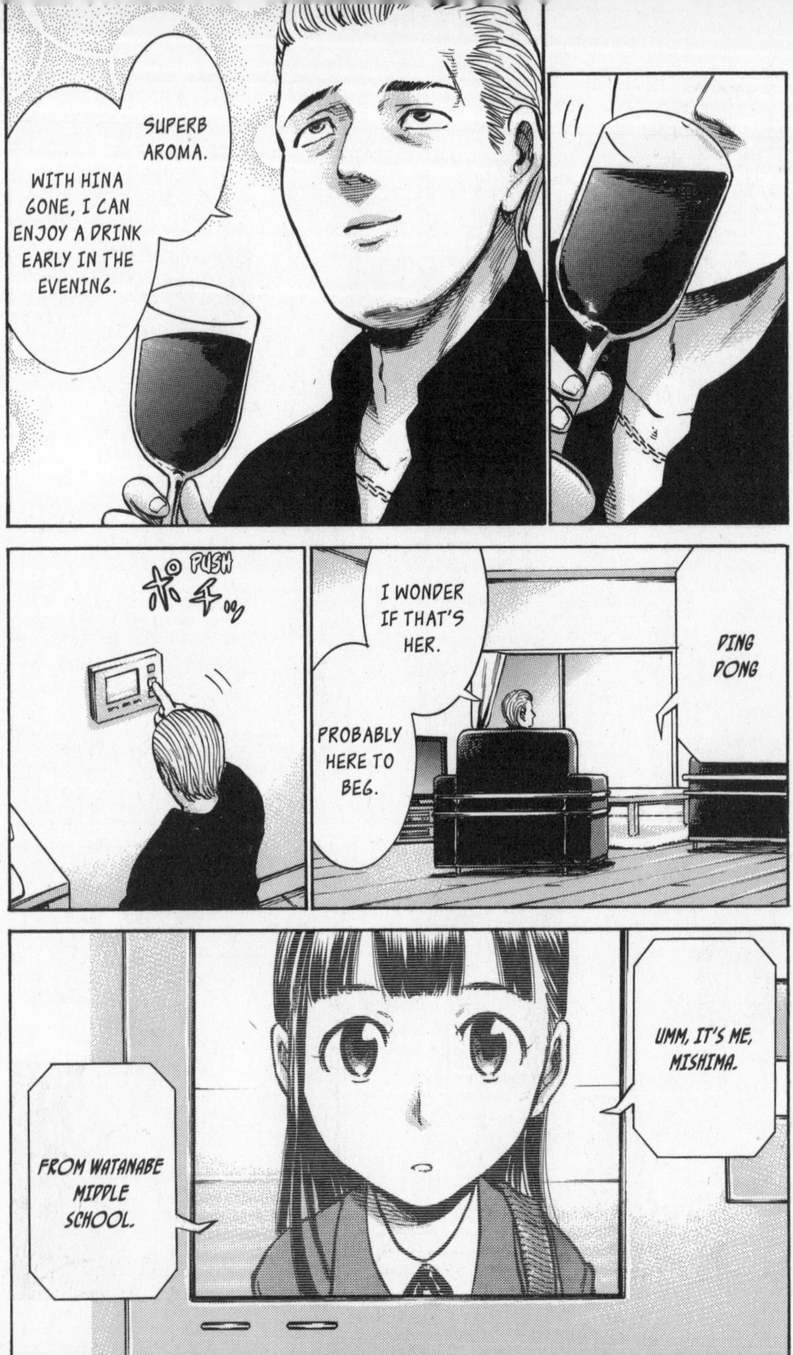
SUPERB AROMA.
WITH HINA GONE, I CAN ENJOY A DRINK EARLY IN THE EVENING.
DING DONG
I WONDER IF THAT'S HER.
PROBABLY HERE TO BEG.
PUSH
UMM, IT'S ME, MISHIMA.
FROM WATANABE MIDDLE SCHOOL.

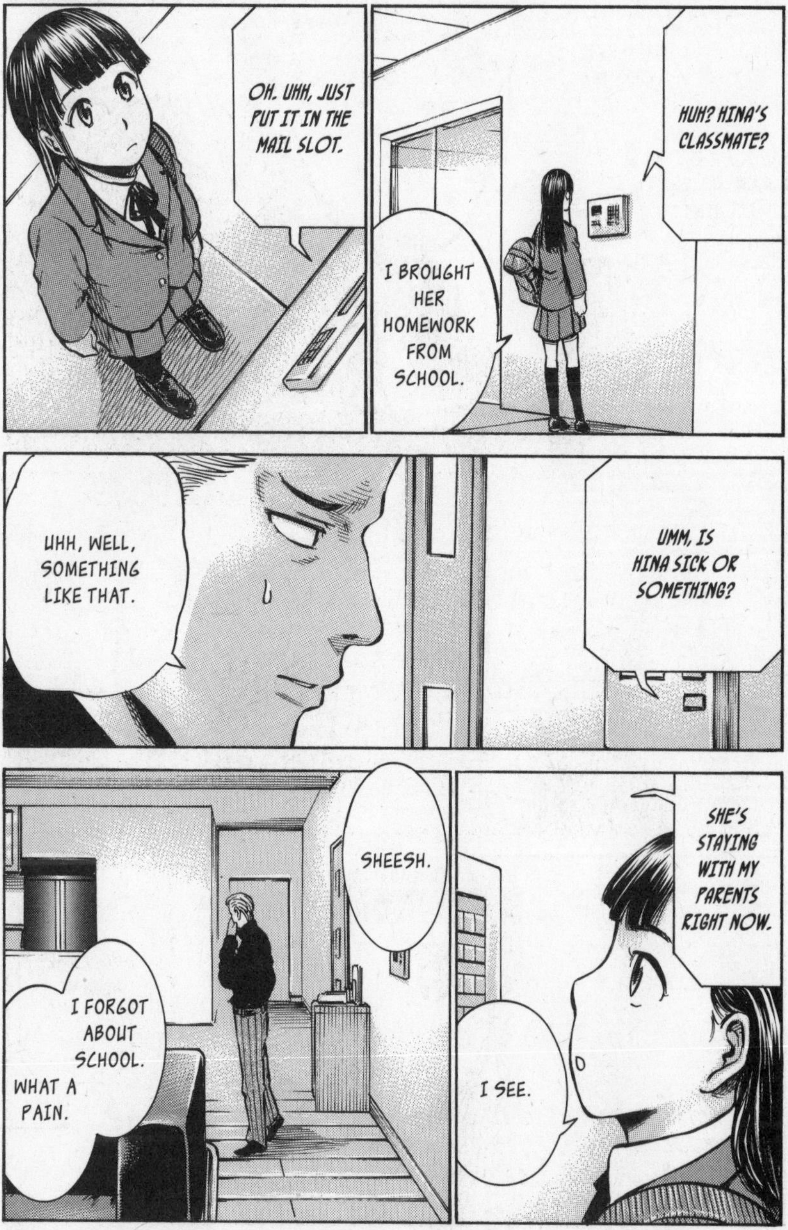
HUH? HINA'S CLASSMATE?
I BROUGHT HER HOMEWORK FROM SCHOOL.
OH. UHH, JUST PUT IT IN THE MAIL SLOT.
UMM, IS HINA SICK OR SOMETHING?
UHH, WELL, SOMETHING LIKE THAT.
SHE'S STAYING WITH MY PARENTS RIGHT NOW.
I SEE.
SHEESH.
I FORGOT ABOUT SCHOOL.
WHAT A PAIN.

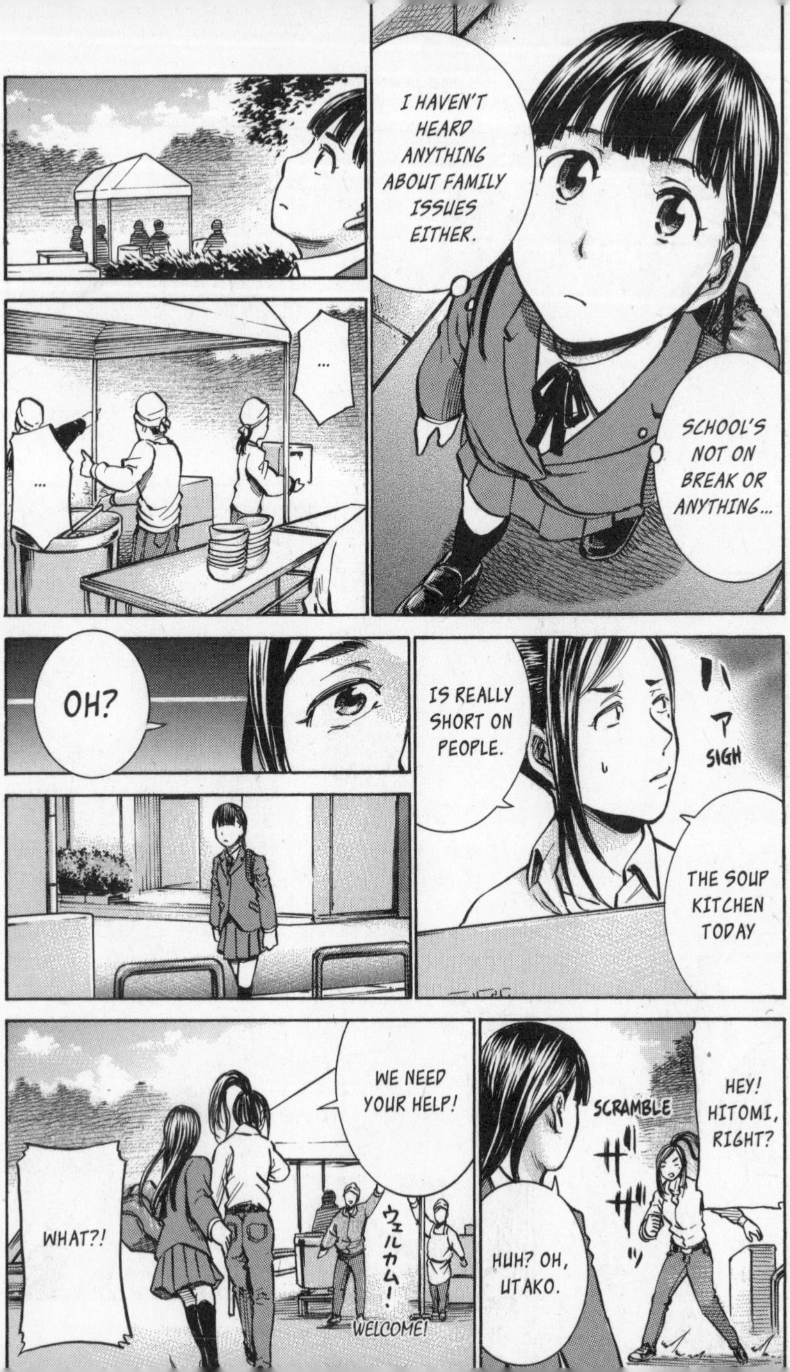
I HAVEN'T HEARD ANYTHING ABOUT FAMILY ISSUES EITHER.
SCHOOL'S NOT ON BREAK OR ANYTHING...
...
...
THE SOUP KITCHEN TODAY
IS REALLY SHORT ON PEOPLE.
ハア
SIGH
OH?
HEY! HITOMI, RIGHT?
SCRAMBLE
ザザッ
HUH? OH, UTAKO.
WE NEED YOUR HELP!
ウェルカム!
WELCOME!
WHAT?!

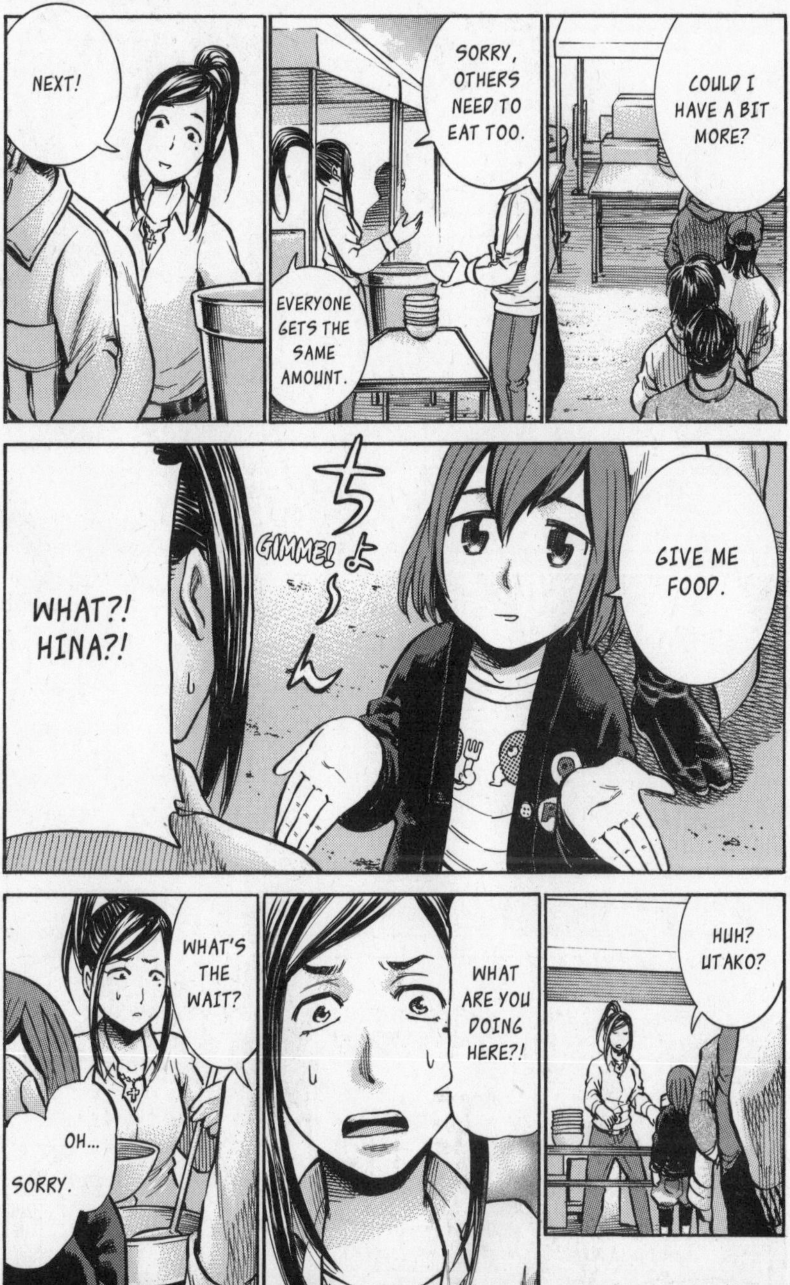
COULD I HAVE A BIT MORE?
SORRY, OTHERS NEED TO EAT TOO.
EVERYONE GETS THE SAME AMOUNT.
NEXT!
GIVE ME FOOD.
GIMME!
WHAT?! HINA?!
HUH? UTAKO?
WHAT ARE YOU DOING HERE?!
WHAT'S THE WAIT?
OH... SORRY.

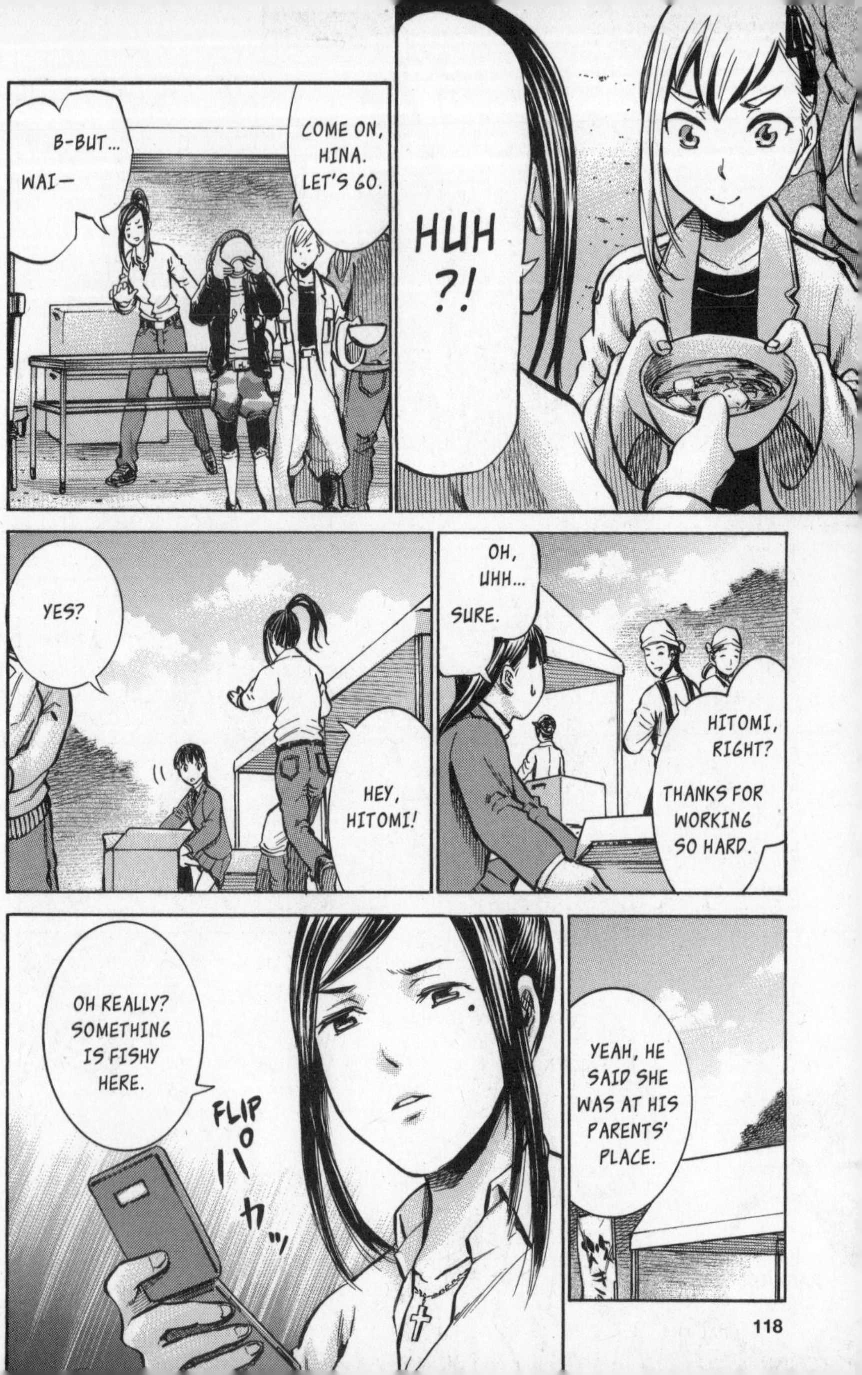
HUH ?!
COME ON, HINA. LET'S GO.
B-BUT... WAI—
HITOMI, RIGHT? THANKS FOR WORKING SO HARD.
OH, UHH... SURE.
HEY, HITOMI!
YES?
YEAH, HE SAID SHE WAS AT HIS PARENTS' PLACE.
OH REALLY? SOMETHING IS FISHY HERE.
FLIP
パカッ

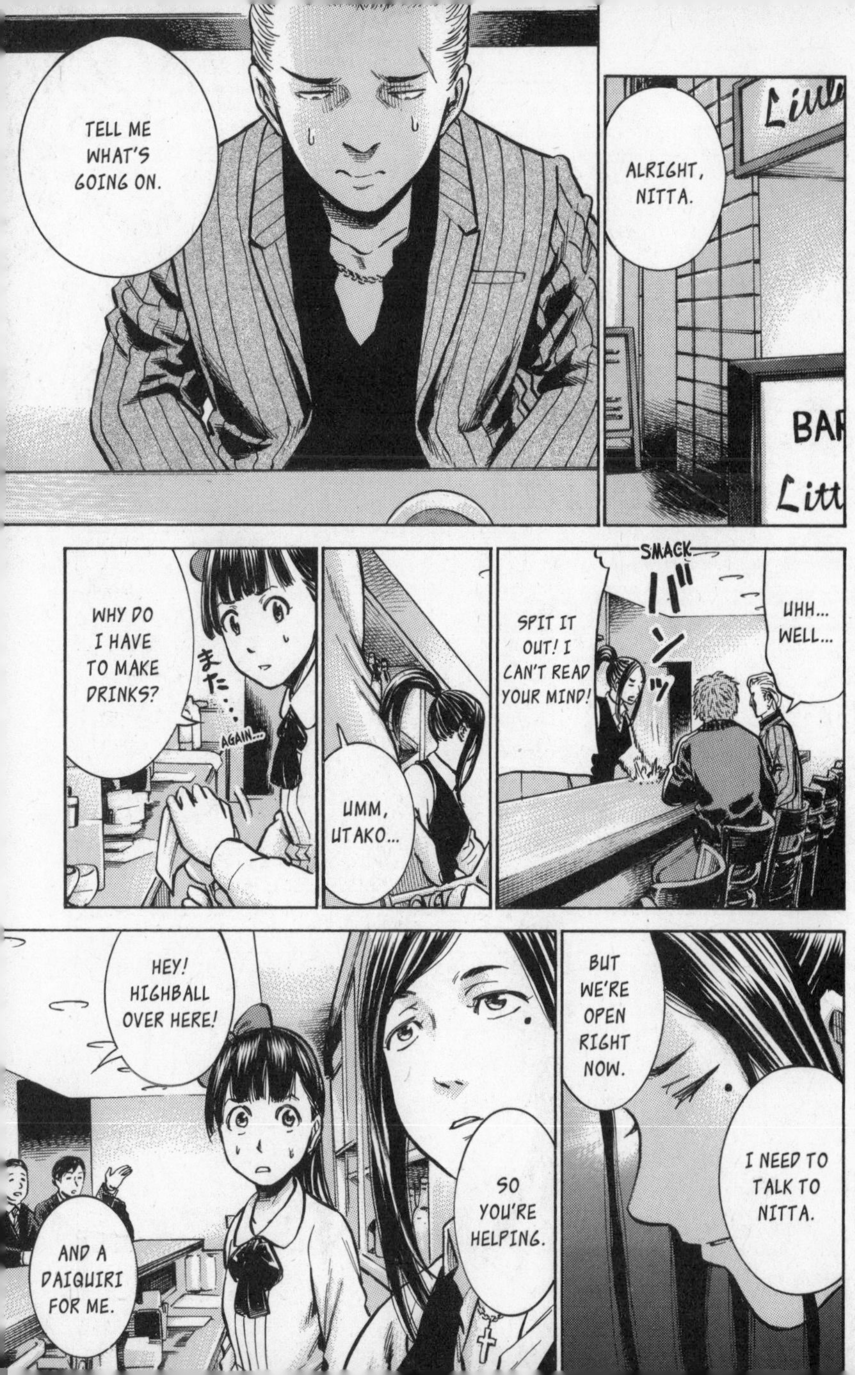

ALRIGHT, NITTA.
BAR
TELL ME WHAT'S GOING ON.
UHH... WELL...
SMACK
バンッ
SPIT IT OUT! I CAN'T READ YOUR MIND!
UMM, UTAKO...
WHY DO I HAVE TO MAKE DRINKS?
また...
AGAIN...
I NEED TO TALK TO NITTA.
BUT WE'RE OPEN RIGHT NOW.
SO YOU'RE HELPING.
HEY! HIGHBALL OVER HERE!
AND A DAIQUIRI FOR ME.

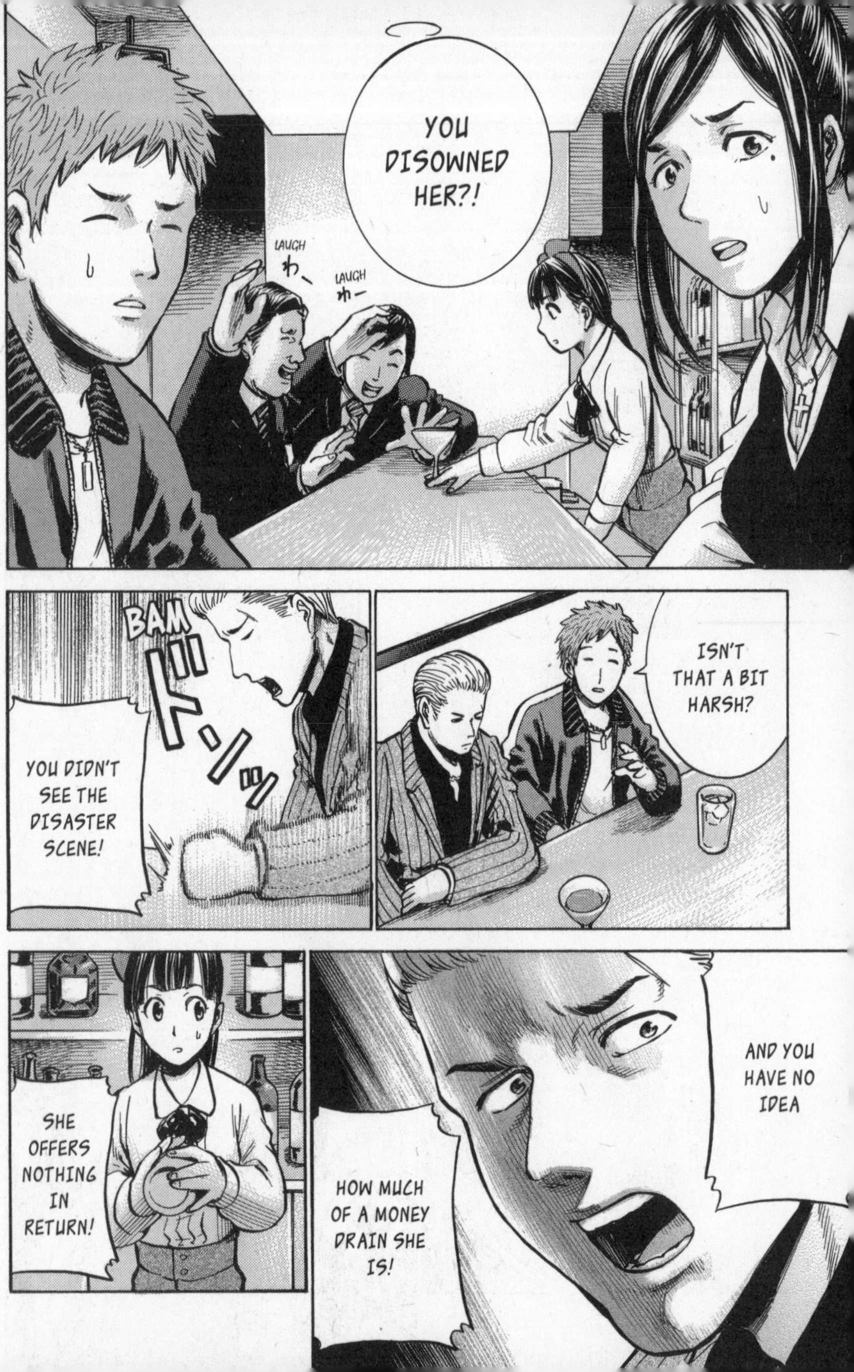
YOU DISOWNED HER?!
LAUGH
わー
LAUGH
わー
ISN'T THAT A BIT HARSH?
BAM
YOU DIDN'T SEE THE DISASTER SCENE!
AND YOU HAVE NO IDEA
HOW MUCH OF A MONEY DRAIN SHE IS!
SHE OFFERS NOTHING IN RETURN!

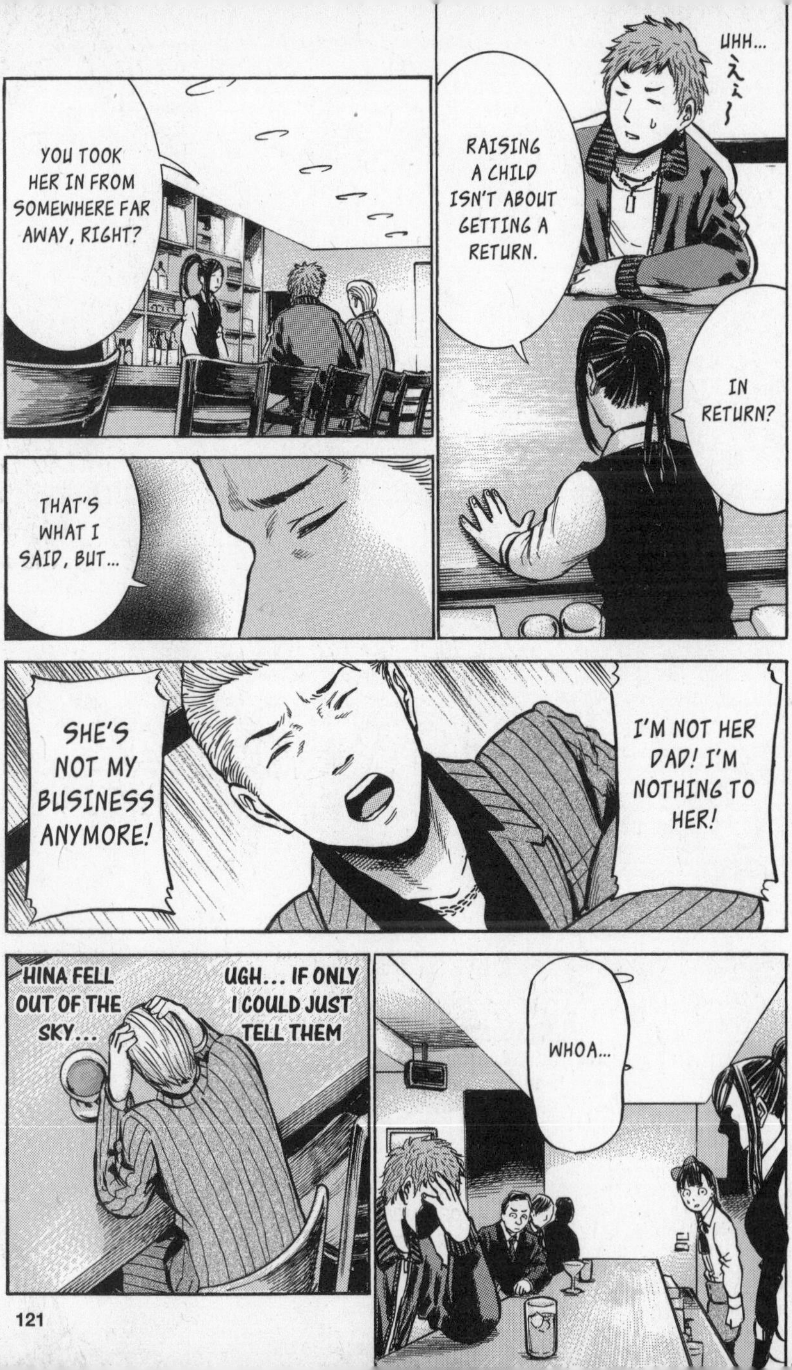
UHH...
えぇ~
RAISING A CHILD ISN'T ABOUT GETTING A RETURN.
IN RETURN?
YOU TOOK HER IN FROM SOMEWHERE FAR AWAY, RIGHT?
THAT'S WHAT I SAID, BUT...
I'M NOT HER DAD! I'M NOTHING TO HER!
SHE'S NOT MY BUSINESS ANYMORE!
WHOA...
UGH... IF ONLY I COULD JUST TELL THEM
HINA FELL OUT OF THE SKY...

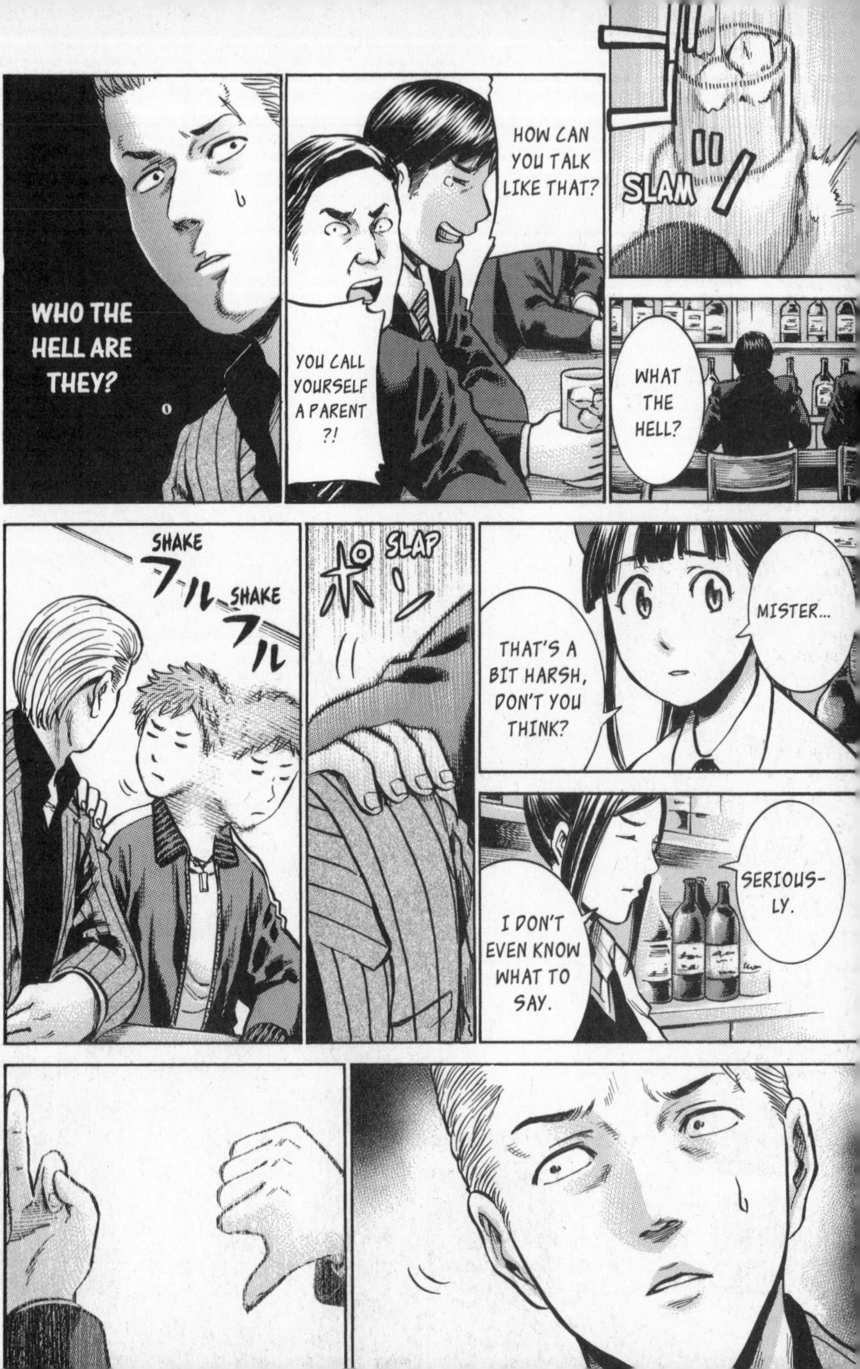
SLAM
WHAT THE HELL?
HOW CAN YOU TALK LIKE THAT?
YOU CALL YOURSELF A PARENT ?!
WHO THE HELL ARE THEY?
MISTER...
THAT'S A BIT HARSH, DON'T YOU THINK?
SERIOUS-LY.
I DON'T EVEN KNOW WHAT TO SAY.
SLAP
ポン
SHAKE
フル
SHAKE
フル

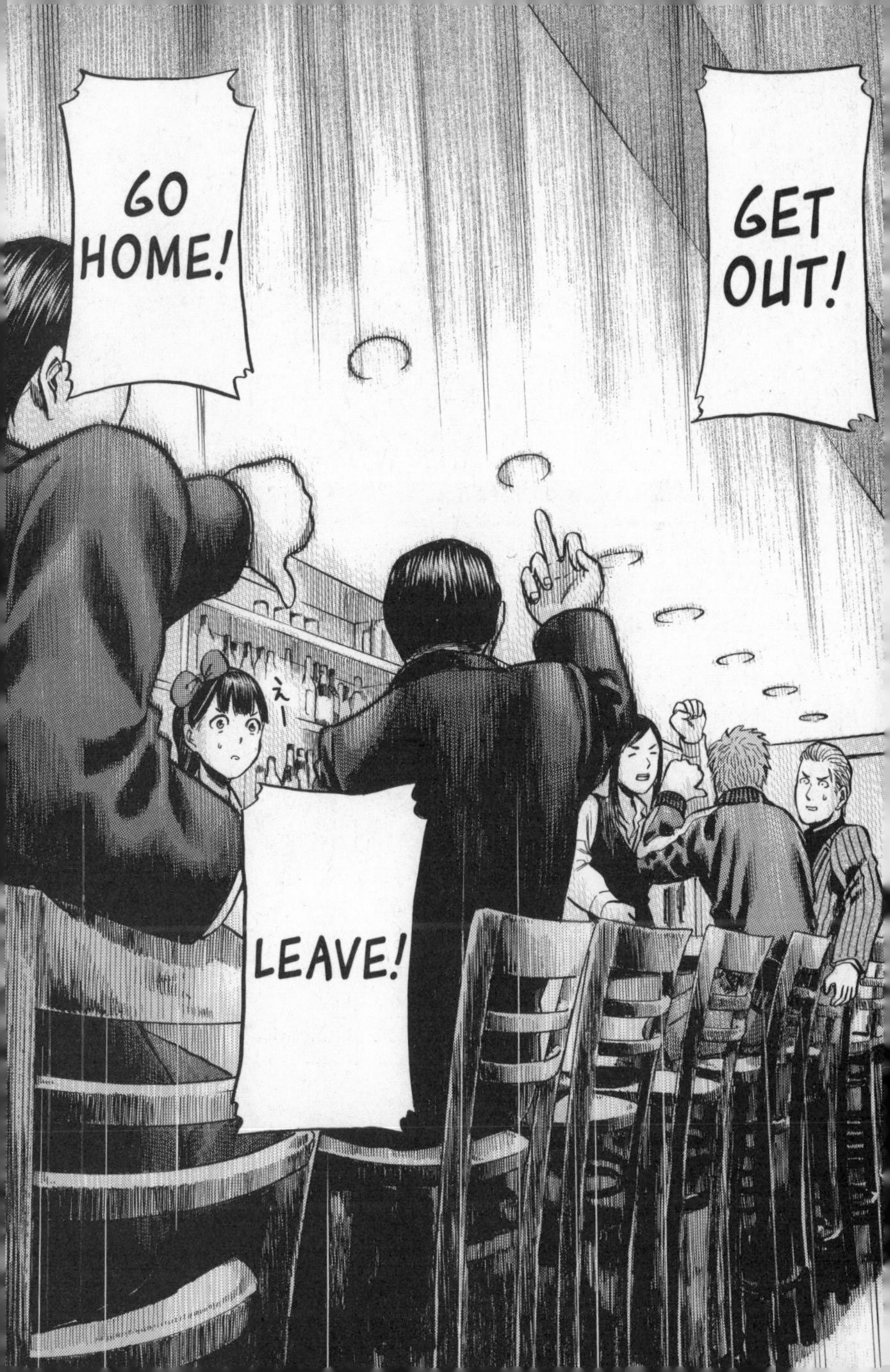
GET OUT!
GO HOME!
え
LEAVE!

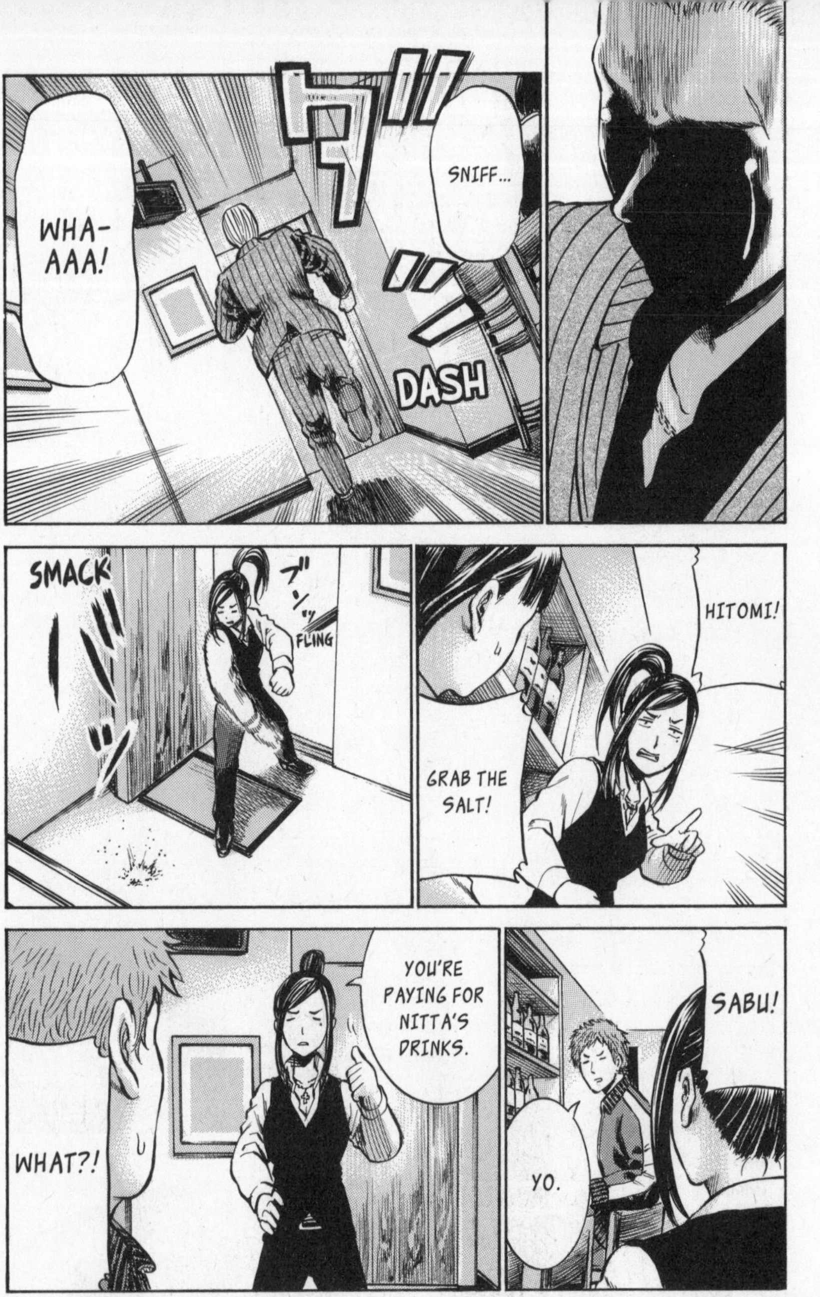
ドッ
SNIFF...
WHA-AAA!
DASH
HITOMI!
GRAB THE SALT!
FLING
SMACK
SABU!
YO.
YOU'RE PAYING FOR NITTA'S DRINKS.
WHAT?!

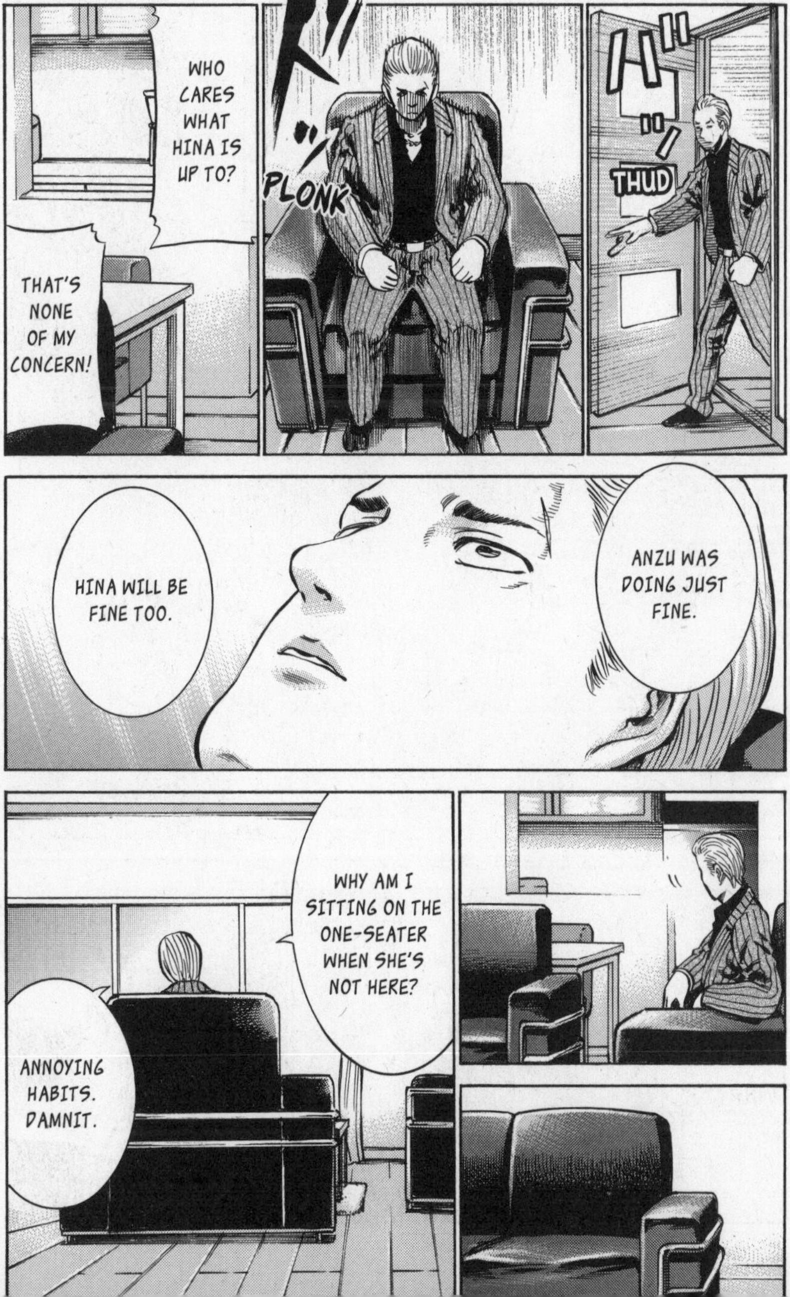
THUD
PLONK
WHO CARES WHAT HINA IS UP TO?
THAT'S NONE OF MY CONCERN!
ANZU WAS DOING JUST FINE.
HINA WILL BE FINE TOO.
WHY AM I SITTING ON THE ONE-SEATER WHEN SHE'S NOT HERE?
ANNOYING HABITS. DAMNIT.

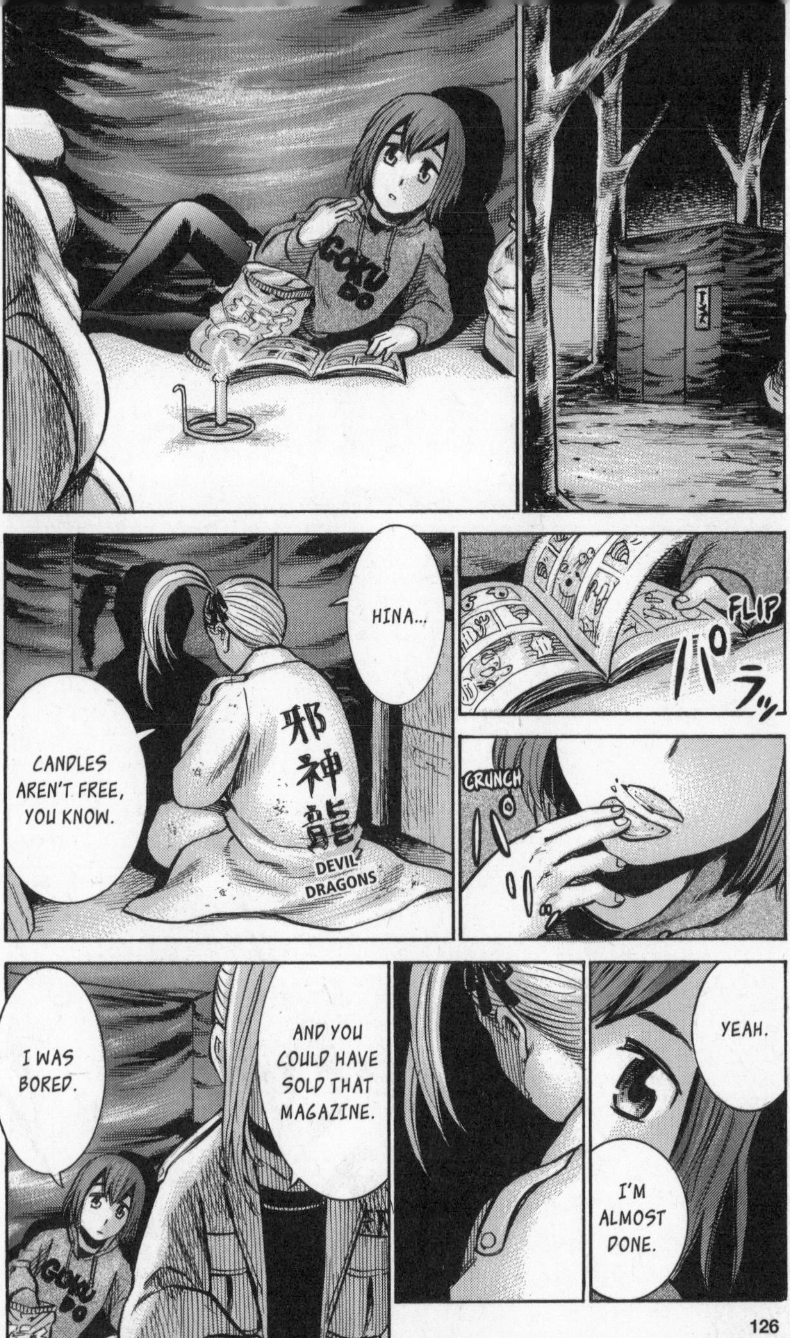
FLIP
パラッ
CRUNCH
HINA...
邪神龍
DEVIL DRAGONS
CANDLES AREN'T FREE, YOU KNOW.
YEAH.
I'M ALMOST DONE.
AND YOU COULD HAVE SOLD THAT MAGAZINE.
I WAS BORED.

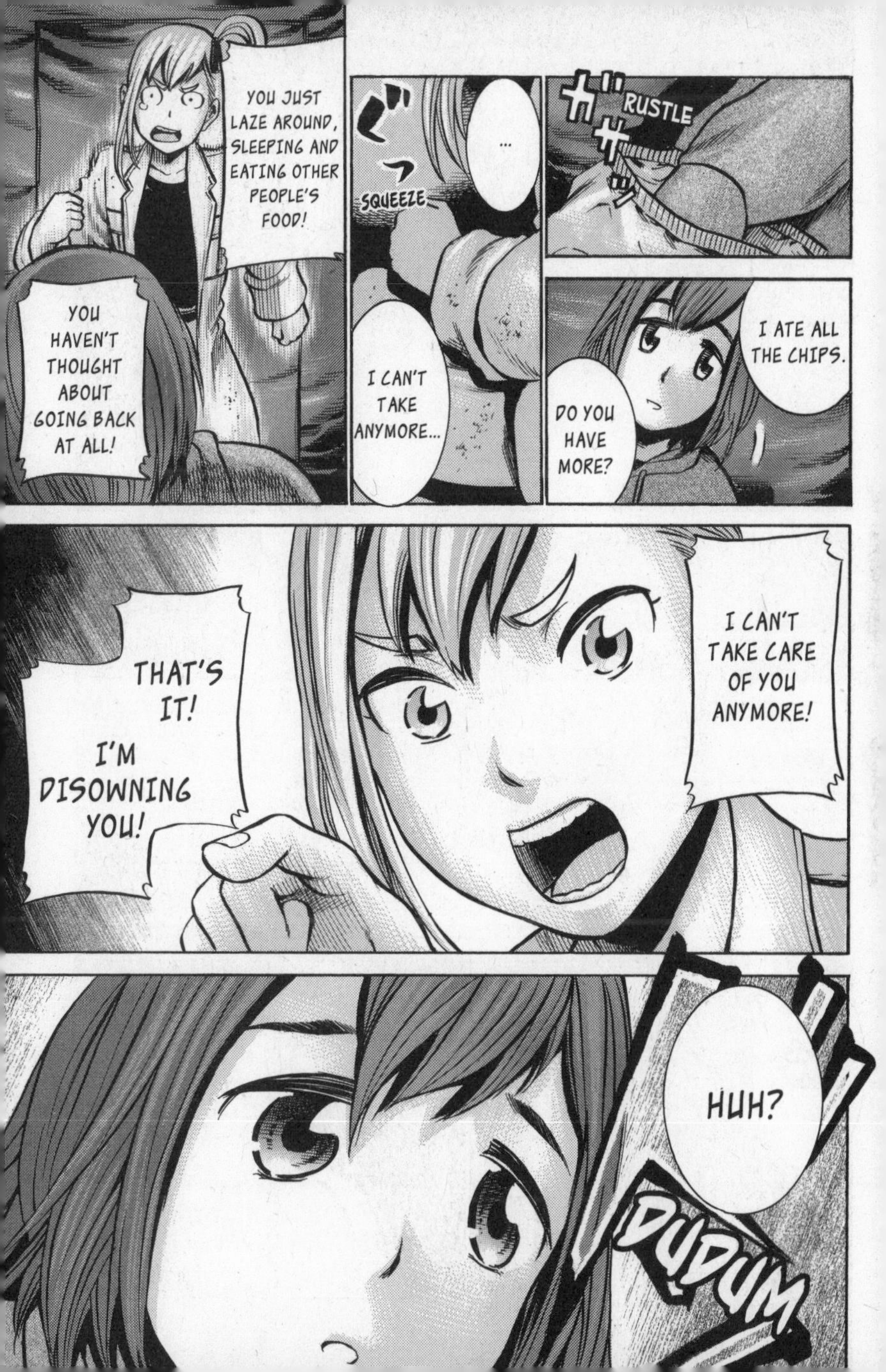
RUSTLE
I ATE ALL THE CHIPS.
DO YOU HAVE MORE?
...
SQUEEZE
I CAN'T TAKE ANYMORE...
YOU JUST LAZE AROUND, SLEEPING AND EATING OTHER PEOPLE'S FOOD!
YOU HAVEN'T THOUGHT ABOUT GOING BACK AT ALL!
I CAN'T TAKE CARE OF YOU ANYMORE!
THAT'S IT!
I'M DISOWNING YOU!
HUH?
DUDUM

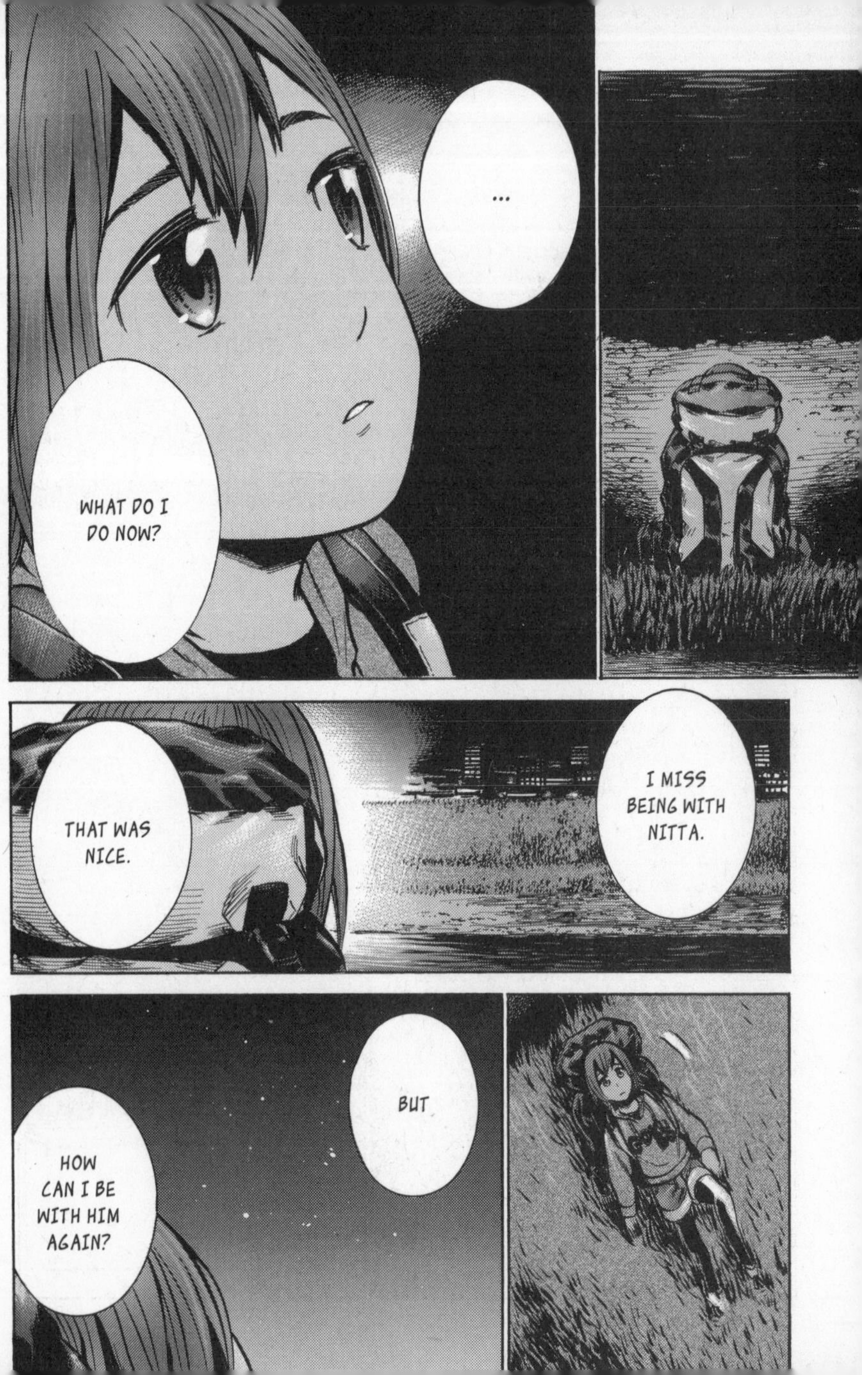
...
WHAT DO I DO NOW?
I MISS BEING WITH NITTA.
THAT WAS NICE.
BUT
HOW CAN I BE WITH HIM AGAIN?

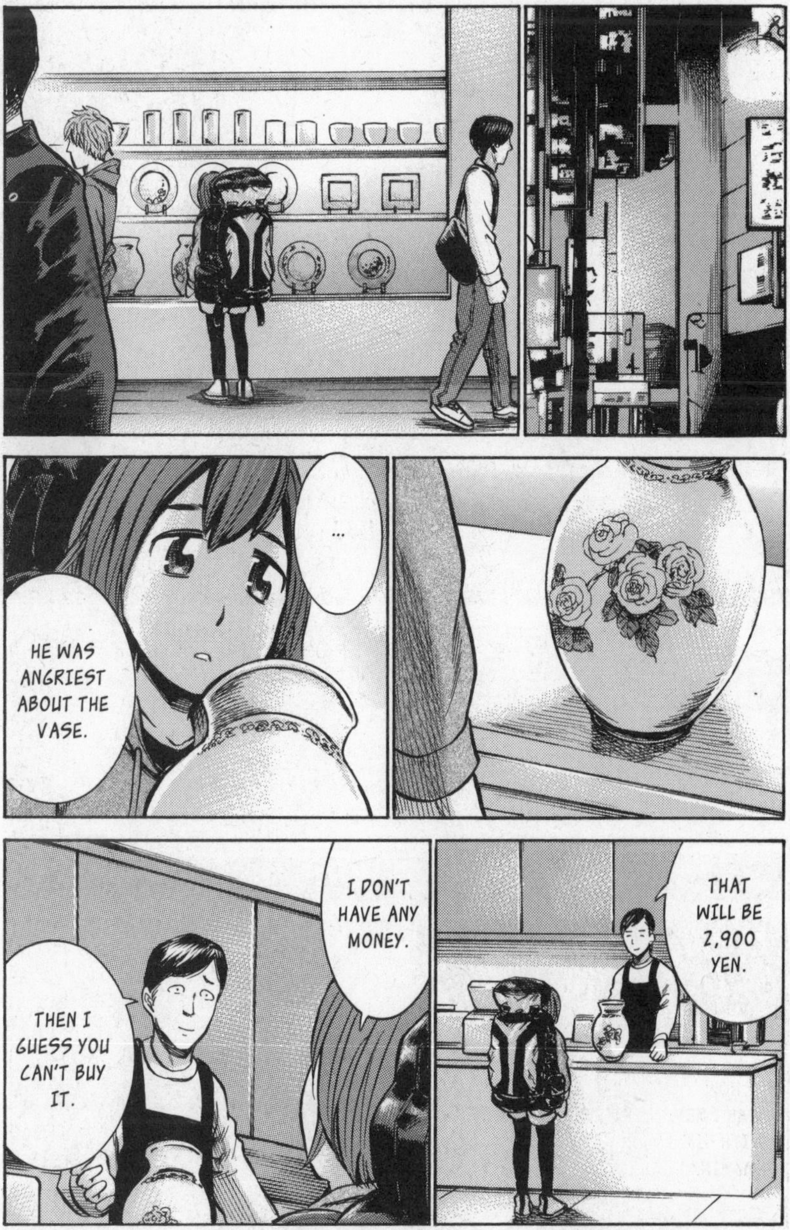
...
HE WAS ANGRIEST ABOUT THE VASE.
THAT WILL BE 2,900 YEN.
I DON'T HAVE ANY MONEY.
THEN I GUESS YOU CAN'T BUY IT.

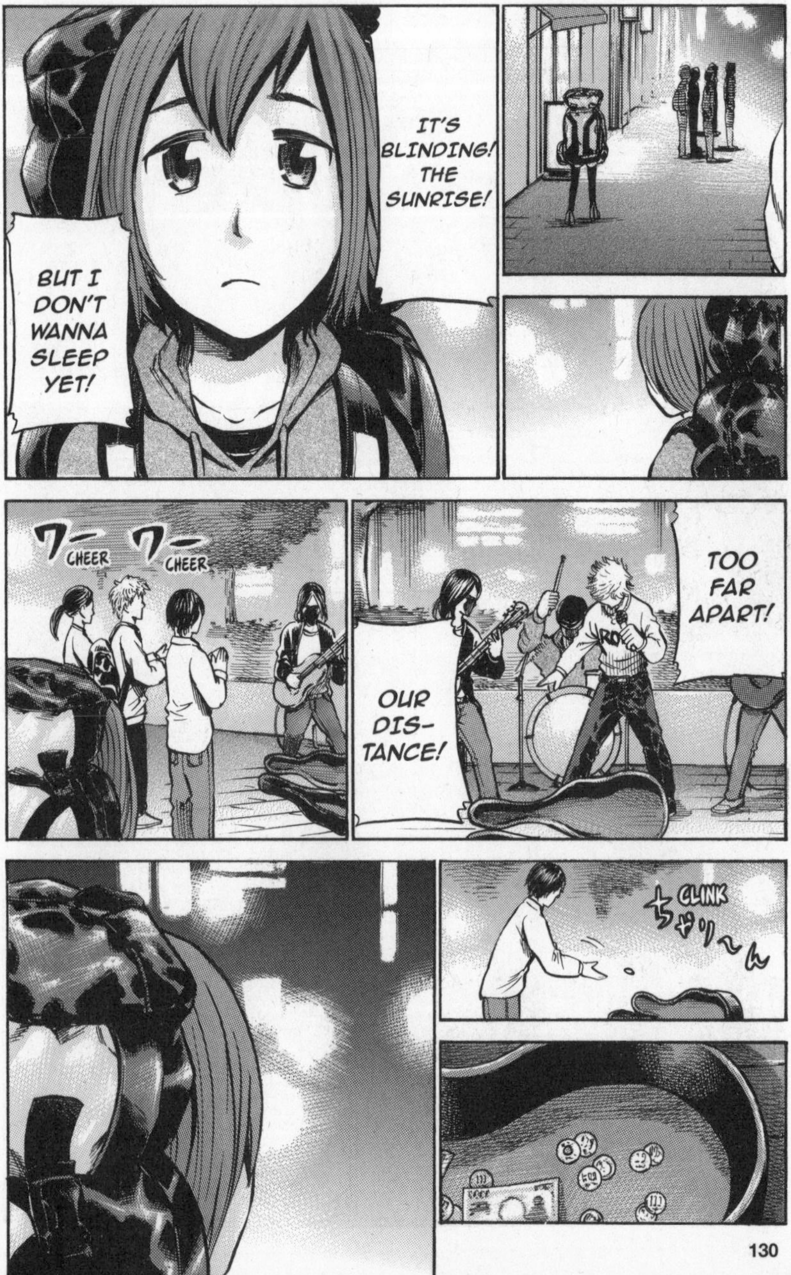
IT'S BLINDING! THE SUNRISE!
BUT I DON'T WANNA SLEEP YET!
TOO FAR APART!
OUR DIS- TANCE!
ワー CHEER
ワー CHEER
ちゃりーん CLINK

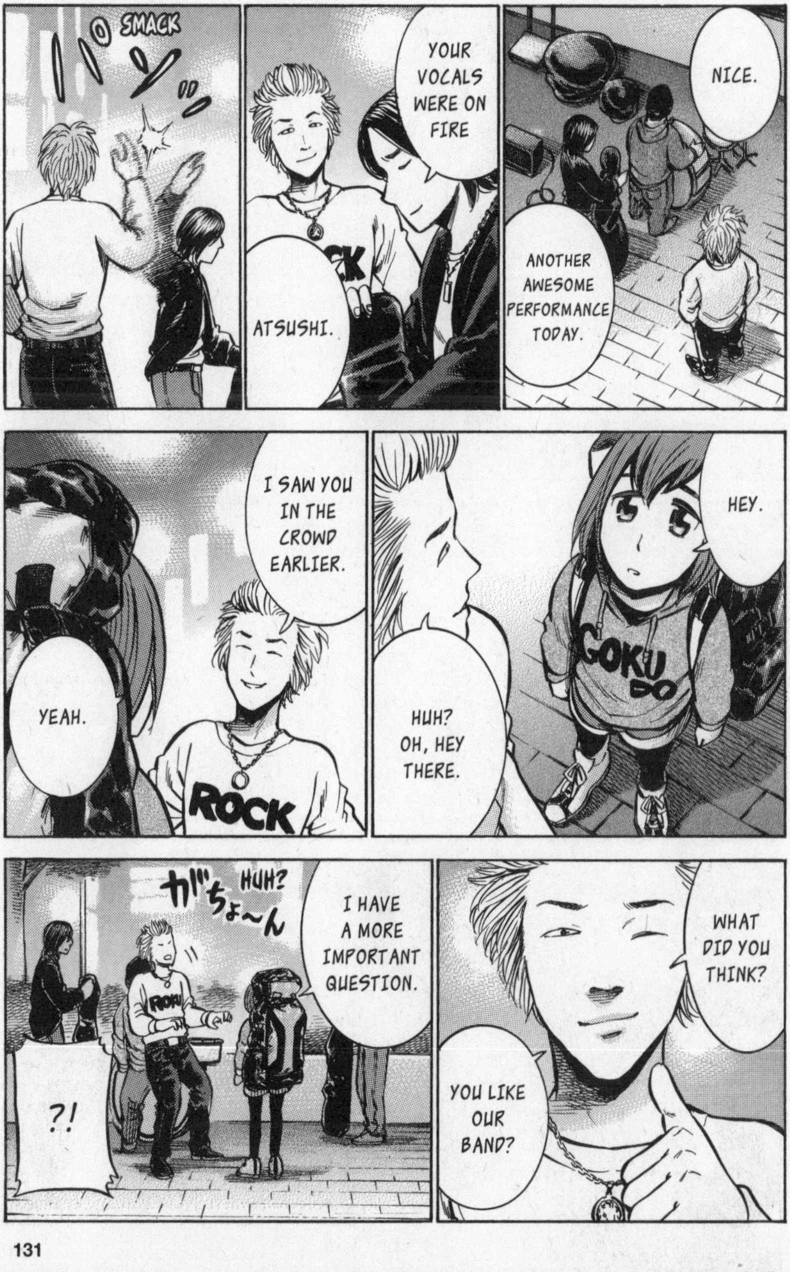
NICE.
ANOTHER AWESOME PERFORMANCE TODAY.
YOUR VOCALS WERE ON FIRE
ATSUSHI.
SMACK
HEY.
HUH? OH, HEY THERE.
I SAW YOU IN THE CROWD EARLIER.
YEAH.
WHAT DID YOU THINK?
YOU LIKE OUR BAND?
I HAVE A MORE IMPORTANT QUESTION.
HUH?
ガちょ～ん
?!

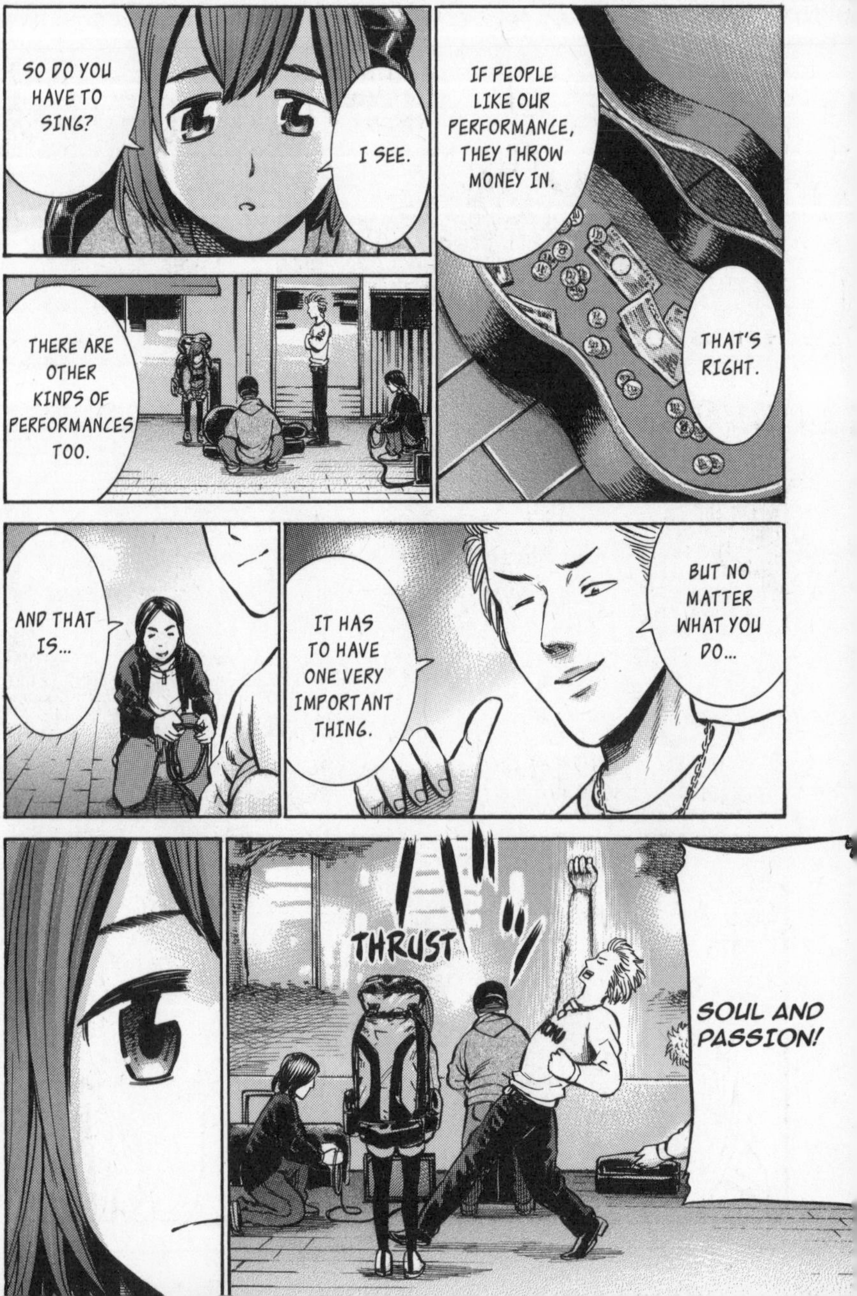
IF PEOPLE LIKE OUR PERFORMANCE, THEY THROW MONEY IN.
THAT'S RIGHT.
I SEE.
SO DO YOU HAVE TO SING?
THERE ARE OTHER KINDS OF PERFORMANCES TOO.
BUT NO MATTER WHAT YOU DO...
IT HAS TO HAVE ONE VERY IMPORTANT THING.
AND THAT IS...
SOUL AND PASSION!
THRUST

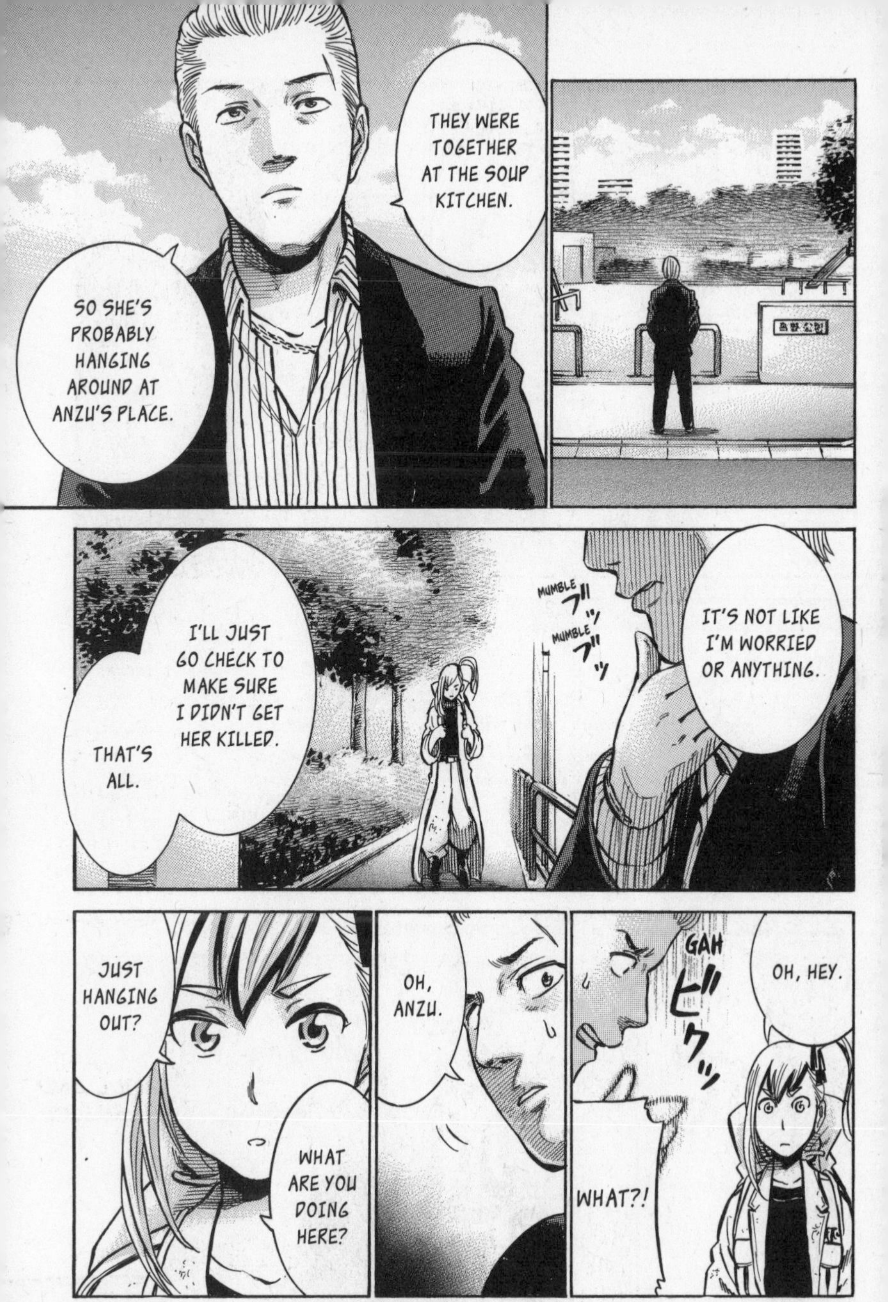
THEY WERE TOGETHER AT THE SOUP KITCHEN.
SO SHE'S PROBABLY HANGING AROUND AT ANZU'S PLACE.
IT'S NOT LIKE I'M WORRIED OR ANYTHING.
MUMBLE ブツ
MUMBLE ブツ
I'LL JUST GO CHECK TO MAKE SURE I DIDN'T GET HER KILLED.
THAT'S ALL.
OH, HEY.
GAH ビクッ
WHAT?!
OH, ANZU.
JUST HANGING OUT?
WHAT ARE YOU DOING HERE?

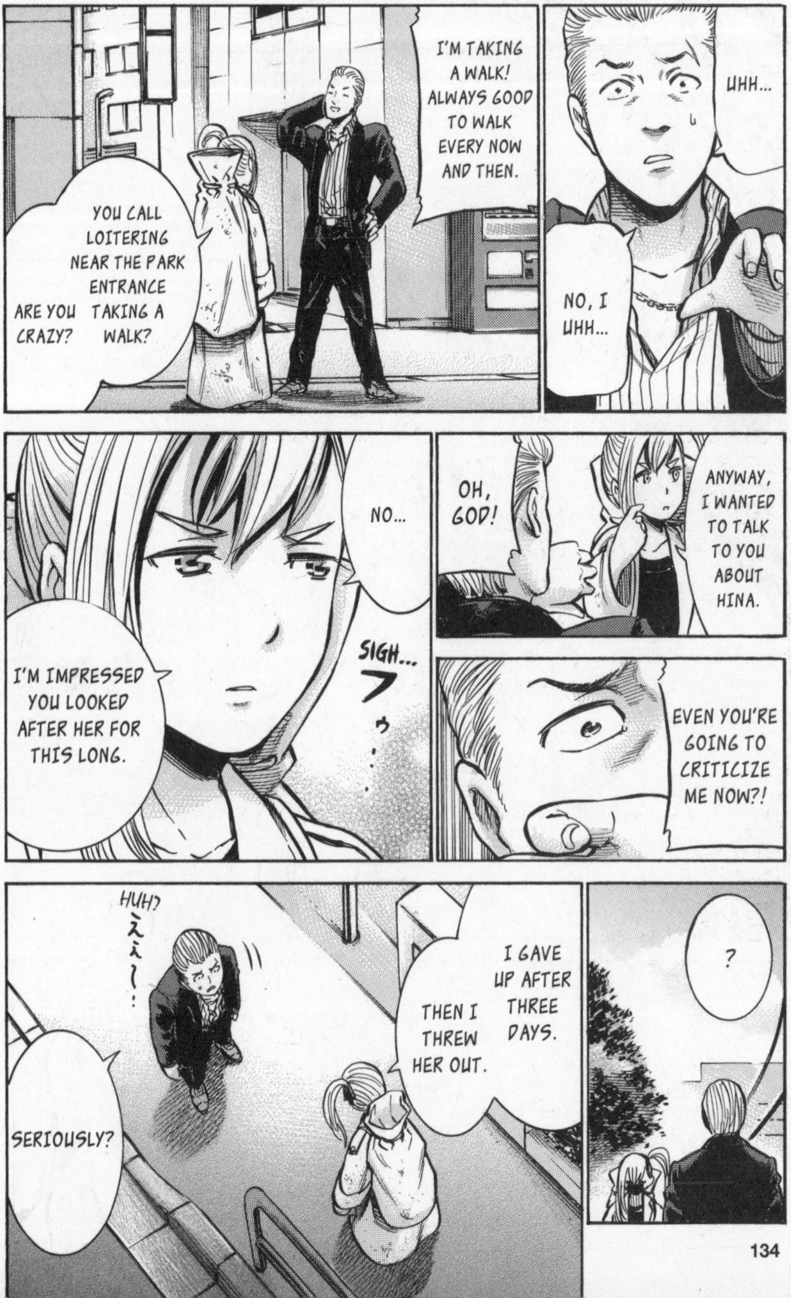
UHH...
NO, I UHH...
I'M TAKING A WALK! ALWAYS GOOD TO WALK EVERY NOW AND THEN.
YOU CALL LOITERING NEAR THE PARK ENTRANCE TAKING A WALK?
ARE YOU CRAZY?
ANYWAY, I WANTED TO TALK TO YOU ABOUT HINA.
OH, GOD!
EVEN YOU'RE GOING TO CRITICIZE ME NOW?!
NO...
SIGH...
フゥ...
I'M IMPRESSED YOU LOOKED AFTER HER FOR THIS LONG.
?
I GAVE UP AFTER THREE DAYS.
THEN I THREW HER OUT.
HUH?
ええ～!
SERIOUSLY?

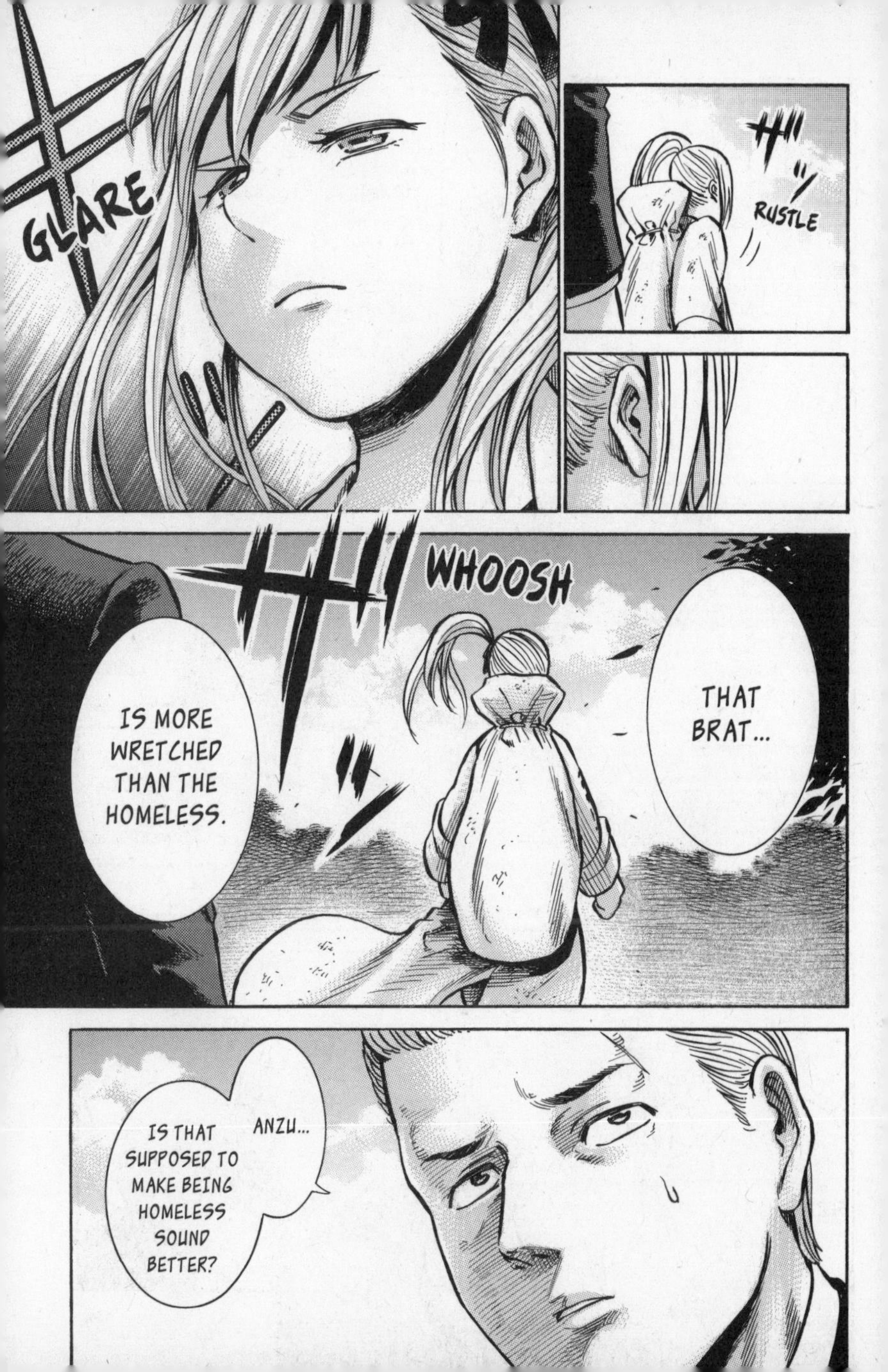
RUSTLE
GLARE
WHOOSH
THAT BRAT...
IS MORE WRETCHED THAN THE HOMELESS.
ANZU...
IS THAT SUPPOSED TO MAKE BEING HOMELESS SOUND BETTER?

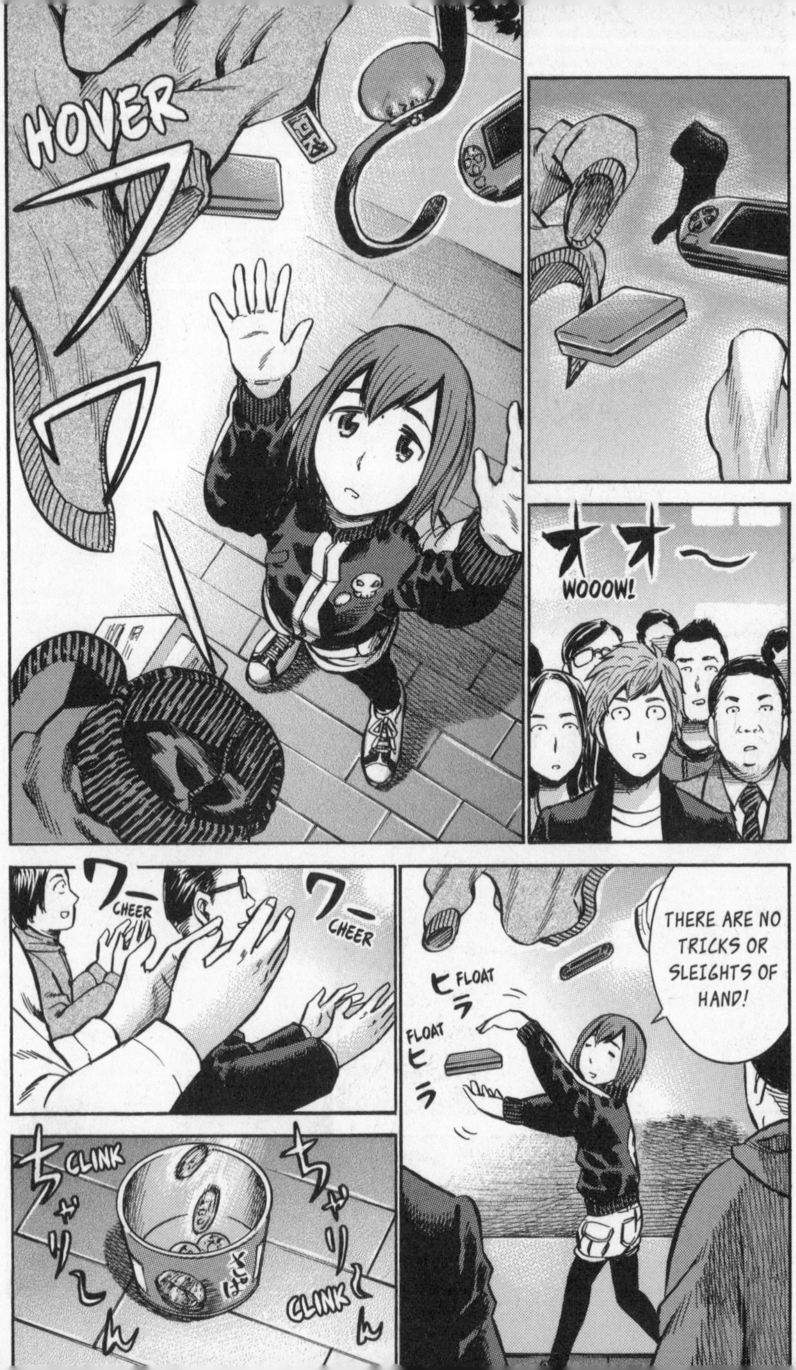
オオ〜
WOOOW!
HOVER
THERE ARE NO TRICKS OR SLEIGHTS OF HAND!
ヒラ
FLOAT
ヒラ
FLOAT
ワー
CHEER
ワー
CHEER
CLINK
CLINK

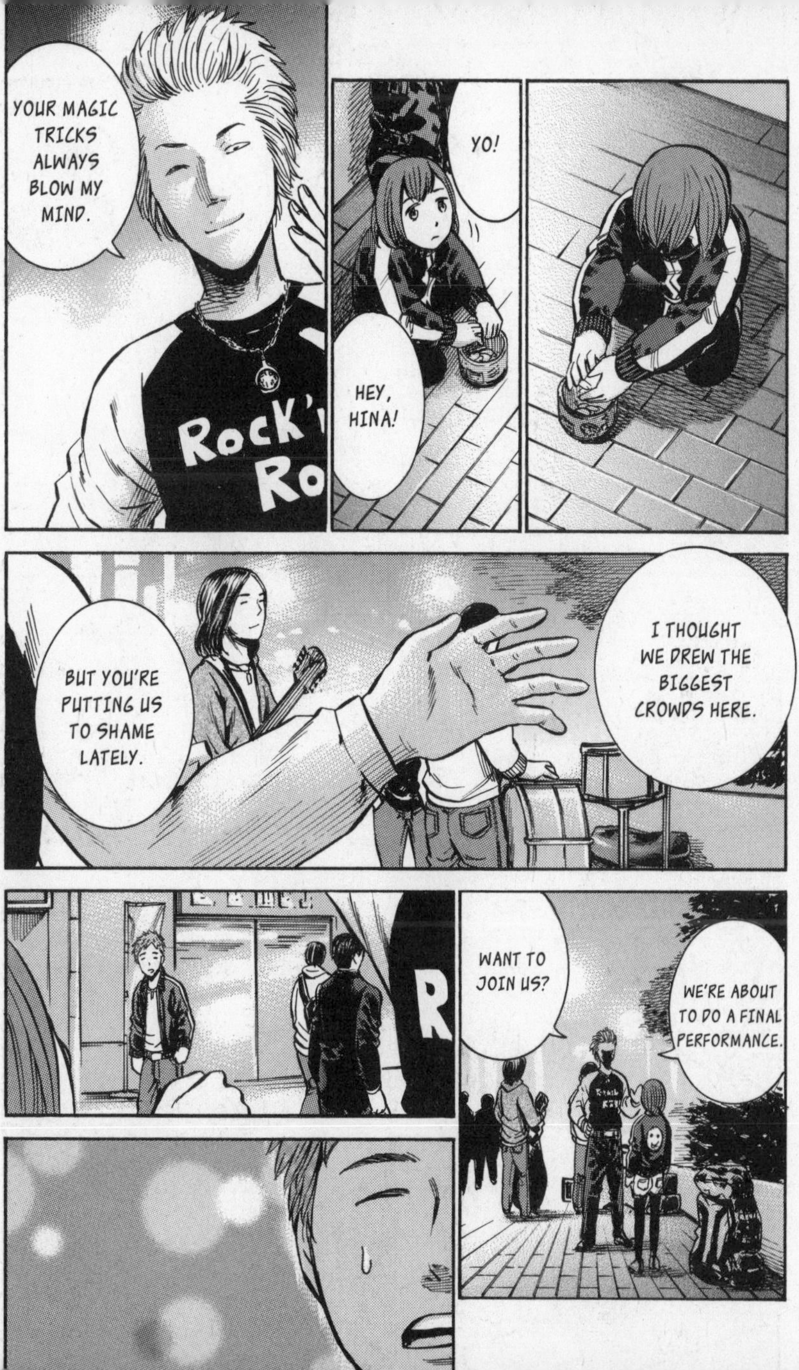
YO!
HEY, HINA!
YOUR MAGIC TRICKS ALWAYS BLOW MY MIND.
I THOUGHT WE DREW THE BIGGEST CROWDS HERE.
BUT YOU'RE PUTTING US TO SHAME LATELY.
WE'RE ABOUT TO DO A FINAL PERFORMANCE.
WANT TO JOIN US?

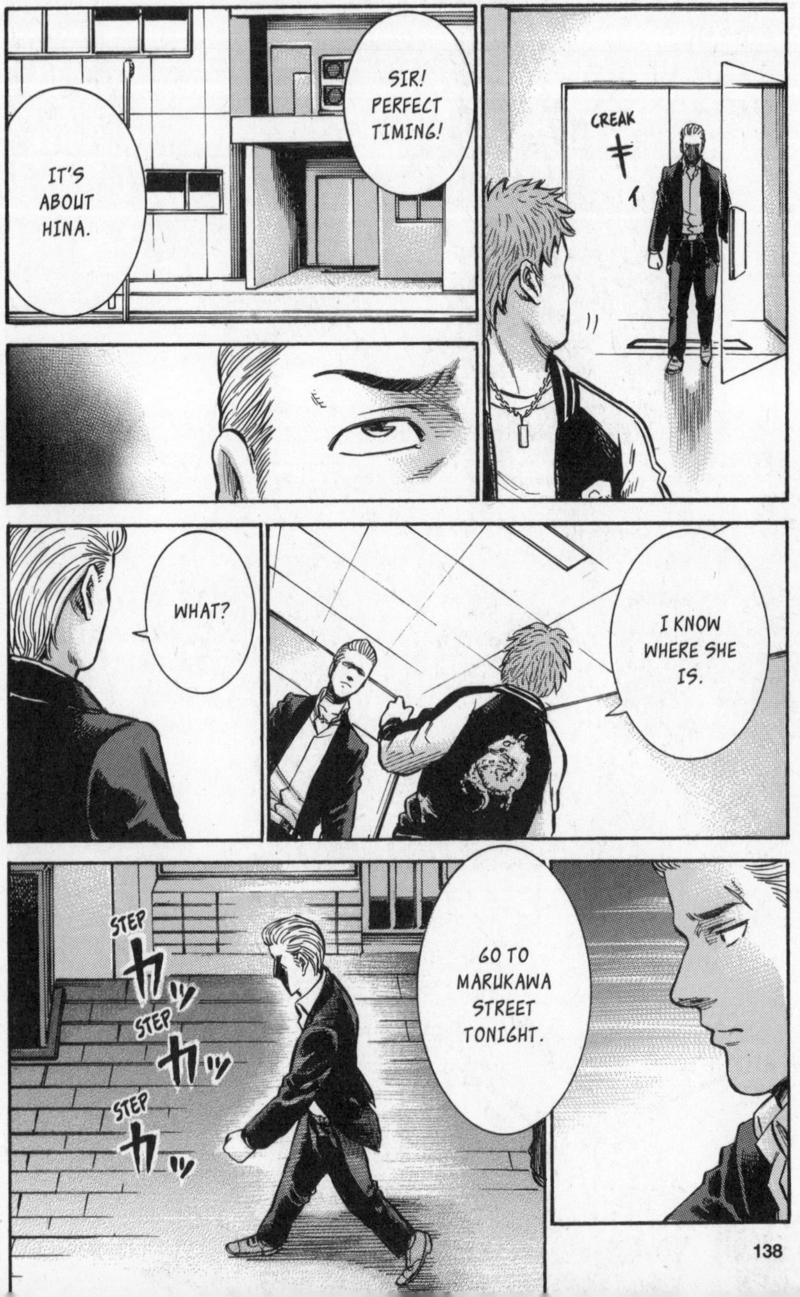
CREAK
SIR! PERFECT TIMING!
IT'S ABOUT HINA.
I KNOW WHERE SHE IS.
WHAT?
GO TO MARUKAWA STREET TONIGHT.
STEP
STEP
STEP

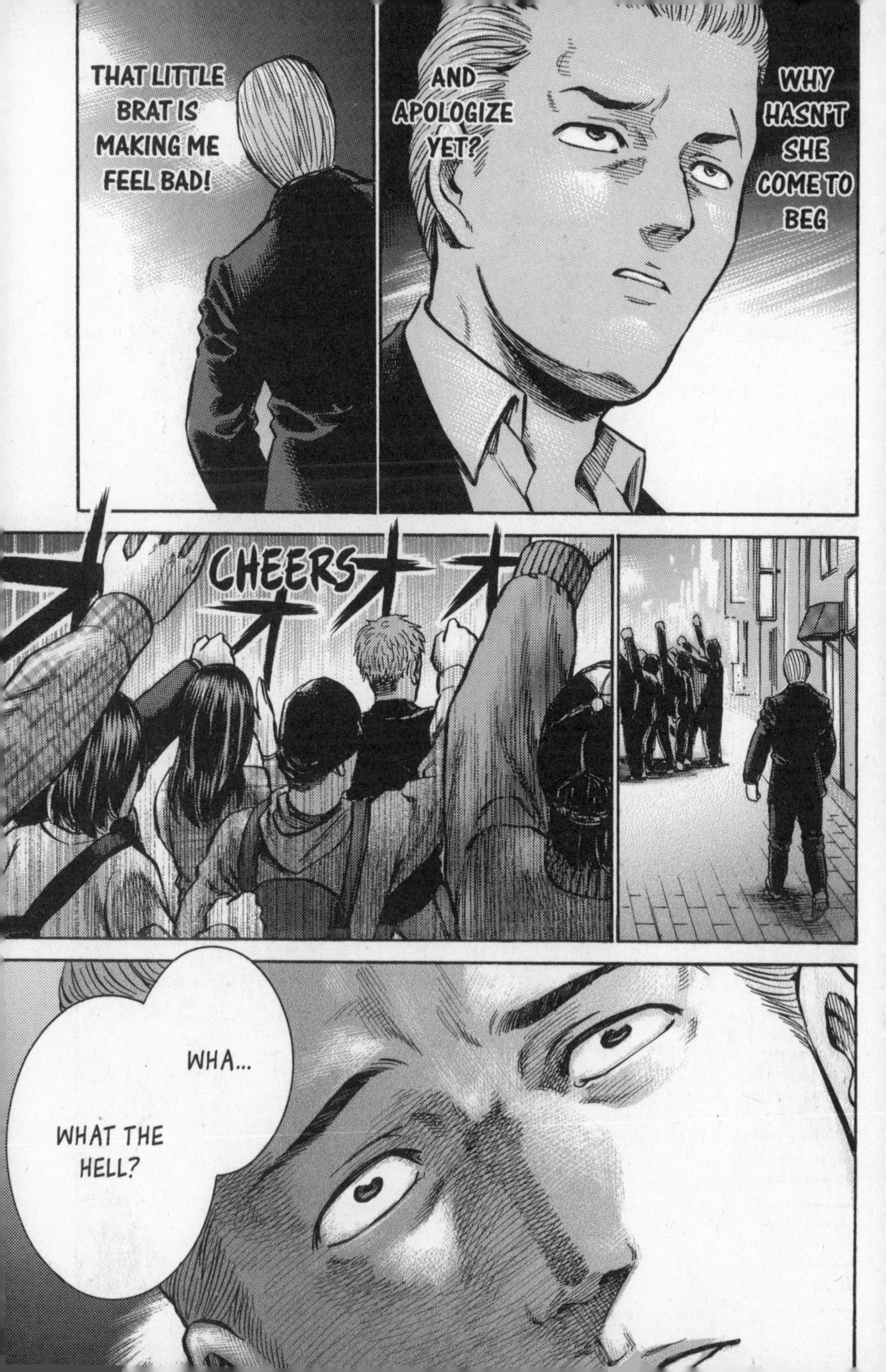
WHY HASN'T SHE COME TO BEG
AND APOLOGIZE YET?
THAT LITTLE BRAT IS MAKING ME FEEL BAD!
CHEERS
WHA...
WHAT THE HELL?

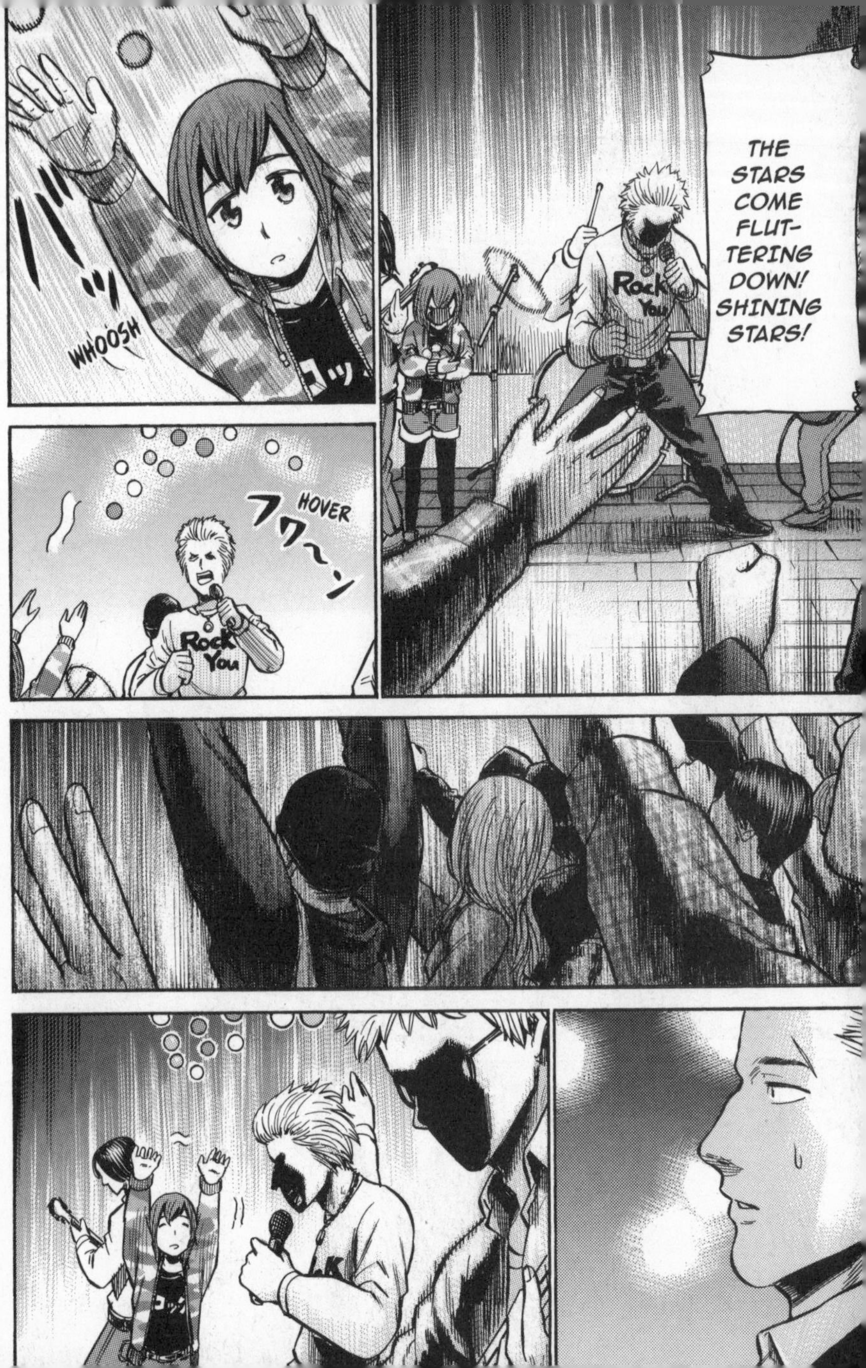
THE STARS COME FLUT-TERING DOWN! SHINING STARS!
WHOOSH
HOVER

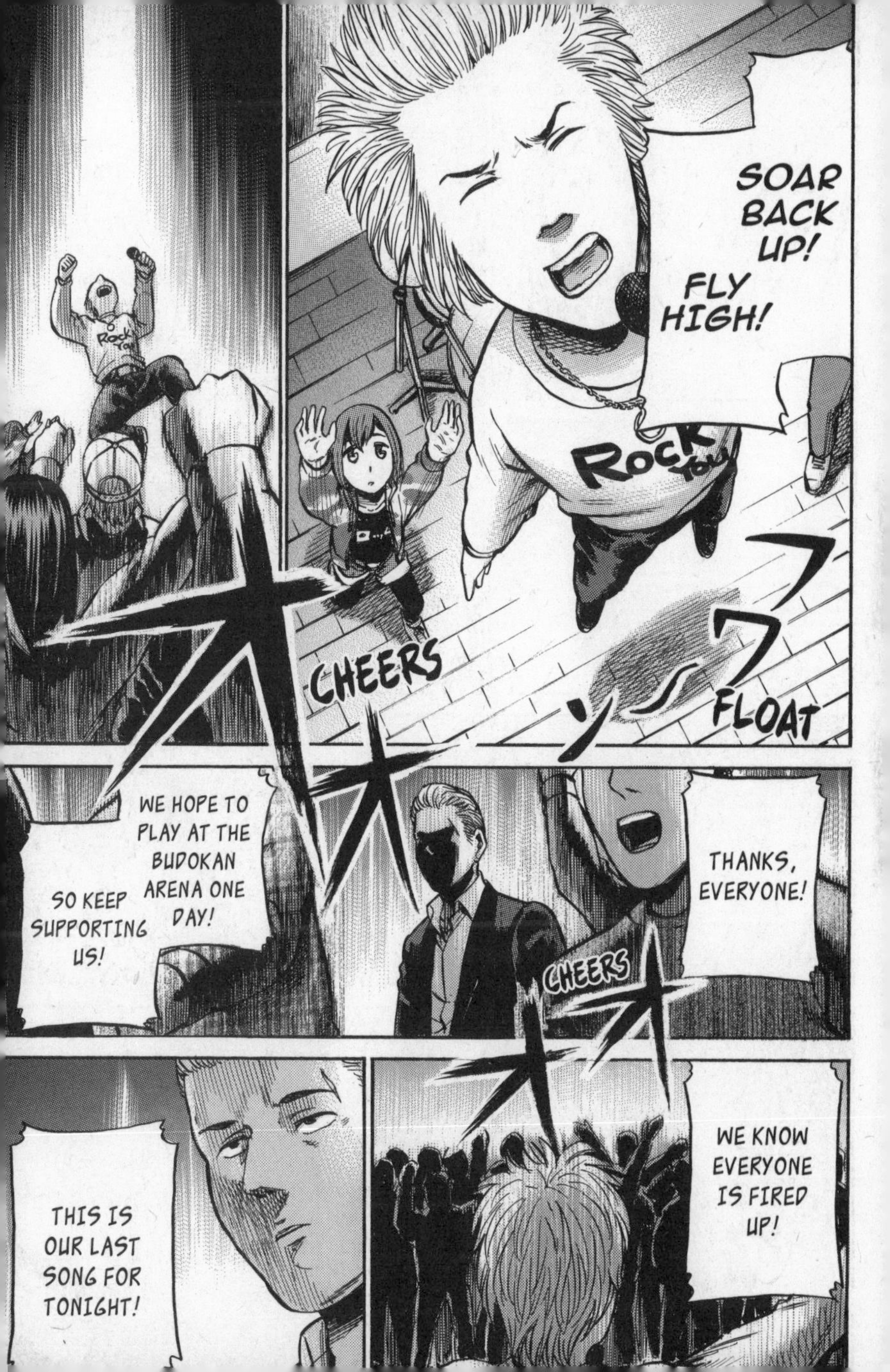
SOAR BACK UP!
FLY HIGH!
ROCK YOU
FLOAT
CHEERS
THANKS, EVERYONE!
CHEERS
WE HOPE TO PLAY AT THE BUDOKAN ARENA ONE DAY!
SO KEEP SUPPORTING US!
WE KNOW EVERYONE IS FIRED UP!
THIS IS OUR LAST SONG FOR TONIGHT!

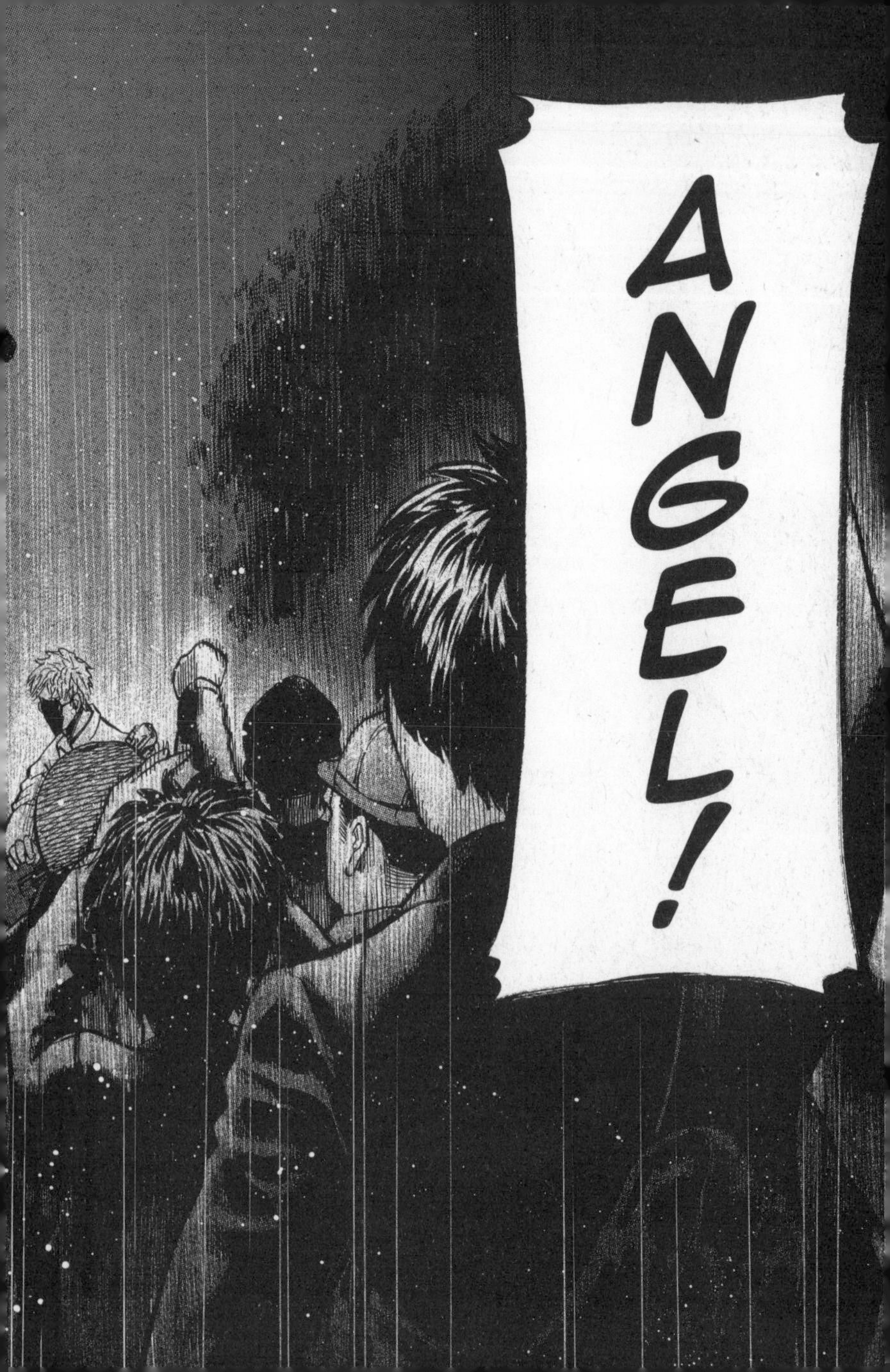
ANGEL!

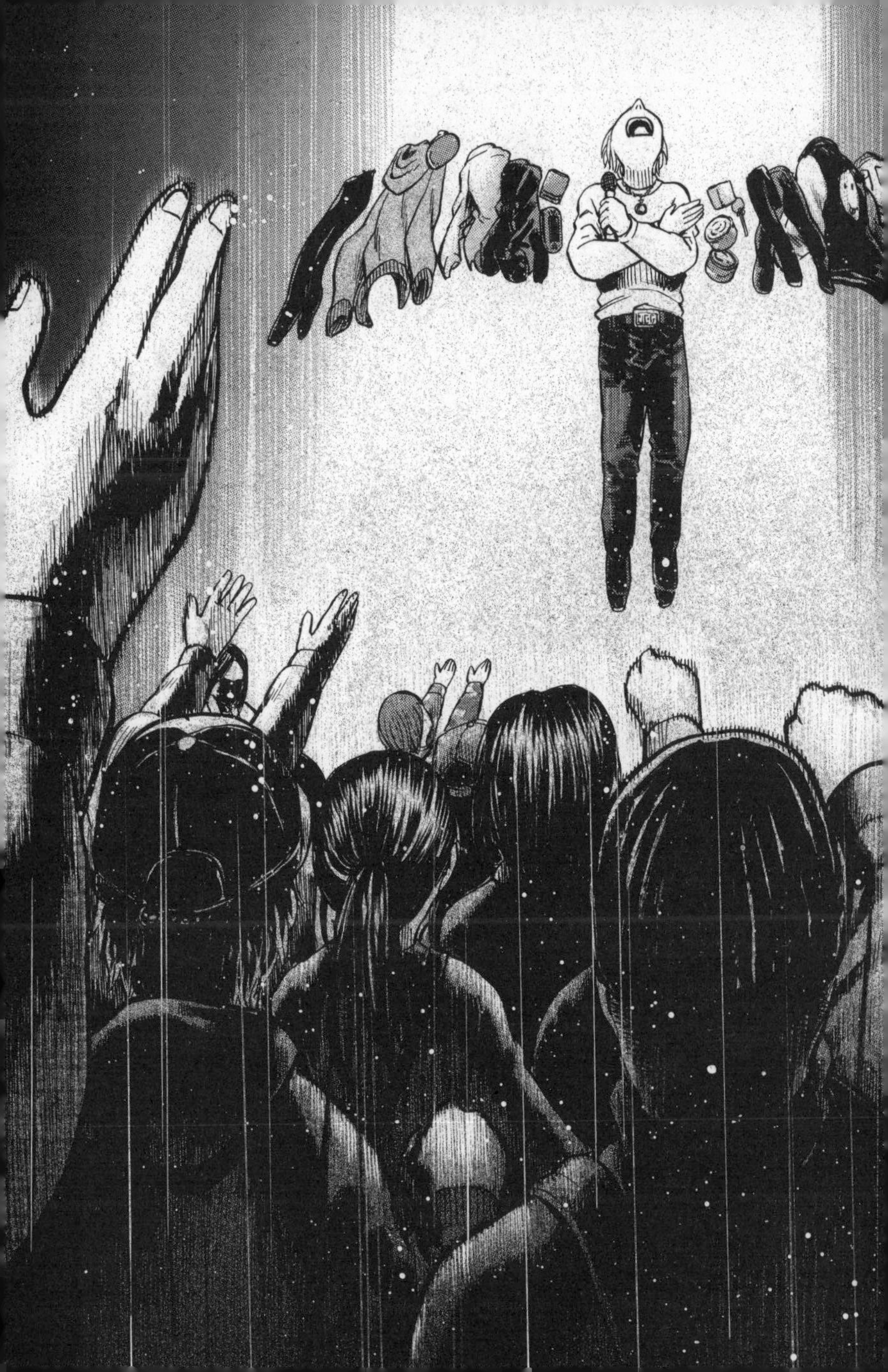

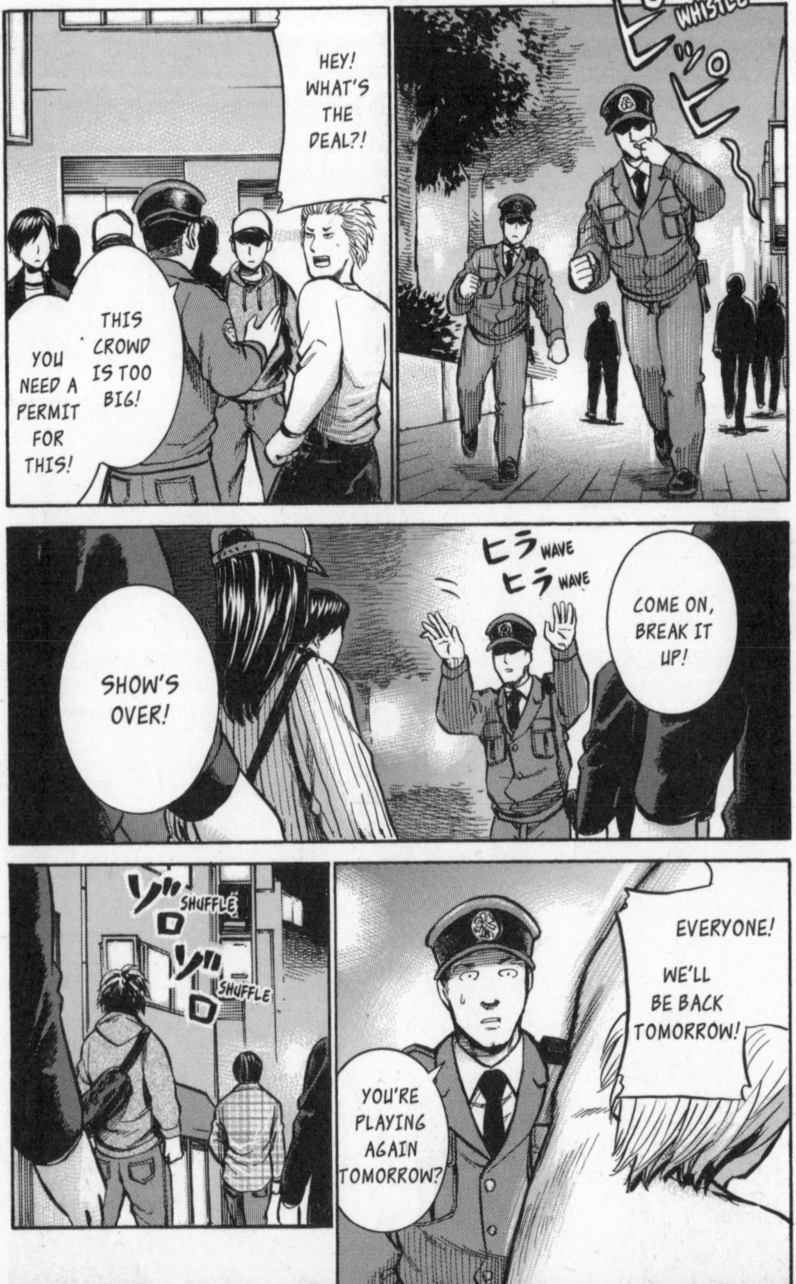
ピッピ WHISTLE
HEY! WHAT'S THE DEAL?!
THIS CROWD IS TOO BIG!
YOU NEED A PERMIT FOR THIS!
ヒラ WAVE ヒラ WAVE
COME ON, BREAK IT UP!
SHOW'S OVER!
EVERYONE! WE'LL BE BACK TOMORROW!
YOU'RE PLAYING AGAIN TOMORROW?
ゾロ SHUFFLE ゾロ SHUFFLE

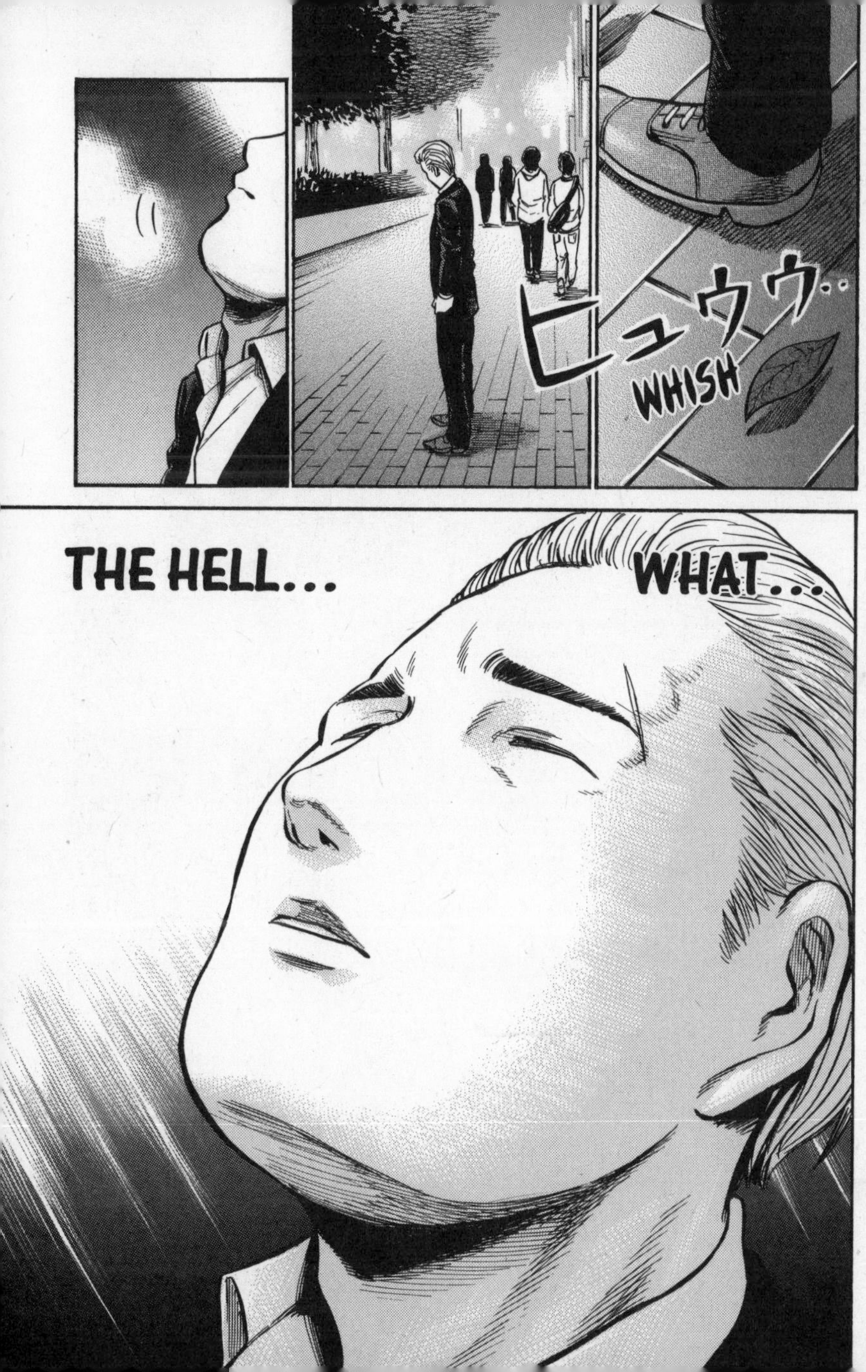
ヒュウウ..
WHISH
WHAT...
THE HELL...

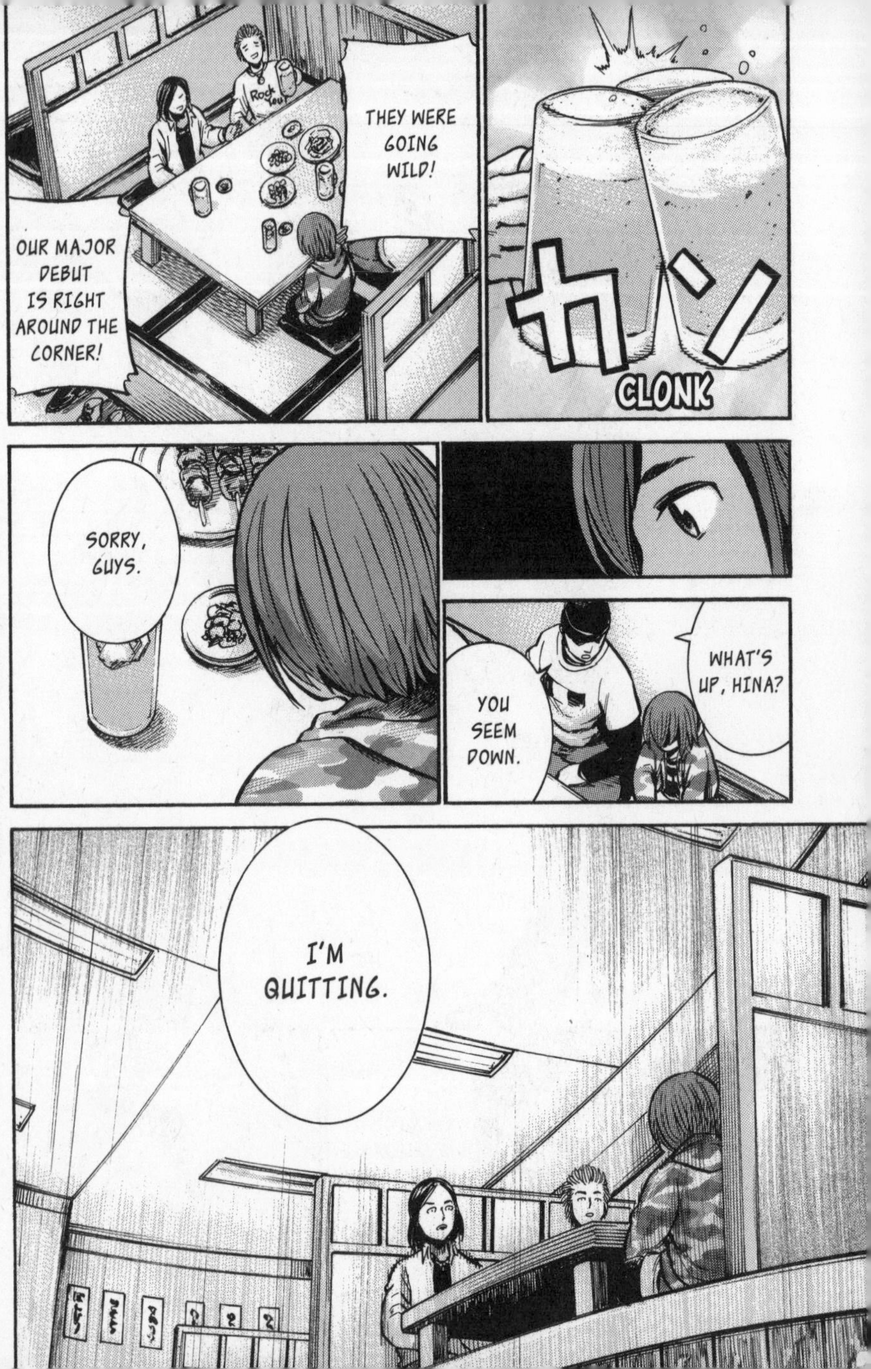
カン
CLONK
THEY WERE GOING WILD!
Rock You
OUR MAJOR DEBUT IS RIGHT AROUND THE CORNER!
WHAT'S UP, HINA?
YOU SEEM DOWN.
SORRY, GUYS.
I'M QUITTING.

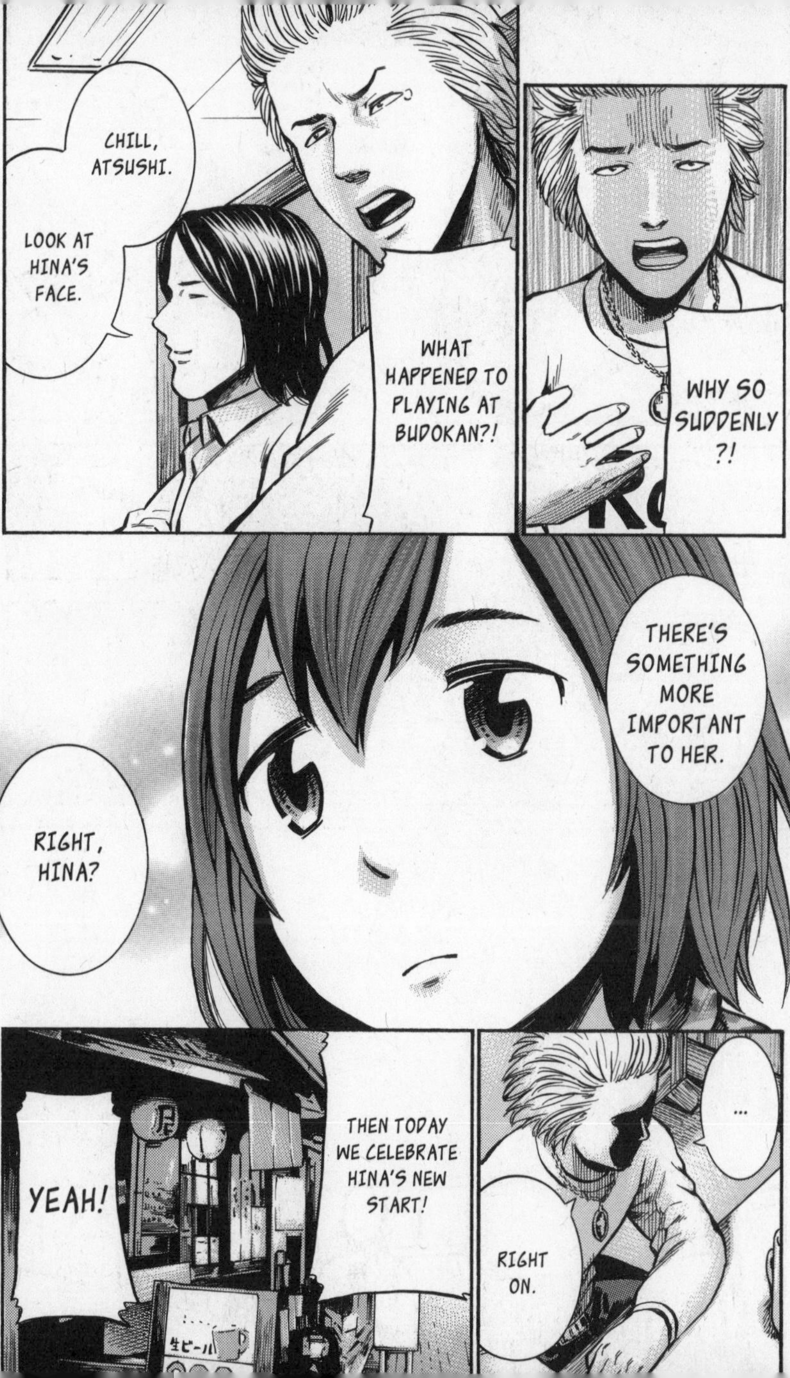
WHY SO SUDDENLY ?!
WHAT HAPPENED TO PLAYING AT BUDOKAN?!
CHILL, ATSUSHI.
LOOK AT HINA'S FACE.
THERE'S SOMETHING MORE IMPORTANT TO HER.
RIGHT, HINA?
...
RIGHT ON.
THEN TODAY WE CELEBRATE HINA'S NEW START!
YEAH!
生ビール

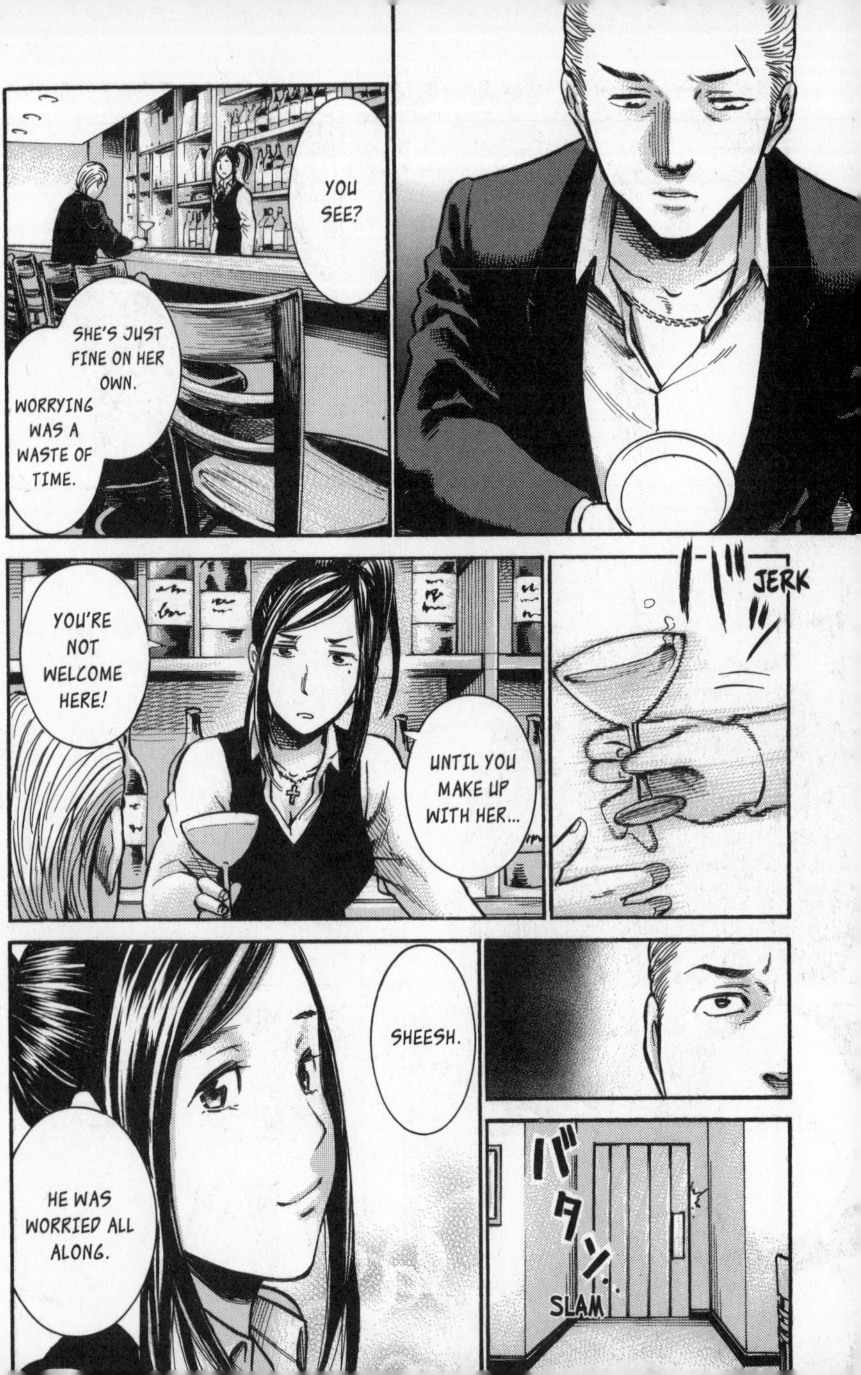
YOU SEE?
SHE'S JUST FINE ON HER OWN.
WORRYING WAS A WASTE OF TIME.
JERK
YOU'RE NOT WELCOME HERE!
UNTIL YOU MAKE UP WITH HER...
バタン
SLAM
SHEESH.
HE WAS WORRIED ALL ALONG.

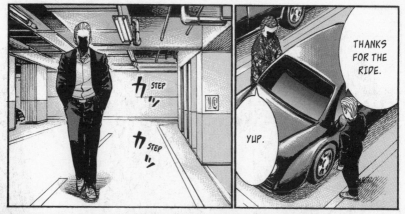

STEP

STEP

THANKS FOR THE RIDE.

YUP.

30

NITTA...

HINA...

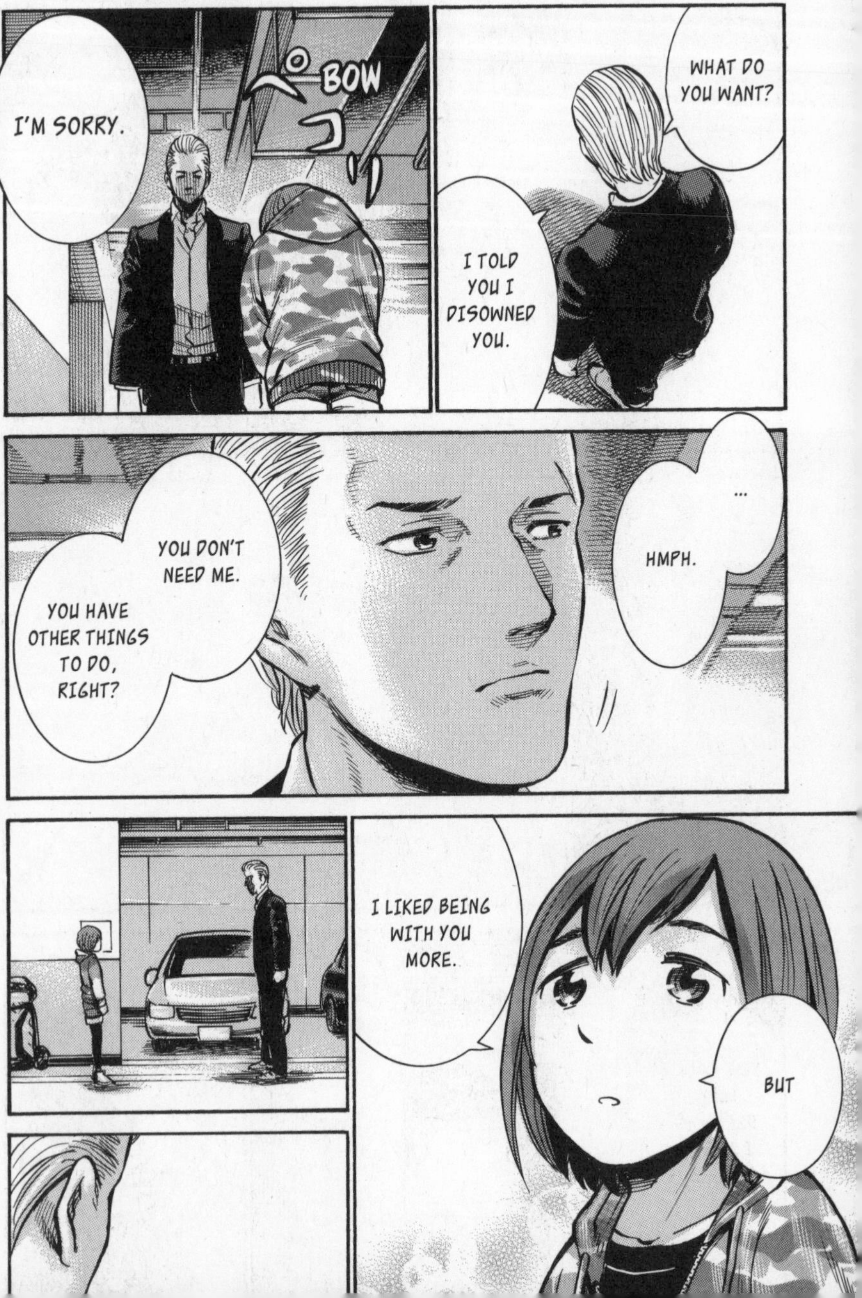
WHAT DO YOU WANT?
I TOLD YOU I DISOWNED YOU.
BOW
I'M SORRY.
...
HMPH.
YOU DON'T NEED ME.
YOU HAVE OTHER THINGS TO DO, RIGHT?
I LIKED BEING WITH YOU MORE.
BUT

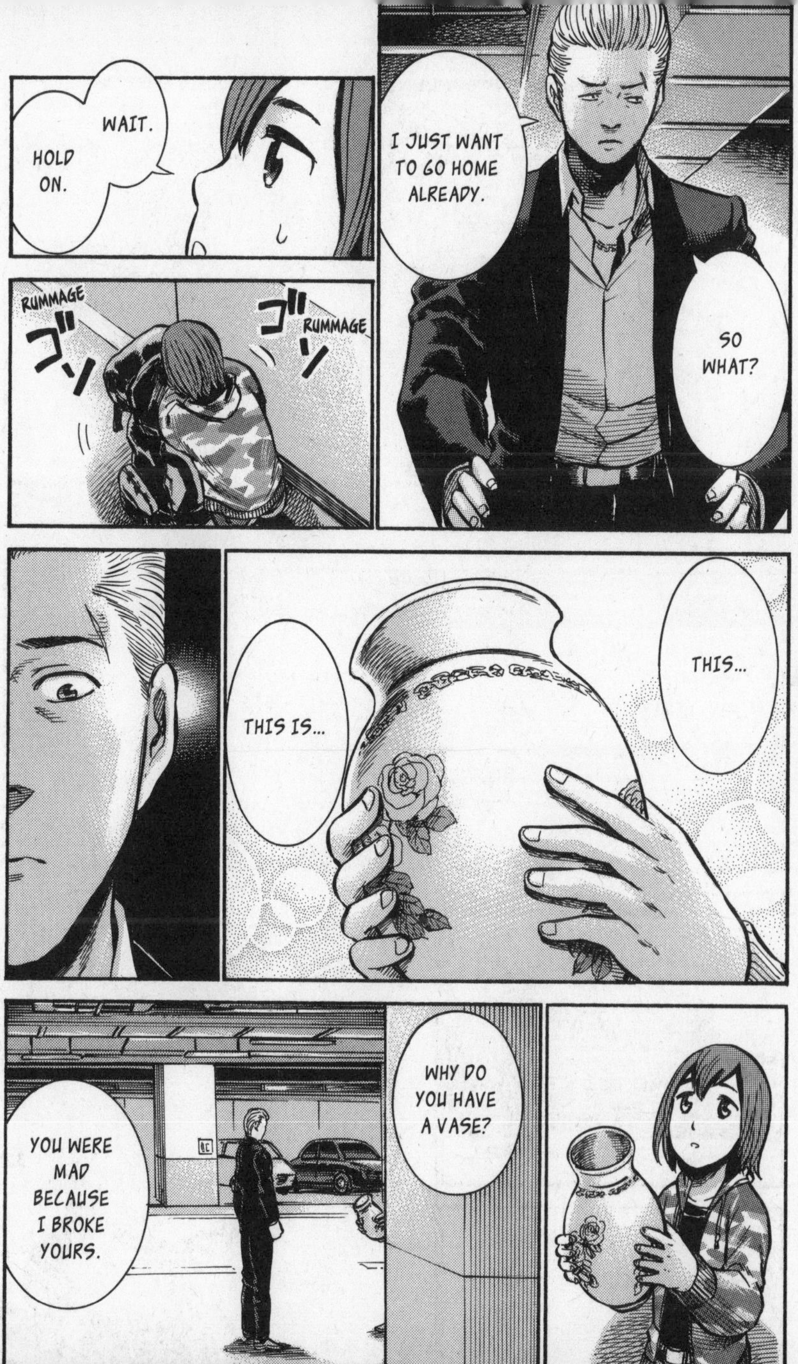
I JUST WANT TO GO HOME ALREADY.
SO WHAT?
WAIT.
HOLD ON.
ゴソ
RUMMAGE
RUMMAGE
ゴソ
THIS...
THIS IS...
WHY DO YOU HAVE A VASE?
YOU WERE MAD BECAUSE I BROKE YOURS.

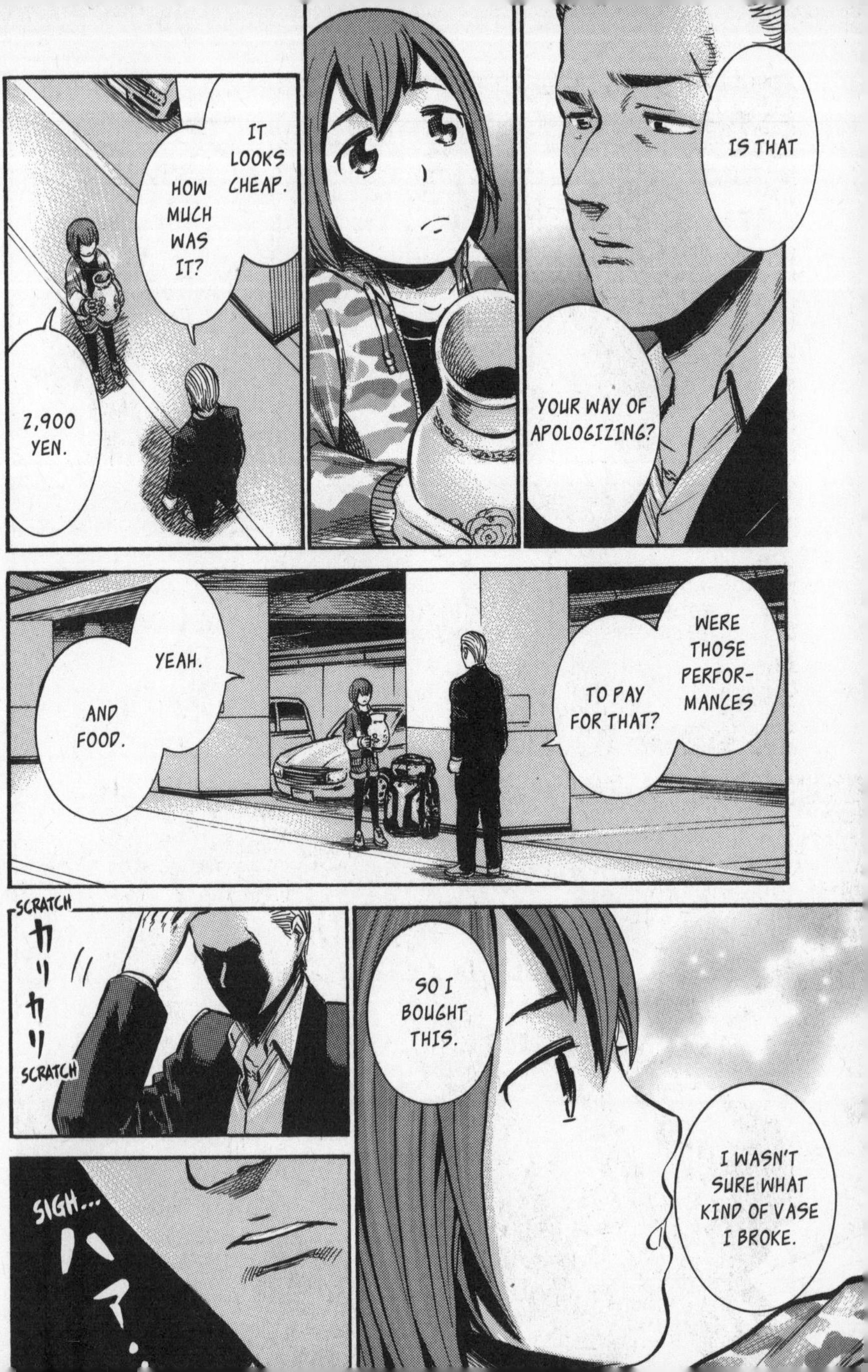
IS THAT
YOUR WAY OF APOLOGIZING?
IT LOOKS CHEAP.
HOW MUCH WAS IT?
2,900 YEN.
WERE THOSE PERFORMANCES
TO PAY FOR THAT?
YEAH.
AND FOOD.
SO I BOUGHT THIS.
I WASN'T SURE WHAT KIND OF VASE I BROKE.
SCRATCH
カリカリ
SCRATCH
SIGH...
ハァ

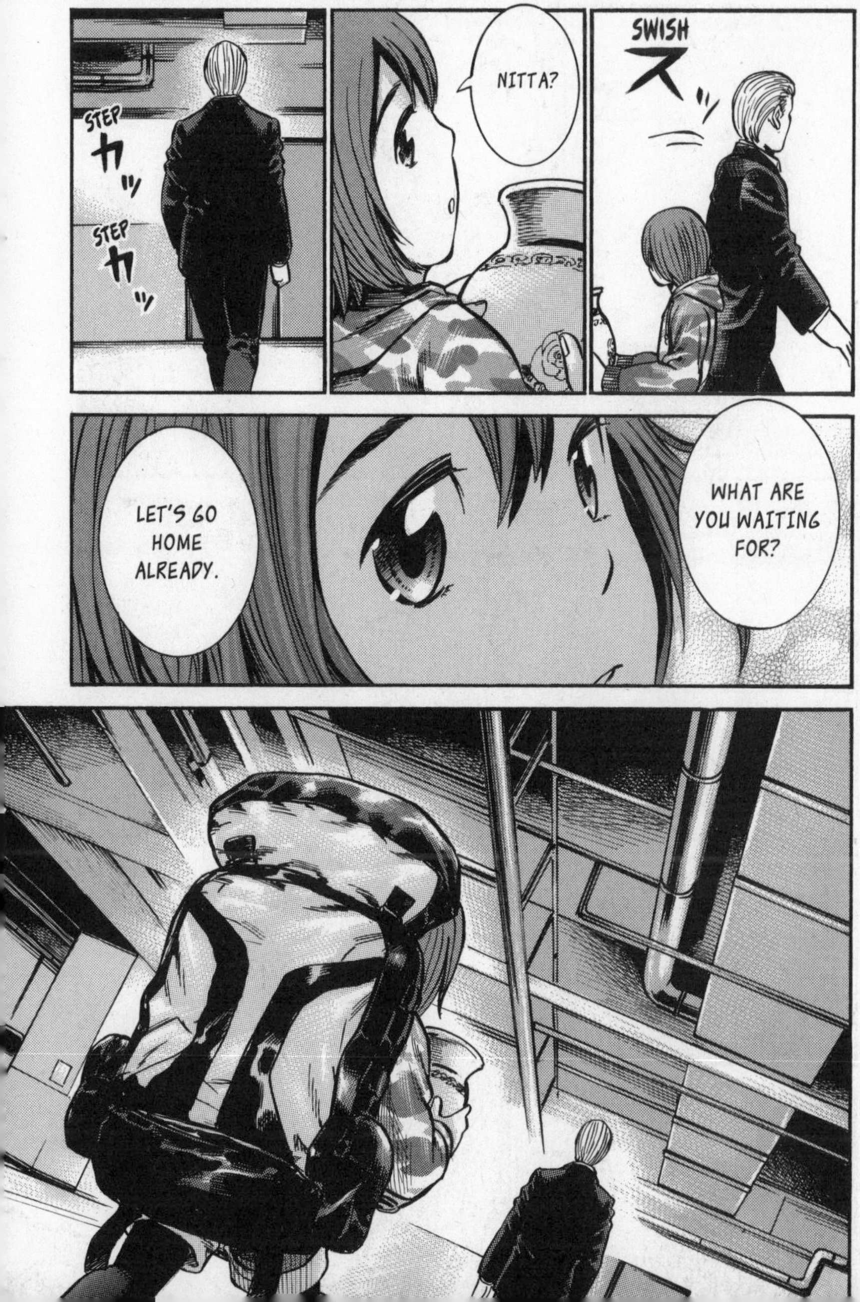
SWISH
スッ
NITTA?
STEP
カッ
STEP
カッ
WHAT ARE YOU WAITING FOR?
LET'S GO HOME ALREADY.

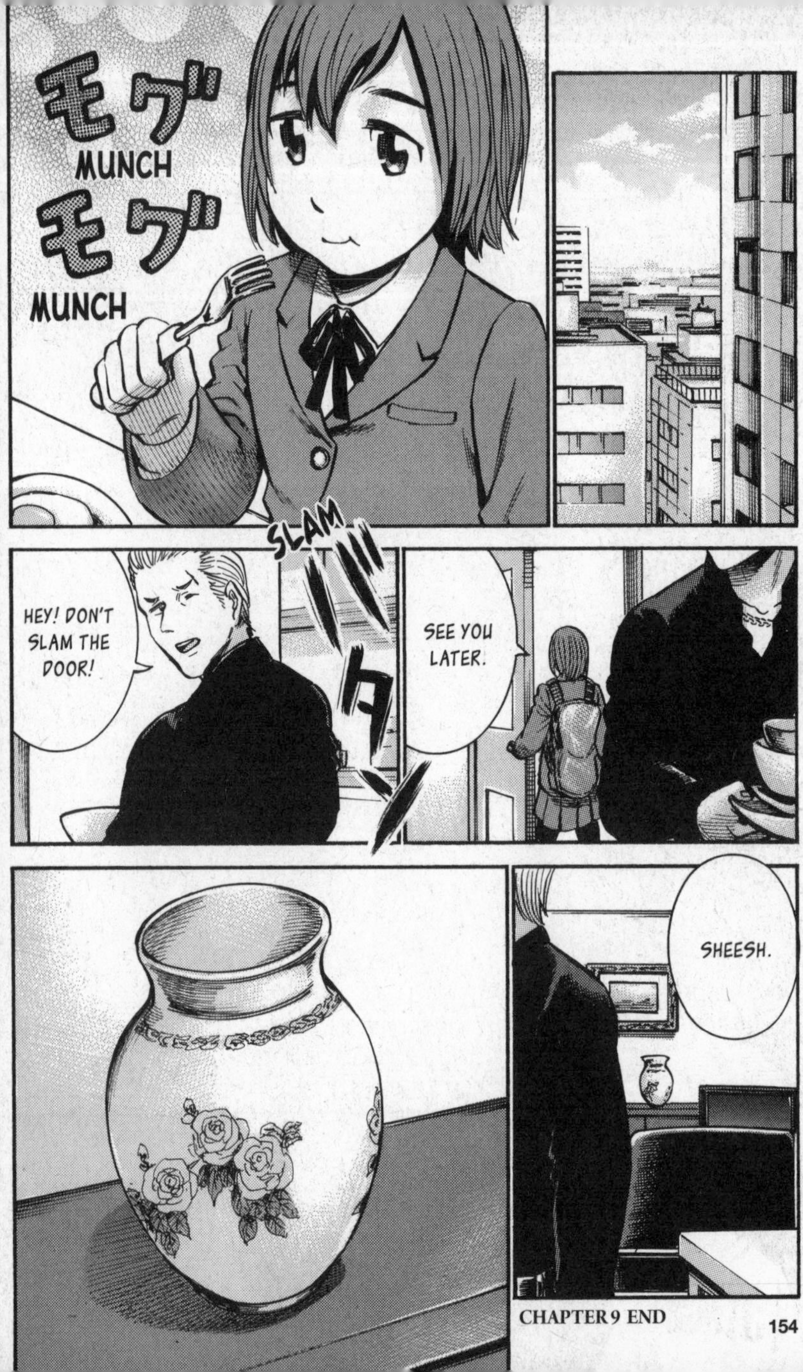
モグ
MUNCH
モグ
MUNCH
SEE YOU LATER.
SLAM
タ
HEY! DON'T SLAM THE DOOR!
SHEESH.

CHAPTER 9 END

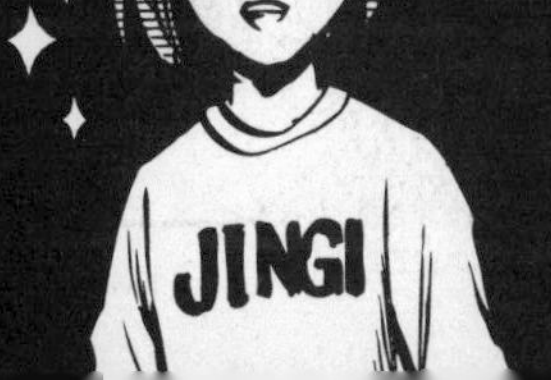
JINGI

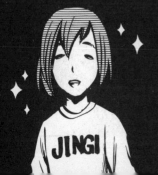

CHAPTER 10
ROAD TO DOMINATION

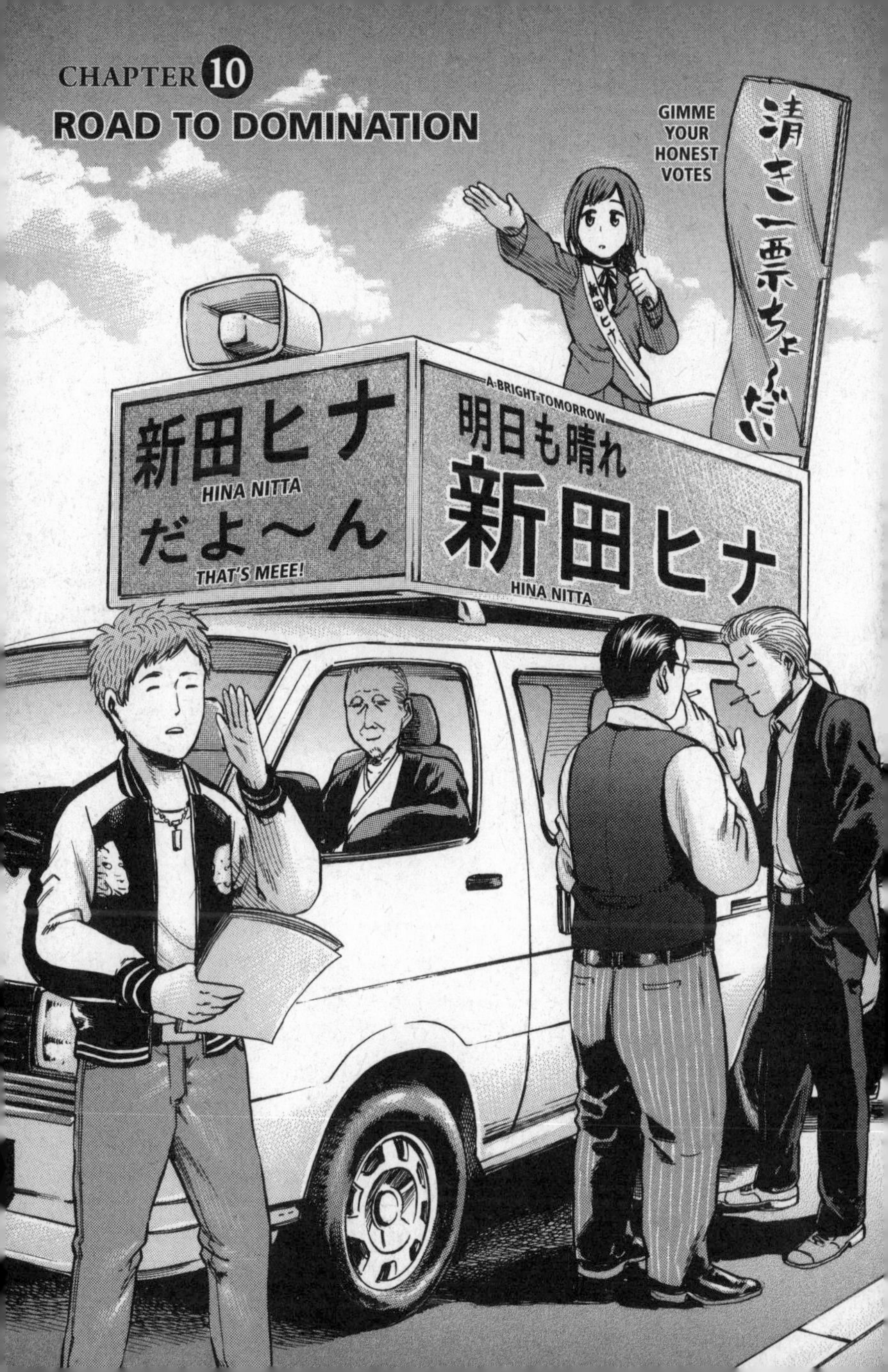

清き一票ちょ〜だい
GIMME YOUR HONEST VOTES
A BRIGHT TOMORROW
明日も晴れ
新田ヒナ
HINA NITTA
新田ヒナ
HINA NITTA
だよ〜ん
THAT'S MEEE!

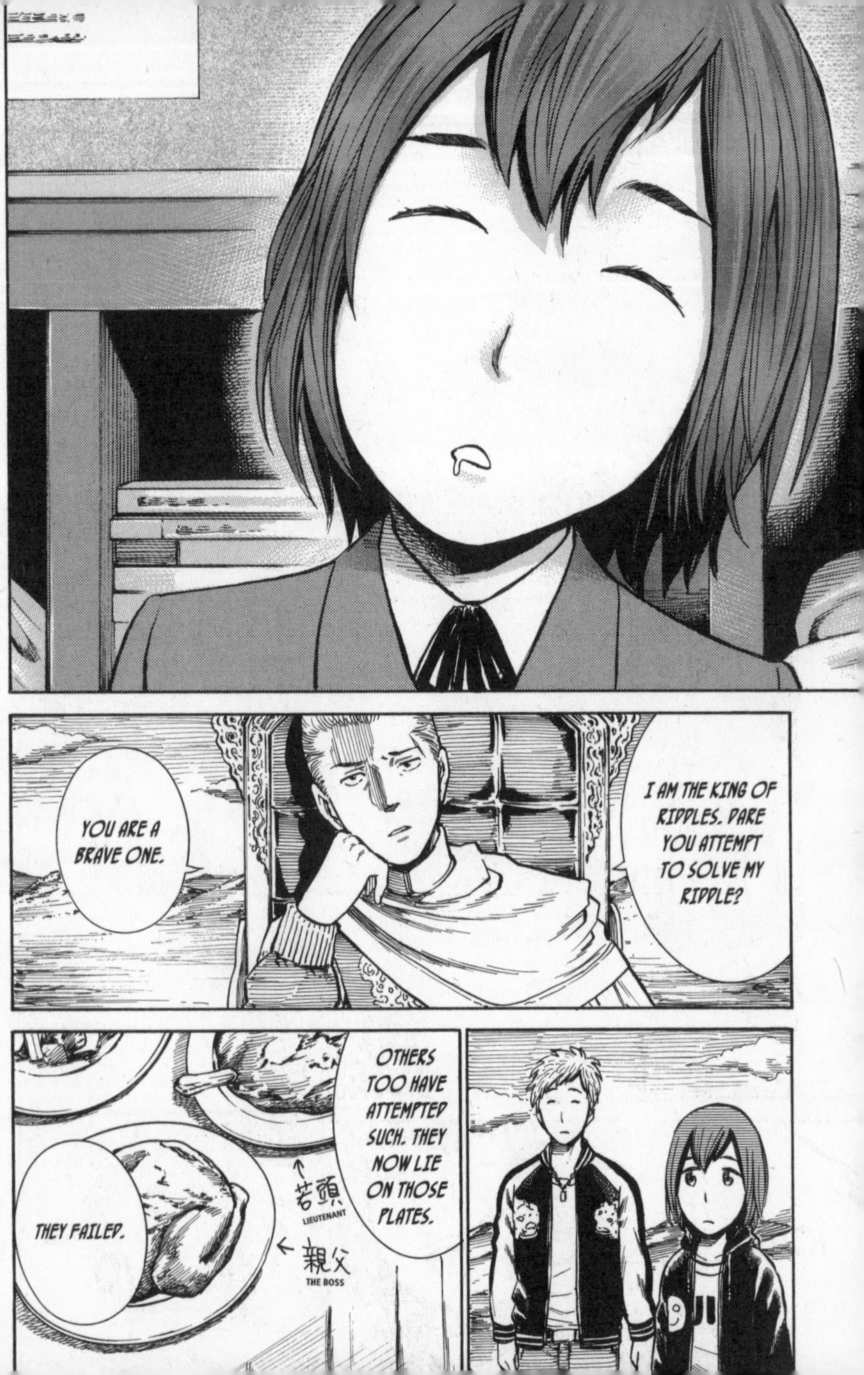
I AM THE KING OF RIDDLES. DARE YOU ATTEMPT TO SOLVE MY RIDDLE?
YOU ARE A BRAVE ONE.
OTHERS TOO HAVE ATTEMPTED SUCH. THEY NOW LIE ON THOSE PLATES.
若頭
LIEUTENANT
親父
THE BOSS
THEY FAILED.

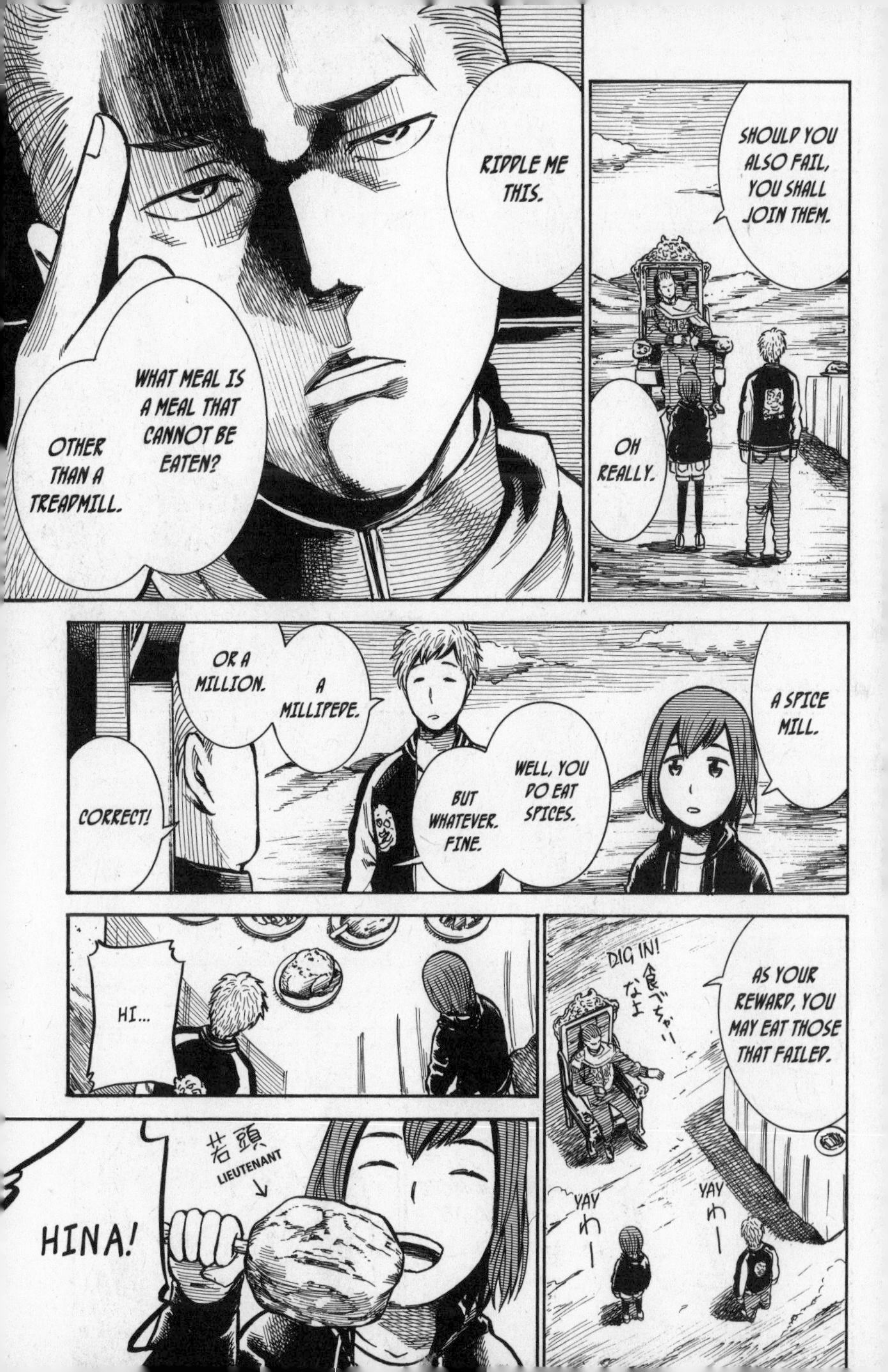
SHOULD YOU ALSO FAIL, YOU SHALL JOIN THEM.
OH REALLY.
RIDDLE ME THIS.
WHAT MEAL IS A MEAL THAT CANNOT BE EATEN?
OTHER THAN A TREADMILL.
A SPICE MILL.
WELL, YOU DO EAT SPICES.
BUT WHATEVER. FINE.
A MILLIPEDE.
OR A MILLION.
CORRECT!
AS YOUR REWARD, YOU MAY EAT THOSE THAT FAILED.
DIG IN!
食べちゃいなよ
YAY
わー
YAY
わー
HI...
若頭
LIEUTENANT
HINA!

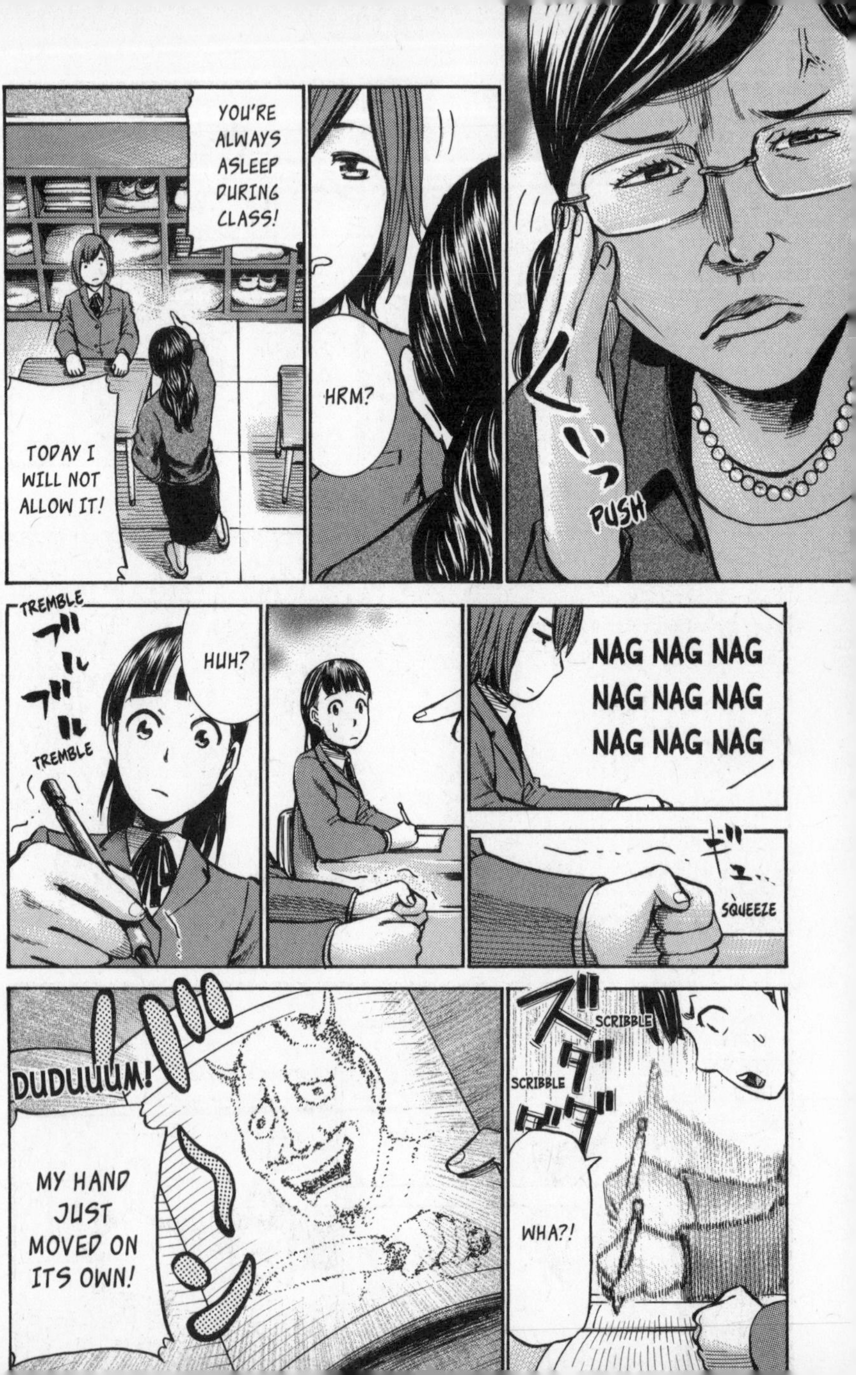
PUSH
HRM?
YOU'RE ALWAYS ASLEEP DURING CLASS!
TODAY I WILL NOT ALLOW IT!
NAG NAG NAG NAG NAG NAG NAG NAG NAG
SQUEEZE
HUH?
TREMBLE
TREMBLE
SCRIBBLE
SCRIBBLE
WHA?!
DUDUUUM!
MY HAND JUST MOVED ON ITS OWN!

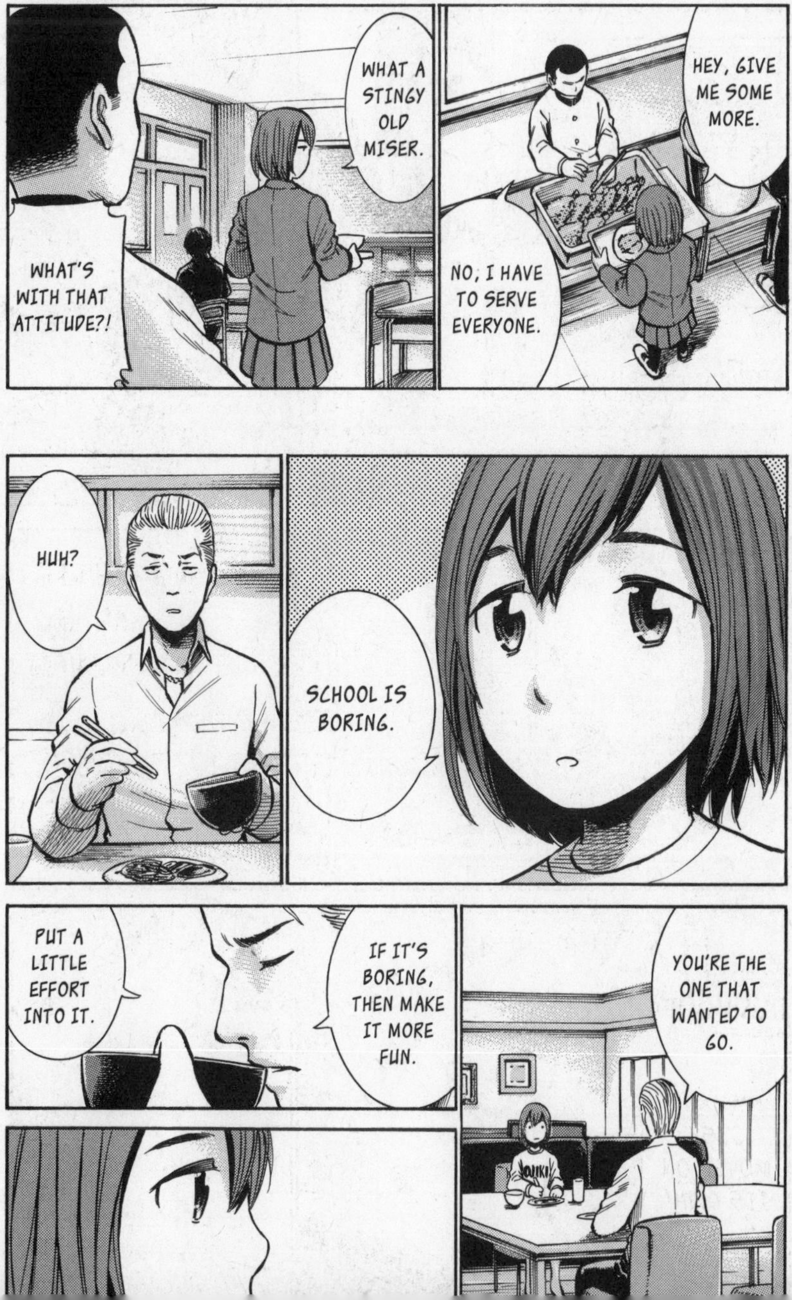
HEY, GIVE ME SOME MORE.
NO, I HAVE TO SERVE EVERYONE.
WHAT A STINGY OLD MISER.
WHAT'S WITH THAT ATTITUDE?!
SCHOOL IS BORING.
HUH?
YOU'RE THE ONE THAT WANTED TO GO.
IF IT'S BORING, THEN MAKE IT MORE FUN.
PUT A LITTLE EFFORT INTO IT.

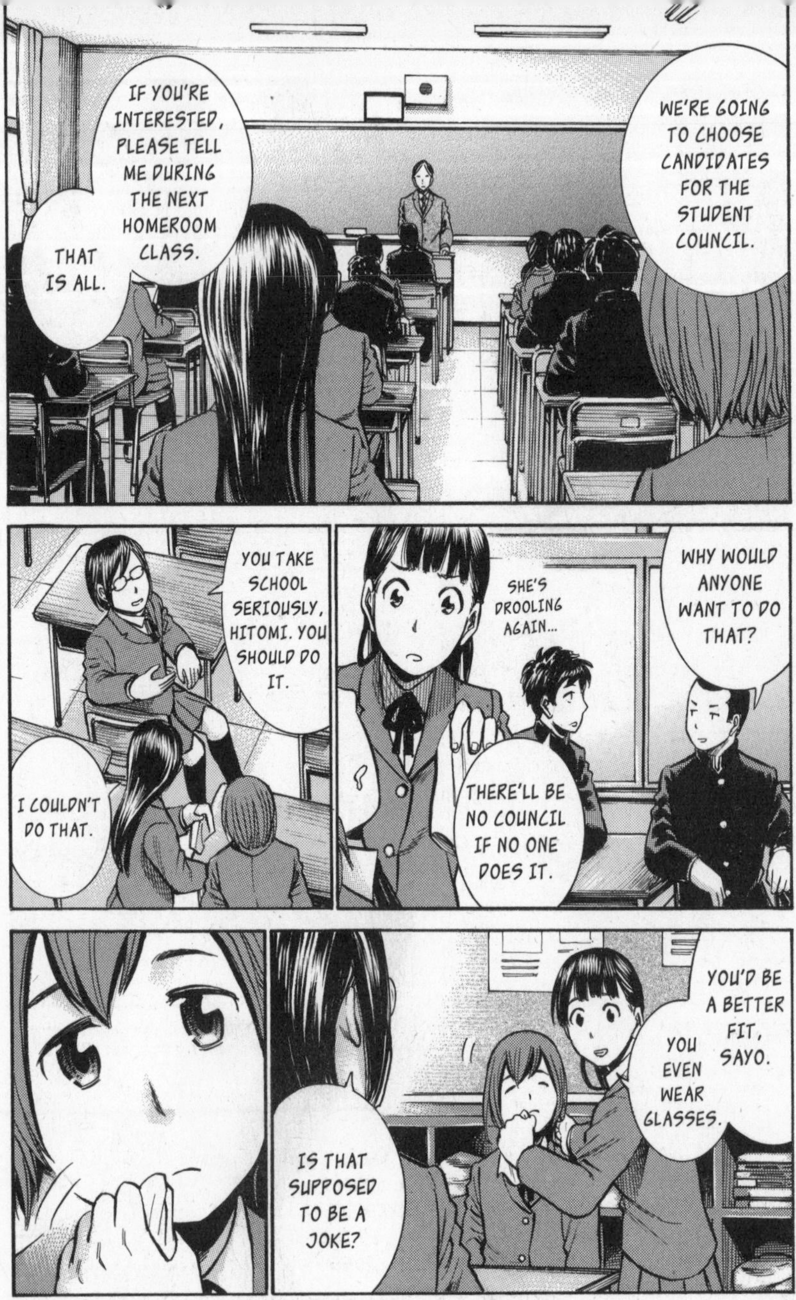
WE'RE GOING TO CHOOSE CANDIDATES FOR THE STUDENT COUNCIL.
IF YOU'RE INTERESTED, PLEASE TELL ME DURING THE NEXT HOMEROOM CLASS.
THAT IS ALL.
WHY WOULD ANYONE WANT TO DO THAT?
SHE'S DROOLING AGAIN...
THERE'LL BE NO COUNCIL IF NO ONE DOES IT.
YOU TAKE SCHOOL SERIOUSLY, HITOMI. YOU SHOULD DO IT.
I COULDN'T DO THAT.
YOU'D BE A BETTER FIT, SAYO.
YOU EVEN WEAR GLASSES.
IS THAT SUPPOSED TO BE A JOKE?

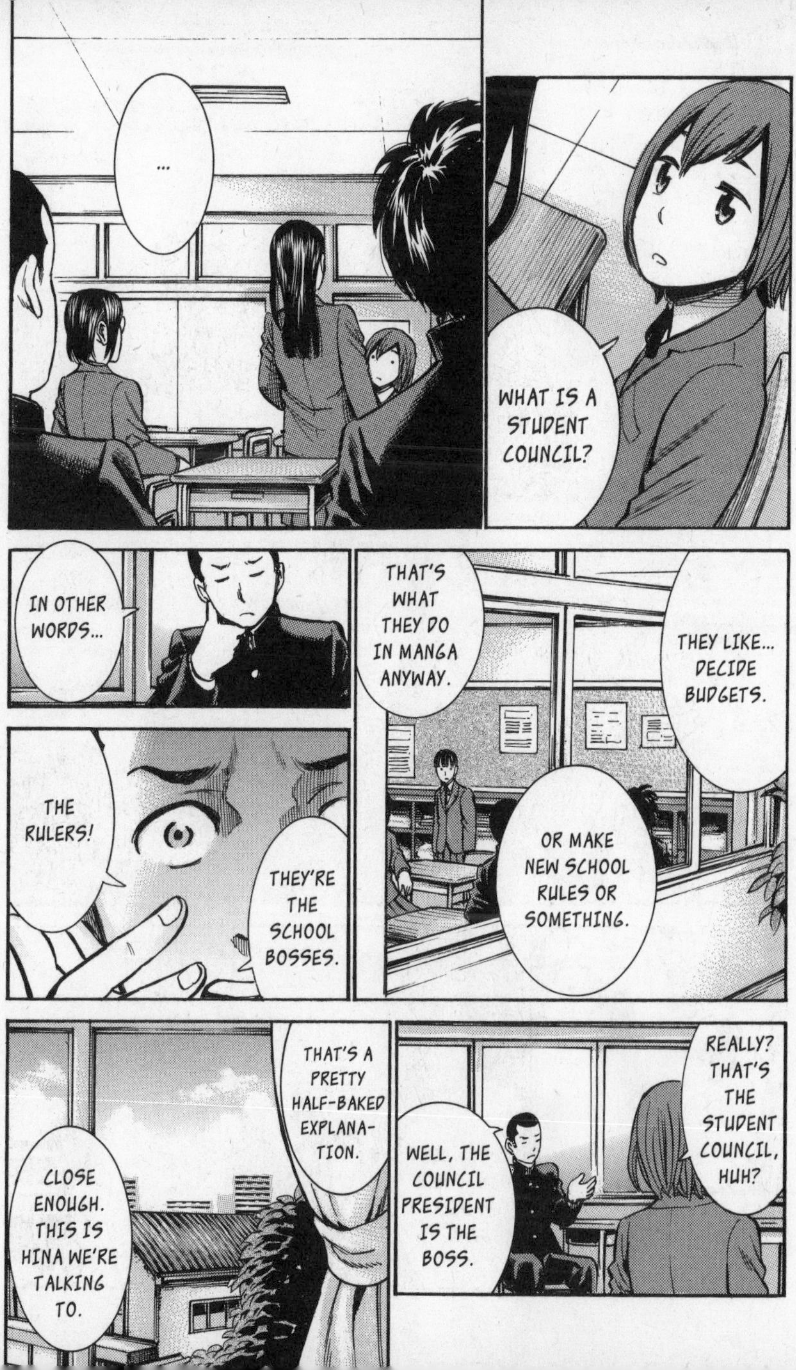
WHAT IS A STUDENT COUNCIL?
...
THEY LIKE... DECIDE BUDGETS.
OR MAKE NEW SCHOOL RULES OR SOMETHING.
THAT'S WHAT THEY DO IN MANGA ANYWAY.
IN OTHER WORDS...
THE RULERS!
THEY'RE THE SCHOOL BOSSES.
REALLY? THAT'S THE STUDENT COUNCIL, HUH?
WELL, THE COUNCIL PRESIDENT IS THE BOSS.
THAT'S A PRETTY HALF-BAKED EXPLANA-TION.
CLOSE ENOUGH. THIS IS HINA WE'RE TALKING TO.

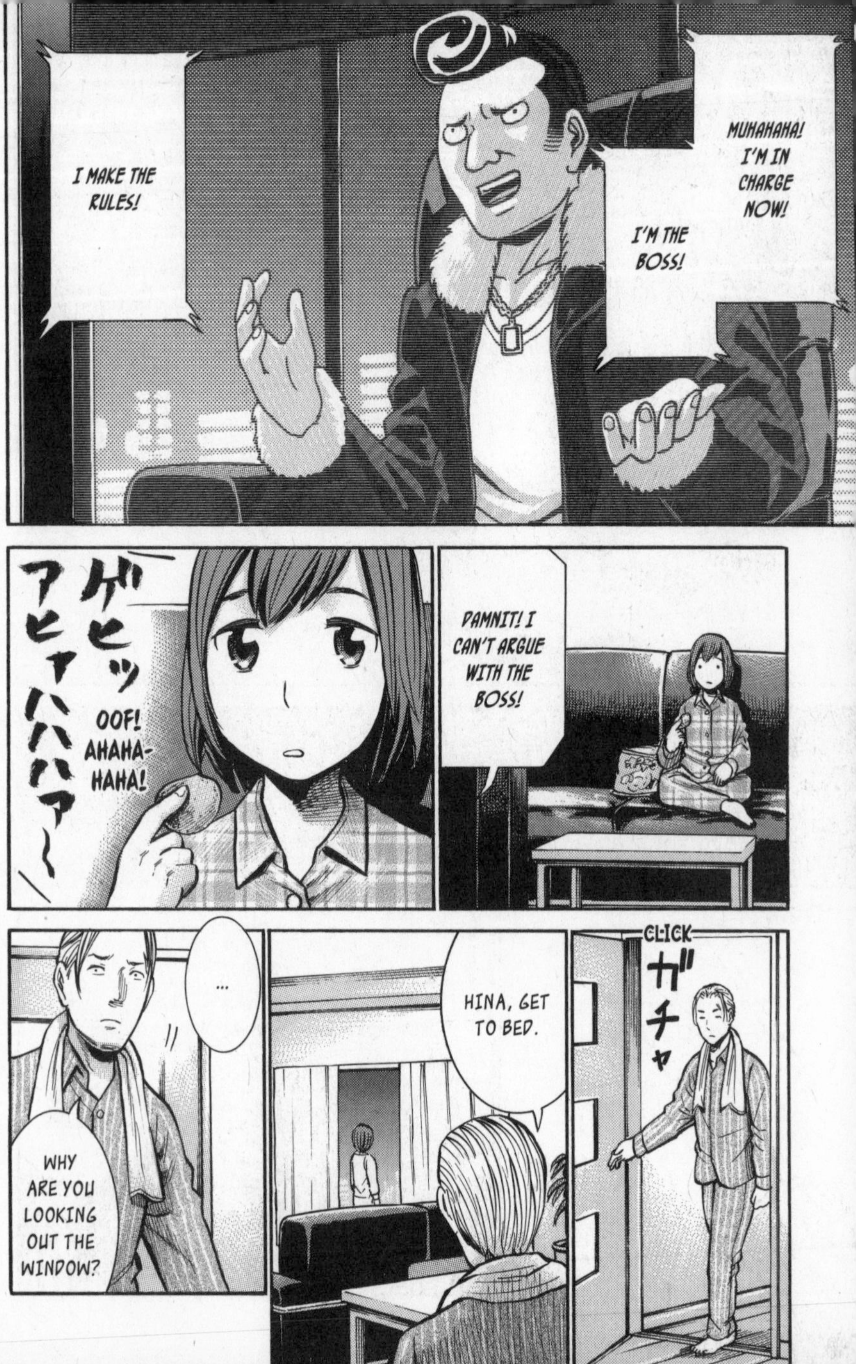
MUHAHAHA! I'M IN CHARGE NOW!
I'M THE BOSS!
I MAKE THE RULES!
DAMNIT! I CAN'T ARGUE WITH THE BOSS!
ゲヒッ
アヒャハハハァ～
OOF! AHAHA-HAHA!
CLICK
ガチャ
HINA, GET TO BED.
...
WHY ARE YOU LOOKING OUT THE WINDOW?

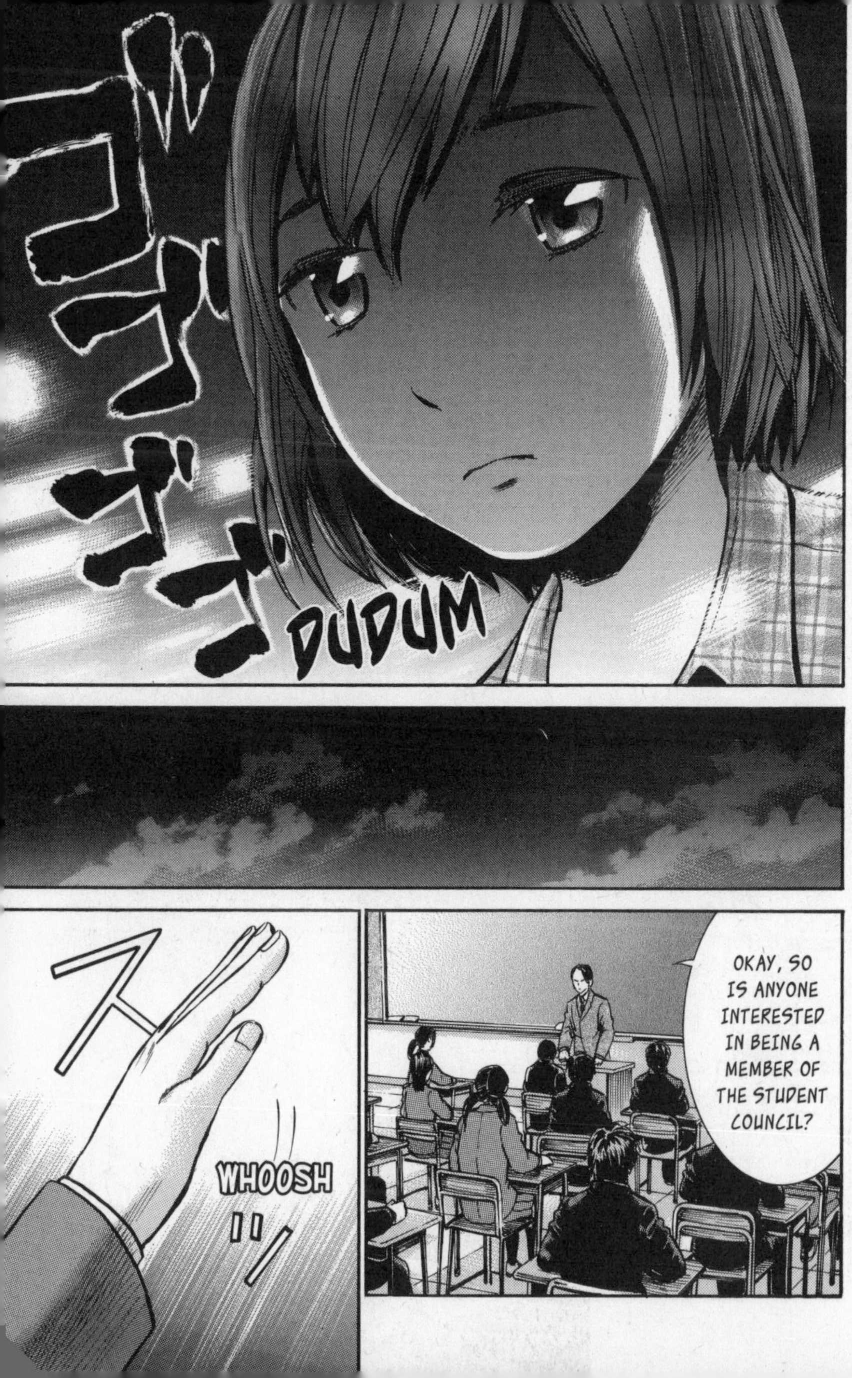
DUDUM
OKAY, SO IS ANYONE INTERESTED IN BEING A MEMBER OF THE STUDENT COUNCIL?
WHOOSH

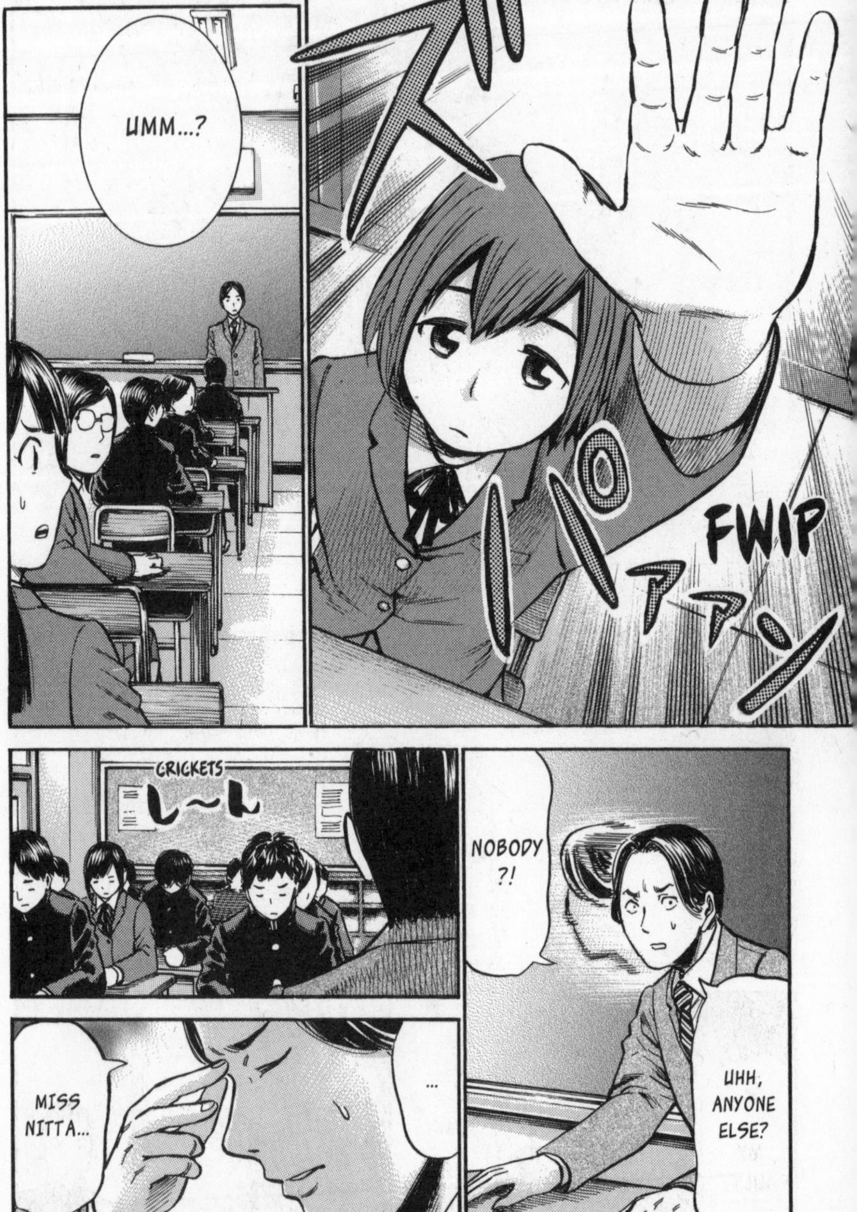
ズ
FWIP
パアアン
UMM...?
NOBODY ?!
UHH, ANYONE ELSE?
CRICKETS
し~ん
...
MISS NITTA...

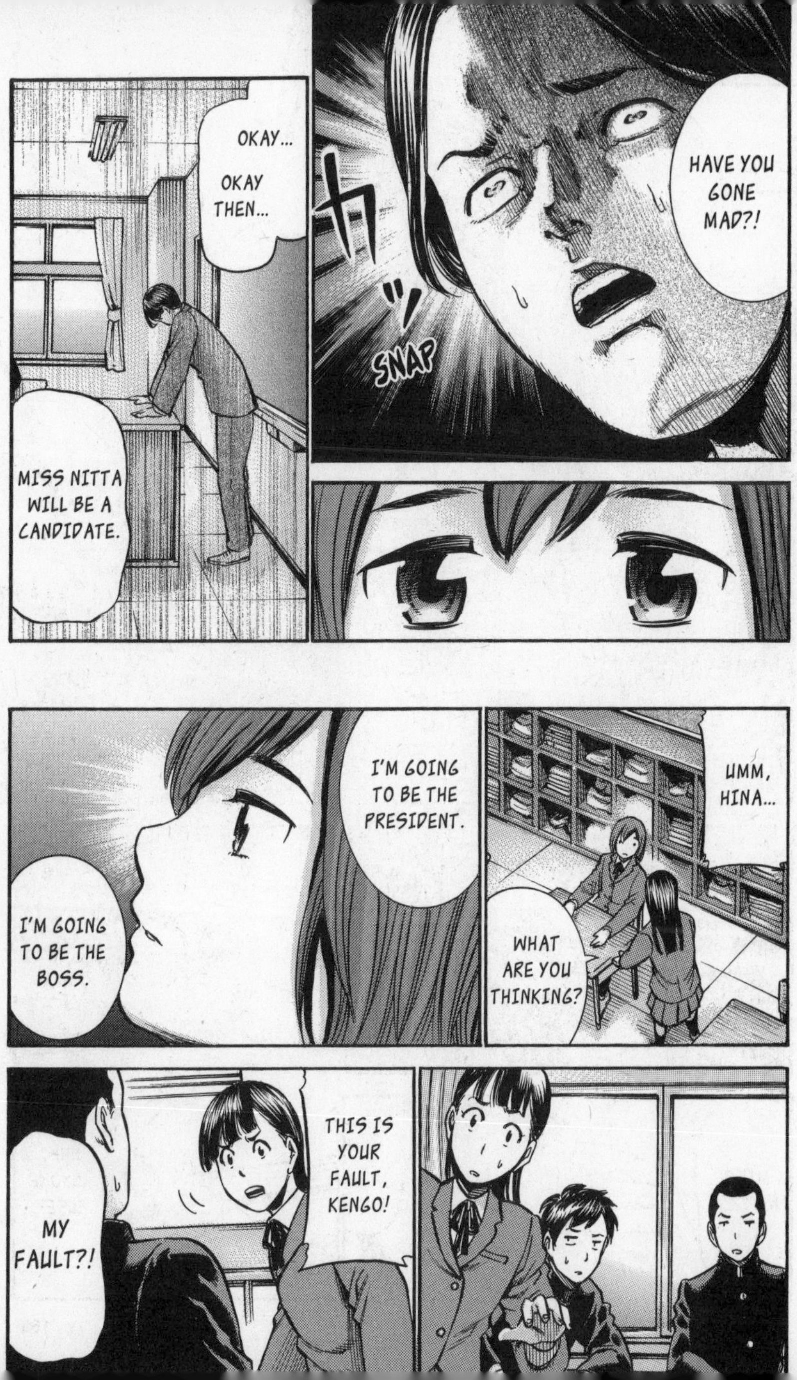
HAVE YOU GONE MAD?!
SNAP
OKAY...
OKAY THEN...
MISS NITTA WILL BE A CANDIDATE.
UMM, HINA...
WHAT ARE YOU THINKING?
I'M GOING TO BE THE PRESIDENT.
I'M GOING TO BE THE BOSS.
THIS IS YOUR FAULT, KENGO!
MY FAULT?!

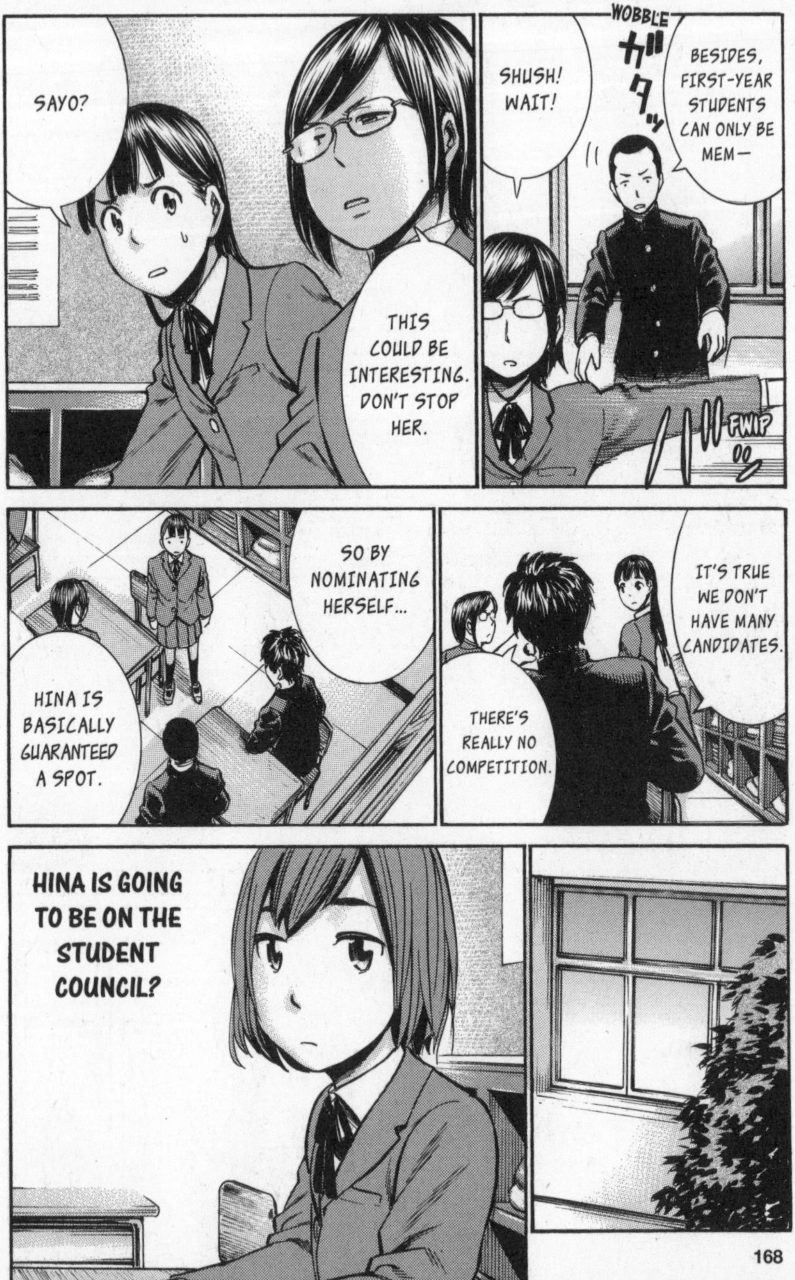
BESIDES, FIRST-YEAR STUDENTS CAN ONLY BE MEM—
WOBBLE
ガタッ
SHUSH! WAIT!
FWIP
SAYO?
THIS COULD BE INTERESTING. DON'T STOP HER.
IT'S TRUE WE DON'T HAVE MANY CANDIDATES.
THERE'S REALLY NO COMPETITION.
SO BY NOMINATING HERSELF...
HINA IS BASICALLY GUARANTEED A SPOT.
HINA IS GOING TO BE ON THE STUDENT COUNCIL?

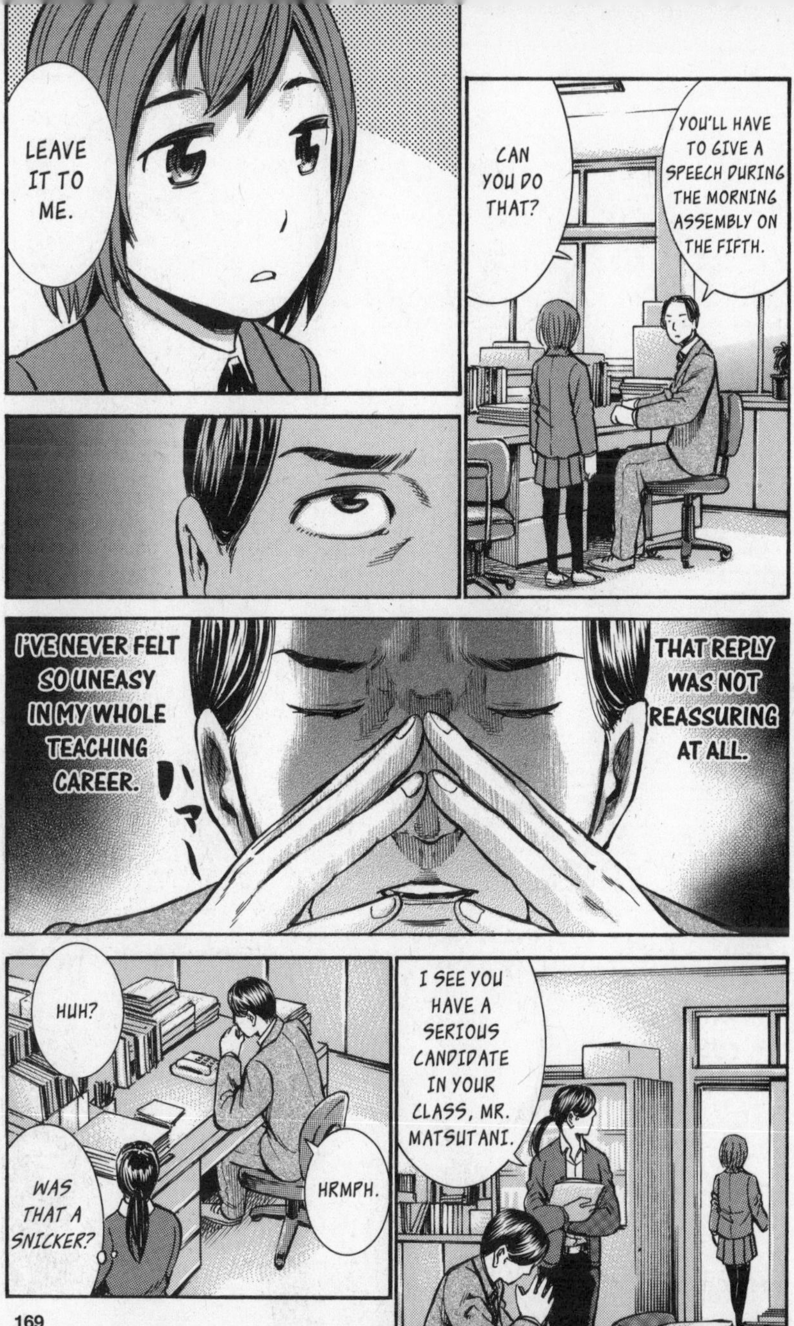

YOU'LL HAVE TO GIVE A SPEECH DURING THE MORNING ASSEMBLY ON THE FIFTH.
CAN YOU DO THAT?
LEAVE IT TO ME.
THAT REPLY WAS NOT REASSURING AT ALL.
I'VE NEVER FELT SO UNEASY IN MY WHOLE TEACHING CAREER.
ハァー
I SEE YOU HAVE A SERIOUS CANDIDATE IN YOUR CLASS, MR. MATSUTANI.
HUH?
HRMPH.
WAS THAT A SNICKER?

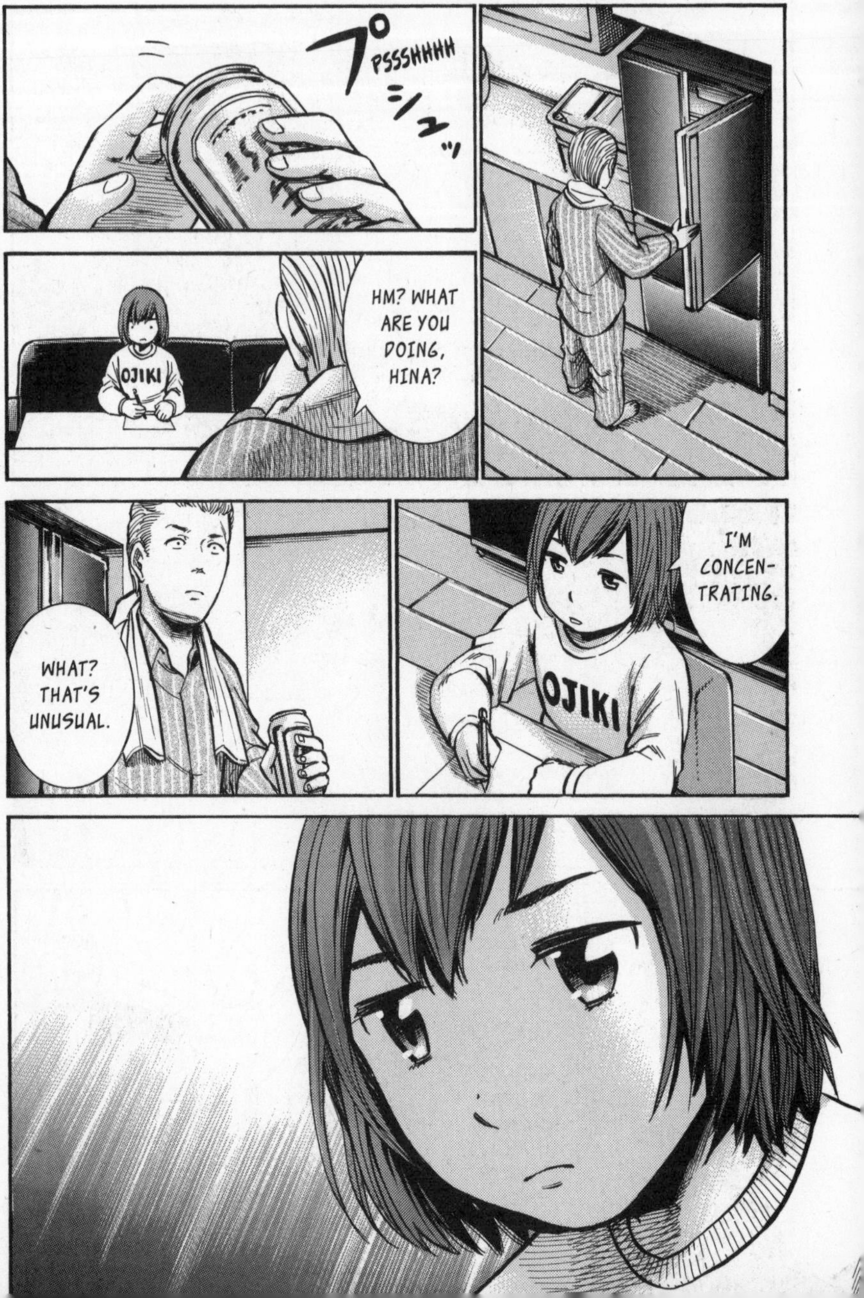
プシュッ
PSSSHHHH
HM? WHAT ARE YOU DOING, HINA?
OJIKI
I'M CONCEN-TRATING.
OJIKI
WHAT? THAT'S UNUSUAL.

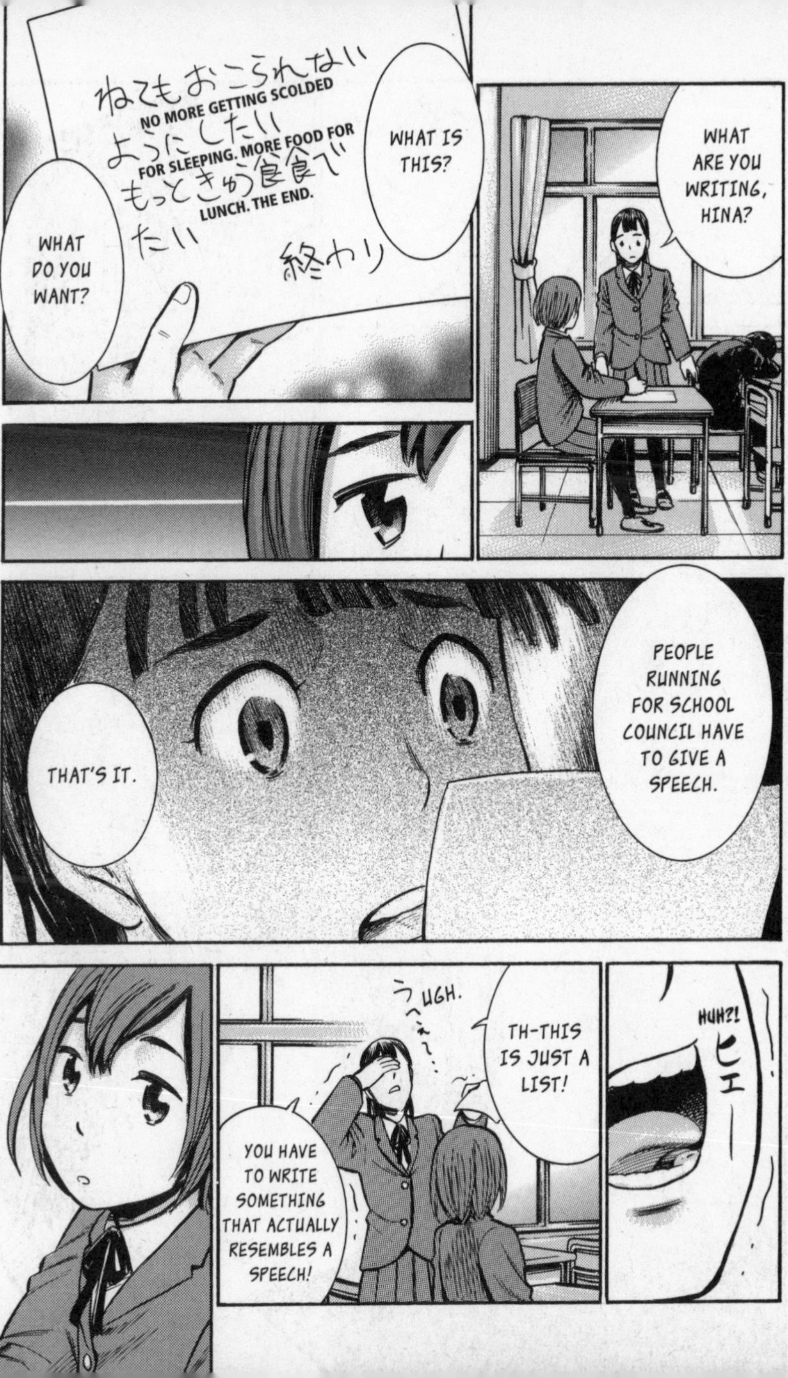
WHAT ARE YOU WRITING, HINA?
WHAT IS THIS?
ねてもおこられないようにしたい
もっときゅう食食べたい
終わり
NO MORE GETTING SCOLDED FOR SLEEPING. MORE FOOD FOR LUNCH. THE END.
WHAT DO YOU WANT?
PEOPLE RUNNING FOR SCHOOL COUNCIL HAVE TO GIVE A SPEECH.
THAT'S IT.
HUH?!
ヒエー
TH-THIS IS JUST A LIST!
うへぇ〜
UGH.
YOU HAVE TO WRITE SOMETHING THAT ACTUALLY RESEMBLES A SPEECH!

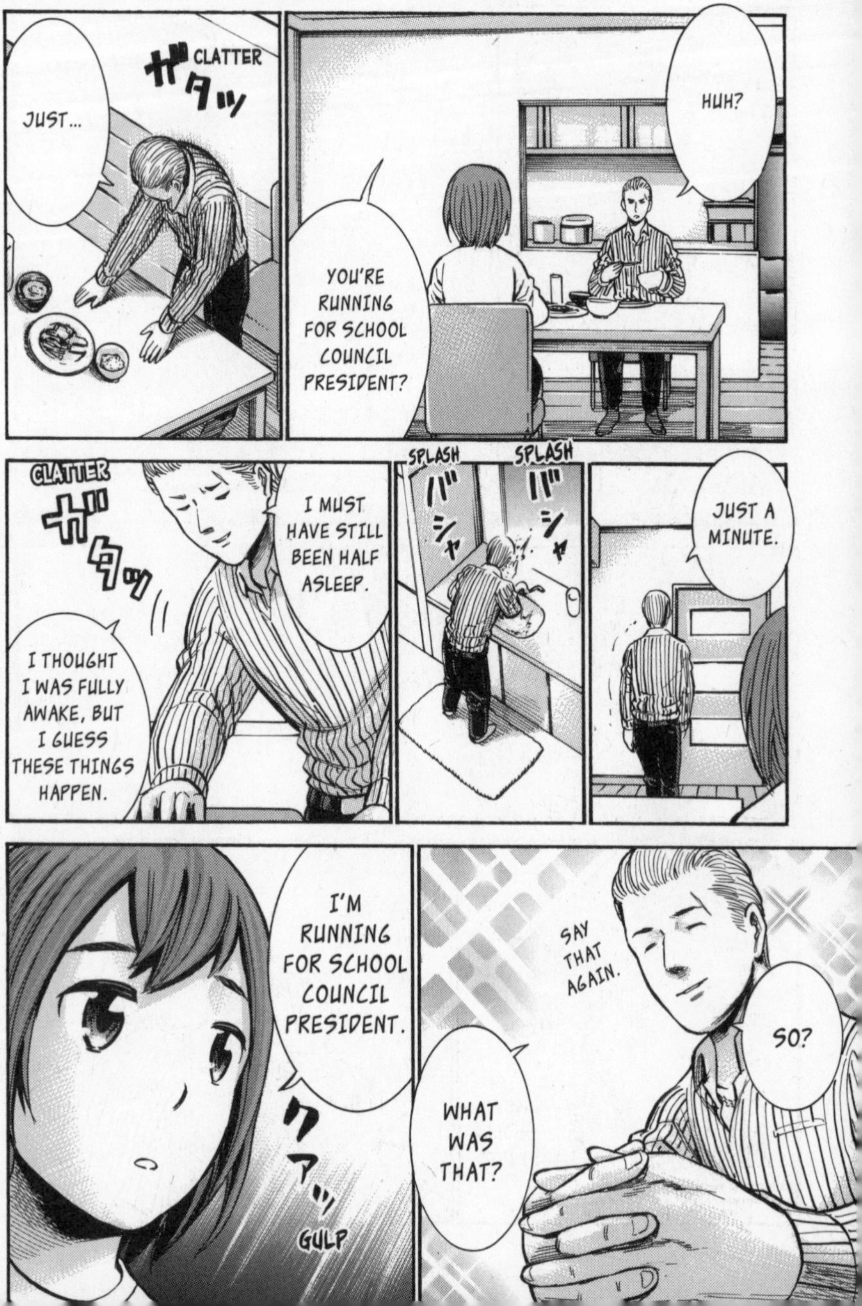
HUH?
YOU'RE RUNNING FOR SCHOOL COUNCIL PRESIDENT?
ガタッ
CLATTER
JUST...
JUST A MINUTE.
バシャ
SPLASH
バシャ
SPLASH
I MUST HAVE STILL BEEN HALF ASLEEP.
CLATTER
ガタッ
I THOUGHT I WAS FULLY AWAKE, BUT I GUESS THESE THINGS HAPPEN.
SO?
WHAT WAS THAT?
SAY THAT AGAIN.
I'M RUNNING FOR SCHOOL COUNCIL PRESIDENT.
GULP

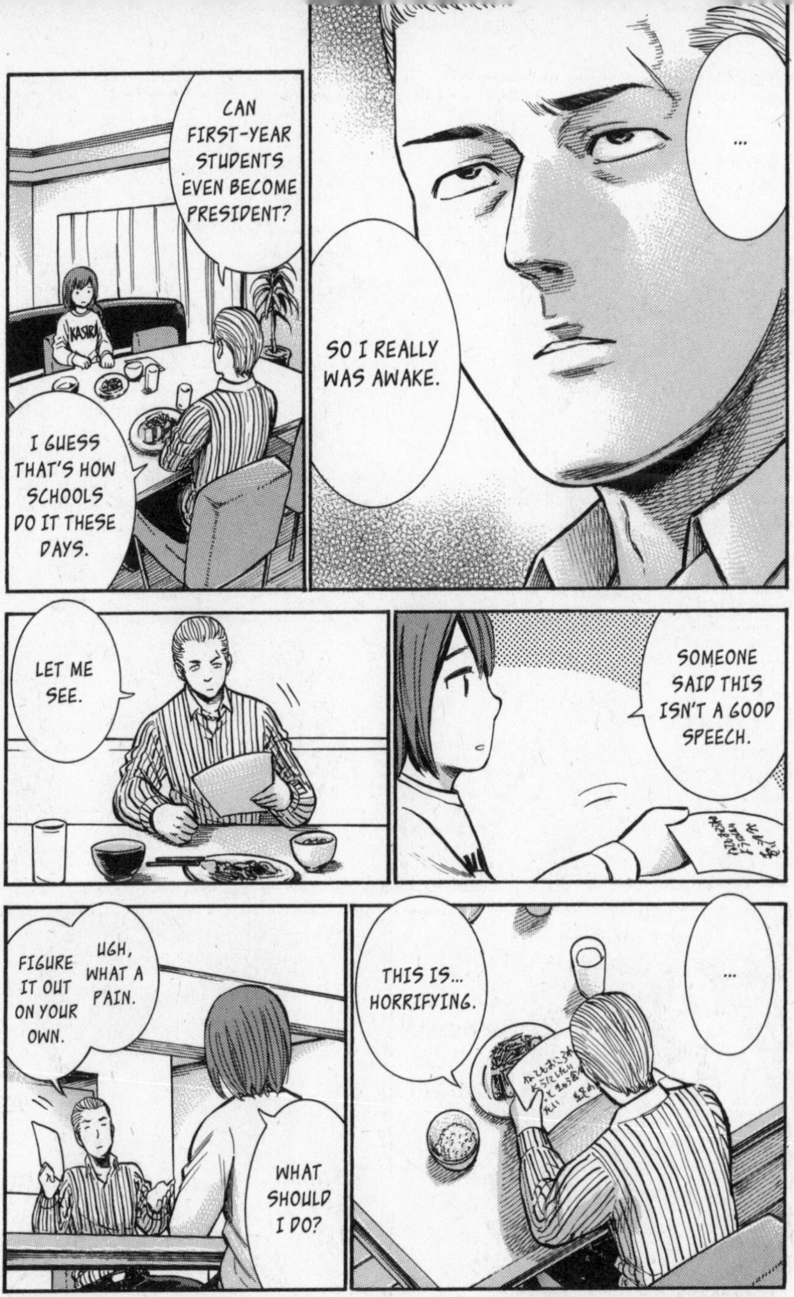
...
SO I REALLY WAS AWAKE.
CAN FIRST-YEAR STUDENTS EVEN BECOME PRESIDENT?
KASIRA
I GUESS THAT'S HOW SCHOOLS DO IT THESE DAYS.
SOMEONE SAID THIS ISN'T A GOOD SPEECH.
LET ME SEE.
...
THIS IS... HORRIFYING.
UGH, WHAT A PAIN.
FIGURE IT OUT ON YOUR OWN.
WHAT SHOULD I DO?

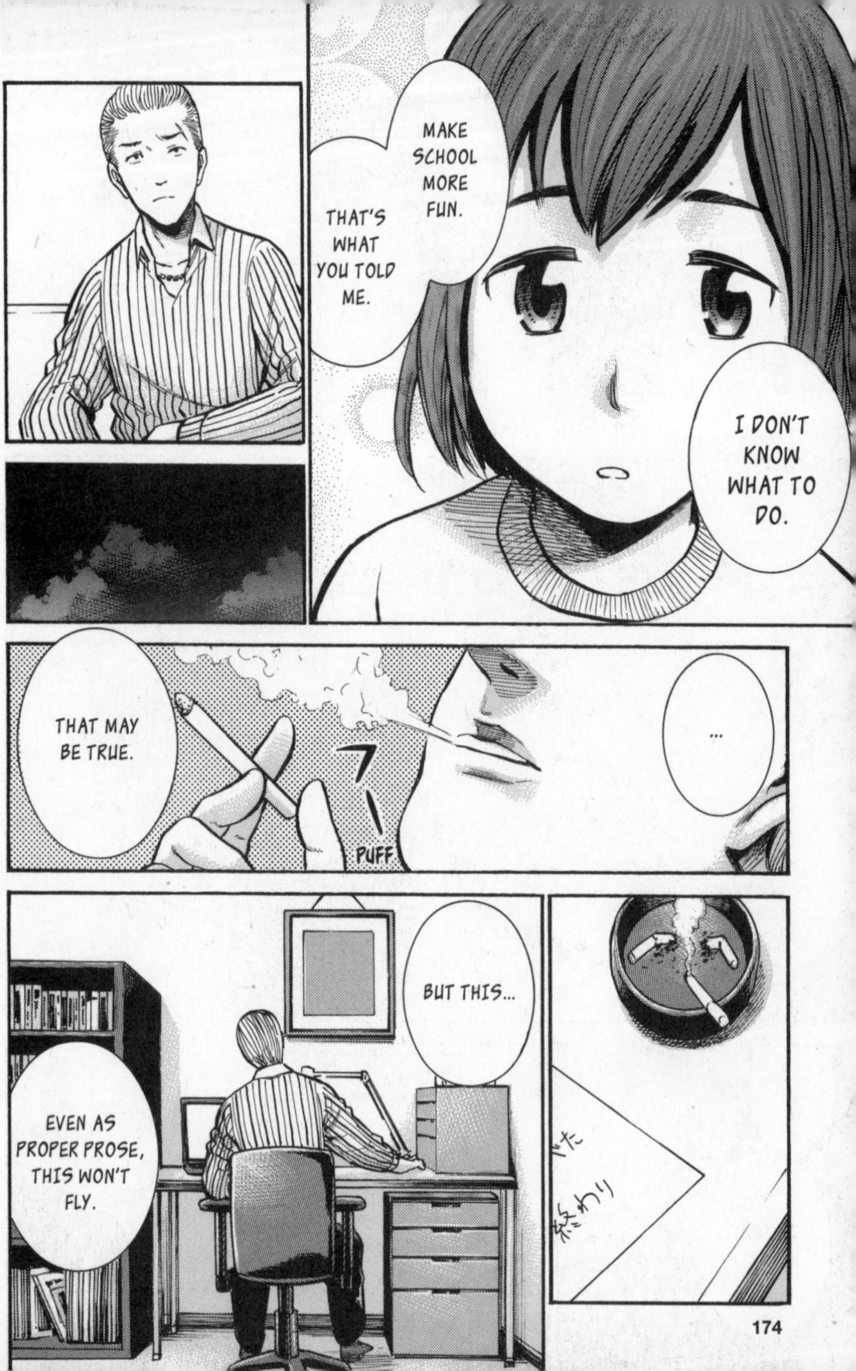
MAKE SCHOOL MORE FUN.
THAT'S WHAT YOU TOLD ME.
I DON'T KNOW WHAT TO DO.
...
PUFF
THAT MAY BE TRUE.
BUT THIS...
EVEN AS PROPER PROSE, THIS WON'T FLY.

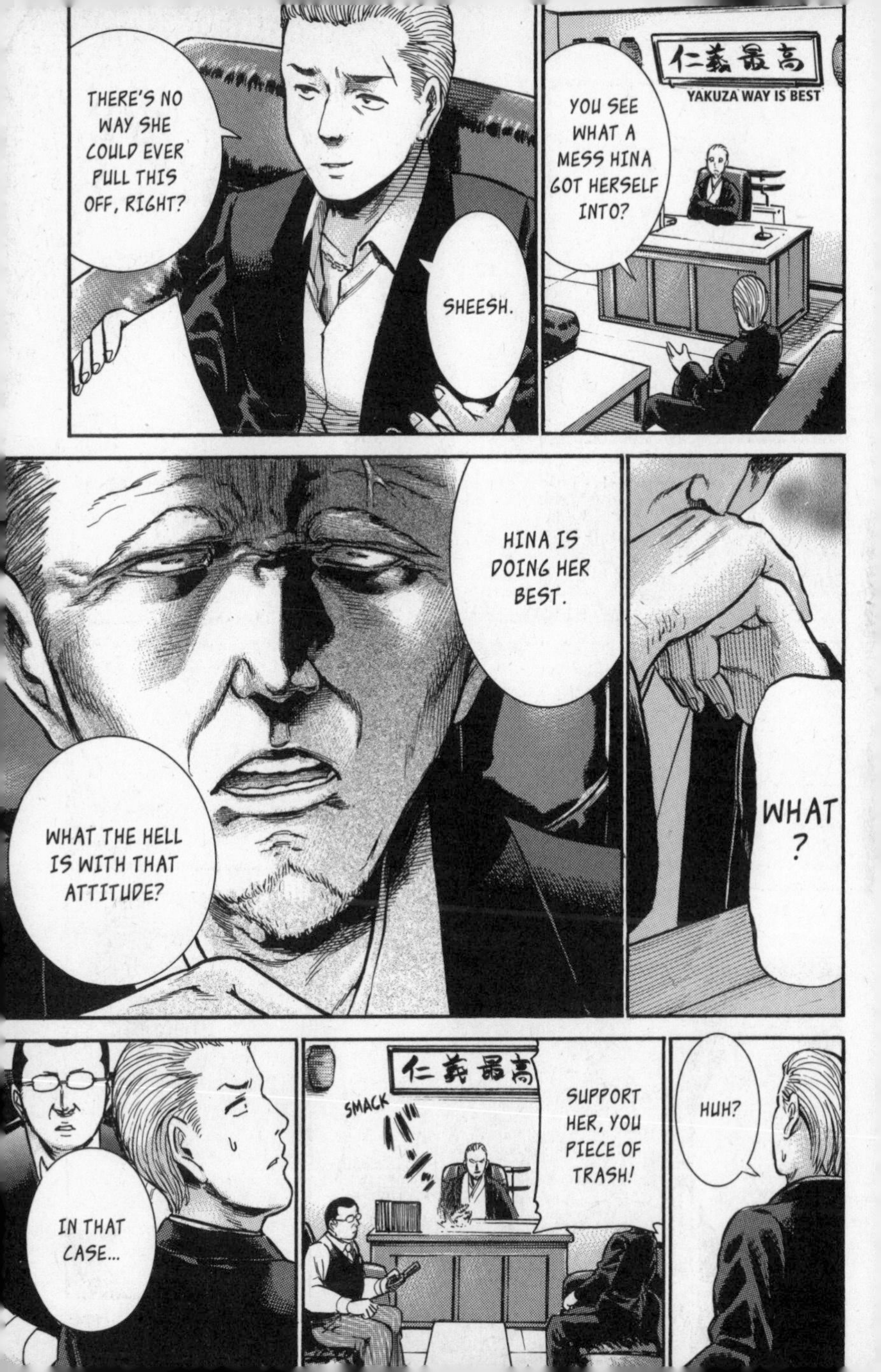
仁義最高
YAKUZA WAY IS BEST
YOU SEE WHAT A MESS HINA GOT HERSELF INTO?
THERE'S NO WAY SHE COULD EVER PULL THIS OFF, RIGHT?
SHEESH.
WHAT?
HINA IS DOING HER BEST.
WHAT THE HELL IS WITH THAT ATTITUDE?
HUH?
仁義最高
SMACK
SUPPORT HER, YOU PIECE OF TRASH!
IN THAT CASE...

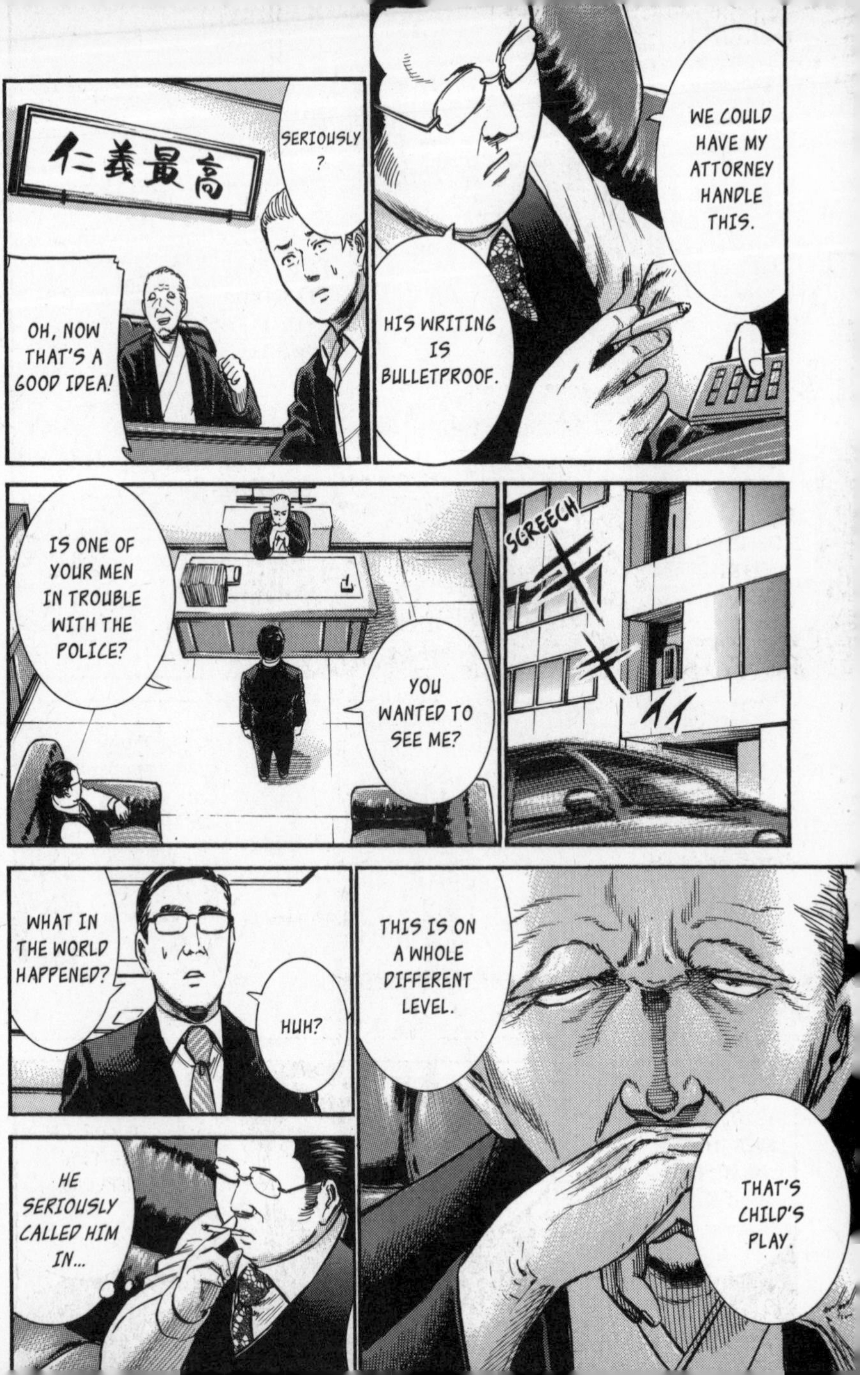
WE COULD HAVE MY ATTORNEY HANDLE THIS.
HIS WRITING IS BULLETPROOF.
SERIOUSLY?
仁義最高
OH, NOW THAT'S A GOOD IDEA!
SCREECH
YOU WANTED TO SEE ME?
IS ONE OF YOUR MEN IN TROUBLE WITH THE POLICE?
THIS IS ON A WHOLE DIFFERENT LEVEL.
THAT'S CHILD'S PLAY.
WHAT IN THE WORLD HAPPENED?
HUH?
HE SERIOUSLY CALLED HIM IN...

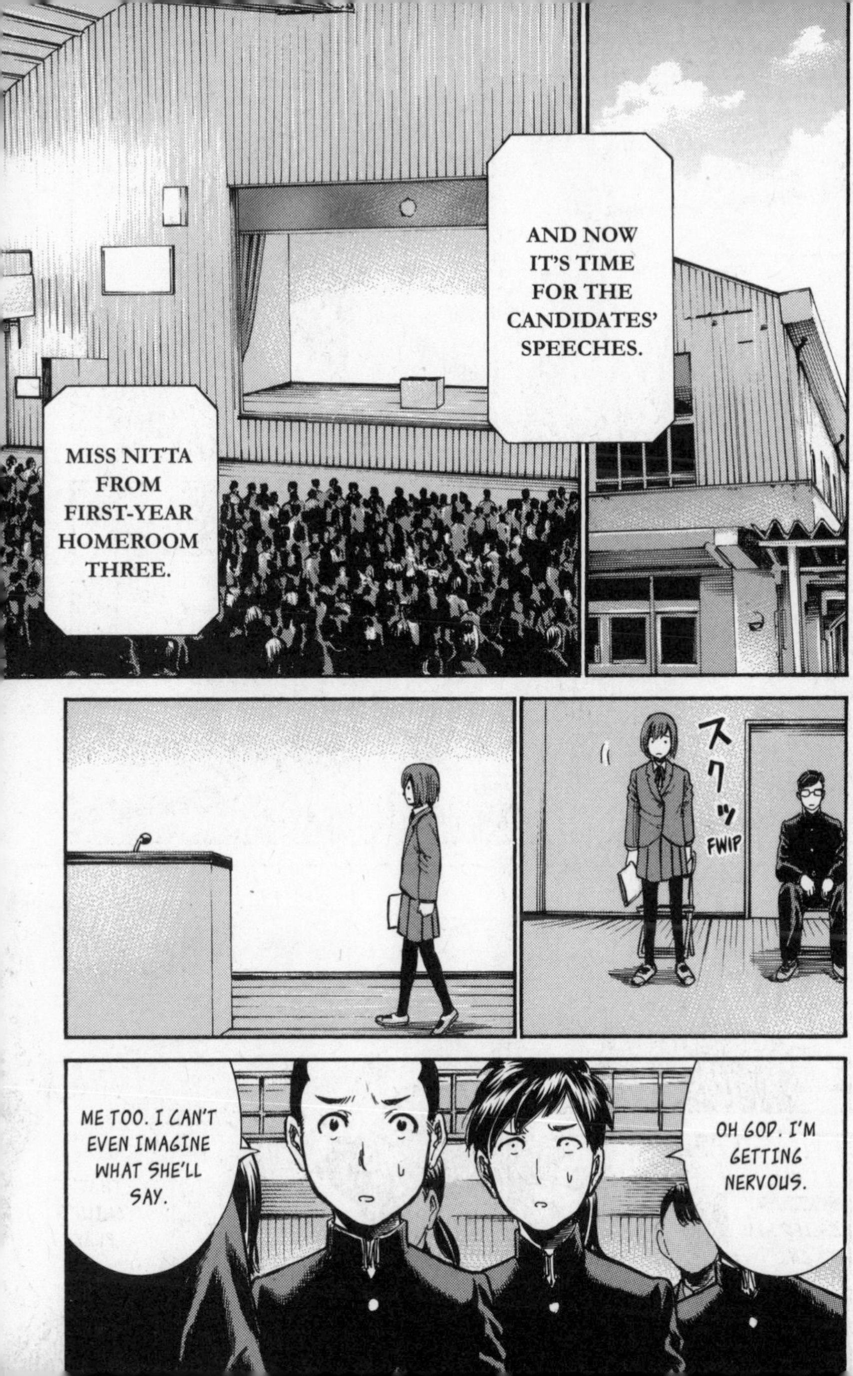
AND NOW IT'S TIME FOR THE CANDIDATES' SPEECHES.
MISS NITTA FROM FIRST-YEAR HOMEROOM THREE.
スクッ
FWIP
OH GOD. I'M GETTING NERVOUS.
ME TOO. I CAN'T EVEN IMAGINE WHAT SHE'LL SAY.

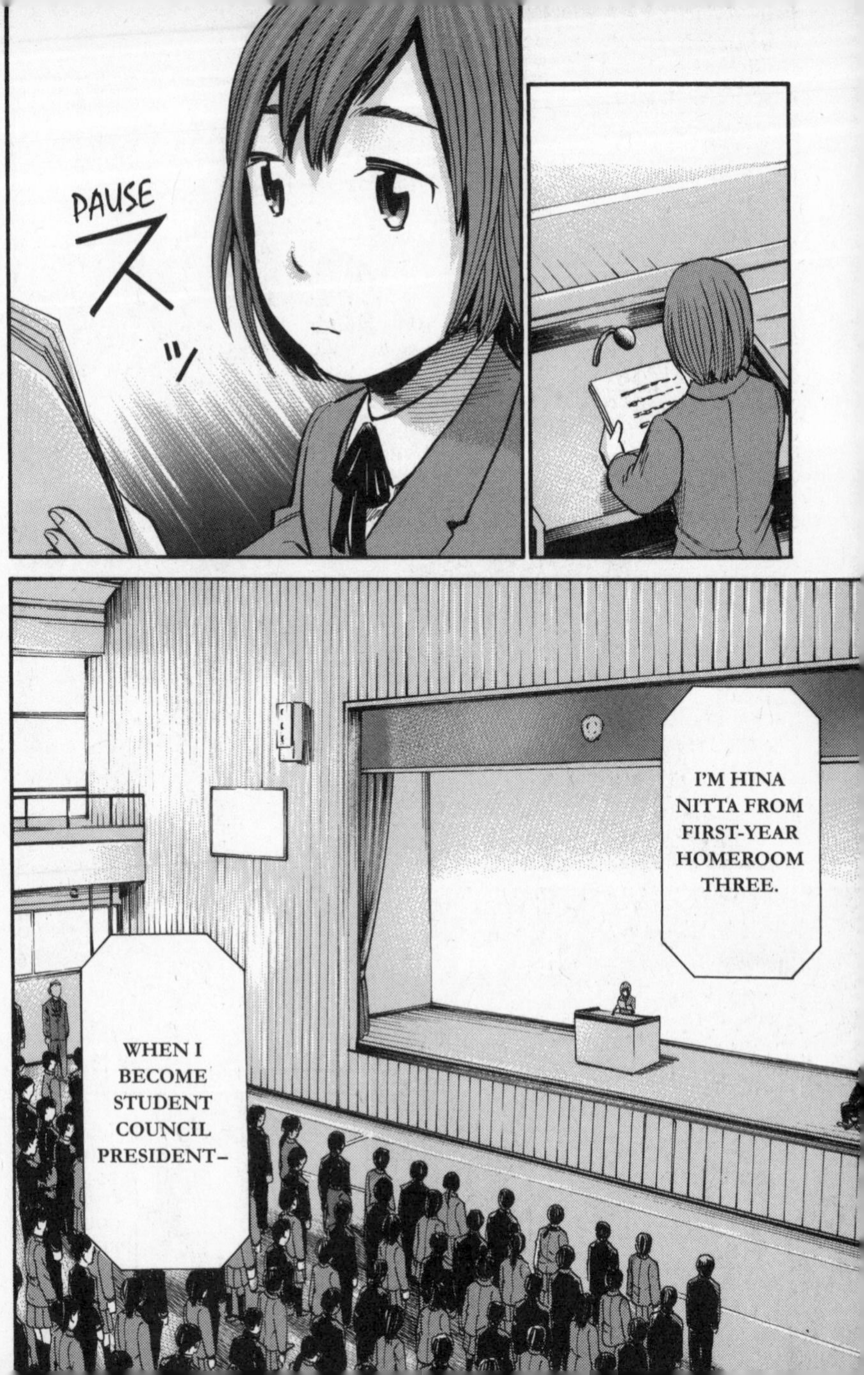
PAUSE
I'M HINA NITTA FROM FIRST-YEAR HOMEROOM THREE.
WHEN I BECOME STUDENT COUNCIL PRESIDENT–

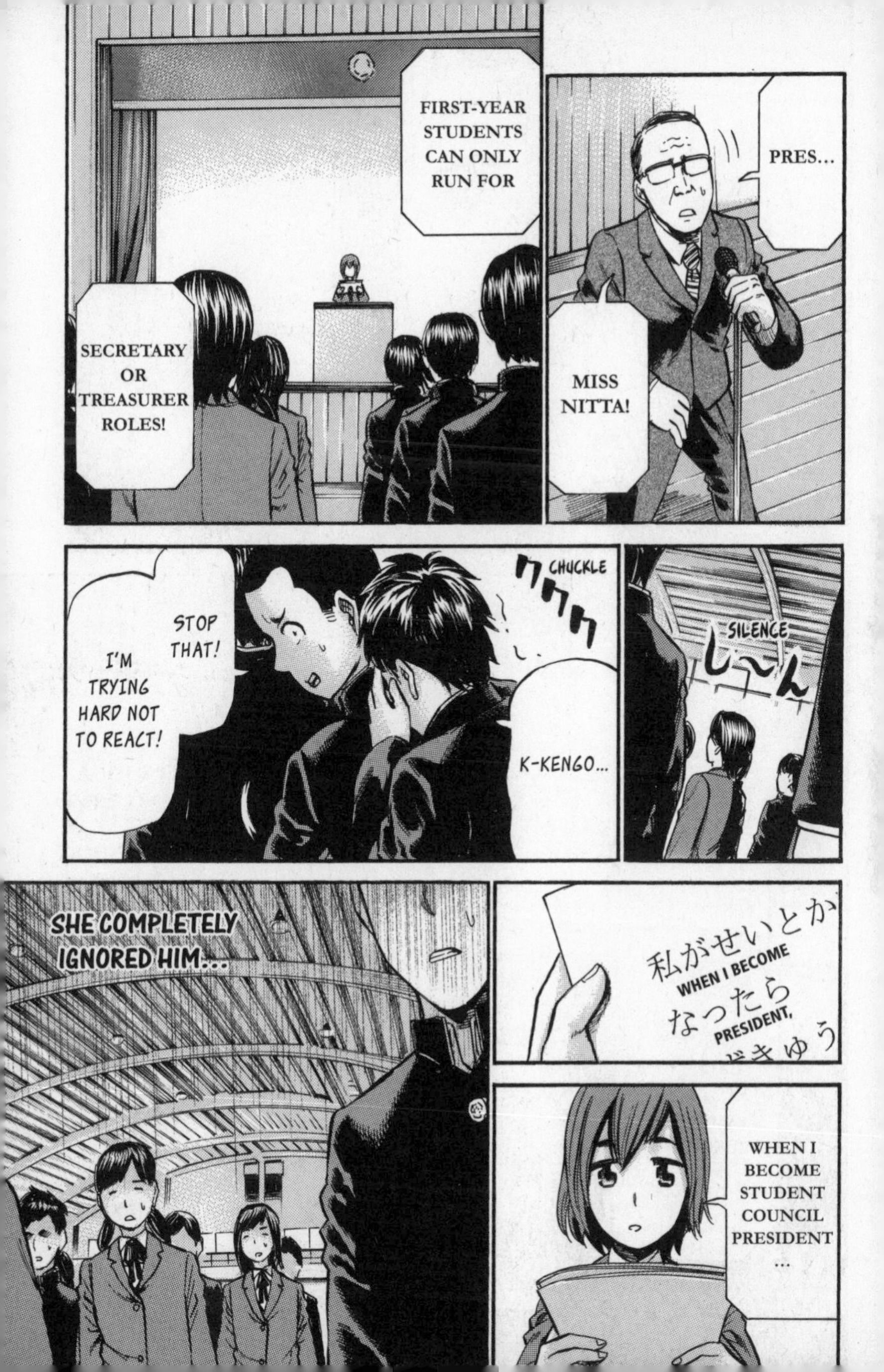
PRES…
MISS NITTA!
FIRST-YEAR STUDENTS CAN ONLY RUN FOR
SECRETARY OR TREASURER ROLES!
SILENCE
しーん
CHUCKLE
K-KENGO…
STOP THAT!
I'M TRYING HARD NOT TO REACT!
私がせいとか
WHEN I BECOME
なったら
PRESIDENT,
WHEN I BECOME STUDENT COUNCIL PRESIDENT…
SHE COMPLETELY IGNORED HIM…

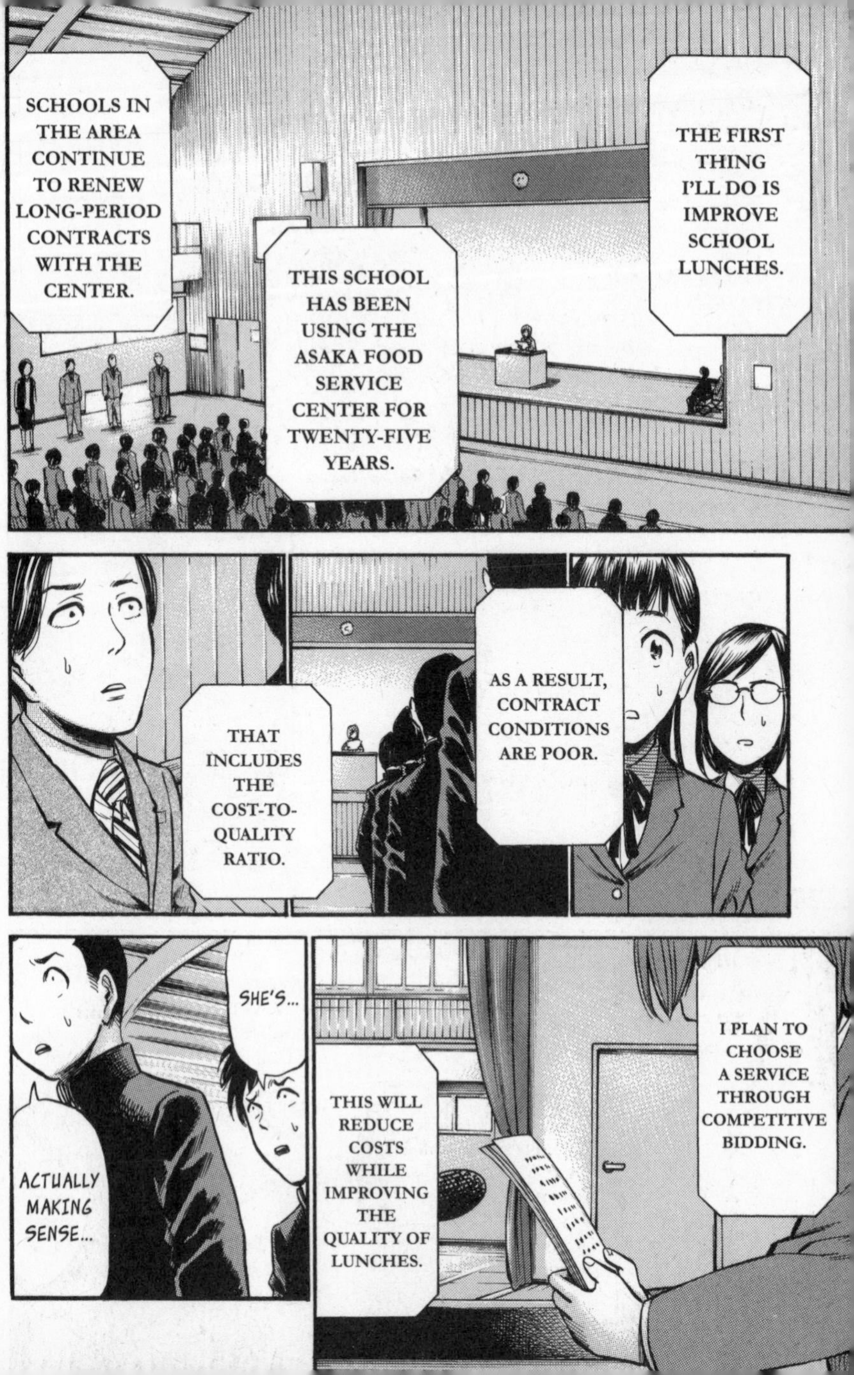
THE FIRST THING I'LL DO IS IMPROVE SCHOOL LUNCHES.
THIS SCHOOL HAS BEEN USING THE ASAKA FOOD SERVICE CENTER FOR TWENTY-FIVE YEARS.
SCHOOLS IN THE AREA CONTINUE TO RENEW LONG-PERIOD CONTRACTS WITH THE CENTER.
AS A RESULT, CONTRACT CONDITIONS ARE POOR.
THAT INCLUDES THE COST-TO-QUALITY RATIO.
I PLAN TO CHOOSE A SERVICE THROUGH COMPETITIVE BIDDING.
THIS WILL REDUCE COSTS WHILE IMPROVING THE QUALITY OF LUNCHES.
SHE'S...
ACTUALLY MAKING SENSE...

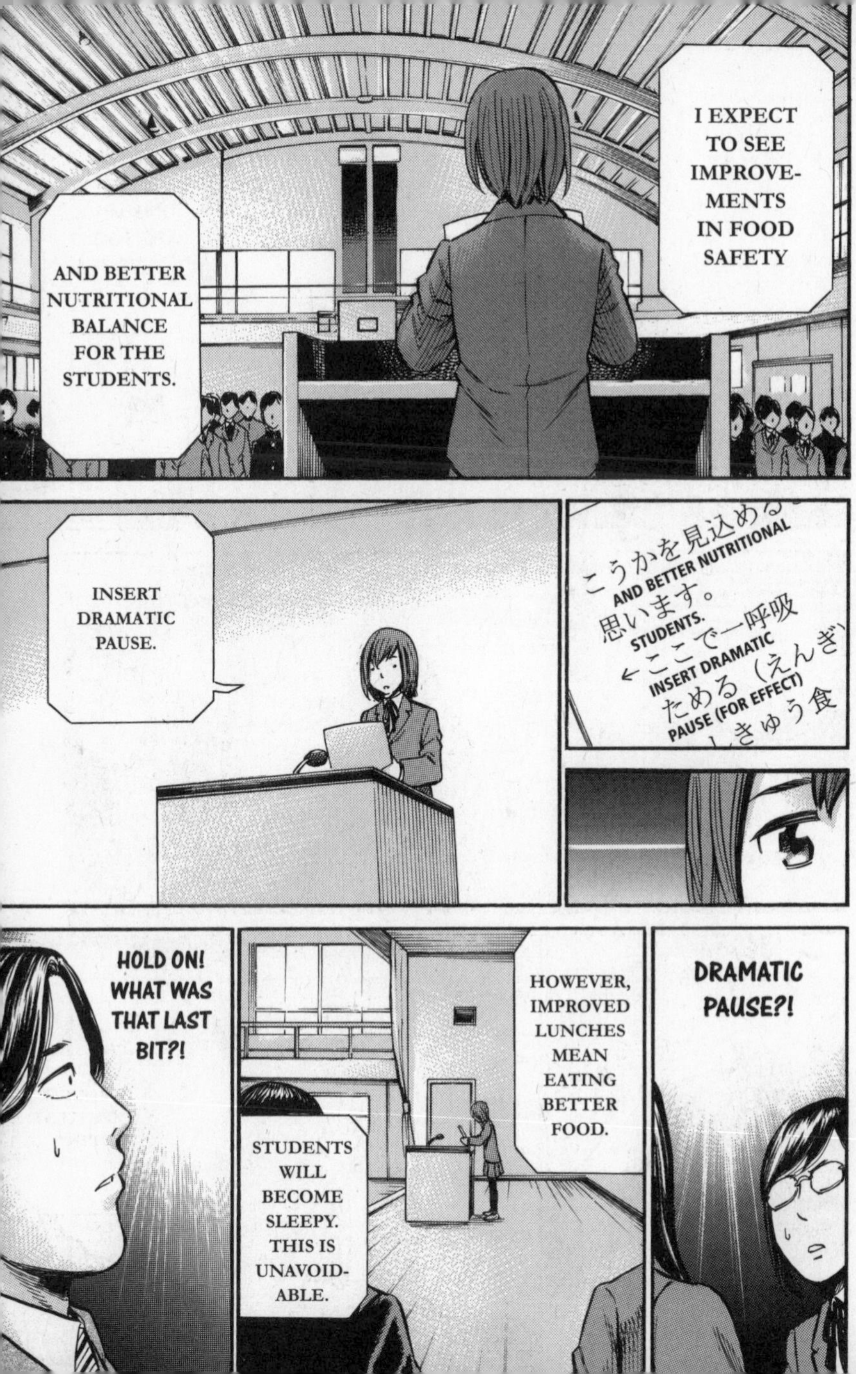
I EXPECT TO SEE IMPROVEMENTS IN FOOD SAFETY
AND BETTER NUTRITIONAL BALANCE FOR THE STUDENTS.
こうかを見込める
AND BETTER NUTRITIONAL
思います。
STUDENTS.
←ここで一呼吸
INSERT DRAMATIC
ためる（えんぎ
PAUSE (FOR EFFECT)
きゅう食
INSERT DRAMATIC PAUSE.
DRAMATIC PAUSE?!
HOWEVER, IMPROVED LUNCHES MEAN EATING BETTER FOOD.
STUDENTS WILL BECOME SLEEPY. THIS IS UNAVOIDABLE.
HOLD ON! WHAT WAS THAT LAST BIT?!

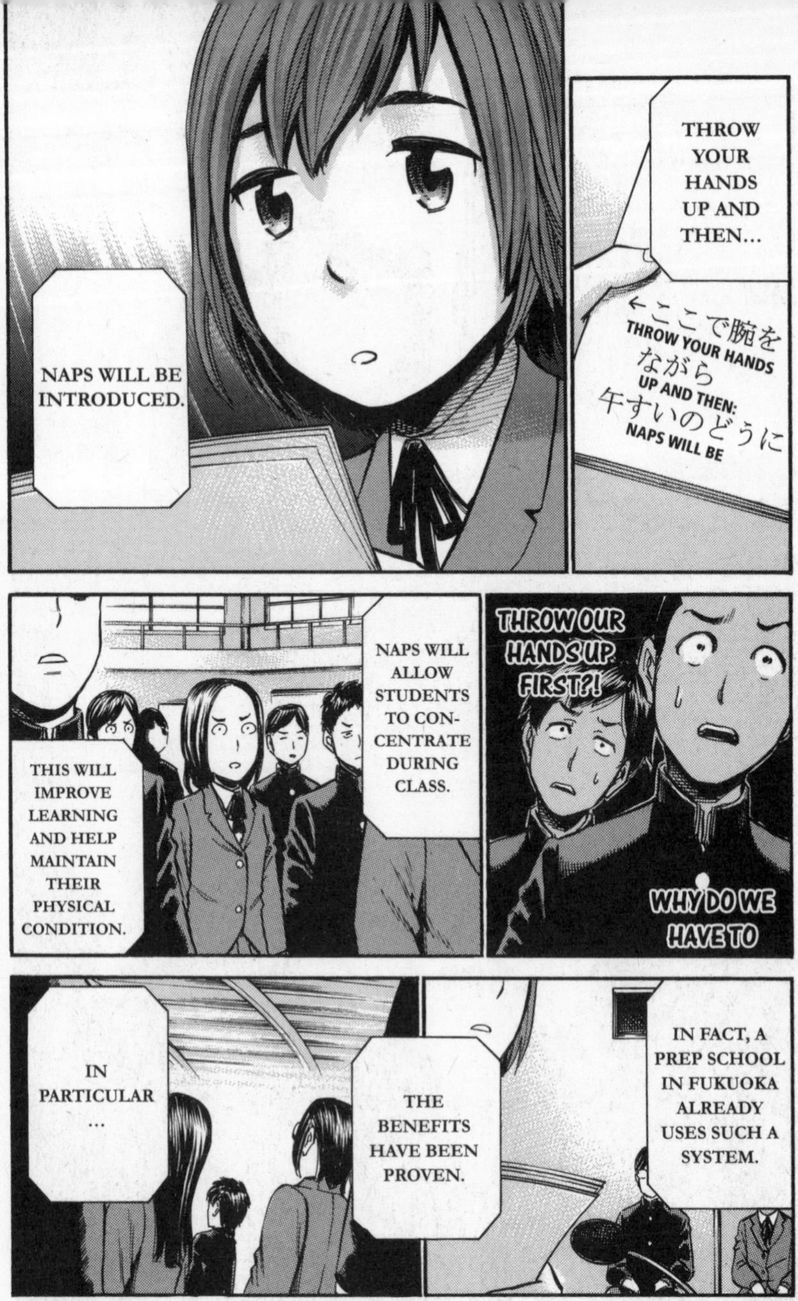
THROW YOUR HANDS UP AND THEN…
←ここで腕を
THROW YOUR HANDS
ながら
UP AND THEN:
午すいのどうに
NAPS WILL BE
NAPS WILL BE INTRODUCED.
THROW OUR HANDS UP FIRST?!
WHY DO WE HAVE TO
NAPS WILL ALLOW STUDENTS TO CON-CENTRATE DURING CLASS.
THIS WILL IMPROVE LEARNING AND HELP MAINTAIN THEIR PHYSICAL CONDITION.
IN FACT, A PREP SCHOOL IN FUKUOKA ALREADY USES SUCH A SYSTEM.
THE BENEFITS HAVE BEEN PROVEN.
IN PARTICULAR …

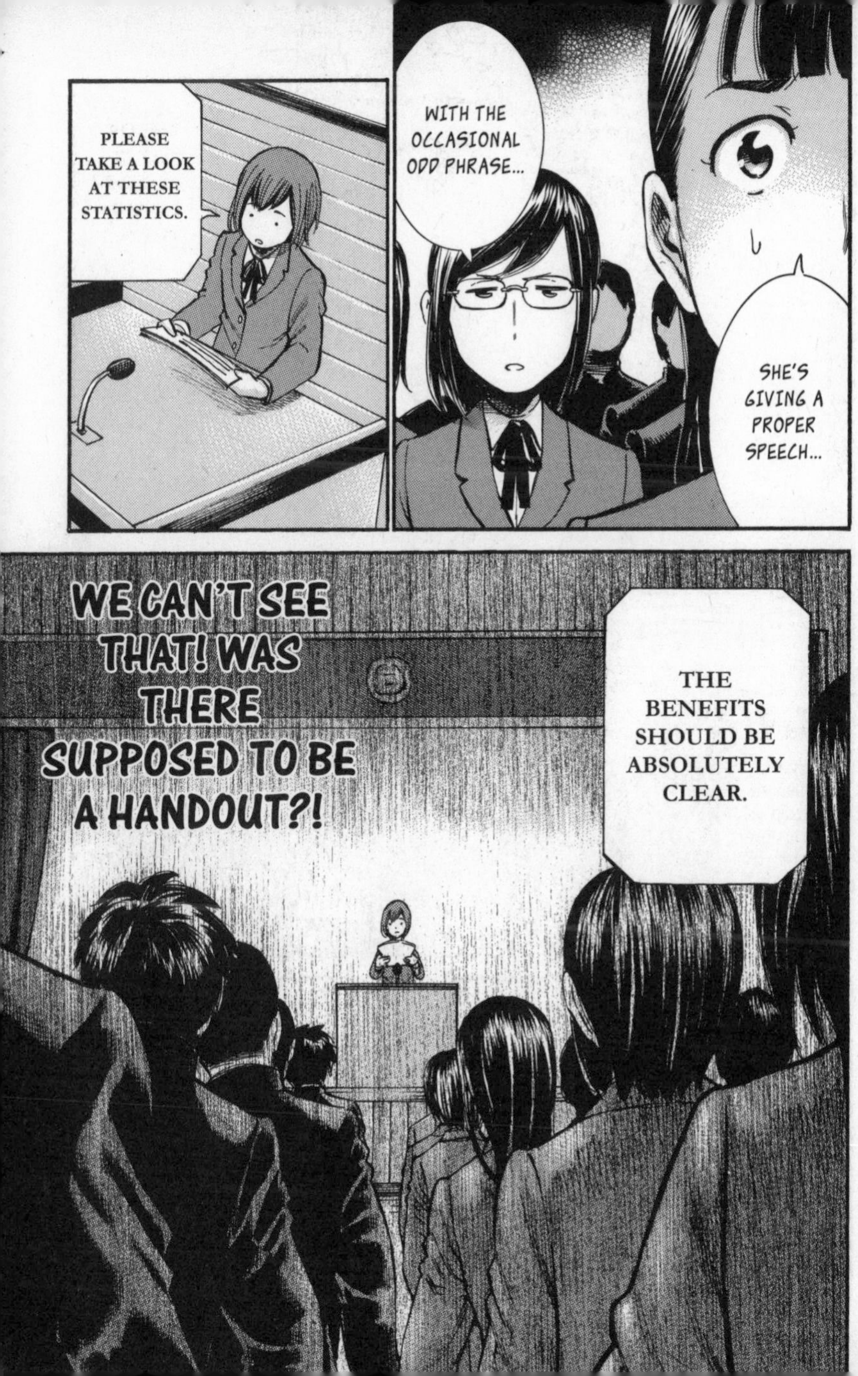
SHE'S GIVING A PROPER SPEECH...
WITH THE OCCASIONAL ODD PHRASE...
PLEASE TAKE A LOOK AT THESE STATISTICS.
THE BENEFITS SHOULD BE ABSOLUTELY CLEAR.
WE CAN'T SEE THAT! WAS THERE SUPPOSED TO BE A HANDOUT?!

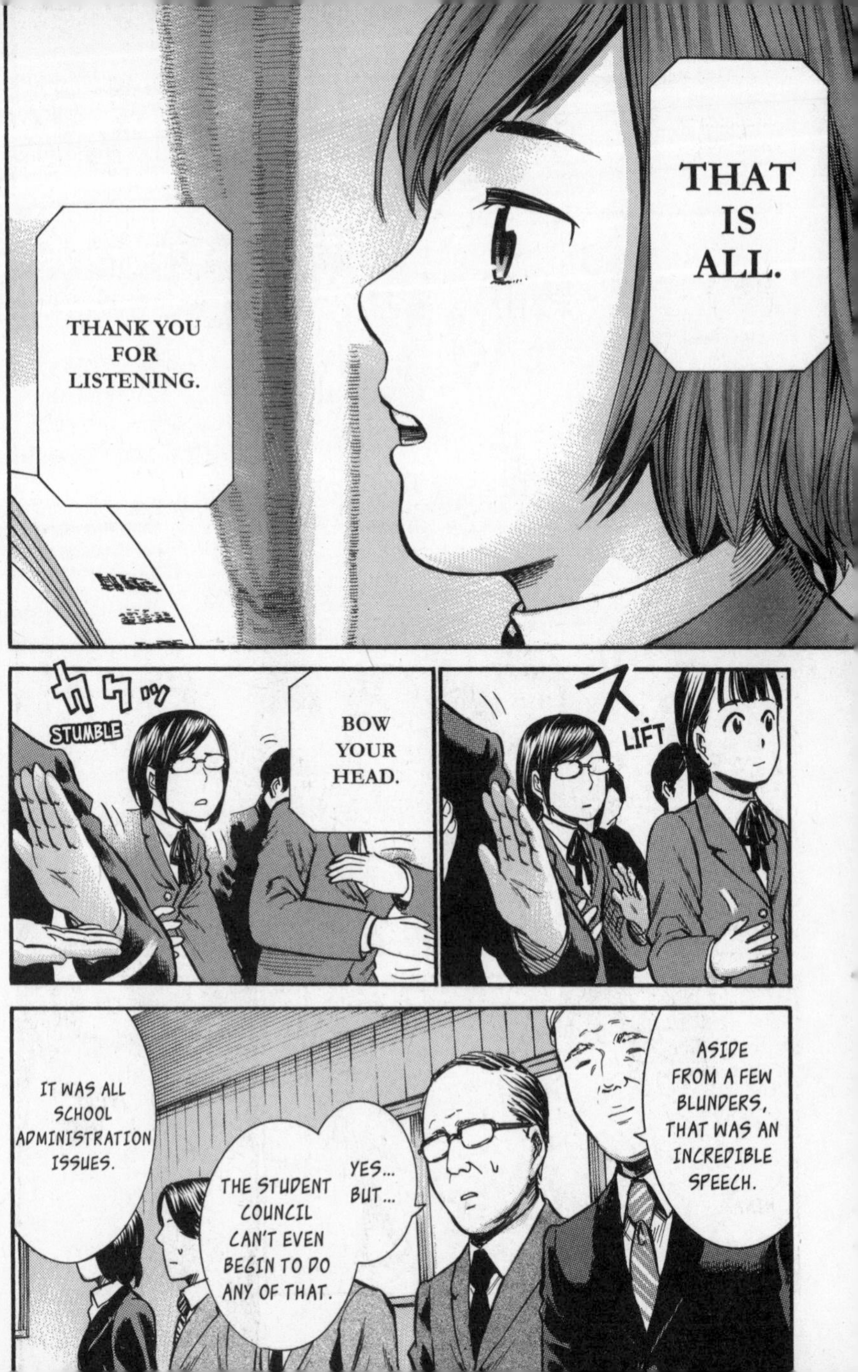
THAT IS ALL.
THANK YOU FOR LISTENING.
ス
LIFT
BOW YOUR HEAD.
カクッ
STUMBLE
ASIDE FROM A FEW BLUNDERS, THAT WAS AN INCREDIBLE SPEECH.
YES... BUT...
THE STUDENT COUNCIL CAN'T EVEN BEGIN TO DO ANY OF THAT.
IT WAS ALL SCHOOL ADMINISTRATION ISSUES.

書記 SECRETARY	安城　吉保 ANJO, YOSHIYASU		
書記 SECRETARY	新田　ヒナ NITTA, HINA		
会計 TREASURER	広瀬　翔平 HIROSE, SHOHEI		

STUDENT COUNCIL
生徒会役員

PRESIDENT 生徒会長		KOGURE 小暮	
副会長 VICE PRESIDENT		北条 HOJO	

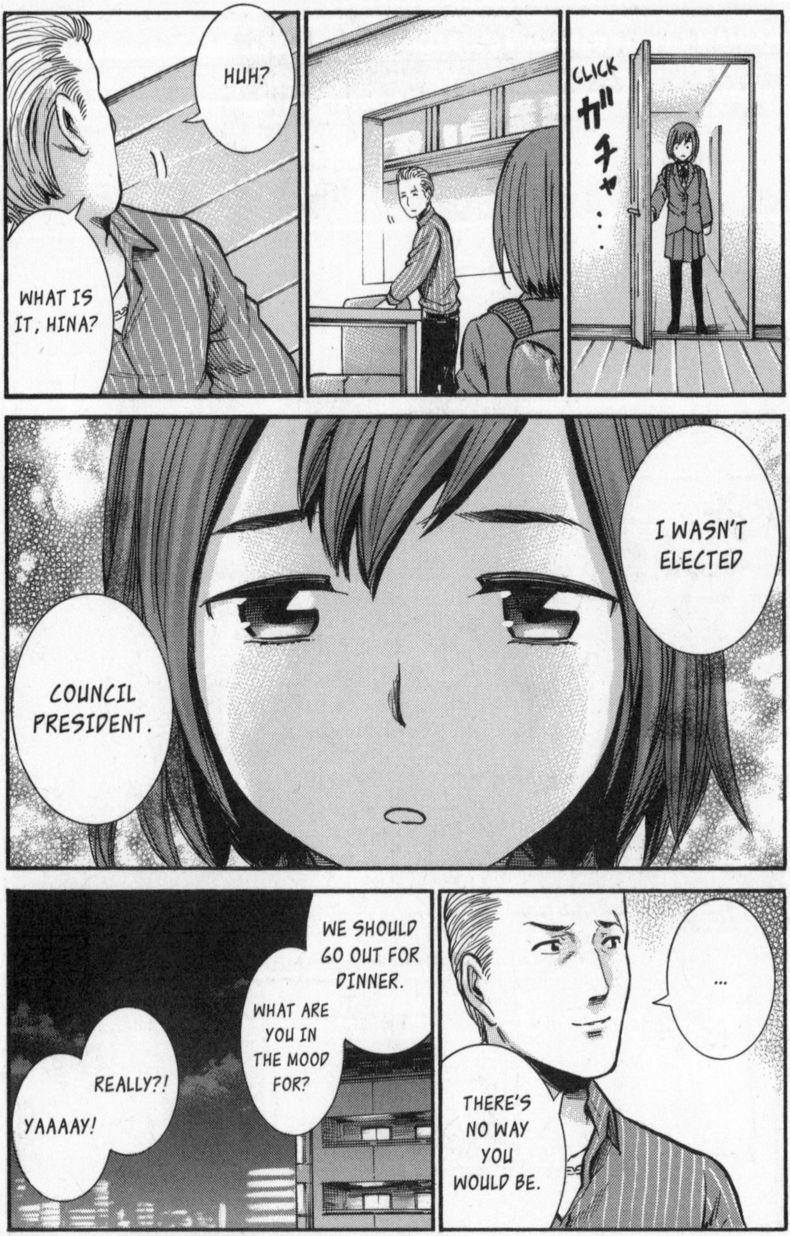
CLICK
ガチャ・・・
HUH?
WHAT IS IT, HINA?
I WASN'T ELECTED
COUNCIL PRESIDENT.
...
THERE'S NO WAY YOU WOULD BE.
WE SHOULD GO OUT FOR DINNER.
WHAT ARE YOU IN THE MOOD FOR?
REALLY?!
YAAAAY!

CHAPTER 10 END

EXTRA 3

KEEP GROWING NO MATTER WHAT HAPPENS

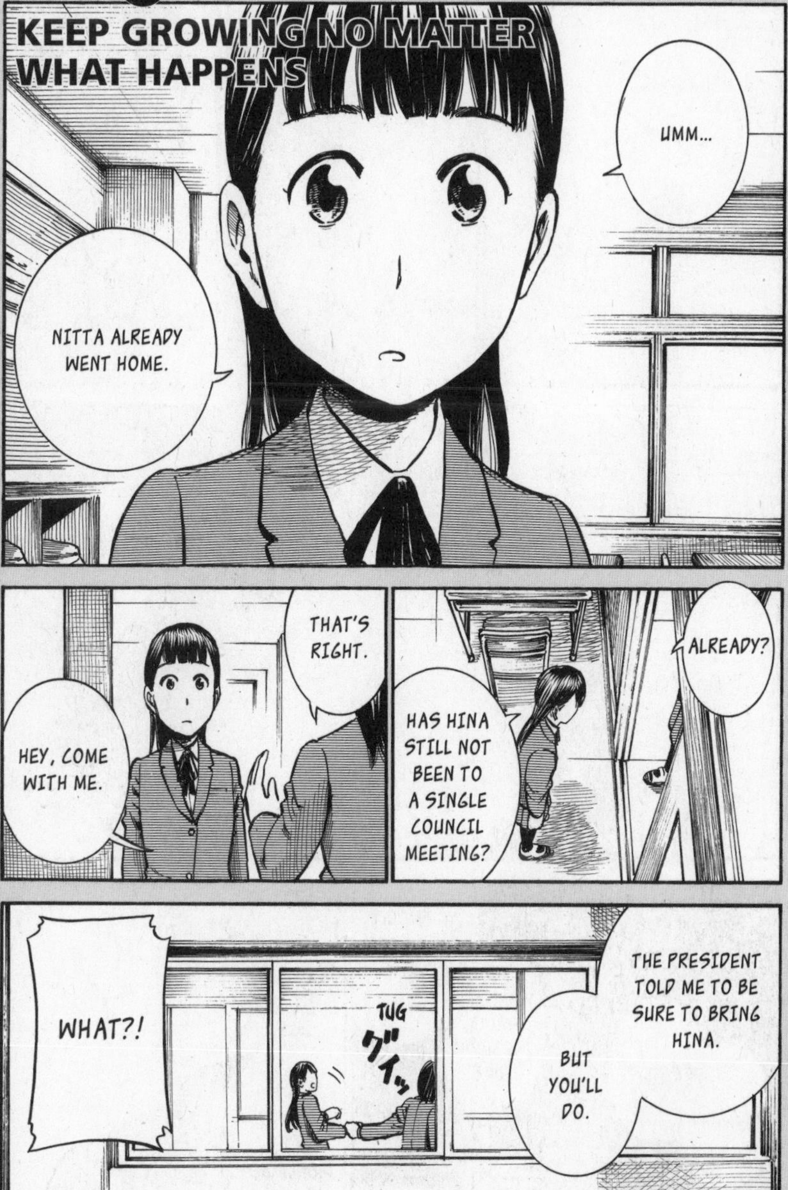

UMM...
NITTA ALREADY WENT HOME.
ALREADY?
HAS HINA STILL NOT BEEN TO A SINGLE COUNCIL MEETING?
THAT'S RIGHT.
HEY, COME WITH ME.
THE PRESIDENT TOLD ME TO BE SURE TO BRING HINA.
BUT YOU'LL DO.
TUG
WHAT?!

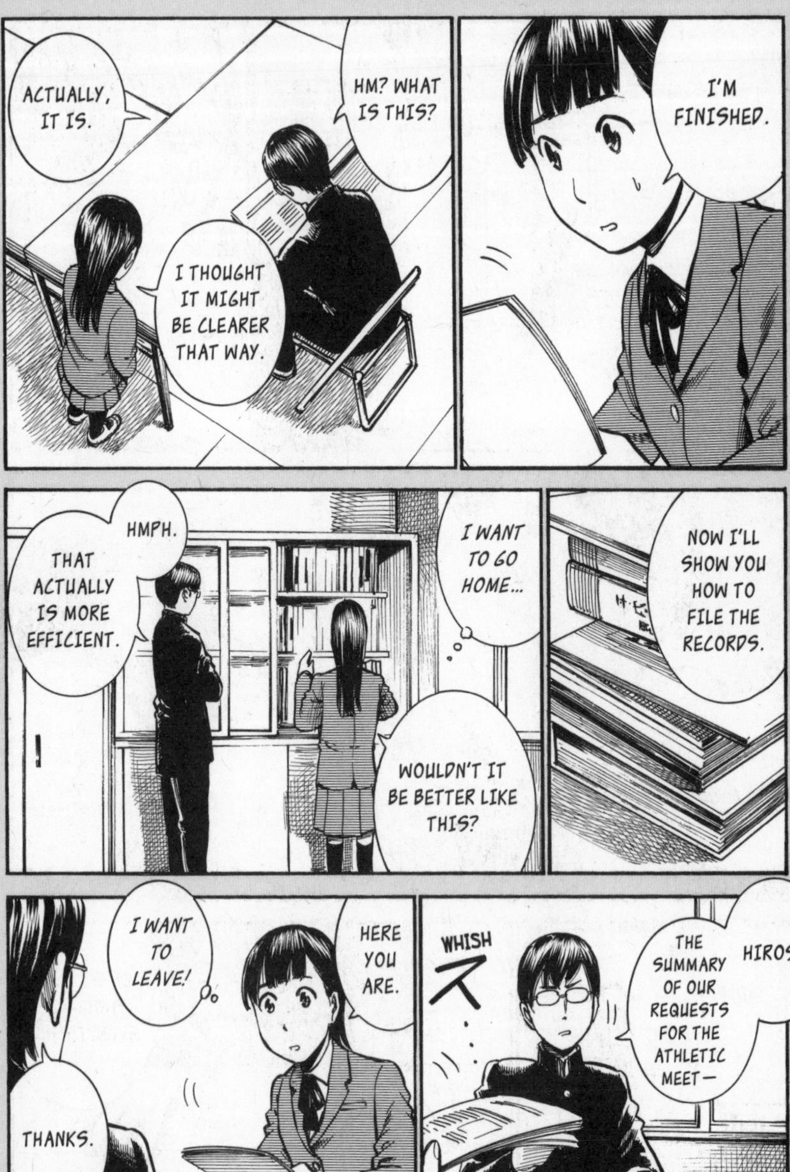

I'M FINISHED.
HM? WHAT IS THIS?
ACTUALLY, IT IS.
I THOUGHT IT MIGHT BE CLEARER THAT WAY.
NOW I'LL SHOW YOU HOW TO FILE THE RECORDS.
I WANT TO GO HOME...
HMPH.
THAT ACTUALLY IS MORE EFFICIENT.
WOULDN'T IT BE BETTER LIKE THIS?
HIROSE.
THE SUMMARY OF OUR REQUESTS FOR THE ATHLETIC MEET—
WHISH
ス
HERE YOU ARE.
I WANT TO LEAVE!
THANKS.

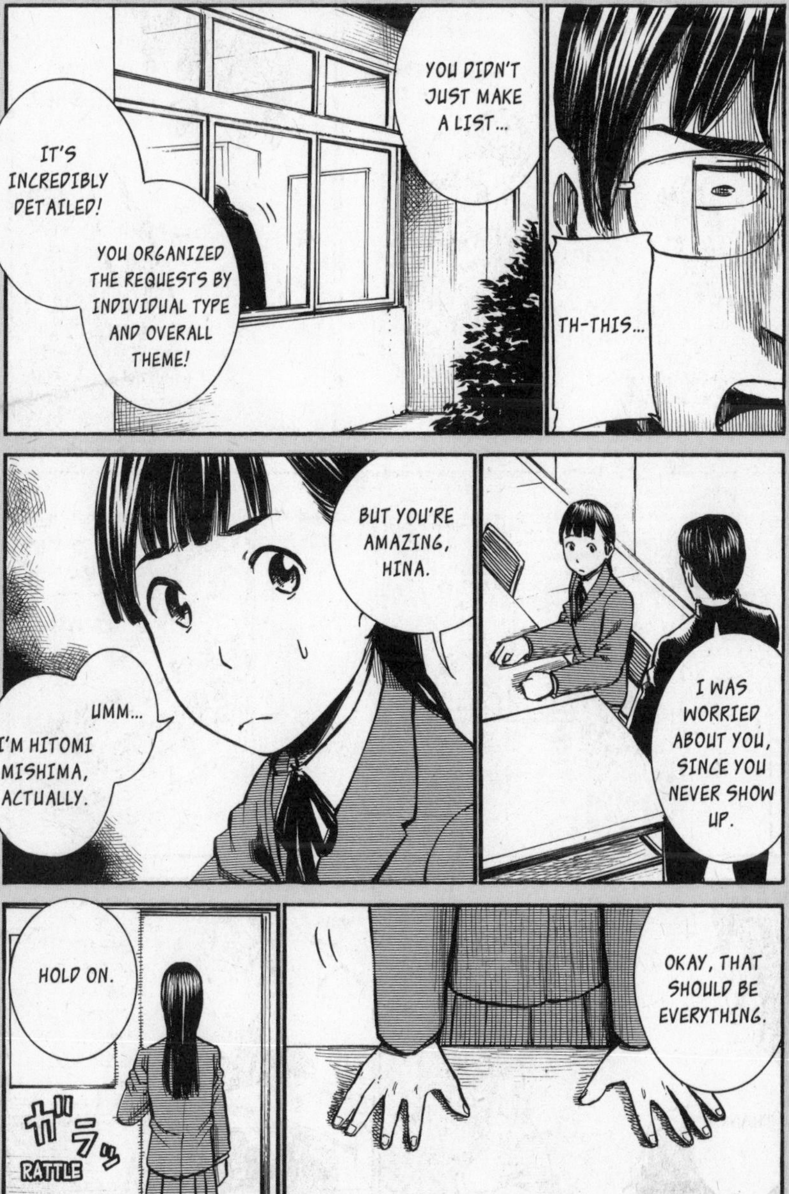
TH-THIS...
YOU DIDN'T JUST MAKE A LIST...
IT'S INCREDIBLY DETAILED!
YOU ORGANIZED THE REQUESTS BY INDIVIDUAL TYPE AND OVERALL THEME!
I WAS WORRIED ABOUT YOU, SINCE YOU NEVER SHOW UP.
BUT YOU'RE AMAZING, HINA.
UMM... I'M HITOMI MISHIMA, ACTUALLY.
OKAY, THAT SHOULD BE EVERYTHING.
HOLD ON.
ガラッ
RATTLE

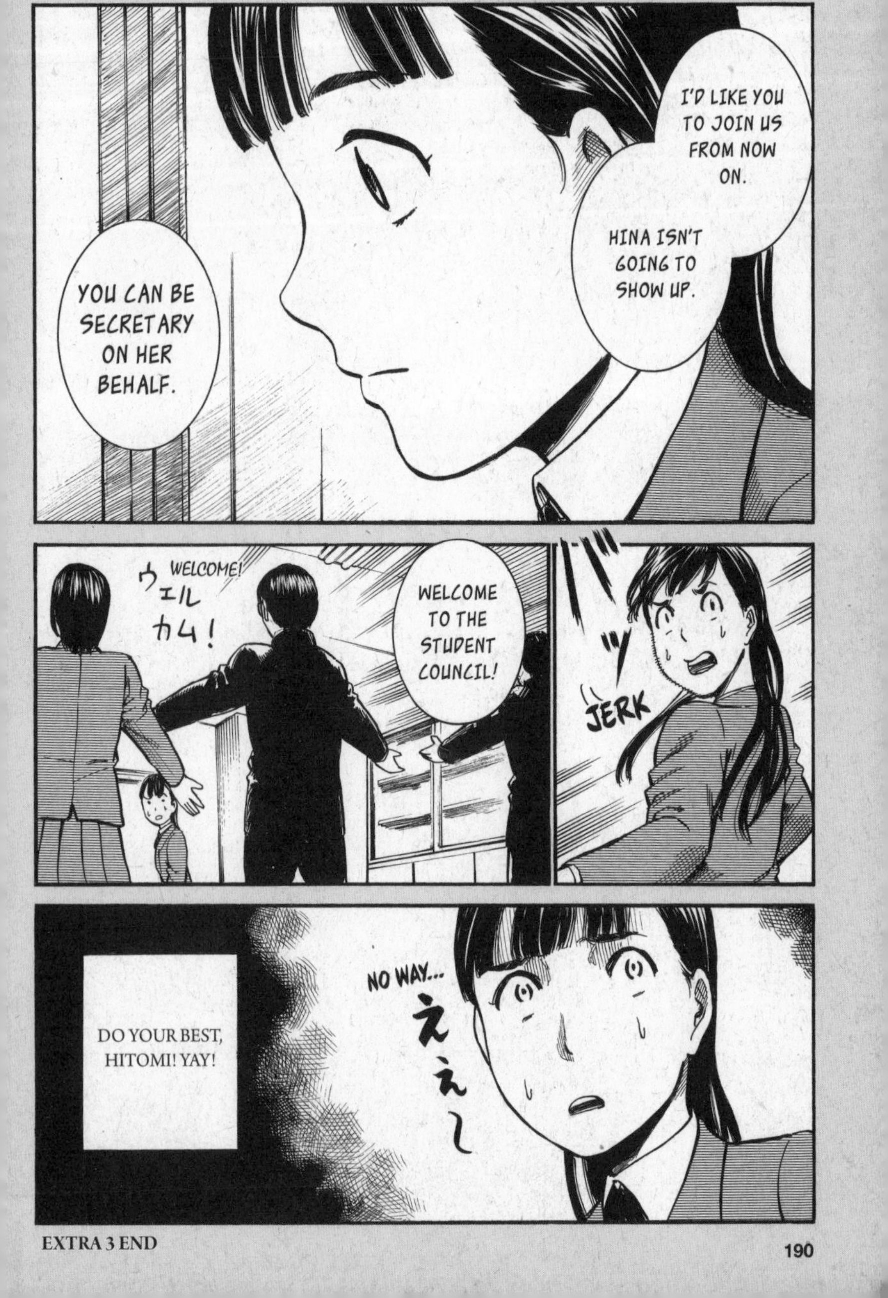
I'D LIKE YOU TO JOIN US FROM NOW ON.
HINA ISN'T GOING TO SHOW UP.
YOU CAN BE SECRETARY ON HER BEHALF.
JERK
WELCOME TO THE STUDENT COUNCIL!
WELCOME!
ウェルカム!
NO WAY...
DO YOUR BEST, HITOMI! YAY!

EXTRA 3 END